THE EMPLOYED MOTHER
IN AMERICA

The Employed Mother in America

BY   *F. Ivan Nye*
Washington State University

Lois Wladis Hoffman
University of Michigan

WITH CONTRIBUTIONS BY

Jean Adamson, Robert O. Blood, Jr., Lee G. Burchinal, James E. Conyers, Elizabeth Douvan, Sheila Feld, David M. Heer, Ethel Alice Hitchcock, Francena L. Nolan, Richard H. Ogles, Joseph B. Perry, Jr., Kathryn S. Powell, Prodipto Roy, Lawrence J. Sharp, Alberta Engvall Siegel, Marion G. Sobol, Lois Meek Stolz

14497

Rand McNally & Company · *Chicago*

Rand McNally Sociology Series
Edgar F. Borgatta, Advisory Editor

Alford, *Party and Society*
Christensen. ed., *Handbook of Marriage and the Family*
Demerath, *Social Class in American Protestantism*
Faris, ed., *Handbook of Modern Sociology*
March, ed., *Handbook of Organizations*
Nye and Hoffman, *The Employed Mother in America*
Scott, *Values and Organizations*
Warren, *The Community in America*

Researchers and practitioners interested in a given social phenomenon often come from several different fields of specialization. Maternal employment, for example, has been studied by psychologists, sociologists, and economists, by social workers, school teachers, and pediatricians. Most researchers publish their findings in journals and books close to their professional identification; i.e., the psychologist publishes in the psychological journals, the sociologist in sociological journals. For research to be maximally fruitful, the scientist must know the relevant work that has preceded his, even though this work was done by someone in another profession. As a result, when the researcher becomes interested in a problem, he has to scour the literature in many fields and is likely to overlook some that might be useful or even crucial to him. A major objective of this book is to gather together the research on the subject of maternal employment. Implied in this aim is a commitment to the advancement of research, which is the integrating theme of this volume.

Not all relevant research was available, nor was there space for all that might have been included. The editors believe, however, that they have succeeded in bringing together most of the social and socio-psychological research completed from 1957 to the cut-off date early in 1962. While we think that the present volume is comprehensive for the time period covered, we have no thought that it brings "the final word" on the employed mother. As it goes to press, researchers are taking the unsolved problems reported and proceeding to additional theoretical and methodological refinements. The

present volume, therefore, is offered as a benchmark for research on the
topic at the time it goes to press.

We are happy to present frames of reference and methodological techniques from sociology, social psychology, economics, and child development.
Although these disciplines share a large number of common assumptions and
interests, each has a unique contribution, and their presentation together
offers one safeguard against disciplinary provincialism.

The book is organized into four sections. Part I serves a broad intro-
ductory function in presenting the basis for the emergence of the employed
mother as a major phenomenon in American life—its cultural, social, socio-
psychological, and psychological rationale. In the process it portrays social,
economic, socio-psychological, and psychological differences between mothers
in and outside the labor force.

Part II presents the rather extensive research dealing with the children
of employed and non-employed mothers. In the concluding chapter of the
section, Dr. Hoffman summarizes and systematizes the research reported in
Part II and briefly presents additional research from studies not included in
this volume. The concluding chapter also gives some attention to methodological problems and techniques and presents some suggestions for needed
further research. Part III compares the marital relationships of employed
and non-employed women. The final chapter in Part III by Professor Blood
provides a partial summary of the section as well as a presentation of his
own research.

Part IV compares the self-feelings, health, and relationships of the two
categories of mothers. In a concluding chapter, Professor Nye summarizes
this research, provides a conceptual formulation for the employed mother,
and suggests some areas for further research. The editors have elected to
perform the functions of a general concluding section in the final chapters
of Parts II and IV.

We are indebted to many people for their contributions to this volume.
First, of course, to the contributing authors who are listed both on the title
page and on the chapters they have contributed. We owe a real debt, also,
to Dr. Edgar Borgatta, Sociology Editor of Rand McNally, for a number of
excellent constructive criticisms and suggestions, which have improved the
volume. William Goode was the editorial consultant. Many of his suggestions
were incorporated with benefit. Dr. Martin Hoffman reviewed Chapters
Two, Six, Fourteen, and Fifteen and made many constructive suggestions.
Errors of commission or omission, of course, remain the responsibility of
the authors.

Professors Hoffman and Nye wish to thank the University of Michigan
and Washington State University, respectively, for making time and
material support available. Support was also forthcoming from Florida

State University in the final stages of the preparation of the manuscript. The research was supported, in part, by several grants from the National Institutes of Health. For permission to reprint previously published materials, we wish to thank *Marriage and Family Living, Child Development, Social Forces, Social Problems, Sociology and Social Research, The Pacific Sociological Review.*

We wish also to thank research assistants Marrietta Downs, Evelyn MacDougal, and Leland Axelson (now Assistant Professor) for assistance in the analysis of the data. Mrs. Bernice Dayton, Mrs. Elizabeth Hunt, and Miss Martha Saterfield assisted in the preparation of the manuscript.

Lois Wladis Hoffman
F. Ivan Nye

Contents

III. THE HUSBAND-WIFE RELATIONSHIP

IV. ADJUSTMENT OF THE MOTHER

PART I

WHY THEY WORK

Chapter One

The Socio-Cultural Setting

F. IVAN NYE AND LOIS WLADIS HOFFMAN

FEW, if any, single changes in family life have as profoundly affected so many families in so few years as the movement of mothers into paid employment. Since 1940 there has been an estimated net increase of 10 million mothers in the labor force. Other millions have taken paid employment for a period of time, but have eventually left it. The reasons of *specific* mothers for taking employment may be explained in terms of individual talents and training, personality needs, or the constellation of beliefs, values, or particular family needs. To appreciate the larger phenomenon of the massive movement of mothers into the labor force, one must consider the rapid and fundamental social and cultural developments which have changed America.

In this chapter, we shall present those socio-cultural changes which appear particularly relevant to the movement of mothers into paid employment. Through a close look at our census and survey data, we will show some of the social characteristics of mothers who are most likely to take paid employment. The motivations of specific families and specific mothers will be the focus of Chapter Two, and their reasons for deciding to stay permanently in or to leave employment after a period of time will be considered in Chapter Three.

CHANGING ECONOMIC ORGANIZATION

Industrialization has brought a continuing shift from family-centered to factory-centered production and a further shift from production to distribution and service functions. Men have physically moved from the farm and family-located tasks to factory and office. Similarly but more slowly, women have left family-located tasks for factory, office, classroom, and service establishments. For single women, this transition appears to have been completed prior to 1940, since the number and proportion of single employed women has declined rather than increased since that date. The shift to employment of married women, particularly mothers, has been slowed by their socializing, service, and affectional functions in the home.

Technological advances in production and distribution have made it possible to fashion and service clothing, to produce vegetables and poultry, and to process food much more economically in factories, on specialized farms, or in service establishments, than in the individual home. These advances have transformed the mother from a vitally important economically contributing member of the family to one whose utility in this respect sometimes approachs the trivial.

As the mother's economic duties continue to be transferred to men and women employed in establishments outside the home, the cost of paying for these tasks has been transferred to the father. From his salary comes the increased cost of food and clothing and the large sums required for mechanized household equipment.

This transfer of economic tasks has left the mother with more time that can be devoted to paid employment outside the home. It has also created additional employment opportunities for married women in the very factories and service establishments which perform her former economic tasks. And, in addition, the cost of paying for these services places an added strain on the income of the father.

At the same time, the proportion of the labor force in occupations requiring physical strength has declined, and the professional, sales, clerical, and service occupations have expanded. This has greatly increased the number of jobs which women can perform as easily as men. The more advanced education of many women has further increased their usefulness to employers. The current relatively younger age at marriage, the increased proportion of young women who are married, and the increased size of the average family (since 1933) mean that if a significant proportion of women are to be employed, mothers must be hired. Finally, more married women have been able to enter the labor force without displacing men because of a high level of employment and an expanding economy.

Cultural change, therefore, has allowed mothers increased free time, has added incentive, and simultaneously has provided extensive employment opportunities. For many women, this has presented an attractive opportunity to play a significant new role.[1]

---

[1] The employment opportunities in combination with their lack of economic productivity at home may even create for some mothers a psychologcal *pressure* to enter employment. This point is considered in more detail in Chapter Two.

FAMILY ORGANIZATION

The modal number of children has changed from an estimated eight in 1790 to three in 1960. In a family of eight children, the period of child-bearing not infrequently encompassed two full decades; currently, the typical pattern spaces the first child two years following marriage with two more children following at intervals of two years. Since the present median age at marriage for women is twenty, the mother typically completes childbearing at twenty-six and sees her last child enter school at thirty-two. This pattern of early marriage and relatively small families has resulted in an increased period of time during which a woman may be employed without leaving preschool children.

FAMILY IDEOLOGY

The family ideology which defined the male role as both the dominant party in family decision-making and the provider of family income has passed through a gradual redefinition. Its early decline may have been causally connected to the gradual entry of single women into the labor force. Since these single women supported themselves financially, they were in a better position to insist on making their own decisions. The achievement of the franchise, changes in property laws, and the entry of women into institutions of higher learning were other landmarks and agents in the emergence of an equalitarian ideology. Moreover, as the proportion of employed married women increased, the relative power of these women increased as well, adding further to the development of an equalitarian ideology.

As a consequence of the wide challenge to the ideology of male supremacy and responsibility, the emergence of the married woman as a second wage-earner posed less of a personal threat to the husband. In the emerging equalitarian ideology, there is no compelling logic to support the position that all income be earned by the husband. The visibility of large and increasing numbers of employed married women further reduced the ego threat to the individual husband.

A modified ideology favoring male dominance still appears to be accepted by most American families. However, this is not entirely inconsistent with the employment of the wife, provided her position is lower than her husband's in the occupational hierarchy and yields a smaller portion of the family income.

Although smaller families and a developing equalitarian family ideology have been favorable to the entry of married women into the labor force, some concepts from child psychology have had a deterrent effect.

The conception of personality as a product of interaction, and primarily interaction within the family, has given added content to the mother's child-rearing responsibilities. Again, a two-way interaction may be involved, in that women who are relinquishing their meaningful economic functions in the home are eager to justify this reduction of economic duties by amplifying their responsibilities in interpersonal relationships. This, in turn, may have led to a preoccupation with the emotional life of the child, the creation of the "child-centered family."

This child-rearing philosophy is, in turn, giving way to one which defers less to the child and expects a larger contribution from him; a philosophy which is not incompatible with the expectation that the child will perform some household tasks, or that, on occasion, the mother will not have time to entertain him, chauffeur him, etc. This philosophy of child-rearing is more compatible with the employment of the mother. Again, it is possible that the development of a "person-centered" in contrast to a "child-centered" family philosophy is being accelerated by the entry of mothers into the labor force. This more recent family philosophy rationalizes the employed mother's definition of her duties much better than does the child-centered philosophy.

THE IMAGE OF THE WORKING MOTHER

Neither the general public nor social scientists were prepared for reports which began to appear in 1955 and the following years that more than a third of the mothers of school-age children were employed. These reports, emanating from census surveys through textbooks, newspapers, and magazines, sharply contradicted the traditional image of the mother.

Social scientists and the general public had been aware of the employment of mothers in World War II, but regarded this as a temporary adaptation to a unique set of wartime conditions.[2] Generally, it was felt that the roles of mother and employee were incompatible and could be reconciled only in an emergency. Futhermore, it was believed that when men returned to the labor force there would be few, if any, positions left for mothers.

The knowledge that in peacetime a large *and increasing* minority of mothers were employed brought a mixed but predominantly negative reaction from professional and lay people. Major social changes normally evoke more negative than positive emotions, as people confuse the familiar with the superior. In this case, even social scientists, for the most part,

---

[2] John Durand foresaw the increased employment of married women with more accuracy (6).

took a negative view. Psychiatric comment was generally negative. Lundberg and Farnham, for example, expressed a particularly pessimistic evaluation (12). Even many sociologists, although committed to the idea that social change should (and must) accompany technological change, tended to lump the increased employment of women along with other trends, such as higher divorce rates, more crime and delinquency, and increased alcoholism and schizophrenia among women. Others, such as Bossard, took a strong negative position, contending that such employment was gravely detrimental to children (2). Many interested laymen, always alert for a simple explanation of the numerous and complex social problems of our times, speculated that the employment of the mother was the principal cause of current social problems. Proposals were made to force mothers out of employment. One of the research projects reported in this volume was financed by a social agency which expected to obtain data which would justify its insistence that mothers leave employment.

Only a small minority of sociologists, Komarovsky (10) and Landis (11) to cite two, took a position favoring the change as providing a wider variety of activities for women and permitting fuller use of their training and talents. For this reason, they felt it might actually improve family life.

In the absence of empirical data, the armchair philosophers have had a heyday. Only recently have there been serious efforts to examine empirically the effects of maternal employment. The question is not a simple one, for it involves questions of which mothers go to work, the conditions surrounding their employment, the age of their children, the attitudes of the working mother and her husband, and the alternative to employment for women. Furthermore, the effects have to be specified rather than lumped together in an evaluative way; that is, it may have a different effect on different aspects of family or community relationships.

EXTENT AND TRENDS OF EMPLOYMENT

Census data show a steadily increasing proportion of women in paid employment over a sixty-year period, but, unfortunately, early reports do not distinguish between women who were mothers and those who were not. Estimates are available from the 1940 census, and after 1948 adequate data indicate the presence and age of children in the family.

There has been a "moderate" increase in the proportion of all women gainfully employed—from 25.7 per cent in 1940 to 34.8 per cent in 1960. By contrast, the proportion of employed married women living with their husbands increased from 14.7 to 30.5 per cent in the same twenty-year period, and the proportion of mothers with children under eighteen increased even more dramatically (Table 1.1).

TABLE 1.1 *Women in the Labor Force, 1940–1960*

MARITAL STATUS	EMPLOYED WOMEN						
	1940	1944	1948	1952	1955	1958	1960
	Number (Millions)						
Single	6.7	7.5	5.9	5.5	5.1	5.4	5.4
Married, living with husband	4.2[1]	6.2	7.6	9.2	10.4	11.8	12.3
No children under 18	2.7		4.4	5.0	5.2	5.7	5.7
Children 6–17 only	1.5[1]	[2]	1.9	2.5	3.2	3.7	4.1
Children 0–5		[2]	1.2	1.7	2.0	2.4	2.5
Widowed, divorced, living apart	2.9	4.7	3.7	4.1	4.6	4.8	4.9
All women	13.9	18.5	17.2	18.8	20.1	22.0	22.6
	Per Cent						
Single	48.1	58.6	51.1	50.0	46.6	45.4	44.1
Married, living with husband	14.7	21.7	22.0	25.3	27.7	30.2	30.5
No children under 18			28.4	30.9	32.7	38.8	34.7
Children 6–17 only	8.6[1]	[2]	26.0	31.1	34.7	37.6	39.0
Children 0–5			10.7	13.9	16.0	18.2	18.6
Widowed, divorced, living apart	35.4	42.0	38.3	38.8	38.5	40.8	40.0
All women	25.7	35.0	31.0	32.7	33.4	35.0	34.8

Sources: *Current Population Reports, Labor Force* (4) and *Special Labor Force Report No. 13* (14).
[1] Estimated. Source: *Women as Workers* (15).
[2] No information available.

Women with children of school age have entered the labor force in greater numbers than mothers of preschool children, but the *rate* of increase of both groups is about equal. The *increase* from 1948 to 1960 is 116 per cent for the mothers of the school-age children and 108 per cent for the mothers of preschool children.

Almost one third of all employed women in 1960 were mothers with children under eighteen. While the latter grew over 400 per cent in absolute numbers in a twenty-year period, single employed women declined in actual numbers, and the widowed, divorced, and separated groups showed only small increases. Within this period, the employed mother changed from a negligible social and economic phenomenon to one that affects almost two in five households in which there are children under eighteen.

In total numbers there were 22 million women aged fourteen or over in the labor force (employed or seeking employment) in 1958, which was 35 per cent of the total female population aged fourteen or older. Of these, slightly more than half were married and living with their husbands, one quarter were single, and one quarter had been married but were now widowed, divorced, or separated (Table 1.1). The highest proportion employed is among the single women (45.4 per cent) and, second, those previously but not now married (40.8 per cent); however, women with children aged six to seventeen and living with husbands are not far behind (37.6 per cent). It should be considered that practically all women with dependent children are within the age range in which women are defined as employable, whereas many single and previously married women are not.

THE CHANGING FACE OF THE EMPLOYED MOTHER

Less obvious changes have occurred in the type of work performed by an employed mother, the type of woman employed, and the type of family from which she comes. The 1940 estimate gave 1.5 million mothers living with husbands as being employed full- or part-time. At a time when unemployment was near 10 million, these women were probably in most cases the only or principal means of support of their families. This assumption is further buttressed by the strong social pressure that existed from business and labor to "spread the jobs" by having no more than one wage-earner in each family. The employed mother typically was forced into employment regardless of the size of her family, specialized education, talents, or personal wishes. Since unemployed men were (and still are) recruited in largest numbers from those with the least education and skills, the mothers involved were likely also to come from the bottom socio-economic strata and were unlikely to have advanced educational or vocational training. Mothers in such educational and socio-economic strata are also more likely to have large families.

In general, the employed mother prior to World War II (as nearly as it can be reconstructed) had several children and was forced into an unskilled, physically tiring, low-paying job by direct economic necessity. Although there undoubtedly were exceptions, this image is in harmony with the available facts (7, chap. 11).

The stereotype has persisted, but the reality has changed in the post-war era, particularly as American society enters the 1960's. Now married women living with husbands are not usually forced into employment because of a need for their income as the principal support for their families. The large majority live with husbands who are employed, and this factor

TABLE 1.2 *Occupations of the Employed Female Population for the United States, 1900–1960*

OCCUPATION	WOMEN WORKING						
	1900	1910	1920	1930	1940	1950	1960
				Per Cent			
Professional, technical, and kindred workers	8.1	9.7	11.6	13.4	12.7	12.2	13.3
Farmers and farm managers	5.8	3.7	3.2	2.4	1.2	.7	.4
Managers, officials and proprietors, exc. farm	1.4	2.0	2.2	2.7	3.2	4.3	4.6
Clerical and kindred workers	4.0	9.2	18.6	20.8	21.4	27.4	30.0
Sales workers	4.3	5.1	6.2	6.8	7.3	8.6	7.2
Craftsmen, foremen, and kindred workers	1.4	1.4	1.2	1.0	1.1	1.5	.9
Operatives and kindred workers	23.8	22.9	20.2	17.4	19.5	19.9	16.1
Private household workers	28.7	24.0	15.7	17.8	18.1	8.8	9.8
Service workers, exc. private household	6.7	8.4	8.1	9.7	11.3	12.6	15.4
Farm laborers and foremen	13.1	12.0	10.3	5.9	2.7	2.9	2.0
Laborers, exc. farm and mine	2.6	1.4	2.3	1.5	1.1	.8	.3
Total	99.0	99.9	100.0	100.0	100.0	99.9	100.0

Source: *Occupational Trends in the United States, 1900 to 1950* (13), and *Special Labor Report No. 13* (14).

allows them to enter employment selectively. Thus working mothers living with their husbands may fall into two possibly overlapping categories— (a) those to whom employment gives an opportunity to use their individual talents and vocational training, and (b) those women who are least likely to experience major conflicts in their responsibilities toward their children or to receive negative reactions from their husbands.

This, together with the rapid upgrading of the occupations of both sexes, has radically changed the kinds of jobs held by employed mothers (Table 1.2). The demand for unskilled and slightly skilled labor has declined sharply. The proportion of women employed as household workers and farm laborers has shown a particularly large decline. In contrast, clerical and kindred workers have shown a tremendous increase, with large gains also in sales workers and managers, officials, and proprietors. However, though professional, technical, and kindred workers increased steadily until 1930, this category has shown a slight decline since then.[3] Paid employment for the most part has become less physically tiring, has more status, yields more income, and is accompanied by better working conditions. In the current situation, mothers are *choosing* employment; they are not being forced into it in any absolute sense.

Better educated mothers are moving into the labor force. Although adequate data prior to World War II are unavailable, present data indicate the employed mothers to be better educated, generally, than those not employed (Table 1.3). For many jobs, for both men and women, high

TABLE 1.3 *Education Level and Employment Status of 1972 Washington Mothers*

EDUCATION	NOT EMPLOYED	PART-TIME EMPLOYED	FULL-TIME EMPLOYED	TOTAL	TOTAL
	Per Cent				*Number*
1–6 years	2.0	1.4	.3	1.6	32
7–9 years	15.1	13.0	8.6	13.7	270
10–12 years	60.9	59.6	64.9	61.4	1211
13–16 years	20.0	24.2	20.1	20.6	407
17 or more	1.9	1.8	6.0	2.6	52
Total	99.9	100.0	99.9	99.9	1972

school graduation is a prerequisite. Increasingly, it is the educated women who have the opportunity for employment.

These opportunities for more highly skilled and educated women cause working women to come from different types of families. Dornbusch and Heer have analyzed 1940 and 1950 census data and have shown that although there was an inverse correlation between the rate of female employment and median male income in 1940, there was a reversal for Caucasian women in 1950. That is, the 1950 data show a higher rate of employment for women in *the more prosperous* communities (5). More recent census releases have also shown a trend toward the increased involvement of the middle-class family. Data prior to 1950 generally show that the lower the income of the husband, the more likely· was the employment of the mother. A 1957 census release indicates that this is no longer true. If there were no children under eighteen, the women whose husbands made an average wage—$4,000 to $5,000 yearly—were most

---

[3] This point is discussed further by Caplow (3, p. 230.)

likely to be employed. If minor children of school age were present, the husband earning $2,000 to $3,000 was most likely to have an employed wife; next came husbands earning $3,000 to $4,000, only slightly below the median male income in that year (Table 1.4).

TABLE 1.4 *Labor Force Status of Wife by Presence of Children and Income of Husband, 1957*

INCOME OF HUSBAND	ALL WOMEN 14 YEARS OF AGE AND OVER TOTAL	WIFE WORKING 20 TO 44 YEARS OF AGE			
		TOTAL	NO CHILDREN UNDER 18	CHILDREN 6 TO 17 ONLY	CHILDREN UNDER 6
			Per Cent		
Total	30.2	31.9	60.4	39.9	18.2
Under $1,000	31.3	42.3	....	45.9	28.2
$1,000 to 1,999	28.7	40.0	59.8	47.3	28.3
2,000 to 2,999	34.3	39.3	59.1	57.3	22.9
3,000 to 3,999	36.0	37.7	63.9	49.4	22.4
4,000 to 4,999	34.2	34.2	64.1	42.8	21.1
5,000 to 5,999	27.9	27.2	59.7	34.7	15.0
6,000 to 6,999	27.8	26.4	57.5	36.7	13.4
7,000 to 9,999	20.5	18.3	53.5	26.9	6.2
10,000 and over	14.6	14.8	....	16.2	9.3

Source: *Current Population Reports, Labor Force,* No. 87 (4).

This trend of maternal employment upward into the middle-class family, is further substantiated by its increasing presence in families in which the husband is engaged in a middle-class occupation (Table 1.6). For example, the highest proportions of married women gainfully employed are found among non-farm proprietors; those following have husbands who are clerical and kindred workers, service workers, operatives, sales workers, laborers (except farm), craftsmen, professionals, farmers and farm managers, non-farm managers and officials, and farm laborers and foremen.

In brief, in two decades the employed mother has passed through two states and into a third. In the first state, she provided sole support for herself and her family; in the second, her husband was employed or partially employed in the lowest income bracket; and at present, her husband is employed with an income only slightly lower than the median for the entire society. During the same period a transition was made from a situation in which women were *forced* into employment with their labor the primary source of family income, to one in which women are *drawn* into employment to raise family living standards or for other reasons. A rapid upgrading of occupations has raised the pay and status of the employed mother. This has required more vocational training, which has involved more and more middle-class families.

SOCIAL DIFFERENCES BETWEEN EMPLOYED AND NOT EMPLOYED

All studies have shown family size to differentiate among women entering employment. In the Washington sample (Table 1.5), the number

TABLE 1.5 *Number of Children and Employment Status of 1976 Washington Mothers*

NUMBER OF CHILDREN BORN OR ADOPTED	NOT EMPLOYED	PART-TIME EMPLOYED	FULL-TIME EMPLOYED	TOTAL	TOTAL
		Per Cent			*Number*
1	3.8	4.3	12.7	5.4	*107*
2	23.1	28.0	34.7	25.7	*509*
3	27.3	27.6	25.2	26.9	*532*
4	24.0	21.9	15.9	22.3	*440*
5	10.3	11.5	4.6	9.5	*188*
6 or more	11.6	6.9	6.9	10.1	*200*
Total	100.1	100.2	100.0	99.9	*1976*

of children averaged one more per family among the non-employed women; moreover, the proportion of families with four or more children is much larger for this group. The difference is even greater with respect to the presence of preschool children in the home—65 per cent for the non-employed compared to 23 per cent for those employed full-time.

The relationship of socio-economic status to employment of mothers is not entirely clear from the census data. Employment of the wives of professional men is low, but it is high for the wives of business owners and proprietors. It is high for wives of men in clerical work but low for wives of agricultural laborers (Table 1.6). These differences appear to stem partly from the availability of suitable work in family-operated businesses and the absence of suitable employment for wives of agricultural laborers; however, they also result from limitations in the census classification. In the Washington study, the Empey scale for measuring occupational prestige was employed. Unlike the census category, it differentiates between businesses of various sizes, assigning lower prestige to those employing pri-

TABLE 1.6   *Labor Force Status of Wives by Occupation of Husband*

OCCUPATION OF HUSBAND	WIVES IN LABOR FORCE Per Cent
All categories	30.9
Farm laborers and foremen	22.4
Non-farm managers and officials	25.4
Farmers and farm managers	26.2
Professional, technical, and kindred workers	27.2
Craftsmen, foremen, and kindred workers	28.9
Laborers, except farm and mine	32.8
Sales workers	33.4
Operatives and kindred workers	34.0
Service workers (inc. private household)	35.7
Clerical and kindred workers	36.6
Non-farm proprietors	36.8

Source: *Current Population Reports, Labor Force* (1).

marily family labor (8). This criterion does discriminate between families in which the mother is or is not employed. A smaller percentage of employed mothers come from families in which the husband is the owner or manager of a large business. That there is some relationship to social class is also indicated in the slightly lower incomes of husbands of employed women (Table 1.4). The Washington data also show that *within* an occupational category the wives of husbands earning less are more likely to be employed. It appears evident, therefore, that although more and more employed mothers are coming from middle and upper socio-economic levels, they are still overrepresented in the lower and lower-middle classes.

Employed mothers as a category have somewhat more education than mothers not in the labor force. In the sample of Washington mothers, the differences are greatest between the proportion of employed and not employed who have junior high or less education (Table 1.3). In the same sample, more employed mothers also had some college education, but the differences are less.[4]

If broken homes are considered as a single category, they are more prevalent among employed mothers. However, when they are divided into those in which the mother has and those in which she has not remarried, the

---

[4] Since "absolute need" is presumably greater for mothers who have no more than a junior high school education, this provides more evidence that more women are choosing than are being forced into employment.

TABLE 1.7 *Marital Status and Employment Status of 1975 Washington Mothers*

Marital Status	NOT EMPLOYED	PART-TIME EMPLOYED	FULL-TIME EMPLOYED	TOTAL	TOTAL
	Per Cent				*Number*
Original marriage	86.3	87.0	74.1	83.8	*1665*
Solo mother	1.8	2.5	13.0	3.8	*76*
Remarriage	11.9	10.5	13.0	11.8	*234*
Total	100.0	100.0	100.1	99.4	*1975*

relationship is quite different for the two. In the Washington study, 13 per cent of the families of the employed mothers and 1 per cent of those of non-employed mothers included no male adult (Table 1.7). Stated another way, over 80 per cent of the female heads of households were employed compared to less than 40 per cent of women who were not heads of households.

Remarriages (in which there is a male head of household) present a very different picture. Almost identical proportions of remarriages were found in the three employment categories (Table 1.7).

Census data (1959) show a higher proportion of non-white women in the labor force; 46.2 per cent of non-white and 34.8 per cent of white women work. This can be refined slightly by taking the age group from thirty-four to forty-four—in which individuals are likely to be married and have dependent children of school age. In this age range, 60.8 per cent of the non-white females were employed compared to 41.1 per cent of the white females (1).

The proportion of women employed reaches its peak in the age range from thirty-five to forty-four, but there is no sharp peak. Rather, a plateau of high employment extends from age twenty through fifty-five. Between the forty-five to fifty-four and fifty-five to sixty-four categories, a substantial decline occurs—from 54.3 to 40.9 per cent employed. For the purposes of the present inquiries, it is of interest that the years of peak employment for women are twenty-five to fifty-four, the same years in which their household and family responsibilities are heaviest. Finally, after sixty-five only 16.5 per cent are employed (1).

SUMMARY

The American mother moved into paid employment in significant numbers during World War II. Contrary to the expectation of American society in general and social scientists in particular, her numbers continued to increase rapidly during the postwar era. By 1960, almost 40 per cent of mothers of children six to seventeen years of age were in the labor force, and almost 20 per cent of those with preschool children were employed.

This massive movement was made possible by: (a) new labor-saving machinery in the home and new inventions and distributive techniques in industry and trade which permitted the mother's economic tasks to be performed more efficiently outside the home; (b) smaller families; and (c) the spread of equalitarian family ideology. The continued dominance of the value of an increased standard of living, broadly defined, provided strong positive motivations.

The rapid upgrading of occupations following World War II created a demand for well-educated women. This increasingly involved not only more middle-class women but, as a consequence, middle-class husbands and children. The employed wife presently is likely to have more education than her non-employed counterpart, but her husband is likely to have a slightly lower occupational level and lower income than the husband of a woman not employed.

By 1955 the continued surge of mothers into paid employment had been noticed by social scientists and laymen alike. The more vocal laymen, in most instances, denounced the trend and even intimated that action should be taken to reverse it. Social scientists were divided and without adequate research from which to generalize.

The contributors of this volume were attracted by a desire to investigate empirically the effects of maternal employment—to line up the facts where there has been only speculation. In the following pages, the findings of nineteen social scientists working alone or in teams are presented with the thought that many researchers employing several frames of reference and different samples and methodological techniques might provide an over-all view of the phenomenon that is more reliable and more exhaustive than any single researcher could achieve.

REFERENCES

1. "Annual Report of the Labor Force, 1958," *Current Population Reports, Labor Force*. United States Department of Commerce, Bureau of the Census. Washington, D.C.: Government Printing Office, 1959.
2. Bossard, James H. S. *The Sociology of Child Development*. New York: Harper, 1954, pp. 282–86.
3. Caplow, Theodore. *The Sociology of Work*. Minneapolis: University of Minnesota Press, 1954.

4. *Current Population Reports, Labor Force.* United States Department of Commerce, Bureau of the Census, Series P-50, Nos. 22, 62, 73, 76, 81, and 87. Washington, D.C.: Government Printing Office.
5. Dornbusch, Sanford M., and Heer, David M. "The Evaluation of Work by Females, 1940–1950," *American Journal of Sociology,* LXIII (July, 1957), 27–30.
6. Durand, John D. "Married Women in the Labor Force," *American Journal of Sociology,* LII (November, 1946), 217–24.
7. Elliott, Mabel A., and Merrill, Francis E. *Social Disorganization.* New York: Harper, 1950.
8. Empey, LaMar T. "Social Class and Occupational Aspiration: A Comparison of Absolute and Relative Measurement," *American Sociological Review,* XXI (December, 1956), 703–9.
9. Kirkpatrick, Clifford. "Inconsistency in Marriage Roles and Marriage Conflict." In Judson and Mary Landis, eds. *Readings in Marriage and the Family.* New York: Prentice-Hall, 1952, pp. 386–92.
10. Komarovsky, Mirra. *Women in the Modern World.* Boston: Little, Brown, 1953.
11. Landis, Paul H. *Making the Most of Marriage.* New York: Appleton-Century-Crofts, 1955.
12. Lundberg, Ferdinand, and Farnham, Marynia F. *Modern Woman, The Lost Sex.* New York: Harper, 1947.
13. *Occupational Trends in the United States, 1900 to 1950.* United States Department of Commerce, Bureau of the Census, Working Paper No. 5. Washington, D.C.: Government Printing Office, 1958.
14. *Special Labor Force Report No. 13.* United States Department of Labor. Washington, D.C.: Government Printing Office, 1961.
15. *Women as Workers.* United States Department of Labor, Women's Bureau, D.-65. Washington, D.C.: Government Printing Office.

Chapter Two

The Decision to Work

LOIS WLADIS HOFFMAN

CHAPTER One sketched the social changes which seem to have been important in bringing about the increase in maternal employment. Linking these changes to maternal employment are many individual decisions—each made by a single woman or family. Yet these decisions, based on personal and seemingly idiosyncratic factors, have a great deal in common, for the families are part of the same society and subject to similar experiences. Mrs. Jones may decide to go to work because she is bored staying at home now that her youngest child is in school. She does not consider the high degree of mechanization of her household or the availability of commercial services, but the boredom she feels may be intimately linked to these factors nonetheless; and because of these, many other women in her position also feel bored. These same factors can influence the decision to work in additional ways. Another woman, for example, may decide to work as a means of supplementing the family income, but this possibility might not have occurred to her if she were indispensable to the operation of her household.

THE STUDY OF MOTIVATION FOR EMPLOYMENT

The actual decision usually involves several motivations and takes into consideration certain barriers to employment as well as facilitating factors, but even a single motivation can often be traced to several social factors. Thus, for example, boredom does not result simply from having surplus time. The Protestant Ethic, which has made work the cornerstone of virtue and leisure frought with anxiety, may also be important. Birth control and

18

the possibility of completing the child-bearing period while the mother is still young are yet other possible social factors. It is also possible that boredom is tied to the fact that the mother is likely to be the only adult at home during the day—the husband being at work and no members of the extended family sharing the same household. The possibilities are many. Individual decisions are based on a complex of social factors which are often so interwoven that it is difficult to trace a particular motivation back to its social origins, even when its prevalence suggests such origins. However, the examination of individual decisions for this purpose should help us understand the functional interrelationships among the various relevant social factors. That is, through the analysis of individual decisions the researcher gains insights about the processes by which certain social events have contributed to the increased employment of mothers.

The study of individual motivations may also enable us to predict the effects maternal employment will have in the future, whether it will continue to increase or start to decline, and what functional substitutes might arise to take its place. In studying individual motivations we often find that two social events which on the surface appear to be unrelated or even contradictory are but two alternative responses to the same need. For example, the recent increase in family size is often seen as an opposite trend to that of increased maternal employment. Possibly, however, these are two solutions to the same problems. One way to fill time and to increase one's sense of contribution is to go to work; another is to have a baby (9).

In addition, and more germane to the present book, studying motivations for employment is necessary for understanding the effects of employment on the family. There are at least two reasons for this. The first is the methodological problem stemming from the fact that the motivations women have for working differentiate them from non-working women even before their employment. The second is a theoretical concern; the effects of employment may be conditioned by the motives underlying it. Both of these problems, self-selection and the interaction between employment and its underlying motives, will come up repeatedly in this book, and so they will be elaborated on here.

SELF-SELECTION

In the social sciences one seldom has the opportunity to utilize a laboratory setting with a before-measure, a stimulus imposed by the experimenter, and an after-measure, all under controlled conditions. Rather, the social scientist must usually be contented with comparing groups of subjects who have selected themselves into the "experimental" or "control" group. This technique always raises questions as to whether the differences obtained between the groups are due to the effects of the stimulus (maternal employment) or merely reflect differences which existed previously and led to "choosing" that stimulus. Thus, for example, if the children of working mothers show a higher incidence of juvenile delinquency, is this due to the employment or to the fact that women who go to work tend to be economically underprivileged, rejecting of their children, or without husbands?

Furthermore, effects of employment can be *obscured* by selective factors. For example, it is possible that mothers who seek employment after the youngest child enters school are the ones who have been the most totally involved with their children, and who therefore feel the greatest need to fill their time once the children are no longer home during the day. If working were to lessen such involvement, this effect would not be apparent in a comparison of working and non-working women since with lessened involvement the working mothers would be the same as those who were not working.

Almost all the studies in this volume have tried to deal with the problem of selective factors, and this requires an answer to the question of how working mothers differ from non-working mothers at the point of making the decision about going to work. To answer this, we must understand why mothers work and what factors enable them to work.

INTERACTION BETWEEN EMPLOYMENT AND UNDERLYING MOTIVES

The other major reason for considering the factors involved in the decision to go to work when studying the effects on the family involves a problem more theoretical than methodological. The effects of employment will depend in part on the meaning it has for the mother and her family. For example, if employment is motivated by the desire to escape the maternal role, the children may be aware of this, and the mother's action may represent rejection to them; whereas a different motivation might arouse a different response from the children. The theory discussed in Chapter Six provides another example: the working mother who enjoys her work may feel guilty and try to compensate by overdoing the maternal role, while the mother who does not enjoy work will be free of guilt and therefore more likely to withdraw from the maternal role. A similar theory could account for Kligler's finding that women who work because of interest in the job are more likely to report that their mother-role performance has improved as a result of employment than are mothers who work for financial reasons (10).

Suggestive of another possible source of interaction between motivation and effects is Glenn's finding that community approval or disapproval of maternal employment depends on the motivations for employment (6). It seems likely that the community attitude toward a mother's employment might, in turn, influence her family's response to it.

In sum, it may not be fruitful to study the effects of maternal employment per se, but rather it may be necessary also to consider the factors involved in the decision to work or not. Maternal employment may be a meaningful variable only when we consider the context within which it takes place.

KINDS OF DATA AVAILABLE ON MATERNAL EMPLOYMENT MOTIVES

Despite the importance of understanding the factors involved in the decision to seek employment, there is little research which has focussed on this problem. Most of the existing data are of two kinds: those showing demographic differences between working and non-working women and those reporting women's responses to direct questions about why they did or did not go to work. The former data exist almost in abundance. It is known, for example, that whether or not a woman works is related to her marital status, husband's income, education, the number of children she has, the age of her children, her place of residence, race, and ethnic background (14). Occasionally two of these variables have been considered simultaneously in relation to maternal employment. For example, the negative relationship between the husband's income and maternal employment is strongest for mothers of small children. For mothers of older children, the relationship is not linear, and the figures suggest that financial need is a less salient reason for employment.[1] Such analyses in which the relationship between maternal employment and another demographic variable is examined, with a third controlled, are unusual, although they are much more useful for theory development than simple two-variable correlations.

An example of a finding that could be theoretically suggestive if examined this way is the relationship between female employment rates and ethnic background. In certain areas, Japanese-American women are the most highly represented in the working force, followed by Negro women, Puerto Rican, "white" women, Chinese, Indian, and Mexican, respectively (14, p. 78). This order does not follow the economic position of these groups in society, nor does it seem to reflect directly such factors as family size. The Puerto Rican group has a relatively high female employment rate and the Mexican group, a low one, although both are predominantly Catholic, Spanish-speaking, and economically underprivileged. This is an interesting finding in itself, but one might gain considerable insight by examining the order of these groups within each of several categories. Is this order the same, for example, for single women, married women without

---

[1] For mothers of older children there is little difference in employment rates according to husband's income if his income is under $5,000. These rates fall sharply in the $5,000 to $10,000 range but rise somewhat in the group where the husband earns over $10,000 (14, p. 72).

children, and married women with children? If so, we would know that it was not merely the reflection of marital status and family size and, further, if the order reflected group attitudes, that these attitudes applied to women in general rather than to mothers only.

The demographic data, then, by showing certain correlates of maternal employment, suggest variables that need to be controlled, but as yet they have not been sufficiently exploited for theoretical purposes.

Data of the second kind—those based on women's responses to direct questions about motivation for employment—often suffer from superficiality. The questions have been simple, and only the first responses given are usually reported. Measuring motivation by the response to a single, direct question is inadequate at best. Motives in general, and certainly motives for maternal employment, are not that simple.

An additional complication is that respondents often feel there is considerable social censure of maternal employment. The direct question is, therefore, apt to put a respondent on the defensive, and as a result she may not readily give her most personal reasons. She would most likely hold back entirely an answer which suggested that she was rejecting her child or working for personal pleasure.

Another reason for the inadequacy of this approach is that the question has an answer that borders on the cliché: "Why do you work?" "For money." Indeed, this is the response overwhelmingly given by women (11, 18, 19, 20, Chapter Three).[2] Somewhere between 55 and 90 per cent of the answers will be in terms of money, depending on the particular sample of women being interviewed, the phrasing of the question, whether it is part of a questionnaire or personal interview, etc. The answer may be worded sometimes as simply "the money," sometimes as monetary need, sometimes as money to repay debts, "money for the children," money for some specific purchase such as a home, extra money, personal money, or the high pay. If the respondent is encouraged to elaborate on her answer, she will usually come forth with additional reasons. At this point, she will often talk about boredom, having insufficient work in the home, being "nervous" at home, and about the positive aspects of the job. Sometimes more specific concerns are added like: "The plant was near enough that I could get home before the kids get back from school."

But such answers as these are still insufficient. What is needed is a focussed interview designed to obtain data on the complexities of the

---

[2] Industrial sociologists have noted that inarticulate and unacceptable frustrations and desires on the part of workers often find expression in the form of wage demands. The tendency for women to say they work for money may be a similar phenomenon. Money may seem to be a more acceptable reason for employment than the satisfaction of a vaguely felt need.

decision.[3] The simpler questions may be useful for specific research purposes, but until more intensive interview procedures are employed, we can only speculate about the factors involved in the decision to work.

THE MOTIVATIONS

The decision to be a working mother may be made thoughtfully and deliberately or so subtly that the actors involved—the decision-makers—do not know a decision has been made. Whichever is the case, the decision may be thought of as having two components—motivations and facilitators. The first are the needs and desires both conscious and unconscious that make maternal employment attractive. The second, which we will take up later, are those factors which make it possible.

MONEY

We have already noted that women give "money" as their major reason for working and, cliché though it may be, it is undoubtedly a major motivation. A bulletin put out by the Women's Bureau of the Department of Labor (18) demonstrates, by calling on the results of many other studies, that working women are often supporting dependents and, in fact, are frequently the sole support of their families. The relationship between father's income and mother's employment has already been mentioned. In addition to the actual size of the income, income satisfaction and *perceived* financial need are important. Sobol found that wives were more likely to enter the working force when their family incomes dropped from their former level than when they remained stable or increased. This finding was statistically significant for each socio-economic level.[4] Just as wives will go to work to maintain their standard of living, they will also take employment to achieve the level of those around them. Thus, if working does not detract from one's social status, families which strive for upward mobility and take as their reference group families with incomes higher than their own, may augment their income through maternal employment. In certain occupational groups such as teaching, the actual income is considerably below the desired style of life—not so much because of mobility strivings as because of education. A school teacher usually hopes that his children can go to college, but he may not be able to afford this unless his wife works. In each of these situations, where there is financial depriva-

---

[3] The focussed interview is discussed in detail by Merton, Fiske, and Kendall (12).

[4] This unpublished finding is reported by Marion G. Sobol in personal communication. It is based on a panel study of urban families carried out by the Economic Behavior Program, Institute for Social Research, University of Michigan, 1954–1957.

tion relative to a particular standard, the mother may enter the labor force out of what she may perceive as financial need.

Sometimes the mother works to pay debts. These debts may have been incurred by necessity—such as when there is prolonged illness—or by credit buying. These situations are like the above except that here the spending precedes the employment, so employment becomes a very real as well as a perceived necessity. The particular order—spending and then working—may be a function of greater resistance to employment, poor financial planning, or even good financial planning (i.e., when the family engages in deficit spending knowing that the mother will go to work at a later and more convenient date). Consideration of how the family managed to get into debt is important in determining the significance of this motive. The distinction between expensive illness and blatant extravagance is, of course, an extreme one. Further, if extravagance is the reason, which parent was the lavish one might be crucial in determining the impact of the employment on the family.

Financial *desires* are also important. Maternal employment has brought an unprecedented level of living to many working-class families. American advertising has succeeded in keeping people's desires for material goods beyond their ability to obtain them. Furthermore, the coveted purchase is often expensive enough to require an extra income, yet inexpensive enough to be obtainable without a permanent commitment by the supplementary wage-earner, and durable enough to make a sustained effort worth while. It is a washing machine, a drier, a car, a down payment on a house, carpeting, or possibly even a mink coat. Among the eighty-nine working mothers of Detroit elementary school children (the sample used for the analysis in Chapters Six and Fifteen) the down-payment on a house was mentioned most frequently. Financial desires also may be non-specific: sometimes the mother works for "pin money." "Pin money" seems to mean money that can be used for incidental luxuries that can be spent without family consultation. It is closely akin to "personal money"—i.e., money which the wife controls and can spend independently.

Any of these monetary motivations can also be tied in with other attitudes that are important to consider. For example, is the financial motivation related to a feeling that the father is a failure? If so, the mother's employment could symbolize his failure for the whole family. On the other hand, the mother's employment could be part of cooperative planning and perceived as a symbol of family unity. Perhaps the working mother is paying penance for her poor management and extravagance. Or, she might want an independent income because of marital difficulties or simply out of a desire for autonomy in an otherwise close and congenial relationship. Clearly, the possible underlying motives are many, and the family climate surrounding employment cannot be automatically inferred from the monetary motive alone.

Money also operates as a motivation for employment in less concrete ways. Because of the availability of jobs, because so many women are working, and because so many have worked at some time in their lives, a woman's time has come to have monetary meaning. A modern woman who bakes her own bread must figure into its cost not only the cost of the ingredients but the cost of her labor. A mother whose children are all in school could spend her day diligently trying to save money by sewing the family's clothes, doing all of her own cooking, canning, cleaning, repair work, and redecorating and still not save enough money to compensate her for her time. It is more economical for her to obtain outside work and use commercial facilities for the needed household services. Goods are produced at less cost by mass production than they can be produced at home. Thus, if her household activities are not intrinsically satisfying, the woman may choose outside employment; and even if they are, she may choose employment because these household activities then become akin to leisure in that she must acknowledge that she does them for pleasure. The mother who does not work may feel that she is actually "spending" money for the privilege of not working, and therefore, particularly where all her children are of school age, she may feel guilty about *not* working. This seems to be a switch from the usual view, but as employment becomes increasingly common and increasingly possible, it may become more fruitful to ask "Why don't mothers work?" than "Why do they work?" The former is also becoming, in some cases, the question that the disapproving neighbors ask. The working mother of adolescent children who does not seem to be neglecting her roles as wife and mother is often admired for "working so hard." The mother of adolescent children who does not work and who can be seen sunning herself in her back yard or visiting with the neighbors, is often the object of disapproval. The Protestant Ethic is still very much with us,[5] and if the mother and wife roles do not fill the working day, it is increasingly felt that this time should be spent in gainful employment.

The notion that a woman's time represents potential wages has led some young wives to consider their salaries in estimating the cost of having a baby. Although it was said partly as a jest, this point was brought home when a young professional woman said to her secretary, "It's all right for you to have a baby; it only costs you $4,000 to quit your job. But it would cost me $9,500, so I can't afford it."

Money operates as a motive for employment in still another way.

---

[5] The existence of the Protestant Ethic in the present day has been brought out in a study by Morse and Weiss (13).

The role of housewife and mother, however important it may be to society, carries with it little opportunity for a sense of achievement, competence, and contribution. The educational system and cultural values have tied feelings of achievement to success in the intellectual or business world. These have been intimately linked to money and the increasing size of the pay check, whether it increases because of inflation, union demands, or promotion. The housewife has none of these rewards. As Riesman (15, p. 300) has said:

> [The housewife] does not find her work explicitly defined and totaled, either as an hour product or a dollar product, in the national census, or in people's minds.

Because of the lack of significance attached to her work, the housewife feels she is incompetent and that her contribution is a small one. No one expresses this more clearly than housewives themselves when they answer the inquiry about their occupation with the poignant phrase, "just a housewife." Bringing home a pay check, whether it is added to the family budget, saved for a rainy day, or used only as pin money, seems, in contrast, to be a sign of competence and a tangible contribution to the family.

THE HOUSEWIFE AND MOTHER ROLES

Although the absence of wages may contribute to the housewife's feeling that her contribution is not great, this is not the whole story. Part of it lies in certain intrinsic aspects of the housekeeping role. Leaving aside temporarily the role of mother, and examining only that of housekeeper, one cannot fail to note the lack of creativity it affords. There is very little skill demanded and very little room for excellence. Take cooking, perhaps the most creative of the household tasks. A woman married about the time of World War I came to marriage well schooled in the art of cooking. Since this art was usually passed on from mother to daughter and developed through trial and error in private kitchens, each woman usually had certain dishes that were hers individually. It was a mysterious art which some could perform well and some could not. In a small community a woman could become famous for her cherry pie, and since the recipe was not written down and the quantity of the ingredients depended on the size of her hand, and the firmness of her "pinch," she usually remained the only person in the community who made pie just like that. Betty Crocker (5) does not depend on the size of a hand but says "seven-eights of a cup of sifted flour." If a guest admires a dish, the generous hostess can say, "page 42 in Betty Crocker." With this message the guest has all of the skill needed to reproduce the dish exactly. With the introduction of package mixes, even the skill of literacy is no longer required, and many a housewife is *saddened* to learn that with a package mix she can make an angle food cake two inches higher than the one she had previously made from one cookbook and twelve left-over egg whites.

If cooking is no longer creative, what is dusting, vacuuming, turning on the washing machine, running the drier, ironing, making beds, and doing 3,500 dishes every month?[6] Furthermore, the repetitive nature of these tasks makes the housewife wonder if it is necessary to do them as often as she does, and indeed, there is some evidence that it is not necessary. A frequent remark by the Detroit mothers in discussing the changes that occurred when they started or quit work was that when they were home all day, they were busy doing housework every minute, but when they were working, they could not see what they were leaving undone.

"I think I'm more efficient [when I work] . . . ; [I] have a better run home. Who was it that said 'if a woman has an hour to do a job she'll get it done in an hour, but if she has all day, it takes all day?' "

"I'm more relaxed [when I work]. The things that used to upset me don't bother me at all—like the house. I don't like it to be dirty but I don't have to run around picking things up like I did."

"I was driving him [husband] and Tim [son] crazy. I can't stand dirt. . . My husband was always after me about how much I clean. I'm just that way. I can't stand dirt and when I'm home I do it all the time."

"I did more work in the house that was unnecessary [when I wasn't working] . . ."

"I get more work done [in the house] really when I'm working [employed] because I know I have to keep up and I don't waste my time doing foolish things—like dusting that table every time I pass it."

"Sure I clean less thoroughly . . . but the house is just as clean."

Of the 178 mothers interviewed in the Detroit study, 108 had started or returned to work after a period of not working. This figure of 108 excludes all situations which were unusual in that the husbands were in the armed services, ill, or unemployed, but includes situations where there were as yet no children. Asked to report changes in their household, 25 per cent reported that they became more efficient in accomplishing household tasks; 46 per cent, that they cleaned less often or less thoroughly; 17

---

[6] The 3,500 dishes per month was estimated for a family of four and reported in an advertisement in *Better Homes and Gardens* (1, p. 160).

per cent, that they stopped ironing certain items which could be simply folded and put away; 22 per cent, that they spent less time on meal preparation; and 50 per cent, that they baked less. This does not mean that the reduced activities were not missed, but it does suggest that much of the work that is done by the full-time housewife is at least not *essential*.

What does it mean to spend one's day in labor that is unskilled, repetitive, and partly non-essential? Della Cyrus (4, p. 392) has expressed this vividly:

> Modern conveniences plus modern high standards, while freeing women from the back-breaking physical labor of the pioneer woman, have increased enormously her petty cleaning-up tasks. The number of things which modern women have to wash and polish and starch and iron and sterilize, and the number of times they have to do it, have multiplied until many housewives spend most of the time cleaning one thing or another, and cannot imagine how the pioneer woman found time to do all she did. If the pioneer woman had spent so much time on the luxury and boredom of cleanliness, she wouldn't have been paying her way, and the modern woman knows in her heart that she isn't paying hers, either.

This is not to say that work on an assembly line is a mad, gay lark, but it does have certain advantages. It takes place outside the home. However unattractive the place of work may be, the fact that there is a change of scenery—in traveling between work and home as well as in actually doing the work—adds a variety to the day. In addition, outside work usually starts and stops at a specified time and the job is "done" when the worker leaves the shop. It usually involves interaction with other adults, not only at coffee breaks, which the housewife may also have, but also during the working hours. In addition, outside work often does offer opportunities for creativity and feelings of contribution and competence. This is clearly true for the professional and social service occupations such as teacher, nurse, and social worker; but it is also true for many white-collar jobs. Being judged as satisfactory on the basis of one's performance and by persons outside the family who are considered to be more objective and who usually have higher social status, add considerably to one's sense of competence. Occupying a particular niche in a large-scale organization, such as that of receptionist or secretary, often makes one feel an essential part of something important. Having contact with important people and distant places (the switchboard operator who places calls to foreign countries) often adds significance to a job. But for all jobs, even the dullest and most routine, there is at least the pay check which says, "You have done work which someone considers worth money" and "You are helping to buy a house by your employment."

Weiss and Samelson (17) asked a national sample of women what activities made them feel useful and important. They found that employed mothers were more likely to mention some aspect of their job than they were to mention either housework or their role in the family as wife and mother. They also found that although about 55 per cent of the mothers who were not employed mentioned housework as one response, only 36 per cent of the employed mothers did.[7] The percentage who mentioned the wife and mother roles, incidentally, was not affected by whether or not the wife worked. These data support the notion that the outside job is indeed an important source of feelings of usefulness and importance. They also suggest that whether or not housework is named as a source of these feelings depends in part on whether there are alternative sources.

But what about the mother role? Isn't this the most creative of all? Very likely it is, and, viewed from the perspective of a lifetime, most mothers would probably say and really feel that here was their most creative endeavor. But in the day-to-day experience of the mother, it is easy to lose sight of this long-range creativity. Changing and washing diapers, picking up toys, putting on snowsuits, and wiping up footprints do not feel creative when they are being done. However, especially when there is a preschool child in the family, there are highly creative moments, there are feelings of being irreplaceable, and there is enough work to easily fill the working day. But when the youngest child enters school, the mother is again left with a day full of housework rather than mothering. The Weiss-Samelson data mentioned above also show that satisfactions from "family inter-relationships," which include the mother role, diminish when the child enters school. While 58 per cent of the non-working mothers of preschool children mention this source of satisfaction, only 41 per cent of the non-working mothers of school children do so.

It is possible that the greater the joys of mothering for a woman, the more empty the days when the children are all in school. Even women who were satisfied with the housewife role before there were children may not be content to return to it. They have been used to a fuller and, in many ways, a richer day, and the house-cleaning tasks may seem less important and more boring than ever.

The period when the youngest child enters school can be very difficult for many mothers. Not only is the child physically absent from the home, but he is less dependent on the mother, and for some women this is a great loss. Just as many women themselves wish to remain dependent, some also

---

[7] Respondents gave more than one response.

wish to have others remain dependent on them. This is a time when mothers often feel they are no longer needed and their major role is over. They may feel, too, that they are growing old or at least that they have lost the vigor of youth. Thus, the mothers who return to work when their youngest child enters school may be motivated not only by practical reasons —i.e., they are now more dispensable to the household—but also by psychological reasons, namely, the dissatisfactions that emerge at this time.

There is yet another reason why this time would be psychologically appropriate for women to return to work. The period when there are preschool children at home can have many frustrating moments for the mother. In addition to the unrewarding work activities mentioned above, the mother's freedom is often considerably restricted. In fact, in one part of the Detroit study, 217 mothers were asked, "How is a woman's life changed by having children?" By far the most common response was that children meant less freedom, particularly that they restricted the mother's freedom of movement. Forty women gave as their first response that children "tie you to the house," "tie you down," or some *very similar* wording. Most of the answers to this question were negative—four times as many gave totally negative responses as gave totally positive. Only half the respondents gave answers that could, *in any part,* be considered positive.[8] Thus, the period when the mother has preschool children may be an extremely frustrating time—a time when she must hold back impulses, defer gratification, and above all, remain physically in the home. For perhaps twelve years, she has had at least one preschool child in the house and been unable to express these frustrations. She did not express them because her role demanded certain behaviors, because she felt that to do a good job she should not, and perhaps because she was not able to acknowledge them to herself. Whatever the reasons, the youngest child's entering school can provide a release for many of the frustrations of the preceding years, and outside employment may be one expression of this release. This motivation is, in a sense, the opposite of the one discussed earlier and would characterize a different group of women. The former involves the notion that the early years of mothering are gratifying and the later years represent a relative dissatisfaction. This one, on the other hand, suggests that the early years are frustrating and the later years allow for the release of these suppressed tensions.

For some women, of course, these tensions are not suppressed. For some the loss of freedom that the preschool child brings to the mother is itself a motivation for employment. For some, the gratifying aspects of

---

[8] There was essentially no difference between working mothers and non-working mothers in the number of positive or negative responses given.

these years are outweighed by the dull day-to-day routines, loneliness and the longing for adult company, boredom with the same physical surroundings, frustration because of the constant requirement that the child's needs have priority over the mother's, the ever presence of the child's needs, the noise level, and the overwhelming sense of personal responsibility. Thus, even in the preschool years, the intrinsically negative aspects of the housewife and mother roles can provide motivations for outside employment.

PERSONALITY FACTORS

Monetary motives for employment and those derived from the housewife and mother roles are, of course, interrelated. And interrelated with both of these are motives derived from personality factors. For example, we have noted that employment may be motivated by aspirations for upward social mobility and also by a desire for a sense of competence. Both of these would be more likely in a woman who has a high need for achievement. It is possible that education and employment for married women relate positively (14; Chapter One; Chapter Ten; Chapter Twenty-Three) not merely because education facilitates employment but also because education is a manifestation of and a stimulation to the achievement motivation. Veroff, Atkinson, Feld, and Gurin (16) found a positive association between education and the need for achievement in women.

A closely related motivation is one that might be thought of as a drive for actualization—to live up to one's creative potential. Personality theorists are divided on whether creativity and self-expression are the sublimation of unsatisfied needs or whether these represent needs of a higher order that can exist only when the more basic needs are satisfied. Whatever the basis, this is a motivation close to the need for achievement which might make some women less satisfied with the housewife and mother roles, particularly with their less challenging and more mundane aspects. To such women these roles seem not to call for the utilization of the women's full potential, and employment may be seen as offering a greater opportunity in this respect. For the professionally trained or talented, this may also involve a feeling of obligation to oneself or to society to use one's skills. For others, it may involve the feeling expressed by Cyrus:

It is a criminal waste for a woman to devote a lifetime
to the cleanliness of a single family (4, p. 393).

More often it simply involves a feeling that the daily activities of the role do not adequately express a woman's energy and capabilities.

Often, too, there is a need for the maximization of gratification rather than potential, a striving for a more fulfilled life but not necessarily through the utilization of one's capacities. This may vary between a questioning and non-acceptance of one's lot, on the one hand, and a wild pursuit of happiness, on the other. The analysis of monetary motivations and the sources of discontent in the housewife and mother roles is meaningful only so long as there is some notion that one has a right to a good life. Thus, the women who seek employment because of some potential for gratification are women who do not simply accept their plight but act to change it. This non-acceptance of one's personal status quo is probably an important prerequisite for the high employment rate of mothers in the United States.

A personality trait often attributed to working women is a need for power or dominance or, in Freudian terms, penis envy. This trait has been associated with the early feminists and is still part of the stereotype—of the professional woman at least. Two of the studies in this book, Chapters Fifteen and Eighteen, attempted to control the predisposition toward dominance on the part of working wives so that the effects of employment on husband-wife power relations could better be investigated.

The belief that "high-power" women will seek employment is based on the traditional association between the notions that a woman's place is in the home and that women should be subordinate to men. The phrase, "kinder, küche, and kirche" is meant not only as a complete list of what the wife's spheres should be, but is also used to symbolize her subordination to her husband. Similarly, the American folk saying, "You gotta keep 'em barefoot in winter and pregnant in summer" is an admonition to husbands that in order to keep a wife subordinate she must be eternally attached to the home.

If the idea that women's place is in the home, and that women should be subordinate are thus linked, it is likely that a person who adheres to one of these ideas would also adhere to the other. Therefore, a mother who does not think her place is only in the home, but seeks a position in the labor force, is likely also to be a woman who has not accepted a subordinate position in the family.

It is one thing, however, to talk about not accepting a subordinate position; it is another to talk about a high power need. The belief that the working woman is a power-striving, unfeminine woman certainly seems to be outdated. First of all, women's employment is too widespread and multi-determined for any particular personality trait to characterize the working group. Furthermore, because it is so widespread it is no longer an appropriate way for a woman to manifest her need for power and masculine strivings; i.e., working is no longer a "manly" thing to do. When working was more uncommon for women, the employed group probably constituted a more homogeneous group. Except for the woman who worked out of sheer economic necessity, the working woman was clearly acting against social pressure. Since there were many factors mitigating against her employment, her motivation must have been particularly strong. In accepting employment she often had to renounce many of the privileges and obligations of being a woman; marriage and children were rarely combined with a career. In many social movements, as in this one, the pioneers are more zealous than persons who join the movement once it is established and acceptable, and these zealots are usually as a group more psychologically homogeneous. To find such a homogeneous group among modern working women, one might go to certain specific occupations which are still considered unfeminine and which have a potential for power expression—for example, women business executives or policewomen. Even these occupations, however, may not include social deviants as extreme as the early feminists.[9]

In any case, empirical evidence does not support the idea that power needs characterize working wives more than non-working wives. Heer (Chapter Eighteen) does not find working and non-working women significantly different on the trait of dominance as measured by the Bernreuter Personality Inventory Test. Gurin, Veroff, and Feld[10] did not find power-need differences as measured by a picture projective. Hoffman (Chapter Fifteen) did not find differences on a male dominance ideology scale. Although these studies show that power need is not a trait of working women as a group, it is still possible that there is a subgroup thus characterized. There are many reasons why a woman might work, and therefore it may be necessary to control on alternative variables to demonstrate the operation of one. For example, one might exclude the women who work out of economic necessity and look for power needs only among those who had a choice; or one could see if these needs characterize particular occupational groups.

There are many other personality factors which also might be involved in the motivation for employment. Women differ with respect to the need for freedom and independence, the need for social contact, the fear of aging and losing vitality. They have different levels of anxiety and anxiety tolerance, and different capacities for performing and enjoying the housewife-mother role.

Personality differences are important in influencing which women go to work at all and which women go to work at one stage in the family cycle rather than another. In addition, they may be important in influencing which women *should* go to work. For example, if a woman with a high need for dominance does not seek outside employment either because of practical considerations or cognitive belief, she may express all of these dominance needs in her relations with her husband and children. If she does go to work,

---

[9] For a discussion of what happened to the feminist movement see A. W. Green, and Eleanor Melnick (7).

[10] This unpublished finding has been reported in personal communication. It is based on a national sample study carried on by the Institute for Social Research, University of Michigan (1959–1960) described in Chapter Twenty-Three.

she may express some of these needs through her job rather than within the family. Or, similarly, if employment makes the mother's life more satisfying, she may be a better wife and mother. In short, the job may sometimes operate as a safety valve whereby frustrations that would otherwise be expressed in the family are avoided or diverted.

The motivations discussed here have been organized according to three categories: money, social role, and personality. This separation is an artificial one, and the three are actually highly interrelated. For example, personality factors will influence whether the monetary conditions and the social role become motivations for employment. Thus, all three categories must be simultaneously considered in any complete analysis of motivations for employment. However, in order to understand the decision about employment more fully and to determine whether the motivations will be translated into behavior, we must also consider a group of factors which we call facilitators.

FACILITATORS

Most of the factors which operate to facilitate maternal employment have already been discussed as social trends in Chapter One. There it was pointed out that the increased mechanization of the household, the greater availability of commercial products and facilities, the smaller number of children in the family, and the relative youth of the mother when the family is complete all operate to release the mother from household responsibilities and make it possible for her to fill the housewife and mother roles as well as the wage-earner role. Changing social attitudes toward maternal employment were also discussed, and these, too, facilitate employment. The working mother need no longer face the social censure that she would have faced thirty years ago. Finally, the changing nature of the jobs available from those that require physical strength to those that require dexterity and special training, and the increased educational opportunities available to American women were discussed. These facilitate employment in that they broaden the job opportunities for women. In this section we will consider these same factors, but here the focus will be not as general social trends, but as factors which affect families differentially.

DEMANDS OF THE HOUSEWIFE AND MOTHER ROLES

Among the many factors which may facilitate or hinder the mother's employment, the largest group includes those which influence the extent to which the woman's time is required for the fulfillment of her roles as housewife and mother. It has already been pointed out, for example, that the mother is more indispensable when there is a preschool child in the home. Thus, having no preschool children facilitates employment. (See Table 1.1.) This situation was discussed above in terms of its motivational aspects, but here we are concerned with it simply as a factor which makes employment more feasible. The age of the children is relevent in two ways: older children require less care, and they can help with household tasks and the care of younger children. The number of children is obviously relevant also because fewer children mean less work. (See Table 1.5.) The physical and mental health of the children is another factor. Not only will the age, number, and health of the children influence the mother's employment, but expectations about these will influence both current employment and the degree of commitment to employment. For example, women who can feel with confidence that they will have no more children, either because of subfecundity or experience with effective family planning, can make a more permanent commitment to their jobs (3).

The extent to which the husband helps with household and child-care tasks is also relevant to the ease with which the mother can work outside the home. Clearly, the "companionship" marriage facilitates maternal employment. The "helping" husband not only lessens the mother's daily household workload, but also provides a resource that can be called upon in emergencies. It should be noted that the mother's expectations about how much her husband would help if she did find employment are as important as his help prior to this event.

The availability of aid from persons outside the conjugal family also enables the mother to seek employment. Thus, extended family ties and physical proximity to relatives is a facilitating factor and working-mother households often include additional relatives, such as a grandparent (8). Neighbors and other friends are often engaged to help look after the children, so primary ties of this sort are also functional. In addition, having paid household workers facilitates employment. Paid help may be part of a general style of life or a direct function of the mother's employment. In either case, it is more likely to be a middle-class than a lower-class pattern. If someone must be hired to replace the mother, the mother must either be capable of earning more than she must pay or she must enjoy her work enough to be willing to work without profit.

The size of the family residence, the degree of mechanization of the household, and the availability of commercial products and services would also seem relevant to the time required by the housewife and mother roles.[11] Thus, for example, the urban apartment with laundry appliances available would seem to be maximally facilitative and the rural farmhouse, mini-

---

[11] In the Detroit study, working and non-working women were not different with respect to any of these variables. Furthermore, the only one mentioned by respondents as a facilitating factor was the degree of mechanization, and that was mentioned by only 5 per cent. Greater use of commercial products and services was an important *response* to employment (e.g., 14 per cent of the 108 women interviewed about changes reported that they started sending their washing and ironing out), but such facilities were equally available to all subjects in this sample since all lived in the same city.

mally. In the United States, however, there is a great deal of standardization with respect to these variables. Certain special facilities, such as child-care centers, are more available in urban and industrial locales, but most commercial services and products have reached even the rural areas.

ATTITUDES

Another group of factors which may operate as barriers or facilitators to the mother's employment includes the attitudes of her family, her community, and herself. Some of the relevant attitudes have already been mentioned or implied. Thus, we have already pointed out the relevance of attitudes about birth control and about the husband's participation in household tasks. Attitudes about children are also important—e.g., attitudes about how essential the mother's constant presence is for the child's development and what the child's share in household tasks should be. The availablity of child-care centers is an expression of the community's attitude, which has value as a facilitator.

In addition to the specific attitudes which operate through their effects on other facilitators, there are general attitudes about the role of women and about whether or not a mother should work. In the Detroit sample, 16 per cent of the eighty-nine working mothers reported that their husbands gave unqualified approval to their working, and 19 per cent reported that their husbands were opposed. For the non-working mothers, 4 per cent reported that their husbands wanted them to work, and 54 per cent, that their husbands were opposed. Most of the working mothers indicated that their husbands approved under the existing circumstances. The husband's approval is important for the family's cooperation and for the solidity of the marriage. Maternal employment is not only disapproved in principle by many persons, but for some it is highly threatening. For some men, their wives' employment would symbolize their own failure to themselves and to the community. This is an interesting kind of barrier to employment because the very conditions that might make a husband concerned with failure, such as actually being an inadequate provider, might also be conditions which would make the woman want to work.

There are also *group* differences in the attitude toward maternal employment, and the attitudes prevailing in a woman's community, ethnic group, or friendship group will operate as facilitators or impediments to her employment.

EMPLOYMENT POSSIBILITIES

Another group of facilitators concerns the mother's ability to get a job, and this depends on the jobs available and her qualifications. The availability of well-paying, part-time jobs obviously facilitates maternal employment.

Convenience of location, the hours involved, and other particulars are also important. These factors are not only influenced by general economic conditions but also by the conditions of the particular area. Cities like Detroit, for example, where heavy industry predominates, usually have a considerably smaller proportion of women employed than cities such as Hartford, where white-collar industries predominate, or other New England towns, where light manufacturing predominates (14).

The woman's skills, education, and training have been mentioned in connection with motivational factors and are also important as facilitative factors. Caplow (2) points out that in considering a woman's eligibilty for employment one must not only consider the amount of training she has had but whether her training might suffer from obsolescence. For example, a woman physicist who has been out of the field for ten years while her children were young might, in some respects, find it more difficult to obtain a job than an untrained woman. If she has not kept pace with new developments she might be unable to find employment as a physicist and unwilling to accept a position which does not use her training at all. Occupations such as that of model or stewardess, where age itself is a handicap, present similar difficulties. However, in general, education and training do facilitate employment and working mothers are better educated than non-working mothers (14; Chapter One, Table 1.3; Chapter Ten, Table 10.2; Chapter Twenty-Three, Table 23.1).

Three kinds of facilitators have been discussed: those which affect the housewife and mother roles, specific and general attitudes of the family and the community, and the opportunities for employment. These factors will distinguish working and non-working mothers. Working mothers compared to non-working mothers have fewer children, older children, husbands who are more active in household and child-care tasks, outside relatives living with the family, attitudes favorable to employment, residence in communities where jobs for women are more available, and higher education. These differences must be considered in any study of the effects of maternal employment on the child. Each of these variables might be independently related to family variables and to child personality. Consequently, group differences between working mothers and non-working mothers could be the result of these prior factors rather than the result of employment per se. This is what is meant by the problem of self-selection, and careful empirical controls must be exercised to isolate the working mother variable.

In addition, just as with the motivational factors, there may be interactions between the particular facilitative variables that operate and the employment variable. Thus, for example, the effect of employment on the family will in part be influenced by the husband's attitude toward this employment.

SUMMARY

In this chapter we have pointed to the importance of studying the factors involved in the mother's decision to work. These factors are important methodologically because differences between working and non-working mothers may be due to their operation rather than to employment itself. They are important theoretically because they may operate as variables which interact with the employment situation and influence its effects on the family.

The monetary motive was given special attention as one which is frequently articulated. It may be based on actual financial need, perceived need, desire, and also on other motives not truly monetary in origin but which become focussed and expressed in monetary terms.

The significance of the housewife and mother roles for employment motivations was considered. Technological advances have made the housewife role less time-consuming and less satisfying. Particularly when the youngest child has entered school, the mother may look to outside employment to fill her day. In addition, certain frustrating aspects of the maternal role itself might motivate some women to seek employment.

Personality variables, such as the needs for achievement, actualization, power, independence, and social contact, and the fear of aging were also considered as motivations for employment. Personality motives, monetary motives, and those that stem from the housewife-mother role are all interrelated.

Factors were also considered which influence the decision to work by making work more feasible. These, called facilitators, include: situational factors which operate to lessen the extent to which the mother is needed in the home; attitudes which operate either indirectly through their effects on the situational factors or directly through their sanctioning of maternal employment; and job opportunities.

REFERENCES

1. *Better Homes and Gardens,* October, 1956.
2. Caplow, Theodore. *The Sociology of Work.* Minneapolis: University of Minnesota Press, 1954.
3. Clare, Jeanne E. "The Relationship of Non-Familial Activities to Fertility Behavior." Unpublished Ph.D. dissertation, University of Michigan, 1957.
4. Cyrus, Della. "Problems of the Modern Homemaker-Mother." In Judson and Mary Landis, eds. *Readings in Marriage and the Family.* New York: Prentice-Hall, 1952, pp. 392–402.

5. General Mills, Inc. *Betty Crocker's Picture Cook Book.* New York: McGraw-Hill, 1956.
6. Glenn, Hortense M. "Attitudes of Women Regarding Gainful Employment of Married Women," *Journal of Home Economics,* LI (April, 1959), 247–52.
7. Green, A. W., and Melnick, Eleanor. "What Has Happened to the Feminist Movement?" In A. W. Gouldner, ed. *Studies in Leadership.* New York: Harper, 1950.
8. Hoffman, Lois Wladis. "Some Effects of the Employment of Mothers on Family Structure." Unpublished Ph.D. dissertation, University of Michigan, 1958.
9. ———. and Wyatt, F. "Social Change and Motivations for Having Larger Families: Some Theoretical Considerations," *Merrill-Palmer Quarterly,* VI (July, 1960), 235–44.
10. Kligler, Deborah H. "The Effects of the Employment of Married Women on Husband and Wife Roles." Unpublished Ph.D. dissertation, Yale University, 1954.
11. LaFollette, Cecile Tipton. *A Study of the Problems of 652 Gainfully Employed Married Women Homemakers.* New York: Teachers College, Columbia University, 1934.
12. Merton, Robert, Fiske, M., and Kendall, Patricia L. *The Focussed Interview.* Glencoe, Ill.: Free Press, 1956.
13. Morse, Nancy C., and Weiss, R. S. "The Function and Meaning of Work and the Job," *American Sociological Review,* XX (April, 1955), 191–98.
14. National Manpower Council. *Womanpower.* New York: Columbia University Press, 1957.
15. Riesman, David, Glazer, Nathan, and Denny, R. *The Lonely Crowd.* New York: Doubleday Anchor Books, 1953.
16. Veroff, Joseph, Atkinson, J. W., Feld, Sheila, and Gurin, Gerald. "The Use of Thematic Apperception to Assess Motivation in a Nation-Wide Interview Study," *Psychological Monographs,* LXXIV, No. 12 (1960), 1–32.
17. Weiss, R. S., and Samelson, Nancy M. "Social Roles of American Women: Their Contribution to a Sense of Usefulness and Importance," *Marriage and Family Living,* XX (November, 1958), 358–66.
18. *Women Workers and their Dependents.* United States Department of Labor, Women's Bureau, Bulletin No. 239. Washington, D.C.: Government Printing Office, 1951.
19. *Women Workers in Ten War Production Areas and their Postwar Employment Plans.* United States Department of Labor, Women's Bureau, Bulletin No. 209. Washington, D.C.: Government Printing Office, 1946.
20. Zweig, F. *Women's Life and Labour.* London: Gollancz, 1952.

Chapter Three

Commitment to Work*

MARION G. SOBOL

CHAPTERS One and Two have dealt with the sociological background for maternal employment and the personal motivations for taking paid employment. This chapter will report on an empirical study which focuses on the mother's commitment to work. Commitment will be measured in terms of the length of time which a woman plans to work. First, the possibilities of change in the percentage of wives who will work in future decades will be investigated. Second, the factors which lead to long-range maternal work commitment will be evaluated.

The behavior of employed married women is hard to predict. Married women frequently move in and out of the labor force. For example, using census data, Lebergott (6) estimated that while only 17 per cent of married women with children under six years were at work in March, 1957, 31 per cent of the women in this category had worked at some time during 1956. In more long-range terms, 25 per cent of all white wives of childbearing age (eighteen to thirty-nine) were at work in the spring of 1955, yet 70 per cent of the wives in this age category had worked at some time during their married lives.

METHODOLOGY

Cross-section studies which relate a particular woman's behavior in the labor force to her family status and to other variables are ideal for the ex-

* Data used in this chapter are drawn from (GAF) "Growth of American Families" study described in the next section of this chapter. The author would like to thank Dr. John Lansing and Dr. James N. Morgan for their valuable suggestions and Dr. George Katona, Dr. Ronald Freedman, and Dr. P. K. Whelpton for permission to use the data from the "Ford Reinterview Study" and "Growth of American Families" study.

ploration of the factors most closely related to work commitment. Using the results of a survey, an individual's work behavior and future plans can be related to sociological, economic, and psychological factors.

The "Study of the Growth of American Families" (GAF), the source of information for this analysis, was conducted by the Survey Research Center of the Institute for Social Research, University of Michigan in the spring of 1955, by professors Ronald Freedman and P. K. Whelpton (2), and sponsored by the Scripps Foundation. The Study contained 2,713 interviews with a stratified random sample of white married women of child-bearing age (eighteen to thirty-nine) living in the United States.[1]

These (GAF) interviews contained full information on family size and future family plans. In addition, they included questions on wives' income, husbands' income, wives' work history prior to and after marriage, wives' reasons for work, and their present work status. Besides the family status and economic questions, each of the wives who was working at the time of the interview was asked:

Do you plan to work permanently or temporarily? How long do you plan to work? (if plans to work temporarily) Do you expect to go back to work some time later on?

Women who were not working at the time of interview were asked:

Do you expect to work at some future time if your husband is well and working? When might that be?

On the basis of answers to these questions about future work plans some rough estimates of future labor force participation will be presented. Subsequently, the answers to these questions about future work will be correlated with economic, sociological, and psychological factors to determine the variables most closely related to work commitment.

The statistical methods used in this study are primarily simple and multiple correlation.[2] By means of simple linear correlation, each factor (such

---

[1] The sampling and interviewing processes are described on pp. 10–16 of Freedman, Whelpton and Campbell (2).

[2] In part of this analysis, simple correlation methods were used. Since many variables are related simultaneously to work commitment a multivariate analysis was necesary to simulate the wife's actual decision-making process. In these multiple regression equations the dependent variable was dichotomous—expects to work or does not expect to work. A probit analysis is ideally suited to this type of data; however it involved many hours of machine computation since it requires an iterative solution. Recent studies have indicated that under certain conditions the results of a least squares multiple regression and a probit analysis do not differ greatly. The least squares analysis of a dichotomous variable which is used for this chapter is called a "linear probability function" and has been employed in many similar economic analyses of cross-section data.

TABLES 3.1   *Correlation Coefficients between Future Work Plans and Selected Variables*

VARIABLE	COEFFICIENT	
	Working Wives	*Non-Working Wives*
Husband's income	—.03	—.08
Wife's income	—.03	
Wife's education	—.09	.02
Wife's work experience prior to marriage	—.07	.08
Children under 6	.06	—.02
Children 6 and older	.11	.02
Expectation of (additional) children	—.13	—.05
Pregnant now	—.14	—.05
Married more than once	.04	.01
Years married	—.14	.04
Professional	.07	
Clerical and sales	.11	
Operative	—.17	
Need to accomplish	.11	
Need to occupy time or to meet people	.12	
Family business	.09	
Chronic and temporary financial problems	.09	
Need to acquire assets	—.10	
Worked since marriage [1]		.19

[1] Appropriate to non-working only.
Note: The sign (—) indicates a negative relation. Thus if we relate husband's income to wife's future work plans (—.03), we see that the higher the husband's income the *less* likely the wife is to work. Note that the correlation coefficients are all rather low. This is often true of survey type data.

as the husband's income, the wife's education) is related to the wife's future work plans, without consideration of the influence of any other factor. For example from Table 3.1, we note that the correlation coefficient between employment as an operative and future work plans of working wives is —.17. This means that women who are employed as operatives are *not* as likely as others to work in the future. We cannot tell from the figures in this table, however, whether a woman's job itself is the most important factor in the determination of whether she will work in the future. It may be that the income of women who work as operatives is so low that they do not feel that working is worth while.

Because a wide variety of factors occurring at the same time influence work plans, a multiple regression analysis which considers all relevant in-

TABLE 3.2 *The Relationship of Selected Variables to Plans to Work in the Future of Married Women*

VARIABLE	PLANS TO WORK		
	WORKING WIVES	WORKING WIVES (REVISED)[1]	NON-WORKING WIVES
	Standardized Regression Coefficients		
Husband's income	—.005		—.010*
Wife's income	.002		
Wife's education	—.007	—.008	.004
Wife's work experience prior to marriage	—.001		.004
Children under 6	.007		—.004
Children 6 or older	.004		.008*
Expectation of (additional) children	—.005		—.007*
Pregnant now	—.010*	—.012*	—.007*
Married more than once	.000		.001
Years married	—.006		.011*
Professional	.002	.001	
Clerical and sales	.004	.004	
Operative	—.011	—.014*	
Need to accomplish	.015*	.017*	
Need to occupy time or to meet people	.014*	.014*	
Family business		.012*	
Chronic and temporary financial problems		.011*	
Need to acquire assets		.004	
Worked since marriage[2]			.018*

* Coefficients are statistically significant at the .05 level. This is a cluster sample; therefore the variance usually computed for simple random samples might be inadequate. Calculations performed by Kish, however, indicate that for this sample, true standard errors were quite similar to simple random sample errors (5).
[1] Revised to study reasons for work more efficiently.
[2] Appropriate to non-working only.
Note: The standardized regression coefficient relating husband's income to wife's future plans is (—.005), which means that the higher the husband's income the *less* likely the wife is to plan a future work career.

fluences *simultaneously* would help determine the factors that have the most important effects. With adjustments for differences in the scaling of variables (standardized regression coefficients), the coefficients of the multiple regression equation can be used to study the *relative importance* of each of the variables we have correlated with work commitment.

Table 3.2 shows the standardized coefficient of each variable. The sign of the coefficient shows the direction of influence (positive or negative) of each variable. The size of the coefficient relative to that of the other variables shows the importance of this variable in determining work commitment.

The correlates of future work plans will be studied separately for wives who are currently working and for those who are not currently working. The information about future work plans is more extensive for working than for non-working wives. We know, for example, if they will retire and return to work at some later date, when they will return, and if they plan to work permanently. Further, for working wives, we know their reasons for work. For wives who are not currently working, the information on future work plans does not provide a notion of *how long* they plan to continue once they return to work. Moreover, we do not know why they plan to work. Thus, to be able to use all available information, working and non-working wives are studied separately.

FUTURE TRENDS IN THE EMPLOYMENT OF MARRIED WOMEN

The United States Labor Department has calculated labor force participation rates for women in different age, child status, and marital status categories (3, p. 18). These rates of labor force participation could be applied to estimates of future population size to predict the percentage of wives who will work in any given year. However, this type of prediction assumes that the same percentage of mothers in each age and family status category will work in future years. If there were a change from current behavior, this type of extrapolation would not account for it.

Future work plans stated by wives offer an opportunity to study future work trends. We can discover whether the wives who are now working plan to continue and whether those who are not working may re-enter the labor force. Moreover if we break down these groups of women into age cohorts we can see if the planned work patterns of the younger generation differ from those of the older generation.

Of the 2,141 wives who are *not working,* approximately 38 per cent indicate that they will work in the future. Generally the time of return is linked to the development of the children. Most of the women who planned to return said they would return when their children were in school.

Among the 672 working wives, approximately 37 per cent plan to work permanently. Another 23 per cent plan to retire (usually to have children) and then to return. The remaining 40 per cent of the working wives plan to retire and not return to work. Most of those who will retire plan to stop working within three years.

If we now combine the results for the working and non-working wives to make estimates for the population as a whole, we have the results presented in Table 3.3.

TABLE 3.3 *Future Work Plans of White Wives of Childbearing Age, Spring 1955*

FUTURE WORK PLANS	WIVES PLANNING TO WORK	
	Per Cent	Number
Currently Working		
Will work permanently	9	247
Will retire and will return to work	5	123
Will retire and may return to work	1	28
Not Currently Working		
Will work	18	488
May work	10	278
Total Planning Future Work Careers	43	1164
Total Not Working Now and Not Planning Future Work Careers[1]	43	1151
Total Working Now but Not Planning Future Careers	14	398
	100	2713

[1] Includes future work careers not ascertained.

Of 2,713 white wives of childbearing age, 1,164 (43 per cent) are contemplating extensive future work careers. Another 398, or 14 per cent, are currently working but plan to retire. The remaining 43 per cent do not plan to re-enter the labor force.

From these data it appears that almost half of the young married women plan extensive future work careers. Since today approximately 30 per cent of all married women are working (10, p. 61), the information that 43 per cent of women in the eighteen-to-thirty-nine age group (where there are the most impediments to work) plan extensive work careers indicates that there should be an increase in the percentage of wives who work in the future. No doubt this will mean an increase in working mothers, too, since so many of these future work plans are linked to the coming of age of children.

Although there is only a twenty-year age difference between the younger and older women studied here, it would be interesting to observe whether the planned work careers of these women differ. For, if the younger wives are more likely to plan to work during their married lives, we will have further indication that the percentage of working wives will increase in the coming decades.

In Table 3.4 we have set out the planned work careers during marriage for women in different age cohorts. It appears that the younger wives are

TABLE 3.4 *Percentage of Women Who Will Work at Some Time During Their Married Lives, by Age Group*

WORK HISTORY	AGE OF WOMEN			
	20–24	*25–29*	*30–34*	*35–39*
Will work during married life[1]	77	75	74	72
May work	3	4	3	3
Will not work	20	21	23	25
Per cent of cases	100	100	100	100
Number of cases	*401*	*697*	*753*	*758*

[1] All women who had already worked, were currently working, or who definitely expected to work, were included in the group "will work during married life."

somewhat more likely to plan work careers than are their older counterparts. Furthermore, this trend toward increased participation among younger age cohorts may be understated, since older women have been married longer and thus have had a greater opportunity to work since marriage. Moreover, older women may be more likely to have developed definite future work plans because they have older children and are therefore closer to the time when work is convenient.

Work prior to marriage is definitely correlated with work after marriage. Younger women were found to be more likely to have worked prior to marriage than their older counterparts.[3] Therefore, on the basis of the relation between work prior to marriage and work after marriage, it can be expected that the younger cohorts would be more likely to work after marriage.

In summary, an increase in the percentage of married women who will work in the future seems likely from three standpoints: (a) a greater percentage of wives of childbearing age have future work plans than are currently working; (b) more younger wives plan future work careers; (c) work participation prior to marriage, which is positively correlated with work experience after marriage, is more common among younger women.

A THEORY OF WORK COMMITMENT

On the basis of wives' work commitment we have inferred that the percentage of wives who work will probably increase. What are the factors which lead a wife to formulate long-range work plans? Influences on work

[3] This has occurred even though women are marrying earlier than previous generations did and even though the level of education for women is rising. From 1940–1947 the median school years completed for females in the U.S. rose from 10.2 to 12.1 (11, p. 109).

decisions can be divided into three major classifications: (a) enabling conditions; (b) facilitating conditions; and (c) precipitating conditions.

Enabling conditions are primarily family status factors which make it easy or difficult to work. For example, it is easier to work when one does not have young children; similarly, it is easier to plan a long-range work career when one has no plans for future family additions.

Facilitating conditions determine how easy it is to find a job.[4] Things which are important here are the level of a wife's education and the extent of her previous work experience. In addition, environmental factors such as rural or urban residence and local labor market conditions (such as local unemployment or boom) will affect the chances of finding suitable work.[5]

Even these two types of conditions are not sufficient to explain a wife's decision to work and her commitment to work. Relative satisfaction with life and with family finances as well as the attitudes that a woman has toward working will also influence her work commitment. These we shall label precipitating conditions—conditions that push her into the labor market.[6] The specific factors we will cover in this chapter are listed in Chart 3–I.

CHART 3–I *Factors Influencing Wives' Future Work Plans*

ENABLING CONDITIONS (FAMILY STATUS)	FACILITATING CONDITIONS (EASE IN OBTAINING WORK)	PRECIPITATING CONDITIONS (RELATIVE DISSATISFACTION)
Family Status	*Previous Experience*	*Financial Factors*
1. Number of children	1. Wife's education	1. Husband's income
2. Age of children	2. Work prior to marriage	2. Wife's income
3. Future child expectations	3. Work since marriage	*Attitudinal Factors*
4. Current pregnancy		1. Life satisfaction
		2. Needs for accomplishment or time occupation

[4] In Chapter Two, the term "facilitators" was used to include both "enabling conditions" and "facilitating conditions." The specification of the term "facilitators" into these two parts was deemed necessary for the analysis presented in this chapter.

[5] A preliminary test showed that there was some relationship between *current* employment status, place of residence, and local labor market conditions. However, these two environmental factors were not related to future work plans, probably because they could not be predicted for future dates. Therefore, these environmental factors have not been analyzed in this chapter.

[6] "Precipitating conditions" correspond to what are called "motivations" in Chapter Two.

In choosing these factors to analyze in connection with work commitment we have made a number of basic hypotheses. We have assumed that jobs offer a number of different kinds of rewards in addition to the income they provide. For example, work may be interesting or give a feeling of accomplishment; it may help one to meet pleasing people; or it may be a device to "keep one busy."

From a recent study of a nationwide sample of urban wives we find that about 43 per cent of *urban working wives* work part-time. Further, about 40 per cent of working wives earned less than $1,000 in 1956 (4). In 1957, wives' income from employment (salary, professional, and self-employment income) was 8.8 per cent of the income of all husband and wife spending units (12). The relatively small income contribution made by the wife seems to indicate that financial considerations may not be the most important determinant of work commitment.

When the various financial reasons for work are compared, we would expect to find that wives are more likely to be commited to work in families that are experiencing financial difficulties than in families where finances have been on an even keel. Thus a past history of income reverses, husband's low income, plus expectations of financial reverses should make a wife more likely to be committed to work. Further, the higher a wife's current income (if she is working), the more likely she should be to continue, because of the greater rewards of her work.

Past experience and training include such factors as the wife's work history prior to marriage, her education, and her work experience after marriage. If a woman has worked prior to marriage, she has job contacts and experience that make it easier to resume her work career. A high level of education would also seem to influence work opportunity. The higher the level of education, the more likely the attainment of a remunerative and intrinsically rewarding job.

Family status variables include the age of children, expectations for additional children, the number of years married, and previous marital history. One would expect that current pregnancy and the expectation of additional children would decrease a woman's future work commitment. Those with older children and no expectation of additional children would be more likely to plan work careers. Finally, women with no children and no expectation of having children would be most likely to plan permanent work careers.

Attitudinal factors include reasons for work and satisfaction with one's life. Financial reasons for work have been mentioned above. Because many wives' financial contributions were relatively small, it seemed that other reasons for work might have a more important relation to work commitment. Satisfaction with the accomplishments derived from work would seem to be a most important precipitating factor in the determination of work commitment. Working to keep busy or to meet people are satisfactions which can be derived from other sources—such as clubs and neighborhood and church activities. Thus these satisfactions would seem to be less important than accomplishment motives. As far as life satisfaction is concerned, wives who are most dissatisfied with their lot are expected to be the most likely to plan future work careers.

Now that we have outlined the basic factors, we shall consider separately the wives who are currently working and those who are currently not working. The two groups must be distinguished because each was asked a different series of questions about working and work plans. Thus, we can consider the occupations and the stated reasons for employment of working women; whereas such data are unavailable for non-working wives.

WORK COMMITMENT OF WORKING WIVES

The following questions were used to ask working wives why they work:

Women have different reasons for working after marriage. Some work because they like to or want a career, some work because it helps to get extra things for the family, some because the family needs income. How is it in your case?

Up to two reasons for work were coded for each wife.

FINANCIAL FACTORS

Financial reasons for work were the most commonly offered. Forty-eight per cent of the wives stated that they worked because "the family needs money [to get along]." Forty-eight per cent said they were working "to buy something." From the large number of women offering financial reasons for work we infer that finances have an important effect on *current work decisions*. Do these same reasons play as large a role in the determination of the length of a wife's expected work career?

If we relate the husband's current income to his wife's future work plans using multiple correlation techniques (Table 3.2), we find no significant relationship. Similarly, we had assumed that the larger the wife's income the less likely she would be to retire. Yet, according to the multiple regression equation, there is no significant relationship between a wife's income and her future work plans.

This may not mean that financial factors have no role in the determination of wives' work commitment. We have examined family finances only from the standpoint of the absolute amount of money earned. An annual income of $5,000 may be satisfactory for one family and sorely inadequate for another. Thus, relating the absolute level of income to work commitment is not sufficient. The desired standard of living may be more influential in determining wives' commitment than the actual family income.

The coefficients for working wives in Table 3.2 indicate two types of financial reasons for work. Some women work to acquire assets. They say, "I'm working to buy a car, refrigerator" or "to educate my child." Other women work because of chronic financial need. They usually say, "I'm working because we need money to get along."

Let us examine the relation between these two types of financial reasons and future work plans. Working to acquire assets is not related to long-range work plans.[7] It would be interesting to determine if this reason changes after women have been employed for a while. Possibly women who work to acquire assets may continue working, if, after a while, they find their jobs rewarding in other ways. Also, it may be that once a woman has purchased her goal she may develop new purchase plans which will keep her employed.

On the other hand, working because the family "needs money" is significantly related to future work plans. Thus, regardless of the absolute level of income, wives in families with chronic low income (low in their own opinion) are likely to plan a long-range work career.

What are the effects of future income expectations on future career plans? When women were questioned about their five-year income expectations, only 2 per cent felt that things would be worse in the next five years. The remaining women felt that things would continue on an even keel or improve. Sixty per cent of the women who expected their finances to deteriorate and who were not working currently planned to work in the future as compared to 39 per cent of the non-working wives with more optimistic financial futures.[8] Since there was such a small group of pessimists, the effect of five-year income expectations on future work plans for the total group was small; however, the difference in the plans of the pessimists and optimists emphasizes the tie between income change and wives' work plans.

In summary, while the actual level of family income is not strongly related to work commitment, the adequacy of family income by the family's standards does influence a wife's work plans. We shall now determine if there are any factors that are more important than relative income levels

---

[7] Evelyn Lomas Feldman advances the notion that in the early years the wife's income enables young couples to live at the standard of living which eventually the husband's income alone, when it reaches its peak, will provide (9, pp. 94–95).

[8] This information is analyzed only for wives who are currently working because it is difficult to tell whether the five-year income change estimate of a working wife includes her own income.

in determining the wives' commitment. Family status questions would seem to be of prime importance since they determine how convenient it will be for a wife to work.

FAMILY STATUS FACTORS

According to the simple and multiple regression analyses, a working wife who has children under six is more likely to plan to work in the future than the working wife with no young children. The working mother with young children is quite strongly attached to the labor force.

Presence of children who are six years or older and expectation of (additional) children are not significantly related to future work plans in the multiple regression equation. Current pregnancy is, however, a strong deterrent to working wives' planning to work in the future. Why is current pregnancy the only deterrent to working wives' future work commitments?

First, most women who are currently pregnant and who have young children are not working at present.[9] Thus, the majority of working wives who are currently pregnant are expecting their first child. Possibly these women have had no chance to make future work plans, are not yet familiar with adequate child care systems, or are now content to assume the roles of mother and housewife.

On the other hand, the women who have children and are currently working have found their family status only a small deterrent to their present work careers. There is little likelihood that as these children mature and become more able to care for themselves they will impose any additional barriers to their mothers' work careers. As far as expectations of additional children are concerned, they do not affect future work plans. Perhaps this is because these working mothers intend to use the same methods of care for additional children that they have used for their other children. Since the classification "plans to work in the future" includes women who plan to retire temporarily and then return to the labor force, these working women may contemplate some form of temporary retirement when their additional children arrive.

Thus, current pregnancy is the only important deterrent to future work plans for wives who are currently working. It is probable that pregnant women may revise their work plans after their children are born, since the future work plans of women with children less than one year old are so much higher than those of women who are currently pregnant.[10]

[9] Thirty-two per cent of pregnant women with no children are working, 3 per cent of pregnant women with a child under one are working, and 8 per cent of pregnant women with a child from one to five are working (GAF Study).

[10] Twelve per cent of pregnant women who have no other children expect to work in the future, while 30 per cent of non-pregnant women who have a child who is younger than one expect to work in the future (GAF Study).

PREVIOUS EXPERIENCE AND TRAINING

We would expect a working woman who has attained a high level of education to be most likely to continue working because her job is likely to be rewarding. However, the multiple regression equation indicates that the higher the wife's level of education, the *less* likely she is to plan a future work career.

Three major occupational categories for married women were studied.[11] They are professional (chiefly teaching and nursing), sales and clerical, and operative. On the basis of social prestige, investment in job training, intrinsic job interest, and salary, one would expect to find professional women most eager to continue working, sales and clerical workers somewhat less eager, and operatives least interested in future work careers.

The order of work commitment (from most committed to least committed) as determined by simple correlation methods is sales and clerical workers, professionals, and finally operatives. In the multiple regression equation, where the effects of all variables in the equations are considered simultaneously, the influence of work in the professions and in sales and clerical fields on future work plans is not significant. In fact, the only significant occupational category is work as an operative. Women who work as operatives are generally *not* planning extensive future work careers.

For wives who are currently working, work experience prior to marriage is not related to future work plans. Probably previous work experience is overshadowed by current work experience. We shall see later, however, that for wives who are not currently working, work experience prior to marriage is a very important correlate of future work plans.

ATTITUDES TOWARD WORK

We have covered financial, family status, and wife's previous training variables—all factors which we had assumed would affect long-range career decisions. As yet, the satisfactions that the job itself may provide have not been covered. When women were asked why they worked, their answers fell into the following categories:

   1. Financial reasons
      a. family income problems—chronic and temporary
      b. acquisition of assets
   2. Quasi-financial reasons
      c. helping in a family business
   3. Non-financial reasons
      d. need for accomplishment outside the home
      e. need to occupy time or to meet people.

[11] Except for service workers, these are the most important occupations for women in the United States—in terms of number employed (10, p. 61).

Financial reasons have been covered above. It was found that working to acquire assets was not correlated with long-range career plans, while working because the "family needs money" was positively correlated with work commitment.

About 5 per cent of the working wives said they were working to help out in a family business. This work has both financial and non-financial aspects. From a non-monetary standpoint, a woman who is employed in a family business has little difficulty choosing convenient work hours. Further, working together in a family enterprise may provide bonds which strengthen the marriage. On the financial side, it may be imperative that the wife work to get the business started. It is difficult to predict how this type of employment will relate to work commitment. On one hand, the wife may retire when the business has been firmly established. Conversely, the wife may become accustomed to her role and continue as long as the family retains the business. The standardized regression coefficients for working women in Table 3.2 indicate that women working in family enterprises are more likely to plan extensive future work careers than women who work because the family "needs money to get along."

Turning now to non-financial reasons for working, we have classified these reasons into two groups.[12] Approximately 140 or 21 per cent of the working wives were classified as working to fill "a need for accomplishment."[13] These women felt that outside employment carried with it a feeling of accomplishment or of doing something important whereas housework did not. In this group were women who said they "worked to have a career," "to feel important," "to do something important," "because they liked work," or "liked the job."

The other non-financial group of reasons included working to keep busy or to meet people. These needs may arise in a number of ways.[14] A woman whose children have reached school age or have married may find that she has unwanted spare time. A childless woman may feel lonely if all her neighbors have children. In some sense, too, all wives are faced with the problem of increasing free time, since the invention of time-saving devices and appliances and the manufacture of food and clothing outside

---

[12] Non-financial motivations for employment are discussed in some detail in Chapter Two.

[13] McClelland and others (8) refer to a similar need in their studies of "need for achievement." However, their categories are based upon answers to projective test questions. It would be valuable to perform a study where answers to projective test questions were correlated with these reasons for work offered by married women.

[14] McClelland and others' category "need for affiliation" is somewhat similar to this category; however, our category is broader since it includes the desire to "keep busy." Furthermore, people are classified into the "need for affiliation" category in McClelland and others' studies on the basis of projective tests (8).

of the home has saved up to 105 work-years per 1,000 women per year (or 1.3 work-months per woman per year) as compared to 1890 (7, pp. 120–23).

From Table 3.2 it appears that even though working to fill a need for accomplishment is not the most common reason offered for working, *it is the reason which is most closely related to work commitment.* Second in importance in determining wives' work commitment is the need to occupy time or to meet people. From these multiple regression coefficients we can now rank-order the reasons for work in terms of their relation to future work plans.

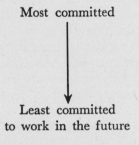

Most committed

Least committed
to work in the future

(1) working to fill a need for accomplishment
(2) working to meet people or to occupy time
(3) helping in a family business
(4) working because the family needs income
(5) working to acquire assets.

REASONS FOR WORK—A FURTHER EXPLORATION

Apart from the deterrent effects of current pregnancy, the most important correlates of work commitment are reasons for work. It is surprising that while financial reasons are positively correlated with future work plans, they are less important than non-financial reasons. The common supposition that married women are working "for the money" does not tell the whole story. Well over one-third of working wives advance reasons other than financial. Further, the women who offer *only* non-financial reasons for work are more likely to plan extended work careers than the women who work for a *combination* of financial and non-financial reasons.[15]

One reason it is surprising to find that women working for non-monetary reasons are more likely to plan to continue than those working because their family needs income is that for the former group, volunteer work, club participation, and PTA activities could fill the needs for time occupation and ·socialization and yet not impose the pledges of punctuality and regularity that are associated with a paid job. It may be that these women appreciate the regularity and order which work commitment brings to their lives. In addition, some of the psychological meanings of the pay check

---

[15] Forty-nine per cent of women who gave financial *and* accomplishment reasons for working expected to work permanently; whereas 63 per cent of the women who gave *only* accomplishment reasons for working expected to work permanently.

which are discussed in Chapter Two may provide the answer to why paid jobs have such a special significance.

Possibly also, financial reasons are not as closely related to work commitment as originally expected because of the optimism of wives. Only 2 per cent of working wives expected to be worse off in five years, while 22 per cent expected to be in the same position. The remaining women expected to be better off. Thus, finances may not seem to be a problem in the imagined future. This is a difficult problem as some of this general optimism may be based on the expectation that they will be working.

Can we use any of this information about the relation between work commitment and reasons for work to enhance our ability to predict the percentage of wives who will work in the future? We know that accomplishment reasons are strongly related to work commitment. Possibly easily measurable demographic characteristics such as education, religious preference, occupation, or husband's income could be used as substitutes for reasons for work in predictive analyses. To investigate this, we shall compare these demographic variables to reasons for work.

Table 3.5 classifies women into reasons-for-work categories on the basis of the first reason they offered for working. From this table we shall attempt to characterize the women who offer each reason.

TABLE 3.5   *Reasons for Work for Working Wives, by Selected Variables*

	REASONS FOR WORKING				
RELATED VARIABLES	Chronic and Temporary Financial Problems	Need to Acquire Assets	Need to Accomplish Outside the Home	Need to Occupy Time or to Meet People	In Family Business
			Per Cent		
Future Work Plans					
Less than 1 year	10 ⎫	20 ⎫	11 ⎫	13 ⎫	0 ⎫
1.0–2.9 years	23 ⎬ 27	29 ⎬ 53	8 ⎬ 24	19 ⎬ 34	23 ⎬ 23
3.0–4.9 years	4 ⎭	4 ⎭	5 ⎭	2 ⎭	0 ⎭
5.0–9.9 years	3	0	2	3	0
Over 10 years	1	–	0	2	5
Other	17	11	11	2	5
Until pregnancy	2	7	9	16	5
Permanently	37	28	51	28	65
Not ascertained	3	1	3	4	0
Per cent of cases	100	100	100	100	100
Number of cases	*262*	*241*	*81*	*45*	*22*

— Less than half of 1 per cent

TABLE 3.5 *Reasons for Work for Working Wives,*
by Selected Variables—Continued

	REASONS FOR WORKING				
RELATED VARIABLES	Chronic and Temporary Financial Problems	Need to Acquire Assets	Need to Accomplish Outside the Home	Need to Occupy Time or to Meet People	In Family Business
			Per Cent		
Plans to Return to Work at Some Later Time					
Yes	31	29	41	14	42
Depends	6	9	5	4	0
No	58	57	46	75	58
Not ascertained	5	5	8	7	0
Per cent of cases	100	100	100	100	100
Number of cases	262	241	81	45	22
Wife's Education					
Grade school	18	8	2	7	9
High school	69	80	65	79	68
College	12	12	33	14	23
Not ascertained	1	0	0	0	0
Per cent of cases	100	100	100	100	100
Number of cases	262	241	81	45	22
Wife's Occupation					
Professional	7	6	25	11	5
Managers, self-employed	4	4	11	4	27
Clerical	32	42	42	45	59
Sales	10	10	4	13	5
Crafts	2	2	0	0	0
Operatives	32	25	11	18	0
Service	13	11	7	9	4
Laborers	–	0	0	0	0
Per cent of cases	100	100	100	100	100
Number of cases	262	241	81	45	22
Has a Child Under 1 Year	5	4	4	2	9

— Less than half of 1 per cent

TABLE 3.5 *Reasons for Work for Working Wives,
by Selected Variables—Continued*

	REASONS FOR WORKING				
RELATED VARIABLES	Chronic and Temporary Financial Problems	Need to Acquire Assets	Need to Accomplish Outside the Home	Need to Occupy Time or to Meet People	In Family Business
			Per Cent		
Has Children					
1–6 Years Old	37	27	36	7	27
Religion					
Catholic	32	32	15	30	33
Jewish	1	4	4	2	–
Protestant	67	64	79	66	62
Other, none	0	0	2	2	5
Per cent of cases	100	100	100	100	100
Number of cases	262	241	81	45	22
Age					
16–25	24	24	25	11	9
26–35	49	52	42	60	36
36–45	27	24	33	29	55
Per cent of cases	100	100	100	100	100
Number of cases	262	241	81	45	22
Club Participation					
Attended meeting in last 3 months (active)	12 ⎫	17 ⎫	21 ⎫	27 ⎫	22 ⎫
Attended—not active	13 ⎬ 26	21 ⎬ 39	27 ⎬ 48	13 ⎬ 40	19 ⎬ 41
Attended—other	1 ⎭	1 ⎭	0 ⎭	0 ⎭	0 ⎭
Didn't attend— not active	10	13	10	11	14
Doesn't belong	64	47	42	49	39
Not ascertained	0	1	0	0	0
Per cent of cases	100	100	100	100	100
Number of cases	262	241	81	45	22

— Less than half of 1 per cent

TABLE 3.5 *Reasons for Work for Working Wives,*
by Selected Variables—Continued

| | REASONS FOR WORKING | | | | |
RELATED VARIABLES	Chronic and Temporary Financial Problems	Need to Acquire Assets	Need to Accomplish Outside the Home	Need to Occupy Time or to Meet People	In Family Business
			Per Cent		
Husband's Income					
Under $1,000	8	1	2	2	5
$1,000–2,999	32	19	19	11	5
3,000–4,999	24	27	23	9	20
5,000–6,999	30	39	35	39	25
7,000–9,999	3	7	16	30	15
over $10,000	0	1	–	2	10
Not ascertained	3	6	5	7	20
Per cent of cases	100	100	100	100	100
Number of cases	262	241	81	45	22
Wife's Income					
Under $1,000	34	30	25	27	41
$1,000–2,999	47	42	48	40	32
3,000–4,999	16	23	24	27	9
5,000–6,999	–	–	1	2	0
7,000 and over	0	0	0	0	0
Not ascertained	3	5	2	6	18
Per cent of cases	100	100	100	100	100
Number of cases	262	241	81	45	22

– Less than half of 1 per cent

The "accomplisher" has a higher level of education than any woman in the other reasons-for-work categories. One-third of the accomplishers have attended college. Twenty-five per cent of the accomplishers are professionals, 11 per cent are managers, and 42 per cent do clerical work. Over a third of the accomplishers have children under six. There are more Protestants among accomplishers than among women in other reasons-for-work categories, suggesting that the need to accomplish may be influenced by the Protestant Ethic. The accomplisher tends to be somewhat older than other women—except for those working in a family business.

The accomplisher is quite an active woman. Almost half of them (they were all working) had attended club meetings within the past three months. The median income of the husbands of accomplishers was comparatively high—between $5,000 and $7,000. Only those working to occupy time had husbands with higher incomes. The incomes of accomplishers themselves, however, seemed to differ little from those of wives working for other reasons.

The woman who works to occupy time or to meet people usually does not have any young children. Only 9 per cent of the "time-occupiers" have children under six, while approximately 38 per cent of women in all other reasons-groups have young children. In education and religious affiliation, the time-occupier differs little from other working wives.

The time-occupier is very heavily concentrated in the age group from twenty-six to thirty-five. She is likely to participate in club activities. The income of her husband is higher than that of the husbands of any other women workers. Surprisingly, the time-occupier's own income is higher than that of any other working wife. This may reflect her ability to work full-time, since she is less likely to have young children. The time-occupier is far more likely to be a saleswoman than are women in any other of the reasons-for-work categories.

We come now to the woman who helps out in a family business. This woman is usually somewhat older than the woman who works for other reasons. Next to the accomplisher, the woman employed in a family business is the most educated working wife. In addition, she is usually active in club work. Over 60 per cent of the "helpers in family businesses" belong to a club.

It is difficult to study the income of husband and wife for women who are working in a family business, as these women often do not receive salaries. Also it is difficult to ascertain private business income in a survey where only the wife answers the financial questions.

The characteristics of the wives who work for financial reasons are quite markedly different. We shall now compare the women who work for the two different financial reasons to each other and to the women who work for non-financial reasons.

The women who work because the family needs money have the lowest educational attainment of all women studied. Further, these women are the most likely to be operatives. The median income of the husbands of women who work because the family needs money is between $3,000 and $5,000. These wives tend to earn as much as women in the other reasons-for-work categories, but fewer receive very high incomes. These women are more likely than others to have children under school age. Women who work for financial reasons do not differ from the general population by age and religious affiliation. The woman who works because of financial need is, however, less likely to be active in club activities than women from any other group.

The final group of women are those who are working to acquire assets. The education of these "asset-acquirers" is similar to that of women who are working to occupy time or to meet people. However, more of these asset-acquirers are employed as operatives.

It was thought that "asset-acquirers" might be women who were working prior to starting a family. From Table 3.5, however, we see that 31 per cent of these women have children of less than school age. Their need to purchase some particular item must be a very strong push, since they must usually arrange for child care. One wonders if this reason (working to buy something) may not often be an excuse for a brief but fairly regular respite from child care.

The median income of the husbands of asset-acquirers is between $5,000 and $7,000. There are relatively few husbands in the very high income brackets. The income, age, and religious affiliation of asset-acquirers seem to differ little from the population of working wives.

In summary, the "accomplisher" has a high level of education and is likely to work in a profession or have a managerial job. The "time-occupier" usually has no children or has no preschool children. She is employed primarily in clerical or sales work or as an operative.

The woman who works in a family business tends to be older than most and almost as well educated as the accomplisher. Possibly her own drive may have been an important factor in the establishment of the business.

The woman working for financial reasons tends to be less educated than the woman who works for other reasons. She is also more likely to be employed as an operative. Thus, even though the incomes of financial workers are as high as those of other women, the fact that the financial workers plan on early retirement may reflect the basically unsatisfying nature of their work.

From this study it appears that education and occupation are not as good in predicting wives' work commitment as working because of a need for accomplishment. (See the multiple and simple correlation coefficients, Tables 3.1 and 3.2.) This implies that some wives with high accomplishment drives may not have had a chance for education and better occupations. However, education and occupation come closest of all other variables to being indicators of a need for accomplishment. The woman who has attended college must have some drive toward achievement. Similarly, the desire and ability to fill professional and managerial roles may indicate drive for achievement. Since education by itself seems to be negatively correlated with future work plans, changes in the percentage of professional women would be a better guide to extensive work commitment. If the percentage of women working as professionals and managers were to increase, a concomitant increase in the percentage of wives with long range work commitment would occur.

WORK COMMITMENT OF WIVES WHO ARE NOT CURRENTLY WORKING

Future work plans of wives who are not currently working are in a sense more interesting than those of employed wives. The wife who is not currently working and who contemplates a work career in the future, plans to *change* her present behavior. We have seen that approximately 39 per cent of wives who are not currently working think that they will probably work in the future. What variables affect these decisions?

The factors listed in Chart 3–I that were related to the plans of working wives, will now be related to those of the non-working wives. The wife's occupation and reasons for working after marriage have been eliminated from this list since this information was not available at the time of interview. A new variable, work experience since marriage, will be related to wives' future work plans. It is to be expected that women who have worked since marriage have recent job contacts, recent work experience, and have had an opportunity at some time to adjust to a dual role. Hence, work experience since marriage should enhance the possibility of a future work career. The same four categories of variables (financial, family status, previous experience and training, and attitudinal) that were related to working wives' plans are related to the plans of non-working wives. These variables are studied by simple regression analysis and reported in Table 3.1 and by multiple regression analysis, reported under non-working wives, Table 3.2.

FINANCIAL FACTORS

The husband's current income is the third most important variable (in the multiple regression analysis) affecting labor force commitment. The lower the husband's current income, the more likely the wife is to expect to work in the future. Past family income and five-year family income expectations are not significantly related to future work plans.

FAMILY STATUS FACTORS

The presence of children under six is a barely significant deterrent to future work plans of non-working wives. On the other hand, women who have children who are six or older are more likely to plan to work in the future than women without children of this age. Perhaps these mothers are experiencing unaccustomed free time now that their children are of school age, and they are therefore eager to work; while those without children who wish to work are probably already employed.

Expectation of additional children in the future and current pregnancy are negatively related to future work plans. However, this relationship is not of major significance since the coefficients and the error terms for these variables are about the same. The year married is positively related to future work plans for non-working wives, indicating that younger wives are more likely to expect to work in the future than older wives. (The oldest wives in this study are no more than forty.)

PAST EXPERIENCE AND TRAINING

Work experience since marriage is the *most important determinant* of future work commitment for non-working wives. This relationship is evident in both the simple and multiple regression analysis. Job contacts and recent experience facilitate obtaining a job. Furthermore, experience since marriage may indicate that the husband approves of his wife's work career. The influence of level of education attained by the wife is far overshadowed by the importance of work experience since marriage in the determination of a wife's commitment to work.

ATTITUDINAL FACTORS

Reasons for working were not available for women who were not working at the time of interview. Therefore, only life satisfaction[16] is studied here. Women who plan to work in the future are somewhat less satisfied with the course of their lives than women who do not plan to work in the future. Thirteen per cent of the women who planned to work were dissatisfied with their lives, while only 8 per cent of the women who did not plan to work were dissatisfied. However, 83 per cent of all non-working wives—those who do and those who do not plan to work—are satisfied that their lives have worked out the way they wanted. Therefore it does not necessarily appear that only dissatisfied women plan to work in the future. Possibly life satisfaction as measured by this question and role satisfaction as measured by reasons for working involve different considerations.

In summary, work experience since marriage is the most important factor related to future work commitment for non-working wives. Second in importance is year married and third is the level of the husband's current income.

Just as with working wives, financial factors are not the most important

---

[16] The question asked was: "Some people feel their lives have worked out just the way they wanted. Others feel that they've really had bad breaks. How do you feel about the way your life is turning out? How do you mean?" This question is not analyzed in the multiple regression equation.

determinants of work commitment. The fact that work experience since marriage is the factor most closely correlated with future work plans seems to indicate again that jobs also offer very important non-financial satisfactions.

REFERENCES

1. "Family Characteristics of Working Wives," *Current Population Reports, Labor Force*. United States Department of Commerce, Bureau of the Census, Series P-50, No. 81. Washington, D.C.: Government Printing Office, 1959.
2. Freedman, Ronald, Whelpton, Pascal K., and Campbell, Arthur. *Family Planning, Sterility and Population Growth*. New York: McGraw-Hill, 1959.
3. Garfinkle, Stuart. *Tables of Working Life for Women*. United States Department of Labor, Bureau of Labor Statistics, Bulletin 1204. Washington, D.C.: Government Printing Office, 1950.
4. Katona, George. *The Powerful Consumer*. New York: McGraw-Hill, 1960.
5. Kish, Leslie. "Confidence Intervals for Clustered Samples," *American Sociological Review*, XXII (April, 1957), 154–65.
6. Lebergott, Stanley. "Population and Labor Force Relationships." Preliminary paper presented at the Conference on the Interrelation of Demographic and Economic Change, Princeton, N.J., December 5–7, 1958. Issued by the National Bureau of Economic Research.
7. Long, Clarence D. *The Labor Force under Changing Income and Employment*. National Bureau of Economic Research. Princeton, N.J.: Princeton University Press, 1958.
8. McClelland, David C., and others. *The Achievement Motive*. New York: Appleton-Century-Crofts, 1953.
9. National Manpower Council. *Womanpower*. New York: Columbia University Press, 1957.
10. ———. *Work in the Lives of Married Women*. New York: Columbia University Press, 1958.
11. *Statistical Abstract of the United States*. United States Department of Commerce, Bureau of the Census. Washington, D.C.: Government Printing Office, 1959.
12. "Survey of Consumer Finances," *Federal Reserve Bulletin*, 1958.

Part II

EFFECTS ON THE CHILDREN

Chapter Four

Dependence and Independence in Children*

ALBERTA ENGVALL SIEGEL, LOIS MEEK STOLZ
ETHEL ALICE HITCHCOCK, AND JEAN ADAMSON

* * *

THE purpose of the present study,[1] conceived as an exploratory investigation, was to identify possible differences between the children of working and nonworking mothers with respect to dependence and independence, and to do so within a research design which permits us to isolate children's characteristics associated with the employment status of their mothers from characteristics associated with other features of their lives and only incidentally associated with maternal employment status.

Various manifestations of dependence and independence in young children were the focus of our study because existing theory and evidence con-

---

* Adapted by the editors of this volume from "Dependence and Independence in the Children of Working Mothers," *Child Development,* XXX (December, 1959), 533–46, by permission of the authors and the publisher. For a more complete report of the data and statistical analysis, the reader is referred to that source.

[1] This study was conducted at Stanford University during 1957–1958 under a grant from the Elizabeth McCormick Memorial Fund to the Committee on Maternal Employment organized by Miss Christine M. Heinig of the American Association of University Women. The authors wish to thank the other members of the Committee —Christine M. Heinig, Margaret McFarland, Leon Yarrow, and Marian Radke Yarrow—as well as Donald Brieland, for suggestions concerning this study. For cooperation in the conduct of the study, we are indebted to the administration, faculty, and parents of the Palo Alto and Sunnyvale School Districts in California. We are especially grateful to Jack Rand, Assistant Superintendent, and John Caffrey, Director of Research, of the Palo Alto School District, and to John Holtorf, Superintendent of the Sunnyvale School District. Frances R. Shaftel of Standford University gave administrative cooperation to this study, and Eleanor Walker Willemsen gave generous assistance in data processing and analysis.

cerning socialization suggest that a child's development with respect to dependency is intimately associated with his relations with his parents and especially with his mother. It seemed reasonable to believe that if maternal employment is indeed a significant factor in the constellation of psychological and social factors which provide a background for the mother-child relation and thus for personality development in the young child, its implications will be greatest for the child's development with respect to dependence and independence. Development in this respect may be presumed to relate to the consistency of the care the child receives, the frequency of his contacts with the caretaker, the number of different people who assume caretaking responsibility for him, the diversity of their child-rearing techniques, and the diversity of their attitudes toward the child. All of these conditions may be quite different for the child of a working mother than for the child of a full-time homemaker.

CORRELATES OF MATERNAL EMPLOYMENT STATUS

To secure information needed for the selection of children to be subjects in the observational study, brief questionnaires were circulated by mail to the mothers of kindergarten children in 17 schools in two large suburban communities. Covered by a letter from the school principal soliciting cooperation, these one-page forms were mailed to 1067 mothers. They were told, "We are cooperating with a research group from Stanford University in collecting data for a study of kindergarten children in relation to adults and other children," and they were asked to use the stamped envelope enclosed in returning the completed questionnaire to the school. The research interest in maternal employment was not mentioned, and certain masking items were included in the questionnaire to attenuate its emphasis on maternal employment. A total of 917 questionnaires were completed and returned, representing an 86 per cent return. From the questionnaire responses it was possible to determine the relation between a woman's employment status and certain other features of her family situation. These survey findings will be reported summarily here.

One of the communities in this study has a large population of college professors and other professionals, but also has the range and diversity of occupational groups typical of many large and well-to-do suburbs in the United States. The other community, also a suburb, has a greater concentration of skilled industrial workers as well as many personnel from a nearby military installation. Both towns are undergoing rapid growth and have many recent arrivals in their populace. A pattern of ethnic segregation by residential area prevails in both communities, and the schools which participated in the study are so located that they drew their pupils overwhelmingly from non-minority families. No ethnic identification of questionnaire respondents was attempted, but our information is that the families circularized included only a sprinkling of minority people, including Negroes and persons of Japanese and Mexican background.

EXTENT OF MATERNAL EMPLOYMENT

At the time of the study, 11 per cent of the mothers of the kindergarten children were employed full time, i.e., 32 or more hours per week. An additional 5 per cent were employed part time, 2 per cent working 16 to 31 hours per week and 3 per cent working 1 to 15 hours per week. The largest single group, 84 per cent of the total number of respondents, were full-time homemakers. These data suggest that, in extent, maternal employment in these communities corresponds closely to the national average (7, p. 69).

The 149 employed mothers were in a wide variety of occupations, ranging from professions (medicine, chemistry, architecture) to relatively unskilled occupations (domestic, laundry, and cannery work). Concentrations of working mothers were observed in teaching, in nursing, in secretarial and clerical work, and in restaurant and factory work.

The total number of months each mother had worked (either full-time or part-time) during the lifetime of her kindergarten-age child was determined. We attempted to classify the employment histories of the mothers, but these histories were so diverse and often so irregular that they defied classification in any reasonable number of groups. Given below are the percentages of respondents whose total number of months of work during the kindergarten-age child's lifetime fell within each of the intervals indicated:

64% had never worked during child's lifetime;
10% had worked from 1 to 6 months during child's lifetime;
7% had worked from 7 to 12 months during child's lifetime;
8% had worked from 13 to 24 months during child's lifetime;
5% had worked from 25 to 36 months during child's lifetime;
3% had worked from 37 to 48 months during child's lifetime;
3% had worked from 49 to 60 months during child's lifetime.

It is evident that but a small minority of these mothers (no more than 3 per cent) had been employed throughout the lifetimes of their kindergarten children, and also that some of the mothers who were full-time homemakers at the time of the survey had worked at some earlier period within the lifetime of the kindergarten child.

MATERNAL EMPLOYMENT AND FAMILY SIZE

In the families surveyed, the median number of children was three. Working mothers were found significantly more often in families with fewer than the median number of children than in families with the median number or more (p < .01). However, among the families of working mothers there was no relation between family size and the number of hours the mother worked per week.

MATERNAL EMPLOYMENT AND AGES OF CHILDREN IN FAMILY

The majority of the families surveyed had preschool-age children in the home: 566 families (62 per cent of the respondents) had at least one child younger than the kindergarten child. Working mothers were found significantly more often in families having no child of preschool age than in families including a preschool-age child (p << .001). However, among the families of working mothers, there was no relation between age composition of family and the number of hours per week the mother worked.

MATERNAL EMPLOYMENT AND FAMILY INTACTNESS

Of the respondents, 95 per cent represented intact homes (homes with united parents), 4 per cent represented homes broken by divorce or separation, and 1 per cent represented homes broken by death of the father.

The proportion of working mothers was higher in nonintact families than in united families (p << .001). This finding does not mean that working mothers were typically from nonintact families, for in fact the great majority of working mothers in the group studied (119 of the 149) were from intact families. Rather, it means that mothers from nonintact families were typically working mothers—of the 49 mothers from nonintact families in our survey, 30 were employed. Interestingly, however, again the number of hours spent at work was not discriminating: working mothers from intact families did not differ in the number of hours they worked per week from working mothers from nonintact families.

It may be appropriate to mention here that family intactness and age composition of family were associated with proportionally more intact families among those with preschool children (p < .001). In addition, family intactness and family size were associated, with proportionately more intact families among those with the median number of children or more than among those with fewer than the median number of children (p < .01).

MATERNAL EMPLOYMENT AND SOCIAL LEVEL OF HUSBAND'S OCCUPATION

Several items in the questionnaire elicited information concerning the occupation and type of work of the child's father. The socioeconomic level of the father's work was rated on the seven-point scale of occupations developed by Hollingshead (4). Such ratings were attempted only for fathers in the 868 intact families concerning whose work the information supplied by the mother was deemed sufficient by two judges rating social level. For 23 intact families the information was judged insufficient, so ratings were made on 845 cases in all.[2]

The fathers from intact families whose occupational levels could be rated were found to be distributed as follows:

Level 1 (higher executives of large concerns, proprietors of
   business valued over $100,000, and major professionals)   17%
Level 2 (business managers in large concerns, proprietors
   of medium-sized businesses, and lesser professionals) ..   15%
Level 3 (administrative personnel, owners of small busi-
   nesses, and minor professionals) 16%
Level 4 (clerical and sales workers, technicians, and own-
   ers of businesses valued under $6,000) 14%
Level 5 (skilled manual employees, small farmers) 23%
Level 6 (machine operators, semiskilled employees, and
   tenant farmers) 12%
Level 7 (unskilled employees and sharecroppers) 3%

To determine whether maternal employment was associated with occupational level of father, we compared·the frequency distribution of occupational levels of husbands of working mothers with the frequency distribution of occupational levels of husbands of nonworking mothers, using the Kolmogorov-Smirnov test for two independent samples (8, pp. 127–36). No significant differences were observed between the two distributions; in the present survey sample, social level of father's occupation and working status of mother were not associated.

It is of some interest to note that there was also no significant association between family size and social level of father's occupation. That is, among intact families, those above the median in social status (as indicated by social position of father's occupation) did not differ in size from families at or below the median in social status.

---

[2] Working independently, two judges first rated occupational level for 164 cases chosen from the total group. Both indicated their "confidence" in each rating. For those ratings of which Judge A was confident, the correlation between the two judges' ratings was $r = .98$. On the basis of this information it was decided that Judge A's ratings of the remainder of the cases would stand in all instances in which she was confident. For those initial ratings of which Judge A was not confident, the correlation between the two judges ratings was $r = .84$. On the basis of this information it was decided that conference ratings would be arrived at by two judges for all of the cases for which Judge A was not confident of her rating. Ratings arrived at under this system constitute the data.

COMPARISON OF CHILDREN OF WORKING AND NONWORKING MOTHERS

On the basis of the information contained in the survey questionnaires, matched pairs of children of working and nonworking mothers were selected. These pairs were observed during the free period of the day in kindergarten. The observations were coded in terms of a number of dependence-independence systems, and the two groups were compared for the frequency with which they exhibited behavior in each of these systems.

SUBJECTS

For inclusion in this comparative study, any child had to meet the following criteria: (a) had been enrolled in his present public school kindergarten for at least three months; (b) had no siblings over 14 years of age; (c) was not a member of any minority group; (d) was born in the United States; (e) was from an intact (united) family. From the group of children who met these initial criteria, the WM Ss (working mother's children) and the non-WM Ss (nonworking mothers' children) were selected.

A child was included among WM Ss if he met the following additional criteria: (a) mother was presently employed full-time, i.e., at least 32 hours a week; (b) mother had been so employed for at least the past six consecutive months. A child was included among the non-WM Ss if he met the following additional criterion: (a) mother had never worked during the lifetime of the subject. (A single work episode of less than a month's duration was not considered to be disqualifying.)

From the pool of potential subjects thus defined, matched pairs, each consisting of a WM S and a matched non-WM S, were selected for inclusion in the observation study according to the following matching criteria: (a) both had to be the same sex; (b) both had to be enrolled in same class at school; (c) the two had to be no more than four months different in age; (d) the two had to be no more than one level different in terms of social status of father's occupation; (e) the two had to belong to families of similar sizes, in terms of number of siblings; and (f) the two had to occupy similar ordinal positions within their own families.

The purpose of applying so many stringent criteria in the selection and matching of Ss was to obtain for comparison a group of WM Ss and a group of non-WM Ss who differed clearly in terms of working statuses and working histories of their mothers but who were directly comparable in terms of other variables which might be relevant to dependence and independence—variables such as age, sex, position in family, place of birth, intactness of family, social level of family, and minority group membership, as well as membership in the same class in school. In fact, the selection and matching criteria listed above represent a relaxation of our initial ones, which called for pairing of subjects holding identical ordinal positions and belonging to families of identical social level. Even with our somewhat relaxed criteria a great many children were disqualified from study, and many more could not be used because no suitable match was available.

In all, 26 matched pairs were obtained, 10 pairs of girls and 16 pairs of boys. In age the 52 Ss ranged from 63 months to 74 months, with an average age of 68.2 for the WM Ss and 67.7 for the non-WM Ss. In terms of social status of father's occupation the range was from level 1 to level 6, with the WM Ss and the non-WM Ss each having a median level of 4. For number of siblings the range was from 0 to 5, with the WM Ss having 1.3 siblings on the average and the non-WM Ss having 1.7.[3]

LOCALE AND TIME OF OBSERVATIONS

All observations of Ss were made in the kindergarten classroom during the free activity period indoors which typically occurred early in the half-day school program. This period lasted at least 30 minutes. Each S was observed for four 15-minute periods, two of these during the first half of the activity period and two during the second half. A WM S and his matched non-WM S were observed on the same day, each for 15 minutes. The purpose of observing both members of a pair on the same day and of systematically alternating the order in which the two were observed was to render as equivalent as possible the situations in which the two members of the pair were observed and thus to clarify the meaning of any possible differences in the behavior of the two.

To assure variability in the observation situations, the four observation periods for any pair were spread over a period of several weeks, and each was set on a different day of the week. It was impossible to maintain constant intervals of time between observations of the various pairs, both because of occasional absences of Ss from school and because of the occurrence of special school events which rendered observation infeasible on certain days. Elapsed time between first and fourth observation for the various pairs ranged from 18 days to 58 days, with a mean of 32 days.

RECORDING OF BEHAVIOR

Detailed written accounts were used to record the child's behavior and pertinent information concerning the behavior of others as they interacted with him. The observer's record was divided into two columns, one for use

---

[3] These differences in average number of siblings, although not large, do reflect the fact that working mothers typically have fewer children than do nonworking mothers—as was indicated in our survey data—and it is therefore very difficult to find exact matches in terms of number of siblings when other matching variables also must be considered. Nonetheless, all but two of the matched pairs of subjects either had the same number of siblings or differed by but one; the two exceptions each differed by two siblings.

in recording the S's behavior and the other for use in describing the situation, a technique which enables the observer to check constantly on the adequacy of her record. The observer attempted to obtain as comprehensive a record as possible, guided by knowledge of the coding system to be used and also by a guide for observers prepared by Stolz (10, pp. 342-43). The observer avoided interaction with the S or with other children and attempted to be unobtrusive in her behavior in the classroom.

Two observers participated in the study, one observing girls and the other observing boys. At no time did the two observers work simultaneously in the same classroom.

PREPARATION OF OBSERVATION RECORDS

In preparation for the coding, the observation records were divided into units. The definition of a unit was adapted from Stevenson (9):

A behavior unit is that portion of behavior which contains: (a) an event (external or internal activity) which is psychologically different from events preceding and following; and (b) the subject's behavior in relation to the event, which is psychologically different from preceding and subsequent behavior (p. 32).

Two modifications were made of Stevenson's definition. First, goal-directedness of the behavior was emphasized, and second, provision was made for interrupted sequences of behavior—sequences in which a child's behavior toward a goal was interrupted and then resumed. Using the notion of overlapping episodes of Barker and Wright (2, p. 260), we provided for the inclusion of units whose segments were not continuous.

CODING AND SCORING OF RECORDS

Each behavior unit, once identified, was classified into one of 10 categories. Nine of these categories represented different behavior systems relevant to dependence and independence; the tenth was a miscellaneous or residual category. The nine behavior systems were: *aggression, conformity, dominance, nurturance, obedience, self-reliance, sociability, submissiveness, succorance.* The basis for breaking down the dependence-independence system into less general categories is presented in Whiting *et al.* (12), to whom we are indebted. The present breakdown represents a revision of theirs, based on later work by B. B. Whiting and others[4] as well as on our experiences in the course of the present study.

---

[4] We are grateful to J. W. M. Whiting and B. B. Whiting for making their recent work available to us.

The relation of the eight systems to dependence and independence is, briefly, that the first system (succorance) is the sort of dependence most characteristic of infancy (but capable of occurring at all later ages as well), and that the other systems represent forms of socially relevant behavior which replace or supplement succorance at later ages and which we feel constitute a more useful classification than the simple dichotomy of dependence versus independence (12, p. 9).

For a discussion of these systems the reader may turn to the field guide (12); the details of their use in the present study are given in Hitchcock (3).

Each of the two observers divided her own records into units and then categorized these units. In addition, each determined whether or not each unit involved interaction with the teacher or another adult. This work was not initiated until all observation records had been collected, a procedure which eliminated the hazard that early experiences in encoding might alter subsequent practices in recording observations.

The information contained in each child's four observation records was combined in the scoring. We determined the percentage of each child's units falling in each of the 10 categories and also the percentage involving interaction with an adult. The percentages constituted the child's scores used in the statistical analysis.

PRECAUTIONS AGAINST BIAS IN OBSERVATION

The structure of the research plan incorporated certain procedures designed to eliminate the possibility that the data might be biased by anyone's beliefs concerning maternal employment and its effects on children. These precautions were:

1. The observer did not know which member of any pair was the WM S and which was the non-WM S. The selection and pairing of Ss was done by another worker than the observer, and the observer was told nothing of the Ss' backgrounds. Classroom teachers were instructed to avoid discussing the children's backgrounds with the observer, and the observers were prepared to remind the teachers to observe this precaution if a reminder were necessary. The observers remained "blind" with respect to their subjects until their analyses of their records were complete, i.e., until every child's scores were ready for statistical analysis.

2. The classroom teacher was not told which S was being observed at any time, nor was she told the nature of the behaviors of interest in the research. These two precautions with respect to the teacher, together with instructions to her to conduct her classes as she might in the absence of any

observer, militated against the possibility that a teacher would treat any S in an unusual or special manner during the observation periods.

RELIABILITY OF OBSERVATIONS

The two observer-coders worked together closely in planning the details of the observation and coding procedures, a collaboration which undoubtedly contributed to the reliability of their independent work.

After each had had some practice in recording observations separately, the two made simultaneous but independent observations of the behavior of two boys, observed successively, in a school activity period. Later, after each had undergone detailed training and practice in the encoding procedure, they independently encoded and scored these boys' records. For the reliability analysis all of the scores obtained for one boy by one observer were ranked, and these ranks were correlated with the ranks of the scores obtained by the other observer for that boy. For one of the boys, this correlation was $rho =$ .80; for the other, it was $rho = .74$ (8, pp. 202–13). These correlations represent interobserver agreement based on a single observation session. It is reasonable to think that such agreement would be higher for the data used, which are based on four observation sessions rather than one.

Due to various restrictions within which this study was conducted, including limitations of observer time, it was not possible for us to make a more thorough investigation of the reliability of our measures.

RESULTS

For descriptive purposes we determined the average percentage of units which fell in each of the categories. These averages are shown in Table 4.1, given separately for boys and girls. Table 4.1 also shows the rank of each average. Although the clear majority of all units was classifiable in one of the nine behavior systems, the tenth (miscellaneous) category contained more units than any single system. This was partly because many concomitant and interrupting behaviors could not be interpreted as to goal. Reference to Table 4.1 will reveal that, among boys, *sociability, succorance,* and *aggression* were the most frequently observed of the dependence-independence systems. For girls, *succorance, obedience,* and *sociability* were the most frequently observed.

The principal analysis of the data was undertaken to discover differences between the children of working and nonworking mothers. Statistical tests were performed separately on the data for boys and the data for girls, as well as on the data for the sexes combined. For each system of behavior a difference score was obtained for each matched pair and a *t* test on the mean difference was performed. The results for the sexes separately are summarized in Table 4.2. Two-sided tests were used in each instance.

TABLE 4.1 *Normative Findings: Relative Frequency of Occurrence of Behavior Units in the Various Systems*

SYSTEM OF BEHAVIOR	BOYS (N = 32)		GIRLS (N = 20)	
	Mean Per Cent of Units in System	Rank of System	Mean Per Cent of Units in System	Rank of System
Aggression	10.30	3	3.08	7
Conformity	6.71	6	5.97	4
Dominance	9.48	4	3.57	6
Nurturance	2.73	9	2.65	8
Obedience	9.13	5	11.36	2
Self-reliance	4.96	8	5.81	5
Sociability	15.02	1	10.82	3
Submissiveness	5.40	7	2.06	9
Succorance	14.40	2	12.80	1
Miscellaneous (unclassifiable)	21.87	(1)	41.92	(1)

As reference to Table 4.2 will reveal, of the 20 tests which were performed, only one revealed differences at a level of significance widely acceptable to research workers. Under the assumption that the groups do not differ at all (i.e., under the null hypothesis), we expect to obtain one "significant" result for every 20 tests performed when we work at the .05 level. This chance expectation is confirmed in the present instance by the

TABLE 4.2 *Group Differences between the Children of Working and Nonworking Mothers with the Sexes Considered Separately*

SYSTEM	BOYS (16 Matched Pairs) Group Higher	GIRLS (10 Matched Pairs) Group Higher
Aggression	non-WM	WM
Conformity	non-WM	WM
Dominance	WM	WM
Nurturance	non-WM	WM
Obedience	WM	non-WM
Self-reliance	non-WM	WM
Sociability	non-WM	WM
Submissiveness	non-WM	non-WM
Succorance	WM	non-WM
Interaction with adults	WM	non-WM*

° Difference statistically significant (indicates .05 or higher level of probability).

finding concerning girls' *interaction with adults.* We must conclude that, when the sexes are considered separately, no differences emerge between the children of working mothers and the children of nonworking mothers.

On the possibility that the above over-all finding was due to the small sizes of the two samples, the data for the two sexes were combined, and *t* tests on the mean differences were performed for the 26 matched pairs thus obtained. The results are presented in Table 4.3. Again, we have no clear indication of group differences; it would be hazardous to attribute one "significant" result out of 10 (the apparent group difference in *dominance* —see Table 4.3) to any but chance factors.

TABLE 4.3   *Group Differences between the Children of Working and Nonworking Mothers with Data from the Sexes Considered Together*

	BOYS AND GIRLS
SYSTEM OF BEHAVIOR	*Group Higher*
Aggression	WM
Conformity	non-WM
Dominance	WM*
Nurturance	non-WM
Obedience	non-WM
Self-reliance	non-WM
Sociability	non-WM
Submissiveness	non-WM
Succorance	WM
Interaction with adults	non-WM

° Difference statistically significant.

A *post hoc* analysis of the data in Table 4.2 yielded a finding meriting attention in future research. Upon inspecting Table 4.2, the reader will notice that the group differences (between WM and non-WM Ss) are some-times in the same direction for both boys and girls and are sometimes in the opposite direction. In *dominance,* for example, the WM boys score higher than the non-WM boys and also the WM girls score higher than the non-WM girls. Similarly, in *submissiveness* both the WM boys and the WM girls score lower than their like-sexed counterparts among non-WM Ss. On the other hand, in *aggression* the WM boys score lower than their matched pairs, whereas the WM girls score higher than their matched pairs, an example of the group differences being in the opposite direction for the two sexes. Under the null hypothesis that only chance factors determine the slight group differences represented in Table 4.2, we would expect the two patterns to occur equally often. That is, we would expect the group differences to be in the same direction for the two sexes about as often as the group differences are in the opposite direction for the two sexes. However, only twice (for *dominance* and for *submissiveness*) were the group differences in the same direction for both sexes; for the other eight variables the group differences were in the opposite direction for the two sexes. This *post hoc* observation suggests that the implications of maternal employment for children, insofar as there are any implications at all, are different for boys than they are for girls. If the data of this study were amenable to a sophisticated statistical analysis, this would appear as an interaction between sex of child and employment status of mother. Whereas the differences between WM Ss and non-Wm Ss are not themselves sufficiently great to be significant, the relative frequency with which these small differences are in the opposite direction for the two sexes is noteworthy.

It should be mentioned that none of the analyses we have presented has involved any direct comparisons of boys with girls. Such comparisons were precluded by the fact that the observations of girls were collected and encoded by a different person than the observations of boys so that any apparent sex differences would represent both sex and observer differences. Our analysis has been concerned entirely with difference scores for matched subjects of the same sex, an approach which eliminated any possible effects of observer differences on our findings.

SUMMARY AND CONCLUSIONS

In previous research evidence concerning differences between the children of working and nonworking mothers, differences associated with mother's employment status have been confounded by differences associated with other factors (family size, family intactness, family income level, etc.) which are themselves associated with mother's employment status. Because of this, it was impossible to determine whether observed differences between the children of working and nonworking mothers reflected the implications of maternal employment for children or whether they reflected the implications of such other factors as divorce, small family size, minority group status, etc. The results of other studies are confounded also by vagueness in the definitions of "working mothers" and by lack of consideration of the work histories of nonworking mothers serving as subjects. The principal purpose of the present study was to eliminate these confoundings by the use of a matching design and then to determine whether the children of working and nonworking mothers differ with respect to behaviors related to dependence and independence.

Our analysis of the gross demographic characteristics of families of working and nonworking mothers, as revealed in replies to the initial questionnaire, revealed that on the average the families of working mothers differed in size, in age composition, and in intactness from the families of nonworking mothers. (Interestingly, none of these factors differentiated between full-time and part-time working mothers.) These findings from the total survey sample reinforced our belief in the importance of using a matching design in a comparison of the children of working and nonworking mothers. Therefore, in the subsample studied the subjects were matched on each of these variables as well as on others. In addition, clear and rather conservative criteria were used in selecting "working" and "nonworking" mothers.

Using a matched pairs design, we have not found differences between the children of working and nonworking mothers with respect to behavior systems related to dependence and independence. Those "significant" differences which did emerge in the analysis are so few that they probably represent chance factors only. Thus, we cannot reject the null hypothesis that working mothers' and nonworking mothers' children are from the same population with respect to dependence and independence. Although nonrejection of the null hypothesis must lead to weaker conclusions than rejection of it, one may surely conclude from these data that maternal employment *per se is* not the overwhelmingly influential factor in children's lives that some have thought it to be.

Needless to say, this conclusion applies only to the age group represented by our subjects. One cannot say what the findings might be if such a study were conducted with younger or older children. Moreover, we have no information concerning the implications of maternal employment during infancy and the earliest years of childhood, since we included among the WM Ss any child whose mother was currently employed full-time and had been so employed for the immediately preceding six months, if the child met the other criteria for inclusion in the study.

To the extent that a mother's working may have implications for her children, *post hoc* inspection of the data of this study suggests that the implications may be different for the two sexes. This finding may be interpretable in terms of the growing evidence that identification processes are different in the two sexes (5), and it suggests the need for further research concerning maternal employment and sex-typing in children.

REFERENCES

1. Adamson, Jean. "A Report of a Study of Kindergarten Girls as Part of an Investigation into the Effects of Maternal Employment." Unpublished Master's thesis, Stanford University, 1958.
2. Barker, R. G., and Wright, H. F. *Midwest and Its Children.* Evanston, Ill.: Row, Peterson, 1954.

3. Hitchcock, Ethel Alice. "The Relationship Between Maternal Employment and Dependent Behavior Observed in Kindergarten Boys." Unpublished Ph.D. dissertation, Stanford University, 1958.
4. Hollingshead, A. B. "Index of Social Position." Mimeographed paper, Department of Sociology, Yale University, 1957.
5. Lynn, D. B. "A Note on Sex Differences in the Development of Masculine and Feminine Identification," *Psychological Review,* LXVI (March, 1959), 126–35.
6. Maccoby, Eleanor E. "Effects upon Children of their Mother's Outside Employment." In National Manpower Council. *Work in the Lives of Married Women.* New York: Columbia University Press, 1958.
7. National Manpower Council. *Womanpower.* New York: Columbia University Press, 1957.
8. Siegel, Sidney. *Nonparametric Statistics for the Behavioral Sciences.* New York: McGraw-Hill, 1956.
9. Stevenson, Nancy G. "A Method for Analyzing Observational Records." Unpublished Master's thesis, Stanford University, 1953.
10. Stolz, Lois Meek, and others. *Father Relations of War-Born Children.* Stanford, Calif.: Stanford University Press, 1954.
11. _____. "Effects of Mother's Employment on Children: Evidence from Research," *Child Development,* XXI (December, 1960), 749–82.
12. Whiting, J. W. M., Child, I. L., Lambert, W. and others. *Field Guide for the Cross-Cultural Study of Socialization.* New York: Social Science Research Council, 1953.

Chapter Five

Anxiety and Anti-Social Behavior in Preschool Children*

F. IVAN NYE, JOSEPH B. PERRY, JR., AND
RICHARD H. OGLES

OF ALL the duties usually expected of the mother, the care of her preschool children is considered the most crucial. Society's concern about this role appears to stem from the belief that the mother's presence is necessary to the satisfaction of the child's physical needs, safety, and emotional needs (2, p. 12; 3; 26; 27). It is assumed that only the biological mother or a permanent mother substitute who is continuously caring for her child can adequately provide for the physical and emotional needs of the child.[1] A number of investigations of children reared in institutions showed that these children were inferior in intellectual, emotional, and even physical development (2, p. 12; 3; 4; 5; 8; 9; 10; 11; 12; 16; 22; 23).

The authors of the studies referred to above center their analyses around the concept of "maternal deprivation." According to Bowlby, there are three types of maternal deprivation:

> [a] the partial deprivation of living with a mother or permanent mother substitute, including a relative, whose attitude towards him is unfavorable,

---

*This study was supported by a grant from the National Institute of Mental Health.
[1] The term "need" is used in the present study in a non-specific sense. We mean by it no more than general conditions for personality development and social relations. Its use in other studies cited on those drawn upon but not given particular reference may be much more specific.

[b] the complete deprivation of losing his mother (or permanent mother substitute) by death, illness, or desertion and having no familiar relatives to care for him,

[c] the complete deprivation of being removed from his mother (or permanent mother substitute) to strangers by medical or social agencies (2, p. 71).

Bowlby further states that young children have on "absolute need" for "continuous care" from their mothers or permanent mother substitutes and that, while the danger of separation diminishes with increasing age, the potential danger for the older child (of three to five) still exists—but is not as great as for younger children (below the age of three) (3).

The types of maternal deprivation may also be characterized, respectively, as follows: psychological isolation, natural separation, imposed separation. Although these are not perhaps mutually exclusive or exhaustive classifications, the underlying implication relates to different types of situations in which the child's needs are not met as well as they would be in a normal family setting.

The consequences of maternal deprivation have been described in the following terms:

> The ill effects of deprivation may vary with its degree. Partial deprivation brings in its train anxiety, excessive need for love, powerful feelings of revenge, and arising from these last, guilt and depression. The young child, still immature in mind and body, cannot cope with all these emotions and drives. The ways in which he responds to these disturbances of his inner life may in the end bring about nervous disorders and instability of character. Complete deprivation . . . has even more far reaching effects on character development and may entirely cripple the capacity to make relationships with other people (2, p. 12).

Nevertheless, it should be obvious that the continuity from complete deprivation to partial deprivation taken as a deduction is inadequately supported and cannot be appropriately treated as a definitional matter; that is, it requires empirical support. Previous studies involve primarily institutionalized and foster-home children and, in most instances, those who have lived in institutions continuously for a period of months or years. The principal distinction made by the investigators between the experience of institutionalized children and those reared in families is that the institutionalized children lacked continuous affection from a particular person—the mother or permanent mother substitute.

Critics of the "maternal deprivation school" question the clarity of its central concept and the adequacy of the above studies. They have suggested that the position constitutes at best a set of hypotheses rather than a well-formulated theory based upon adequate research. The maternal deprivation group has been criticized particularly for generalizing its findings to the children of working mothers: i.e., to a different type of situation from those which they have studied (16, 29).

Some recent studies in which the institutions were managed by professionally-trained personnel in university or federal government agencies disclosed results more favorable to the children reared in these agencies (1, 6, 14, 19, 20, 23). In most of these studies, children were left in nurseries only during the day. Some studies reported a *favorable* effect from the nursery school experience. Consequently, some investigators have concluded that this experience is beneficial to personality development. For example, as a result of research conducted in two nurseries operated for the benefit of mothers working in war industry, Koshuk said:

> . . . experiences in these two nursery schools have operated to reduce tensions and to improve emotional-social adjustment in the young child in a society of his peers—and that this effect is most marked for those children reported to present most home behavior difficulties at entrance. This in turn, it seems, must operate to strengthen family living, especially if there is any indication of carry-over to the home situation (14).

A minority of sociologists are of the opinion that if the mother-child relation results in the continuous subservience of the mother to the needs of small children, such a relationship may be frustrating to her and therefore provide a somewhat unhealthy emotional atmosphere in the home. (This is discussed in Chapter Twenty-Four of the present book.) Some investigators have felt that more playmates and contact with other adults were directly beneficial to the child (1, 13, 14). The import of these nursery studies clearly reveals the importance of specifying situational variables which may be significant in determining whether or not "maternal deprivation" (or the effect thereof) is exhibited *in a particular situation.*

THE PROBLEM

The objective of this paper is to consider the question of whether the employment of mothers of preschool children is accompanied by personality damage to these children. If personality damage appeared significantly more often among children of employed than among the children of non-employed mothers, it might be inferred that the employment of mothers results in "partial deprivation": i.e., the inadequate meeting of the children's needs, with its consequences. Although we have redefined "partial deprivation" (since it does not emphasize psychological isolation or rejection as much as physical separation), its use seems to be consonant with the bases of the classification mentioned above: i.e., specifying a situation where the child's relation with the major care-giver is perhaps impaired through separation.

This, then, is a test of generalizations from the findings of studies of institutionalized children to the children of employed mothers. There is also an attempt to develop empirical relationships which might provide the basis for an alternative to the maternal deprivation position, to clarify the issues between the opposed positions discussed above, and, by providing a limitation to the application of the maternal deprivation concept, to specify more clearly the conditions under which it may occur.

METHODOLOGY

The anti-social behavior items tie the present study to the nursery school approach (although it is in the family setting) and the withdrawing tendency and nervous symptoms items are similar to the characteristics mentioned by Bowlby. Although these scales are, in general, intended to serve as indicators of the child's personality characteristics, the similarity with the above approaches should give them more systematic import.

THE SAMPLE

A preliminary study of census data revealed that only one city in eastern Washington, Spokane, had enough families with children aged three or four to assure an adequate sample of families with full-time employed mothers. Spokane is a city of some 200,000, a trade and service center to eastern Washington and northern Idaho. It employs about the same proportion of women as the average of cities in its class in the United States and is not obviously atypical in other social characteristics.

An area probability sample of blocks was drawn from Spokane and a specified urbanized area north of the city limits, and all mothers of children aged three to five living in these blocks and currently employed full-time were interviewed. In order to obtain the control group, it was decided to interview the non-working mothers of children aged three to five who lived nearest to the employed mothers.[2] An examination of the

---

[2] Evidence came to light at the close of the study which indicated that some interviewers had not followed this instruction precisely, so that in a few instances a non-employed mother other than the one who lived nearest the working mother was interviewed. It is possible that non-employed mothers who were the most accessible to the interviewer and the most extroverted might have been interviewed in disproportionate numbers. In the section on the findings, a discussion of possible bias from this source will be given.

characteristics of the respondents—age, education level, and occupation of the husband—revealed these to be very similar for employed and non-employed mothers.

The interviewers were women similar in age to the respondents. All were from Spokane but were assigned to areas other than their own neighborhoods. None was herself employed just prior to the study. None had preschool children. The interviewers were trained and supervised by the second author.

Usable interviews were collected from 104 mothers employed fulltime, 104 mothers not employed, and 82 mother substitutes. Four callbacks were made in an effort to contact respondents. If they were not contacted in the four attempts, they were not included. Three per cent of those contacted refused to be interviewed. All the families were Caucasian.

THE CRITERIA

One difficulty in the measurement of adjustment of preschool children is the inability of children to read written materials. It was believed that verbal replies to direct interview questions might have insufficient reliability. Projective techniques were considered at length but were rejected because of the lack of available people trained to administer them, the problems of interpretation, expense, and possible problems of securing necessary cooperation from parents under the circumstances of the study. It was decided to interview the mothers and the babysitters separately, employing structured schedules. This provided two reports concerning the behavior of each of the children.

Three hypothesized dimensions of behavior were selected for study: anti-social behavior, withdrawing behavior, and nervous symptoms. Anti-social behavior is defined quite loosely as trespassing upon the rights of others. Withdrawing tendencies refer to unusual fears and insecurities; while nervous symptoms are considered indicative of anxiety. The current study of adjustment is limited to these three specific areas.[3]

ANTI-SOCIAL BEHAVIOR

In an attempt to measure anti-social behavior, ten items were con-

---

[3] The present study focuses upon only one aspect of the total adjustment system of the family. Such other relations as father-child, mother-father, family-community, etc. would, in all likelihood, have to be specified and empirically delineated before "adjustment" could be viewed as a fruitful systematizing concept in our usage. This is to say that, although we have not delineated all these various aspects of "adjustment," hence giving that word a very incomplete meaning in this study, we allow for an "openness of meaning" in our conception which further research might fill in.

structed. The respondent was allowed to respond in degree of frequency from "very frequently" to "never."

1. Is he obedient?
2. Does he help around the house when requested?
3. Is he destructive?
4. Does he have "temper tantrums"?
5. In playing with his brothers and sisters, if any, does he cooperate with them?
6. In playing with other children does he cooperate with them?
7. Does he quarrel with other children?
8. Does he fight physically with other children?
9. Does he wander away from home?
10. Does he take objects that don't belong to him with intent to keep them?

The ten items were dichotomized and scaled, employing Stone's adaptation of the Ford technique (28). Items 1, 5, and 7 were eliminated because of non-random or excessive error. The remaining seven items were rescaled. The coefficient of reproducibility was .84. The items generally met the criteria of a quasi-scale, with the exception that there was some non-random error in them. The child who was scored well-adjusted would be one who rarely fights physically, is generally helpful and cooperative, has few temper tantrums, does not wander away from home frequently, and does not make a practice of taking and keeping the property of others. That is, he knows something of social expectations, and he is learning to orient his behavior in keeping with them.

WITHDRAWING TENDENCIES

The following nine items were constructed with the objective of measuring withdrawing tendencies:

1. Is he in general shy around children?
2. Is he in general shy around adults?
3. Does he prefer to be by himself?
4. Does he have any fears of domestic animals?
5. Does he have any fears of particular types of people?
6. Does he have any fears of wild animals?
7. Does he express the belief that people don't like him?
8. Does he watch others play rather than joining the group?
9. Is he affectionate in his home relationships?

Item five contained excessive error and item six too many non-responses. These were dropped and the remaining items rescaled. The coefficient of reproducibility was .84. The other criteria of a quasi-scale were met and the items were used as a measure of withdrawing tendencies.

NERVOUS SYMPTOMS

Sixteen items were employed to test for nervous symptoms. These items were interpreted as providing a measure of anxiety which could be appropriatetly applied to the age group studied, although they were not validated for this specific age group. These items were based upon the literature which is concerned with preschool children.

1. Has he had any major illness in the past six months?
2. Does he have any allergies?
3. Does he have disturbing or unpleasant dreams?
4. Is he restless in his sleep?
5. Does he wet his bed?
6. Does he wet or soil his clothes during the day?
7. Does he stammer or stutter when talking?
8. Does he follow you around and hang onto you?
9. Does he seek your full attention?
10. Does he suffer from colds?
11. Does he seem nervous?
12. Does he suffer with upset stomach?
13. Does he seem to be tired without apparent reason?
14. In regard to foods, does he have (how many) dislikes?
15. Does he put thumb or fingers in mouth?
16. Does he have any special nervous mannerisms?

Items 1, 2, 3, 7, 9, 10, 12, 13, and 14 were dropped because of excessive or non-random error. The remaining seven items were rescaled with a coefficient of reproducibility of .85. The items met the criteria of a quasi-scale except that one item revealed some non-random error.

The same lists of items concerning the child were scaled for the mother substitutes with better success in that there was little non-random error. All items in each adjustment scale were included in measures which met the criteria for a quasi-scale with reproducibilities ranging from .85 to .90.

Some positive interrelationship of criteria was anticipated and found: anti-social behavior and nervous symptoms, .37; anti-social behavior and withdrawal tendencies, .26; nervous symptoms and withdrawal tendencies, .31. The associations indicate some common element in the three criteria.

After the criteria with mothers and mother substitutes were scaled, the total scores obtained from the mothers and mother substitutes were cross-tabulated in a three-by-three table. The corrected coefficients of contingency of reports by mothers and mother substitutes were .46 for nervous symptoms, .33 for withdrawing tendencies and .55 for anti-social behavior. The measures were expected to correlate more highly than they did, since the same child was observed by both reporters.

A re-examination of the phenomena measured led to the conclusion that although the behavior of the child in care of the mother and the behavior of the child in the care of the mother substitute is related, there is a basic difference in the fact that the child is interacting and responding in different social situations. In order to use this technique of independent judgments with maximum effectiveness, the judges should observe identical behavior.

The instruments have face or logical validity, and the dimensions measured are among those recognized in previous research. The scaling tests give evidence that a dominant dimension is measured. Satisfactory tests of pragmatic validity are not available, except that a significant relationship between mother and mother substitute ratings was found.

In the data on mothers some non-random scale error is present which was not found in the evaluations of the mother substitutes. This may reflect the presence of an element of defensiveness in rating one's own child. The scaling tests provide some evidence of reliability, since reliability is a prerequisite of scalability.

CONTROL OF INTERFERING VARIABLES

Since the primary objective was the evaluation of the influence of the employment of the mother on the adjustment of the child, it was desirable to have the two categories of families as nearly alike as possible in other respects.

The problem called for a cross-section of the city population but financial resources permitted no more than 300 interviews, which had to be divided among employed mothers, non-employed mothers, and mother substitutes. This did not permit control of variables through subsampling or through separate analyses within subsamples.

To meet these conditions a design which has been termed "ecological matching" was employed. Ecological matching requires that for each individual in the experimental group, the nearest individual (spatially) be taken in the control category. It was expected that this would have the effect of roughly equating individuals by socio-economic level, family cycle, and spatial mobility. Employed and non-employed were compared by marital status, occupation of husband, education of husband, income of husband, and age, education, and religious preference of the wife. On none of these was a statistically significant difference found. The samples were adequately matched in terms of these relevant sociological characteristics.

An attempt was made to determine whether the basic attitudes of the mother toward the child differed in the two categories of mothers. This was done because some writers have taken the position that mothers who work have hostile and rejecting attitudes toward their children. Thirteen items, designed to measure attitudes of acceptance of and satisfaction with the child, were developed. An item analysis found two items distinguished between employed and non-employed. These items were the number of reasons volunteered for wanting more children and number of things found enjoyable in children. Both of these favored the employed mothers, as did the non-significant differences on nine of the other eleven items and the total score computed from seven items. On the basis of these data it was not possible to conclude that the employed mothers were more rejecting or less affectionate toward their children than the non-employed mothers.

Finally, it was believed that employed mothers might attempt to compensate or "make up" to their children for working by giving them extra attention, toys, desserts, and otherwise catering excessively to their wants, and also that the children might be more demanding of their mother's time. Six items were devised to measure such "compensating behavior." These were found to form an acceptable quasi-scale. The supposition that employed mothers might compensate did not prove to be tenable. A cross-tabulation of these scores with employment status produced almost no differences between families in which the mothers were and those in which they were not employed.

FINDINGS

The idea of partial maternal deprivation advanced by the "maternal deprivation" school at least implicitly leads to the prediction that the children of mothers employed full-time would display more nervous, withdrawing, and anti-social behavior than those whose mothers were not employed. Since there was considerable contrary evidence, the writers decided to test these ideas without themselves taking that position. Therefore, a two-tailed test was employed.

Employment status was cross-tabulated with psychosomatic symptoms, anti-social behavior, and withdrawing behavior (Tables 5.1, 5.2, and 5.3). Differences between the children of employed and non-employed mothers

TABLE 5.1 *Maternal Employment Status and Psychosomatic Symptoms in Preschool Children**

PSYCHOSOMATIC SYMPTOMS	MATERNAL EMPLOYMENT STATUS			
SCALE TYPES[1]	NOT EMPLOYED	EMPLOYED *Per Cent*	ALL	TOTAL *Number*
0–2	15.4	19.4	17.4	*36*
3–5	47.1	35.9	41.5	*86*
6–8	37.5	44.7	41.1	*85*
Total	100.0	100.0	100.0	*207*

° Differences are statistically non-significant.
[1] High scores indicate absence of symptoms.

TABLE 5.2 *Maternal Employment Status and Anti-Social Behavior in Preschool Children**

ANTI-SOCIAL BEHAVIOR	MATERNAL EMPLOYMENT STATUS[1]			
SCALE TYPES[1]	NOT EMPLOYED	EMPLOYED	ALL	TOTAL
		Per Cent		Number
0–2	12.5	19.2	15.8	33
3–5	38.5	38.5	38.5	80
6–7	49.0	42.3	45.7	95
Total	100.0	100.0	100.0	208

* Differences are statistically non-significant.
[1] High scores indicate absence of anti-social behavior.

TABLE 5.3 *Maternal Employment Status and Withdrawing Behavior in Preschool Children**

WITHDRAWING BEHAVIOR	MATERNAL EMPLOYMENT STATUS			
SCALE TYPES[1]	NOT EMPLOYED	EMPLOYED	ALL	TOTAL
		Per Cent		Number
0–2	9.6	9.6	9.6	20
3–5	45.2	47.1	46.2	96
5–8	45.2	43.3	44.2	92
Total	100.0	100.0	100.0	208

* Differences are statistically non-significant.
[1] High scores indicate absence of withdrawing behavior.

are non-significant. The differences are not consistent in direction. Differences in psychosomatic symptoms seem to favor children of the employed mothers; whereas the withdrawing and antisocial tendency scales are slightly favorable to the children of the non-employed mothers. The differences are so slight that it is not possible to reject the hypothesis of no difference between the preschool children of employed and non-employed mothers. The absence of differences may, of course, be due to limitations in the measurement instruments, although the instruments conform to the standards of measurement in the area.

It was noted that some interviewers did not adhere strictly to the instructions to interview the non-employed mother living nearest the employed mother. If this affected the characteristics of the non-employed group, it might have resulted in oversampling the more extroverted non-employed mothers and those who had resided for a longer period in the area, with the possible result of favoring the composition of the non-employed group. If the findings had significantly favored the children of the non-employed mother, they might have been suspect, but in the absence of differences, this circumstance appears to be unimportant.

SUMMARY

The idea of Bowlby and others that frequent separation of mother and small child has unfavorable effects on the child's development and personality functioning was tested. The results did not support this position. But this research is only a partial test, since it involves separation of children from their mothers only some eight to ten hours five days of the week. The idea of partial deprivation, however, seems to include separation of this type. This project gives additional support to the conclusions of several studies of nursery schools that such experience of separation is not necessarily damaging to the children. Rather, situational factors appear to be relevant to the appropriateness of applying the deprivation concept.

The present research adds evidence also that the working mother is not one who typically rejects her children emotionally or neglects their needs. Differences found are, in fact, in the opposite direction. No evidence was found that employed mothers of preschool children feel that they must "compensate" to their children for the loss of time and attention. In short, the adjustment of the children in the different relational settings was not significantly different.

DISCUSSION

In the literature on maternal deprivation some research studies suggest that "complete" and, to a lesser extent, "partial" deprivation is damaging to the physical, mental, and emotional development of the child. These results have sometimes been generalized to the children of employed mothers who leave their children in the care of other persons while they are at work. Other research studies suggest that it might be the type and quality of care that create problems rather than the fact that someone other than the mother or permanent mother substitute is responsible for the care of the child. Among the latter works are nursery studies described above, Spiro's research on the kibbutz (24, 25), and Mead's work on child rearing in Samoa (18).

The findings presented in this paper suggest that, by itself, the employment of mothers of preschool children does not damage the children. It is believed that generalization of the results of studies of institutionalized children to the children of employed mothers should be avoided. In particular, whatever validity the maternal deprivation approach has in an institutional setting, its relevance to various other situational settings requires empirical testing and (where it falls down) alternative formulations.

REFERENCES

1. Andrus, R., and Horowitz, E. L. "Effects of Nursery School Training: Insecurity Feelings," *Child Development,* IX (June, 1938), 169–74.
2. Bowlby, John. *Child Care and the Growth of Love.* London: Pelican Books, 1953.
3. ———. *Maternal Care and Mental Health.* Geneva, Switzerland: World Health Organization, 1952.
4. Freud, Anna, and Burlingham, Dorothy. *Infants without Families.* New York: International University Press, 1944.
5. ———. *War and Children.* New York: International University Press, 1943.
6. Glass, Netta. "Eating, Sleeping and Elimination Habits in Children Attending Day Nurseries and Children Cared for at Home by Mothers," *American Journal of Orthopsychiatry,* XIX (October, 1949), 697–711.
7. Goldfarb, William. "The Effects of Psychological Deprivation in Infancy and Subsequent Stimulation," *American Journal of Psychiatry,* CII (July, 1945), 18–33.
8. ———. "Psychological Privation in Infancy and Subsequent Adjustment," *American Journal of Orthopsychiatry,* XV (April, 1945), 247–55.
9. ———. "Variations in Adolescent Adjustment of Institutionally-Reared Children," *American Journal of Orthopsychiatry,* XVII (July, 1947), 449–57.
10. ———. "Infant Rearing and Problem Behavior," *American Journal of Orthopsychiatry,* XIII (April, 1943), 249–65.
11. ———. "The Effects of Early Institutional Care on Adolescent Personality," *Child Development,* XIV (December, 1943), 213–23.
12. ———. Heinicke, Christopher. "Some Effects of Separating Two-Year-Old Children from their Parents," *Human Relations,* IX (May, 1956), 106–76.
13. Joel, Walther. "The Influence of Nursery School Education upon Behavior Maturity," *Journal of Experimental Education,* VIII (December, 1939), 164–65.
14. Koshuk, Ruth P. "Developmental Records of 500 Nursery School Children," *Journal of Experimental Education,* XVI (December, 1947), 134–48.

15. Levy, Ruth. "Effects of Institutional vs. Boarding Home Care on a Group of Infants," *Journal of Personality,* XV (March, 1947), 233–41.

16. Mead, Margaret. "Some Theoretical Considerations on the Problem of Mother-Child Separation," *American Journal of Orthopsychiatry,* XXIV (July, 1954), 477.

17. –––––––. *Coming of Age in Samoa.* London: Jonathan Cape, 1929.

18. –––––––. "Life in Bali." In Kenneth Soddy, ed. *Mental Health and Infant Development.* New York: Basic Books, 1956, pp. 174–79.

19. Pease, Damaris, and Gardner, Bruce D. *Non-Continuous Mothering and the Development of Children.* Department of Child Development, Iowa State College, Progress Report No. 3, August, 1958.

20. Portenier, Lillian. "The Psychological Field as a Determinant of the Behavior and Attitudes of Preschool Children," *Journal of Genetic Psychology,* LXII (June, 1943), 327–33.

21. Riemer, Morris. "The Effect on Character Development of Prolonged or Frequent Absence of Parents," *Mental Hygiene,* XXXIII (April, 1949), 297.

22. Ripin, Rowena. "A Comparative Study of the Development of Infants in an Institution with Those in Homes of Low Socio-economic Status," *Psychological Bulletin,* XXX (October, 1933), 680–81.

23. Siegal, Alberta Engvall, and others. "Dependence and Independence in the Children of Working Mothers," *Child Development,* XXX (December, 1959), 533–46. Reprinted as Chapter Four of the present book.

24. Spiro, Melford. *Kibbutz: Venture in Utopia.* Cambridge: Harvard University Press, 1956.

25. Spiro, Melford, and Spiro, A. G. *Children of the Kibbutz.* Cambridge: Harvard University Press, 1958.

26. Spitz, Rene A. "An Inquiry into the Genesis of Psychiatric Conditions in Early Childhood." In Ruth S. Eissler and others, eds. *The Psychoanalytic Study of the Child.* New York: International Universities Press, 1945, I, 53–74.

27. –––––––, and Wolf, Donald. "Anaclitic Depression: An Inquiry into the Genesis of Psychiatric Conditions in Early Childhood." In Ruth S. Eissler and others, eds. *The Psychoanalytic Study of the Child.* New York: International Universities Press, 1946, II, 313–41.

28. Stone, C. L. *A Machine Method for Scaling As Many As Twelve Dichotomies.* Washington Agricultural Experimental Station Circular No. 329, August, 1958.

29. Stone, L. J. "A Critique of Studies of Infant Isolation," *Child Development,* XXV (March, 1954), 9–20.

Chapter Six

Mother's Enjoyment of Work and Effects on the Child*

LOIS WLADIS HOFFMAN

EMPIRICAL studies of the effects of maternal employment have long suffered from a paucity of adequate controls. It was the lack of controls, for example, which led to the long standing belief that maternal employment was strongly associated with juvenile delinquency. In fact, both maternal employment and delinquency were associated with social class and with broken homes; and when the latter variables were controlled the relationship disappeared, suggesting it had been a spurious one (3).

Yet, the new studies on maternal employment, despite their more adequate controls, have often produced more confusion than clarification. Maternal employment has been associated with *less* delinquency, *more* delinquency, withdrawal behavior, dominance behavior, and nothing at all (1, 4, 9, 10, Chapter Four). Furthermore, there are existing theories to account for each of these findings. Thus, delinquent and hostile-assertive behavior might result from parental neglect and lack of sufficient discipline due to the mother's absence from the home; from hostility on the part of the child at being deserted; or, in conjunction with Henry's notion (5) that father discipline leads to the expression of hostility outward whereas mother discipline leads to intrapunitiveness, from father discipline replacing mother discipline.

Withdrawal and dependency responses by the child might also be expected. Loss of mother through death or hospitalization has been associated

* Reprinted from *Child Development*, XXXII (March, 1961), 187–97, by permission of the publisher. The research was supported by a grant from the National Institute of Mental Health.

with overdependency—the young child perhaps seeking in this crisis a return of the maternal relationship he had in the past. Something similar might occur as the result of the mother's spending a great deal of time outside the home working. Still another reason for withdrawal and dependency might be that the working mother feels guilty about working outside the home and responds with a pattern of "smother love" or overprotection. Such a pattern could alleviate the mother's guilt. In addition, if it is true that working mothers have greater power needs than nonworking mothers, this pattern would also be appropriate for expressing power over the child in a way that appears to be benign and admirable.

Some, such as Cyrus (2), would expect working mothers to be less frustrated and more capable of warm interaction. Others would say that the energy output required by trying to fill two jobs would make the mothers more irritable with their children.

Instead of speculating as to which of these theories is correct, the present paper will suggest and illustrate an approach in which the question is: *When does one pattern operate and when does another?*

Each theory assumes something about the working situation that is sometimes, but not always, correct; and, when certain assumptions hold, different mother-child interactions will result and the child will be affected accordingly. One important factor implicit in several of the theories involves the question of whether or not the mother enjoys her employment. It is this difference that the present study has selected for focus. It was expected that the effects of employment on the mother-child relationship, and consequently on the child, would be different when the working mother enjoyed work than when she did not.

Two of the theories mentioned above, the "guilt-overprotection" theory and the "neglect" theory, lead to very different predictions about the mother's behavior toward the child, and, although both theories predict that the working mother's child will be disturbed, the pattern of disturbance predicted is very different. Both these theories served as guides in the present investigation. The "guilt-overprotection" theory was expected to operate for the working women who enjoyed work, and the "neglect" theory for the working women who did not enjoy work.

Only the working woman who enjoys her employment should be guilty about it, and as such it was predicted that such a woman would try to compensate for her employment by showing a great deal of affection toward the child, disciplining the child adequately to leniently, and being careful that the child should not be inconvenienced by the fact that she works, e.g., by having to help with household tasks. The child correspondingly should be relatively nonhostile, nonassertive, and, if this parental pattern were carried to the point of overprotection, somewhat withdrawn and passive. The working woman who dislikes her work should, on the other hand, be quite guiltless. As such, she was expected to show more of a withdrawal from the maternal role—showing less positive affect and less disciplining. She should feel freer to inconvenience the child—specifically to expect the child to help with household tasks. The child, feeling somewhat resentful, and lacking sufficient discipline, was expected to be assertive and hostile. The predictions were, then, that both groups would show different patterns than when the mother was not employed, but that these differences would not be the same.

PROCEDURE

The sample included 176 white, *intact* families with at least one child in the third through sixth grades of three elementary schools in Detroit. There were 88 working-mother families and 88 nonworking-mother families matched on occupation of father, sex of child, and ordinal position, including the important status of being an only child. Except for sex of child, all matched variables were selected because they were known to be related to maternal employment (Chapter Fifteen) and because it was believed they might be related to the dependent variables. Pairs of families were matched by sex of child so that it might be possible to examine the relationship between maternal employment and the dependent variable separately for boys and girls, to be certain that combining was legitimate. All statistical comparisons are between working and nonworking populations, and with a few exceptions which will be pointed out later, *all comparisons are for matched pairs.*

The data reported here are based on questionnaires filled out by the children, interviews with the mothers, teacher ratings, and a classroom sociometric. Each of these measures will be taken up in turn when the findings are presented.

In the interview with the mothers, the working mothers were asked "How do you feel about working?" These answers were coded as to the predominance of positive or negative attitudes toward work. Responses to this question were on the positive side for most respondents. Sixty-five respondents were classified as liking work, and twenty-three as disliking it.

All hypotheses were tested separately for the two groups, i.e., by comparing the 65 mothers who liked work with their 65 matched nonworking counterparts and the 23 mothers who disliked work with their 23 matched nonworking counterparts. Significance tests for differences included the t-test for correlated means where the data were quantitative, sign tests where the data were qualitative, and the t-test for proportions where the data could not be analyzed by pairs.

RESULTS

Table 6.1 summarizes the results dealing with the mother's affect and behavior toward the child. The first comparison deals with the child's perception of the mother as a source of positive affect. The child had been asked to indicate the persons who, from his own experience, best fitted each of a series of verbs, such as "praises" and "smiles," and to indicate the degree of fitness of person to verb. The perception of positive affect in the mother-child relationship was measured by the extent to which the child associated "mother" with the following words: "praises," "smiles," "listens," "helps," "explains." As can be seen in Table 6.1, where the working mother indicates a positive attitude toward her work, the child associates more positive affect with the mother than do children in the matched group of nonworking women. This difference is significant. When we compare the children of working mothers who have negative attitudes toward their work to the nonworking group, we find the opposite relationship although it is not a significant one.[1]

TABLE 6.1 *Mother's Affect and Behavior toward Child: Working–Nonworking Comparisons by Attitude Toward Work*

VARIABLE	WORKING MOTHERS WITH POSITIVE ATTITUDE TOWARD WORK	WORKING MOTHERS WITH NEGATIVE ATTITUDE TOWARD WORK
Child's Report		
Positive affect from mother	More than nonworking*	Less than nonworking
Coerciveness from mother	Less than nonworking	Less than nonworking*
Mother's Report		
Severity of discipline[1]	Less than nonworking*	No difference
Power assertion by the mother[1]	Less than nonworking	Less than nonworking*
Mother's feelings of sympathy[1]	More than nonworking*	No difference
Mother's feelings of hostility[1]	Less than nonworking*	Less than nonworking

Note: Findings reported in all tables are based on the t-test for significance of difference between correlated means except where indicated.
* Significant at the .05 level, one-tailed test.
[1] Comparisons not possible between matched pairs. Each working group therefore compared to pooled sample of nonworking mothers and the t-test for significance of difference between proportions used.

[1] The direction of the relationship is reported even where differences are small; so, except for the significant relationships, differences can be due to chance variation.

The second set of findings deals with the child's perception of coerciveness on the part of the mother. This variable was similarly measured using the words "threatens," "punishes," and "hits." The table shows that the working mother is less likely than the nonworking mother to be associated with coerciveness in both groups, and that the relationship is significant for the working mothers who dislike work.

The remaining findings in this table are based on the mother's report. In the interview, mothers were asked to give detailed accounts of two recent occasions when they wanted the child to do something that the child did not want to do. These descriptive accounts were coded for degree of severity of discipline, degree of power assertion over the child, sympathy, and hostility. Unfortunately, these descriptions were not available on all of the matched nonworking respondents. To have a large enough N, it was therefore necessary to pool the nonworking respondents and compare the two groups of working women separately with this pooled group. These are not, then, matched comparisons, although the working and nonworking groups are, on the whole, comparable with respect to the matching variables. The findings show that where the mother has positive attitudes toward employment she is less severe in her discipline, uses less power-assertive influence techniques, and feels more sympathy and less hostility during the interaction than is the case with the nonworking group. For the working mothers with negative attitudes toward employment there is less power assertion and somewhat less hostility.

Taking the findings in Table 6.1 as a whole they tend to support the hypothesis that the working woman who gains pleasure from her work shows the child more affection and uses milder discipline. Although she is emotionally involved in the discipline situation, the involvement is to a great extent one of sympathy for the child. The working mother who does not enjoy her work, and whom we would expect to be relatively guilt-free thereby, also shows a tendency toward mild discipline. However, here it is not part of a larger pattern which includes affection and sympathy toward the child. Instead, it seems to be part of a general pattern of less involvement with the child. This suggests that the dislike-work group tends to withdraw from the maternal role.

Table 6.2 deals with the child's participation in tasks. This was measured by the child's responses to a form of the "Doing Things" questionnaire developed by Herbst (6), in which the child is asked to report the extent of his participation in several household tasks (20 tasks in this case). As expected, the children of the working mothers who do not enjoy their work participate more in household tasks than do the children of the nonworking mothers; the children of the working mothers who enjoy work participate less. This is in keeping with the notion that the mothers who enjoy work go

TABLE 6.2   *Child's Participation in Household Tasks:*
Working–Nonworking Comparisons by Attitude toward Work

VARIABLE	WORKING MOTHERS WITH POSITIVE ATTITUDE TOWARD WORK	WORKING MOTHERS WITH NEGATIVE ATTITUDE TOWARD WORK
Child's Report Regular participation in household tasks	Less than nonworking	More than nonworking*

* Significant at the .05 level, one-tailed test.

out of their way to avoid inconveniencing their children because of their employment.

Table 6.3 deals with the child's behavior. The child's assertiveness toward the mother is based on the mother's account of the conflict situations in which she wanted the child to do something that the child did not want to do. The child's behavior was considered assertive when he directly indicated that he did not wish to comply and that he did not expect to do so. These behaviors included requests such as "Is it all right to stay up until the end of this program?" as well as statements of intention such as "No. I am not going to bed until the end of this program" where the context made it clear that the child was not "just talking." Pleading, crying, complying with complaints or silent anger, and devious attempts to obtain ends ("I have a stomach-ache.") were all considered less assertive. The child's tendency to play with younger children is based on the mother's report that his playmates were "mostly older," "mostly younger," or "the same age." The remaining variables reported in Table 6.3 are based on teacher ratings. These ratings are described more fully elsewhere (8).

It was hypothesized that the children of working mothers who have positive attitudes toward employment would be nonhostile, nonassertive, and possibly withdrawn and passive as compared with their nonworking counterparts; but that the children of working women who do not like work would be assertive and hostile. The data seem to bear this out. The children whose mothers like work differ in their general lack of initiative-taking and tend to play with children younger than themselves. The children whose mothers do not like work, on the other hand, show assertive behavior toward their mothers and toward their peers. This assertiveness toward peers includes aggressiveness, use of physical force, and less impulse control in general. Only teacher dependency does not operate as expected, the boys in both groups showing more dependency, significantly more in the dislike-work group.

Both the "guilt-overprotection" theory and the "neglect" theory lead to

TABLE 6.3 *Child's Behavior: Working–Nonworking Comparisons by Attitude Toward Work*

VARIABLE	WORKING MOTHERS WITH POSITIVE ATTITUDE TOWARD WORK	WORKING MOTHERS WITH NEGATIVE ATTITUDE TOWARD WORK
Mother's Report		
Child's assertiveness toward mother[1]	No difference	More than nonworking*
Child's playing with younger children rather than own age or older[2]	More than nonworking*	No difference
Teacher's Report		
Initiation of friendships	Less than nonworking*	Less than nonworking
Influence attempts made to peers	Less than nonworking	More than nonworking
Influence success with peers	Less than nonworking*	No difference
Teacher dependency (girls)	No difference	No difference
Teacher dependency (boys)	More than nonworking	More than nonworking†
Aggressiveness	No difference	More than nonworking
Use of physical force	Less than nonworking	More than nonworking*
Impulse control	No difference	Less than nonworking*

° Significant at the .05 level, one-tailed test.
† Significant at the .05 level, two-tailed test, difference not predicted.
[1] Comparisons not possible between matched pairs. Each working group therefore compared to pooled sample of non-working mothers and the t-test for significance of difference between proportions used.
[2] Sign test used for this variable.

the prediction that the children of working mothers will be more disturbed in general than the children of nonworking mothers. This was tested by comparing the matched pairs on the use of nonadaptive responses to frustration, intellectual performance, and sociometric ratings by classmates. The results of these tests are reported in Table 6.4. The first measure was based on a teacher rating of how the child typically reacts to frustration. "Realistic acceptance of insolvable problem" and "attacks problem directly" were considered adaptive responses, while responses such as "cries," "goes to pieces," "blames others," and "becomes over-critical of self" were considered nonadaptive. Both groups of working-mother children were more likely to use nonadaptive responses to frustration. They also showed lower intellectual performance and were somewhat less liked by the other children in the class.

The lower intellectual performance of children whose mothers work is a particularly interesting finding. Being low on performance may be a func-

TABLE 6.4 *Child's Adjustment: Working–Nonworking Comparisons by Attitude Toward Work*

VARIABLE	WORKING MOTHERS WITH POSITIVE ATTITUDE TOWARD WORK	WORKING MOTHERS WITH NEGATIVE ATTITUDE TOWARD WORK
Teacher's Report		
Nonadaptive response to frustration[1]	More than nonworking	More than nonworking*
Intellectual performance	Less than nonworking*	Less than nonworking*
Classroom Sociometric		
Liking by others	Less than nonworking	Less than nonworking

° Significant at the .05 level, one-tailed test.
[1] Sign test used for this variable.

tion of low ability or low motivation. If it is true that the working mothers who like work are guilty about their employment and consequently over-protect their children, then the intellectual *ability* of their children may be impaired. Mothers who solve their children's problems for them may hamper their intellectual development by depriving them of valuable problem-solving experience. Thus, these children would be expected to be low on ability as well as performance. The low performance of the dislike-work children, on the other hand, might be part of the rebellious pattern that seems to characterize this group; here we would not necessarily expect low ability. Scores on the Primary Learning Aptitude Test, for third graders, and the Detroit Alpha Intelligence Test for fourth, fifth, and sixth graders were available. The expectations were borne out. Only the children whose mothers were positive about their work obtained lower scores on these tests than their nonworking counterparts, and this difference was significant. The others showed no such difference.

SUMMARY AND CONCLUSIONS

The overall pattern of findings suggests that the working mother who likes working is relatively high on positive affect toward the child, uses mild discipline, and tends to avoid inconveniencing the child with household tasks; the child is relatively nonassertive and ineffective. The working mother who dislikes working, on the other hand, seems less involved with the child altogether and obtains the child's help with tasks; the child is assertive and hostile.

The data do not show conclusively that the reason for these different patterns is the presence or absence of guilt in the mother, but they are consistent with such an interpretation. If one were to argue that the causality is reversed, that the attitude toward work is a function of the effect of employment on the child, or that happier women produce happier children, it would not be consistent with the fact that both groups of working-mother children show indications of maladjustment. It is only that they show different *syndromes* of maladjustment. Furthermore, in Table 6.5 it can be seen that the attitude toward employment is in large part a function of the particular job the woman holds.[2]

It is interesting to note in Table 6.5 that while attitude toward employment is not purely a function of social class, there is somewhat of a tendency for higher status jobs to be well liked. Because middle-class women, compared to lower-class, can obtain higher status jobs, because their employment is likely to be choice rather than necessity, and because there is probably greater anxiety about child rearing in the middle class, it is likely that guilt and overprotection are more a middle-class response to maternal employment, while neglect is more a lower-class response.

TABLE 6.5 *Attitude toward Work by Occupation*

OCCUPATION	WORKING MOTHERS WITH POSITIVE ATTITUDE TOWARD WORK	WORKING MOTHERS WITH NEGATIVE ATTITUDE TOWARD WORK
Professional and semiprofessional e.g., teacher, social worker, registered nurse	14	1
Skilled, e.g., secretary, bookkeeper	11	7
Sales	14	0
Waitress	1	4
Semiskilled or unskilled factory and clerical	20	10
Domestic	5	1
Total	65	23

The real purpose of this paper, however, is not so much to elaborate on any particular theory as to suggest an approach to the study of the effects of maternal employment. The need to control spurious variables has been established. The problem now is to differentiate the all-inclusive variable of

---

[2] The data presented in Table 6.5 are consistent with the data reported by Weiss and Samelson (12). Their data also show, for example, a positive attitude toward employment on the part of domestic workers.

maternal employment into more specified categories. Only in this way can we come to understand the processes by means of which employment affects the child. If one wants to know whether or not the sheer absence of the mother from the home is the important variable, then one should subdivide the working women according to the number of hours they are away from home while the child is there. If one wants to know the importance of the adequacy of supervision, then one should subdivide the women according to whether or not the substitute supervision provided is adequate. One might feel that the important variable is the father's reaction to the mother's employment. In this case the working women can be subdivided according to some measure of the father's attitudinal or behaviorial response to his wife's employment. In short, by selecting a particular aspect of mother's employment, differentiating the working mothers according to this variable, and examining the differences between working and nonworking groups separately, one can make a more formidable step toward understanding the crucial aspects of maternal employment in relation to the child.

There are still other advantages of this kind of approach. When the working-mother group is not differentiated, it includes a heterogeneous group and, as such, the working-nonworking comparisons will obscure differences due to counteracting subgroup relationships. For example, in the data reported here, since one group of working-mother children was less assertive and the other group was more assertive, the two tendencies cancelled one another out. Thus, when the total group of working-mother children were compared with the matched nonworking group, there appeared to be no differences in child assertiveness. The same is true for the participation of children in household tasks.

Another kind of error that can result from failure to differentiate the working mothers is when what seems to be a single pattern of findings actually includes two or more distinct patterns. For example, when the total groups were compared, working mothers' children were found to play more with younger children and also to show less impulse control. Doing separate analyses for the two groups of working mothers, however, revealed that these results did not come from the same subjects. Although it was not true of the present data to any great extent, it would be possible for a pattern to emerge from the general working-nonworking comparisons which actually characterized neither the total group nor any single subgroup, but was entirely a coincidence of findings contributed by different clusters of subjects.

One final point should be made. In most working-mother studies, relationships are examined between maternal employment and some aspect of the child's behavior *directly*, without considering the intervening variables such as the effect of maternal employment on parent-child relations, family structure, or other aspects of family life. The jump between maternal employment and child behavior is too broad to be covered in one leap. One must first understand the various steps that intervene.

In summary, this paper suggests that maternal employment has a different effect on the mother-child relationship and on the child's behavior depending on whether or not the mother enjoys working. The purpose in doing this analysis was to show that greater understanding of the effects of maternal employment will come about when working mothers are differentiated along some theoretically relevant dimension, and when the effects on family life, as well as on the child, are examined.

REFERENCES

1. Bandura, A., and Walters, R. H. *Adolescent Aggression.* New York: Ronald Press, 1959.
2. Cyrus, Della. "Problems of the Modern Homemaker-Mother." In Judson and Mary Landis, eds. *Readings in Marriage and the Family.* New York: Prentice-Hall, 1952, pp. 392–402.
3. Glueck, Sheldon, and Glueck, Eleanor. "Working Mothers and Delinquency," *Mental Hygiene,* XLI (July, 1957), 327–52.
4. Hand, Horace. "Working Mothers and Maladjusted Children," *Journal of Educational Sociology,* XXX (January, 1957), 245–46.
5. Henry, A. F. "Sibling Structure and Perception of the Disciplinary Roles of Parents," *Sociometry,* XX (March, 1957), 67–74.
6. Herbst, P. G. "Analysis and Measurement of a Situation: The Child in the Family," *Human Relations,* VI, No. 2 (1953), 113–40.
7. Hoffman, Lois Wladis. "Effects of the Employment of Mothers on Parental Power Relations and the Division of Household Tasks," *Marriage and Family Living,* XXII (February, 1960), 27–35. Reprinted as Chapter Fifteen of the present book.
8. ———. Rosen, S. and Lippitt, R. "Parental Coerciveness, Child Autonomy and Child's Role at School," *Sociometry,* XXIII (March, 1960), 15–22.
9. Nye, F. Ivan. *Family Relationships and Delinquent Behavior.* New York: John Wiley, 1958.
10. Rouman, Jack. "School Children's Problems as Related to Parental Factors," *Journal of Educational Research,* L (October, 1956), 105–12.
11. Siegel, Alberta Engvall, Stolz, Lois Meek, Hitchcock, Ethel Alice, and Adamson, Jean. "Dependence and Independence in the Children of Working Mothers," *Child Development,* XXX (December, 1959), 533–47. Reprinted as Chapter Four of the present book.
12. Weiss, Robert S., and Samelson, Nancy M. "Social Roles of American Women: Their Contribution to a Sense of Usefulness and Importance," *Marriage and Family Living,* XX (November, 1958), 358–66.

Chapter Seven

Personality Characteristics of Children*

LEE G. BURCHINAL

THEORETICAL FORMULATION

IT IS frequently asserted that maternal employment probably has a detrimental effect on the personality development and social adjustment of children, especially if the mother works during the first several years of the child's life. Often employment of the mother is said to produce maternal deprivation (3, 10, 22). However, simply analogizing from the results of studies of extreme deprivation to situations involving the impact of the employment of mothers upon the personality development of "normal" children in otherwise "normal" homes appears questionable.

Observation of other cultures indicates that child-rearing functions can be handled in a wide variety of ways (14). The child-care arrangements in the Israeli kibbutz demonstrate that the child-mother relationship may be severed, provided adequate substitute care is available, without causing the child to suffer any apparent detrimental effects. Other research indicates that a multiple-mothering experience does not necessarily lead to retarded or distorted personality development in infants and young children (1, 9).

* Expansion by the author of an article of the same title by Lee G. Burchinal and Jack Rossman from *Marriage and Family Living*, XXIII (November, 1961), pp. 334–40, by permission of the publisher. This is a report on Project 1425 of the Iowa Agricultural and Home Economics Experiment Station, Iowa State University, Ames, Iowa. The project was jointly supported by the Division of Child Welfare of the Iowa State Department of Social Welfare and the Agricultural and Home Economics Experiment Station of Iowa State University. Additional information on the methodology and some more detailed data pertaining to this project are available elsewhere (5, 6, 20).

These conflicting theoretical bases for considering the possible effects of maternal employment on the development of children offer little foundation for developing hypotheses to guide investigation. Despite the number of studies cited earlier, there is no adequate body of empirical findings related to this problem.[1]

In view of the lack of theoretical consistency and the paucity of empirical results in this area, two null hypotheses were developed for the purposes of this investigation:

(a) There is no relationship between maternal employment and selected personality characteristics of children.

(b) There is no relationship between maternal employment and measures of school adjustment and social relations of the children.

Operational definitions of dependent variables and operational hypotheses are presented in the next section. Working mothers are not classified as employed full-time or part-time—in contrast to full-time homemakers; instead, five measures based on the number of months the mother worked during selected periods in the life of her child are used. Theoretical formulations of the psychoanalytic and maternal-deprivation frames of reference emphasize the importance of the mother-child relationship during the early years of the child's life. Separation of the child from the mother during the first several years is generally considered more damaging to the subsequent growth and development of the child than separation during later periods of life. To test this hypothesis, the number of months the mothers worked during the first three, second three, and first six years of the children's lives are recorded separately. Employment during the past thirty months is used as the contemporary index of the independent variable. Thirty months is used because collection of data began during the month of June, 1959; therefore the six months of that year and the twenty-four months of the two preceding years are included in the contemporary measure. The total number of months employed during the life of the child is the fifth operational form of the maternal employment variable.

These measures of maternal employment have two limitations, but little could have been done to eliminate them. The distinctions between regular and sporadic employment and between full-time and part-time employment are lost, primarily because of the recall features involved in obtaining data for the first three measures and for the entire life measure of the independent variable (maternal employment). Mothers were asked only for the total number of months employed during each year of the selected periods in their children's lives.

---

[1] For further citations, see the reports in Part III of this book.

The dependent variables (children's behaviors) were obtained from questionnaire responses and school records. For convenience, the operational form of these variables is presented later in the "findings" section of the report. If maternal employment has a detrimental effect which may be observed with or in spite of the interaction of other variables with the indipendent and dependent variables, the selected personality characteristics of the children will be negatively associated with maternal employment. All of the selected personality characteristics are considered indices of personality development reflecting some aspect of the mental health status and peer group relations of the children.

With the exception of the intelligence scores, which are included in the analyses primarily because they were available, the school-related data—achievement scores, grades, records of absenteeism and tardiness, and school activity scores—are all treated as indices of social adjustments in the context of the school as a social system. The community social participation scores are considered to be indicators of social development as well. Again, if maternal employment has a detrimental effect, assuming a simple model of relation between maternal employment and personality development and social relationship variables, the associations between the maternal employment variables and the children's social relations variables should be negative. More elaborate specification of the relations between the dependent and independent variables lies beyond the scope of this report.

METHOD

Families were first selected on the basis of the children, because they were readily available in school. Two grade levels, seventh and eleventh, were used to determine whether the children's adjustment in the early and late adolescent periods was affected by maternal employment during their early and/or present lives. Cedar Rapids, the second largest metropolitan area in Iowa, was chosen as the locale for the investigation for three reasons: (a) sample selection in one metropolitan area was more economical than one from a larger geographical area; (b) Cedar Rapids contains the widest diversification of industry of any Iowa metropolitan area and provides a wide range of employment for women; and (c) the Cedar Rapids school system was willing to cooperate in the investigation.

About 98 per cent all students in the seventh and eleventh grades in Cedar Rapids completed the questionnaire from which data were taken for all the dependent variables used in this investigation. On the basis of information from name-and-address cards, a second, three-page questionnaire, containing, among other things, questions about the parents' marital histories, educational levels, current occupations, and a detailed table for the employment history of the mother, was mailed to each of the families. After the usual follow-up letters and supplemental interviews with families who had not returned questionnaires, 91 per cent of the original 1,824 parental questionnaires were completed. The number of cases was reduced after some questionnaires, either parental or child, were deleted after careful editing and several control variables were imposed.

Several controls were used in all analyses. These included the grade level and sex of the children. Non-white families and families in which the child was not living with both of his biological parents were deleted from the sample. Age, sex, race, and parental marital status are known to be related to the dependent or independent variables or to both, and hence they were controlled.

Socio-economic status is also considered as a possible control variable. Much research documents the association of socio-economic measures with the types of child-adjustment variables used in this investigation (4, 21). Some research indicates that family socio-economic status is also related to the employment of wives and mothers (2, 8, 16). In the present study, low negative relations were obtained between (a) the educational levels of fathers and mothers; (b) between social status scores based on the husbands' occupations and education (12); and the degree of employment of wives in each of the five selected periods of the children's lives. The Pearsonian correlations ranged between .0 and .23. Inspection of frequency or percentage distributions indicated that these relationships were linear. This was substantiated by the calculation of correlation ratios for the relations between status scores and employment of mothers during the past thirty months. The departures of the eta coefficients from the comparable zero-order coefficients were not statistically significant. Only one of the ten correlation ratios based on the relations between the educational levels of the fathers and maternal employment during the five periods for the two sample families having a seventh or eleventh grade child, was significantly greater than the corresponding Pearsonian correlation coefficients. Because only low level relationships were observed between the socio-economic status and the maternal employment variables, it was decided to obtain the zero-order relationship between each independent and dependent variable first, and, if generally significant results in the predicted direction were obtained, to use partial correlation analysis for controlling on the socio-economic status level.

FINDINGS

We have stated the two general hypotheses formulated for this investigation. Complete statement of operational hypotheses upon which the assessment of these general hypotheses rests would require undue repetition.

Therefore, data are organized under headings appropriate to the two general null hypotheses; specific operational hypotheses are not provided. The total results for each of the two sets of findings are used to determine whether the general null hypotheses should be accepted or rejected.

1. MATERNAL EMPLOYMENT AND SELECTED PERSONALITY
   CHARACTERISTICS OF CHILDREN

The bulk of the data related to personality characteristics of the children was derived from indices developed from forty-four questions similar to those included in several of the personality inventories and the emotionality scale of the Minnesota Test of Personality (7). Each question was followed by three responses—"Yes," "No," and "Don't know"—which were scored as two for "Yes," one for "Don't know," and zero for "No." Eleven scores were derived by sorting items into homogeneous pools on the basis of the agreement of three judges. These scores were based on the following items and are referred to by the following descriptive titles:

(1) Obsessional feeling

Do ideas run through your head so you cannot sleep?

Do you have difficulty getting to sleep even when there are no noises to disturb you?

Does some particular useless thought keep coming into your mind to bother you?

(2) Oversensitivity to others

Does criticism disturb you greatly?

Are your feelings easily hurt?

Are you sorry for the things you do?

(3) Excessive introspection

Do you feel just miserable?

Do you feel self-conscious because of your personal appearance?

Do you worry too long over humiliating experiences?

(4) Upper respiratory complaints (psychosomatic)

Do you have difficulty in breathing through your nose?

Do you take colds rather easily from other people?

Do you have difficulty in getting rid of a cold?

Do you have colds?

(5) Envy and withdrawal

Do you envy the happiness that others seem to enjoy?

Do you feel lonesome, even when you are with people?

(6) Head and eye complaints (psychosomatic)

Are your eyes very sensitive to light?

Do you have headaches?

Are you subject to eye strain?

Do you have shooting pains in your head?

(7) Illness proneness (psychosomatic)

Has it been necessary for you to have medical attention?

Do you find it necessary to watch your health carefully?

Have you been ill during the past 10 years?

Have you been absent from school because of illness?

(8) Nervous symptoms

Do you consider yourself a rather nervous person?

(9) Fatigue

Do you feel fatigued when you get up in the morning?

Do you feel very tired toward the end of the day?

Do you feel tired most of the time?

(10) Mood fluctuations

Do you have up and down moods without apparent cause?

Do you have spells of the "blues"?

Do you get upset easily?

Do you get excited easily?

(11) Anxiety and fright

Do you worry over possible misfortune?

Does it frighten you when you have to see a doctor about some illness?

Are you frightened by lightning?

Ten further questions were each considered as a separate variable related to a personality development characteristic of the children. Two other questions completed data on personality-related characteristics of the children. They were: "How many of your schoolmates do you like?" and "In comparison with other persons in your school how well do you think you are liked by your schoolmates?" The responses to each of these questions were scored from one to five.

Correlation coefficients between each of the indices of maternal employment and the above measures of personality characteristics of children were used as the basis for testing the first general null hypothesis. Table 7.1 shows the estimates of association between the maternal employment indices and the eleven scores; those in Table 7.2 report the estimates of the association between the maternal employment indices and the twelve separate-item responses.

Of the fifty-five correlation coefficients calculated for each grade and sex sample, only seventeen were statistically significant: two for seventh grade boys; three for eleventh grade boys; four for seventh grade girls; and eight for eleventh grade girls. All the significant results supported an association between maternal employment and greater personality disturbance in the children. In each sample, the several other correlation coefficients which approached significance were also in the same direction. However, the overwhelming majority (92 per cent) of coefficients were non-significant.

TABLE 7.1 *Correlations among Maternal Employment Indices and Personality Scores by the Grade Level and Sex of the Children*

MATERNAL EMPLOYMENT DURING GIVEN PERIODS IN THE CHILD'S LIFE	PERSONALITY SCORES			
	OBSESSIONAL FEELINGS	OVER-SENSITIVITY TO OTHERS	EXCESSIVE INTROSPECTION	UPPER RESPIRATORY COMPLAINTS
Seventh Grade Boys (N = 370)				
1 to 3 years	.04	—.03	—.04	—.01
4 to 6 years	.00	—.02	.00	—.06
1 to 6 years	.02	—.03	—.02	—.05
Last 30 months	—.01	—.06	—.02	—.04
Entire life	.00	—.02	.00	—.06
Eleventh Grade Boys (N = 283)				
1 to 3 years	—.03	—.03	.01	.03
4 to 6 years	.00	—.04	.07	.05
1 to 6 years	—.01	—.04	.04	.04
Last 30 months	.05	—.07	.07	.06
Entire life	.01	—.11	.07	.04
Seventh Grade Girls (N = 351)				
1 to 3 years	.03	.05	—.03	.07
4 to 6 years	.03	.00	—.09	.06
1 to 6 years	.04	.03	—.07	.08
Last 30 months	.00	.05	—.02	.05
Entire life	.02	.03	—.09	.06
Eleventh Grade Girls (N = 245)				
1 to 3 years	—.03	—.03	—.04	.11
4 to 6 years	.04	.03	—.03	.20*
1 to 6 years	.00	.01	—.03	.18*
Last 30 months	.05	—.07	.04	.02
Entire life	.05	—.03	—.03	.12

° Correlation coefficients are statistically significant. The size of the correlation required for significance varied from .10 to .13 because of the variation in the number of cases from 245 to 370.

Even where significant, however, the magnitude of the correlations was uniformly low. The level of significance for the correlations varied from .10 to .13. The observed significant correlations ranged from .10 to .13 for boys and from .12 to .20 for girls.

In summary the correlations of Table 7.1 were mostly non-significant, and, where significant, the coefficients were low and showed little pattern with respect to either independent or dependent variables. These data offer no basis for rejecting the first hypothesis.

TABLE 7.1 *Correlations among Maternal Employment Indices, and Personality Scores by the Grade Level and Sex of the Children*

MATERNAL EMPLOYMENT DURING GIVEN PERIODS IN THE CHILD'S LIFE	PERSONALITY SCORES						
	ENVY, WITH DRAWAL	HEAD AND EYE COMPLAINTS	ILLNESS PRONENESS	NERVOUS SYMPTOMS	FATIGUE	MOOD FLUCTUATIONS	ANXIETY AND FRIGHT
Seventh Grade Boys (N = 370)							
1 to 3 years	.07	.02	.02	.03	—.03	.06	.06
4 to 6 years	.10*	.08	.09	—.01	—.07	.08	.08
1 to 6 years	.09	.07	.08	.00	—.05	.08	.07
Last 30 months	.06	.02	.06	—.07	.03	—.01	.01
Entire life	.11*	.08	.04	—.02	—.03	.06	.04
Eleventh Grade Boys (N = 283)							
1 to 3 years	.08	—.08	.01	.09	.05	.00	—.04
4 to 6 years	.13*	.05	.01	.03	.13*	.00	.01
1 to 6 years	.12*	—.02	.01	.06	.10	.00	—.01
Last 30 months	—.02	.03	.07	.04	.08	.04	.06
Entire life	.03	.04	.05	—.04	.08	.02	.00
Seventh Grade Girls (N = 351)							
1 to 3 years	.09	.08	.03	—.01	.03	.05	.06
4 to 6 years	.06	.16*	.05	—.02	.01	.06	.02
1 to 6 years	.09	.14*	.05	—.02	.02	.06	.04
Last 30 months	.02	.12*	.00	—.05	—.03	.01	—.01
Entire life	.03	.16*	.02	—.03	—.03	.03	.02
Eleventh Grade Girls (N = 245)							
1 to 3 years	—.01	.07	.09	.08	.11	.06	—.02
4 to 6 years	—.02	.07	.01	.15*	.05	.09	—.01
1 to 6 years	—.02	.08	.14*	.13*	.09	.09	—.03
Last 30 months	.06	.12	.08	.10	.00	—.07	—.05
Entire life	.06	.17*	.13*	.13*	.01	.07	.03

* Correlation coefficients are statistically significant. The size of the correlation required for significance varied from .10 to .13 because of the variation in the number of cases from 245 to 370.

The twelve separate items are referred to in abbreviated form along the top of Table 7.2. From left to right in the table, the complete forms of the item are: "Do you get angry easily?" "Were you ill much of the time during childhood?" "Do things go wrong for you from no fault of your own?" "Do you get discouraged easily?" "Are you bothered by the feeling that things are not real?" "Have you been depressed because of low marks in school?" "Do you daydream?" "Do you have conflicting moods of love and hate for members of your family?" "Do you feel that your parents are

TABLE 7.2 *Correlations among Maternal Employment Variables and Personality Item Responses by the Grade Level and Sex of the Children*

MATERNAL EMPLOYMENT DURING GIVEN PERIODS IN THE CHILD'S LIFE	PERSONALITY ITEM RESPONSES					
	ANGER EASILY	ILL IN CHILD-HOOD	THINGS GO WRONG	EASILY DIS-COURAGED	FEELINGS NOT REAL	DEPRESSED OVER LOW MARKS
	Correlation Coefficients					
Seventh Grade Boys (N = 370)						
1 to 3 years	.01	—.04	.01	—.01	—.01	.05
4 to 6 years	.01	.00	.08	.03	.00	.06
1 to 6 years	.00	—.02	.06	.01	.00	.06
Last 30 months	—.07	.03	.03	—.05	—.02	.01
Entire life	—.01	—.01	.07	.00	.00	.04
Eleventh Grade Boys (283)						
1 to 3 years	—.01	—.02	.00	—.06	.04	—.05
4 to 6 years	—.01	—.02	.01	—.07	.14*	—.03
1 to 6 years	—.01	—.02	.00	—.08	.10	—.05
Last 30 months	.11	.02	.15*	—.04	.01	.06
Entire life	.04	—.04	.04	—.11	.04	.04
Seventh Grade Girls (N = 351)						
1 to 3 years	.06	—.03	.00	.05	.04	.15*
4 to 6 years	.05	—.04	—.05	—.03	.07	.19*
1 to 6 years	.07	—.04	—.03	.01	.06	.20*
Last 30 months	.05	—.05	—.02	.05	.01	.08
Entire life	.05	—.04	—.04	—.01	.06	.19*
Eleventh Grade Girls (N = 245)						
1 to 3 years	—.10	—.01	.03	.09	—.04	.09
4 to 6 years	—.07	—.07	.11	.05	—.03	—.01
1 to 6 years	—.10	—.04	.07	.08	—.04	.05
Last 30 months	.06	.02	.04	.00	—.03	—.04
Entire life	—.02	—.01	.17*	.08	—.05	.03

* Correlation coefficients are statistically significant. The size of the correlation required for significance varied from .10 to .13 because of the variation in the number of cases from 245 to 370.

disappointed in you?" "Do you suffer discomfort from gas in the stomach or intestines?" The last two columns cover the number of schoolmates you like and who you think like you, items mentioned above.

Only 11 of the total 240 correlation coefficients listed in Table 7.2 were statistically significant—7 for the two girls' samples and 4 for the two boys' samples. Among the boys, three different dependent variables and three different independent variables were significantly correlated. Among the

TABLE 7.2 *Correlations among Maternal Employment Variables and Personality Item Responses by the Grade Level and Sex of the Children*

MATERNAL EMPLOYMENT DURING GIVEN PERIODS IN THE CHILD'S LIFE	PERSONALITY ITEM RESPONSES					
	DAY-DREAM	LOVE AND HATE FAMILY	PARENTS DISAPPOINTED IN YOU	GASTRO-INTESTINAL PAINS	SCHOOL-MATES YOU LIKE	SCHOOL-MATES LIKE YOU
	Correlation Coefficients					
Seventh Grade Boys (N = 370)						
1 to 3 years	.04	.02	—.01	.05	.07	.02
4 to 6 years	.11*	.02	.04	—.01	.05	.01
1 to 6 years	.09	.02	.02	.00	.06	.02
Last 30 months	.07	.01	.04	.06	.05	—.05
Entire life	.11*	.03	.03	.01	.05	.01
Eleventh Grade Boys (283)						
1 to 3 years	.05	—.01	—.03	—.01	—.03	—.03
4 to 6 years	.03	.02	.07	—.05	—.10	—.07
1 to 6 years	.05	.01	.02	—.03	—.07	—.06
Last 30 months	.04	—.02	.02	.01	.01	—.10
Entire life	.08	.00	.06	—.03	—.06	—.10
Seventh Grade Girls (N = 351)						
1 to 3 years	.03	.01	.06	.05	.01	.00
4 to 6 years	.04	—.01	—.06	.02	.03	.09
1 to 6 years	.04	—.01	—.01	.04	.03	.06
Last 30 months	.02	—.03	—.03	.06	.05	.00
Entire life	.06	—.03	—.03	.00	.01	.05
Eleventh Grade Girls (N = 245)						
1 to 3 years	.15*	—.01	—.02	.04	.01	—.03
4 to 6 years	.13*	.03	.02	—.08	.06	—.01
1 to 6 years	.17*	.01	.00	—.02	.03	—.02
Last 30 months	.09	.10	.09	—.07	—.02	—.06
Entire life	.09	.08	.08	—.04	.08	—.06

* Correlation coefficients are statistically significant. The size of the correlation required for significance varied from .10 to .13 because of the variation in the number of cases from 245 to 370.

girls, significant coefficients were found in relation to "depressed over low marks" for younger girls and "daydreaming" for older girls. Again, all the correlations were positive but low. The highest coefficient was .20.

Since all the foregoing significant results were quite low, partial correlation analysis controlling on the socio-economic level was not employed. On the basis of the results given in Tables 7.1 and 7.2, the first hypothesis is not rejected. We turn now to the second hypothesis.

2. SCHOOL AND SOCIAL ADJUSTMENT

Correlations among the five maternal employment indices and the intelligence scores, achievement scores, grades, days absent, days tardy, school activity participation scores, and community activity participation scores are presented in Table 7.3. Data for the first five variables were obtained from school records. The intelligence scores were derived from the Otis Quick-Scoring Form (19). Achievement levels for the junior high school students were measured by the median score on the Stanford Achievement Test (13); those of the senior high school students were measured from the Iowa Test of Educational Development (15). School grades were calculated as a mean from 0 to 4.0 for all grades received during the previous year. The total number of days was used as the measure of absenteeism or tardiness. School activity scores were developed from a ten-item index based upon participation in community organizations appropriate for the age levels of the children.

If maternal employment is negatively associated with school and social variables, negative correlations should be observed for all relations except those involving the absentee and tardy variables. For the latter, high values indicate undesirable behavior; while for the former, high values indicate desirable behavior.

Twenty-two of the 140 correlation coefficients given in Table 7.3 were statistically significant. All of the independent and dependent variables were involved in significant correlations; but, aside from three specific combinations, there was little pattern of association in the results.

First, three of the four correlations between the maternal employment variables and the intelligence scores of the seventh grade boys were statistically significant. Although low, all correlations were negative. However, relations among the maternal employment variables and the intelligence scores of the other three samples of children were uniformly non-significant. Therefore, little theoretical or substantive significance can be attached to the significant results found for the seventh grade boys' sample.

A second concentration of significant results occurred in relation to school grades; two significant correlations were observed for the eleventh grade boys, three for the seventh grade girls, and one for the eleventh grade girls. However, there were only six significant correlations among twenty relations which were tested, and these correlations were low (the largest was —.17). Finally, among the eleventh grade girls, six of the ten correlations involving tardiness or absenteeism were statistically significant. Again, however, the correlations were low, ranging from .14 to .23.

The slight patterning of results on some of the dependent variables required further analysis. Partial correlations were determined for the relations between the last thirty months variable and the dependent variables.

TABLE 7.3 Correlations among Maternal Employment Variables and School and Social Adjustment Variables by the Grade Level and Sex of the Children

MATERNAL EMPLOYMENT DURING GIVEN PERIODS IN THE CHILD'S LIFE	INTELLIGENCE	ACHIEVEMENT	SOCIAL ADJUSTMENT VARIABLES				
			SCHOOL GRADES	DAYS ABSENT	DAYS TARDY	PARTICIPATION IN SCHOOL ACTIVITIES	PARTICIPATION IN NONSCHOOL ACTIVITIES
			Correlation Coefficients				
Seventh Grade Boys (N = 363)							
1 to 3 years	.01	.01	.03	−.06	−.03	−.01	.02
4 to 6 years	−.14*	−.10*	−.05	−.05	−.01	.03	−.01
1 to 6 years	−.11*	−.07	−.02	−.06	−.02	.01	.01
Last 30 months	−.13*	−.06	−.04	.02	.03	−.01	.03
Entire life	−.13*	−.07	−.03	−.07	.00	.04	.03
Eleventh Grade Boys (N = 278)							
1 to 3 years	.07	.01	.02	−.01	.00	−.09	.01
4 to 6 years	.06	.01	−.05	.11	.03	−.08	−.04
1 to 6 years	.07	.02	−.02	.06	.02	−.10	−.02
Last 30 months	−.04	−.12*	−.17*	.11	.05	−.13*	−.02
Entire life	−.01	−.07	−.12*	.12*	.03	−.12*	−.09
Seventh Grade Girls (N = 345)							
1 to 3 years	−.08	−.11*	−.10*	−.03	−.02	.04	−.05
4 to 6 years	−.03	−.05	−.08	.00	−.05	.03	.00
1 to 6 years	−.06	−.09	−.10*	−.02	−.04	.04	−.03
Last 30 months	.00	−.03	−.05	−.02	−.05	.01	.04
Entire life	−.03	−.09	−.10*	−.04	−.05	.03	.01
Eleventh Grade Girls (N = 242)							
1 to 3 years	.10	.10	.03	−.03	.05	.05	−.02
4 to 6 years	−.01	.05	−.05	.10	.23*	.01	−.12
1 to 6 years	.05	.09	−.01	.08	.17*	.04	−.09
Last 30 months	−.02	−.07	−.15*	.14*	.16*	−.01	−.12
Entire life	−.04	−.03	−.09	.14*	.16*	.02	−.12

* Correlation coefficients are statistically significant. The size of the correlation required for significance varied from .10 to .12 because of the variation in the number of cases from 245 to 370.

Only the last thirty months variable was used in these analyses because this independent variable would correspond most closely with the period for which the socio-economic scores were appropriate. Because of social mobility patterns, the socio-economic scores were considered not to be appropriately related to whether the mother worked during earlier periods. When the partial correlations were determined, the significant zero-order correlations between the employment variable and (a) the intelligence scores for the seventh grade boys, and (b) the grades, absenteeism, and tardiness for the eleventh grade girls, were reduced below the level of statistical significance. The only partial correlation to remain significant was between recent maternal employment and the grades of eleventh grade boys with the control on socio-economic level. The coefficient was −.12, having been reduced from −.17 for the association without controlling on the status level variable.

The partial correlation analyses removed virtually all of the major support which was found for the second hypothesis. Therefore, the second null hypothesis was also accepted.

SUMMARY AND DISCUSSION

This study tested a number of operational hypotheses derived from two general hypotheses about this association of maternal employment to the personality development and social adjustment of children. Cause-and-effect connotations are obvious and would have become the major focus of discussion if sufficient support had been found for the rejection of the null hypotheses. However, this was not the case. Because significant correlations between the five maternal employment indices and the dependent variables were so few in number, low in magnitude, and generally scattered among different variables, the significant coefficients are better interpreted as chance, not substantively significant, relationships.

Therefore, it would appear that maternal employment during the specified periods of the children's lives has no apparent relationship with the selected characteristics of the children. Notably, this conclusion holds for the relationship between maternal employment during the first three, second three, and first six years of the children's lives and dependent variables measured during the early and late adolescent periods of the children's lives. Within the limitations of the methodology used, apparently maternal employment per se cannot be considered an index of maternal deprivation having consequent detrimental effects on the development of children. If maternal employment during preschool years of the children's lives has negative effects upon the children's growth and development, these effects are not observed at later periods in the development process—not, at least, by the techniques used in this study. This conclusion holds for both sexes and for two periods of development.

The several sets of results which were significant and appeared to have some degree of replication were at least partly attributable to the socio-economic level and disappeared when this control was applied. For instance, it would have been reasonable to interpret the association between maternal employment and school absenteeism and tardiness among older girls as an indication that these girls had to assume greater domestic roles which at least partially conflicted with their school attendance. However, the greater proportion of employed mothers of girls from lower social class levels apparently was involved in these correlations. There were slight negative correlations between socio-economic level and absenteeism and tardiness. Hence, the pattern of correlation between maternal employment and school absenteeism or tardiness among older girls could not be attributed to maternal employment conditions, but apparently reflected normative standards toward school attendance associated with social class differentials and possibly reinforced by domestic demands arising from the employment of mothers.

These results are valid at the "mass" level for the population studied. The four grade and sex samples were similarly composed of white students from primary-marriage families. Significant positive or negative correlations between maternal employment indices and the dependent variables may be observed for subclasses of families and children within these larger samples.

If the data were obtained for the mothers', attitudes toward child-rearing, motivations for employment, competency to handle home and work roles, the children's perception and evaluations of their mothers' employment, the adequacy of substitute care for younger children, the fathers' attitudes toward the mothers' employment, and family integration and family adaptability, to mention just a few variables, and if appropriate designs were developed to test the relations between maternal employment and dependent child development variables within the context of these or related family relationship variables, different results might be obtained. However, the results provide data in a field where results are desired but have been almost totally lacking until recently and must be interpreted at a general level. Although questions may be raised about the validity and reliability of some of the measures used in this study, the consistency of the results strengthens the basis of interpretation. Because large samples were employed, the present results probably can be generalized to similar populations in similar urban areas.

On the basis of the data obtained, the conclusion of this study coincides exactly with that of another study reported in the present book conducted with kindergarten children: "one may surely conclude from these data that maternal employment per se is not the overwhelmingly influential factor in children's lives that some have thought it to be" (Chapter Four, p. 80). Scattered data from several other investigations generally support this conclusion. Nye (18) found no differences in psychosomatic scores among controlled samples of children whose mothers were and were not employed. Burchinal (5) has reported non-significant differences between anxiety scores of children whose mothers were employed and of children whose mothers were not employed. Nolan and Tuttle (17) reported non-significant differences in school grades and rated adjustment characteristics of children of employed and non-employed mothers. Hand (11) also failed to observe any significant differences in personality adjustment between children whose mothers were employed and those whose mothers were full-time homemakers.

However, results of one recent, carefully reasoned, and well-designed study are at variance with the null differences obtained in these other investigations. Hoffman (Chapter Six) found that children of employed mothers showed lower intellectual performances than the children of non-working mothers. Depending on whether their mothers enjoyed or disliked their work, the children differed, and in different ways, from children in control groups whose mothers were not employed. Research on the relations among maternal employment, other family-related variables, and the developmental characteristics of children is just now developing in a serious manner. The call for additional research in this area deserves more attention than its trite usage generally implies.

REFERENCES

1. Abugosh, Alegria. "Noncontinuous Mothering and Psychological Development of Children 8 to 17 Years of Age." Unpublished Master's thesis, Iowa State University, 1957.

2. Bell, Daniel. "The Great Back-to-Work Movement," *Fortune* (July, 1956), pp. 90–93, 168, 170, 172.

3. Bowlby, John. *Maternal Care and Mental Health*. Geneva, Switzerland: World Health Organization, Monograph No. 2, 1952.

4. Burchinal, Lee G. "Social Status, Measured Intelligence, Achievement, and Personality Adjustment of Rural Iowa Girls," *Sociometry*, XXII (March, 1959), 75–80.

5. _____. *Maternal Employment, Family Relations and Selected Personality, School-Related and Social-Development Characteristics of Children*, Bulletin 497. Ames, Iowa: Agricultural and Home Economics Experiment Station, October, 1961.

6. Carpenter, Chester J. "Maternal Employment and Personality Development of Children." Unpublished Master's thesis, Iowa State University, 1959.

7. Darley, John G., and McNamara, Walter J. *Minnesota Personality Scale*. New York: Psychological Corporation, 1941.

8. "Family Characteristics of Working Wives," *Current Population Reports, Labor Forces.* United States Department of Commerce, Bureau of the Census, Series P-50, No. 81. Washington, D.C.: Government Printing Office, 1957.

9. Gardner, D. Bruce, Hawkes, Glenn R., and Burchinal, Lee G. "Noncontinuous Mothering in Infancy and Development in Later Childhood." *Child Development,* XXXII (June, 1961), 225–34.

10. Goldfarb, William. "Emotional and Intellectual Consequences of Psychological Deprivation in Infancy." In Paul H. Hock and Joseph Zubin. *Psychopathology of Childhood.* New York: Grune & Stratton, 1955, pp. 105–19.

11. Hand, Horace G. "Working Mothers and Maladjusted Children," *Journal of Educational Sociology,* XXX (January, 1957), 245–46.

12. Hollingshead, A. B. "Index of Social Position." Mimeographed paper, Department of Sociology, Yale University, 1957.

13. Kelly, Truman L. and others. *Stanford Achievement Test.* Yonkers, N.Y.: World Book Company, 1953.

14. Kenkel, William F. *Family in Perspective.* New York: Appleton-Century-Crofts, 1960.

15. Lindquist, E. F. *Iowa Test of Educational Development.* Chicago: Science Research Associates, 1948.

16. National Manpower Council. *Work in the Lives of Married Women.* New York: Columbia University Press, 1958.

17. Nolan, Francena L., and Tuttle, Dawn H. *Certain Practices, Satisfactions, and Difficulties in Families with Employed Homemakers.* Pennsylvania Experiment Station, Bulletin 655, University Park Penna.: Pennsylvania State University, August, 1959. An expansion of this article is reprinted as Chapter Eight of the present book.

18. Nye, F. Ivan. "Employment Status of Mothers and Adjustment of Adolescent Children," *Marriage and Family Living,* XXI (August, 1959), 240–44. Reprinted as Chapter Ten of the present book.

19. Otis, A. S. *Otis Quick-Scoring Mental Ability Tests.* Yonkers, N.Y.: World Book Co., 1939.

20. Rossman, Jack E. "Relations of Maternal Employment to Children's Scholastic Achievement and Social Participation." Unpublished Master's thesis, Iowa State University, 1960.

21. Sewell, William H., and Haller, A. O. "Social Status and the Personality Adjustment of the Child," *Sociometry,* XIX (June, 1956), 114–25.

22. Spitz, Rene. "The Influence of Mother–Child Relationship and Its Disturbance." In Kenneth Soddy, ed. *Mental Health and Infant Development.* New York: Basic Books, 1956, I, 103–8.

Chapter Eight

Effects on Rural Children*

FRANCENA L. NOLAN

A VITAL function of the family is the socialization of the children. Much opposition to maternal employment derives from the assumption that the mother role is inherently incompatible with the worker role. Working mothers are thought to neglect their children and to contribute to the children's poor performance in school.

The purpose of this study was to discover the arrangements made by employed mothers for child care at such critical times as after school and during the children's illnesses and to ascertain the impact of the mothers' employment on school performance (see Chapter Seventeen for a description of the sample and methodology).

AFTER SCHOOL

Contrary to popular belief, the majority of children with employed mothers were supervised after school. The practice of leaving children in the care of an older sibling was followed by only 8 per cent of employed mothers. In 61 per cent of the families, the children were under the care of an adult, (25 per cent were in the care of the father or mother; 23 per cent, another relative; and 13 per cent, a sitter). Another 33 per cent

---

* Expanded from Francena L. Nolan and Dawn H. Tuttle, "Certain Practices, Satisfactions and Difficulties in Families with Employed Homemakers," Bulletin 655, Pennsylvania Agricultural Experiment Station, 1959. This study was conducted by the Department of Home Management, Housing and Home Art, College of Home Economics and Department of Agricultural Economics and Rural Sociology, Pennsylvania Agricultural Experiment Station; Project 1259. Project Leader, Francena L. Nolan.

of employed homemakers (nineteen families) said it was not necessary to make special arrangements. In sixteen of these families, the children were in high school and no longer needed close supervision after school.

ILLNESS OF CHILD

One-half of the employed homemakers stayed home when the child was ill, and 26 per cent had some other person stay with the child. Twenty-two per cent indicated that it was usually not necessary to make special arrangements because their children were not often seriously ill or because many were teenagers able to care for themselves.

SCHOOL PERFORMANCE

The child's performance in school is an often-used indication of parental success in child-rearing. Adequate performance within the limits of the

TABLE 8.1 *Performance in School of Children from Homes with Employed and Non-Employed Mothers*

PERFORMANCE IN SCHOOL	CHILDREN 6 TO 11	CHILDREN 12 AND OVER
	Mean Scores	
Academic Achievement		
Employed homemaker	2.54	2.85 ⎱ *
Full-time homemaker	2.39	2.51 ⎰
Relation of Ability to Achievement		
Employed homemaker	3.08	3.25
Full-time homemaker	3.10	3.17
Acceptance by Peers		
Employed homemaker	3.22	3.36 ⎱ *
Full-time homemaker	3.07	3.08 ⎰
Acceptance of Teachers' Supervision		
Employed homemaker	3.61	3.27
Full-time homemaker	3.44	3.09
Evidence of Home Training		
Employed homemaker	2.68	2.85
Full-time homemaker	2.89	2.68
Number of Cases		
Employed homemaker	*40.00*	*49.00*
Full-time homemaker	*124.00*	*157.00*

Scoring—4, high; 1, low.
* Statistically significant.

child's abilities is the expected pattern. Teachers can observe children over long periods of time and in many situations. One would certainly suppose that detrimental effects of maternal employment on children would be reflected in school behavior.

Teachers were asked to rate their pupils on a four-point scale (four high, one low) in the following areas: academic achievement, relation between child's ability and his achievement, acceptance by peers, acceptance of teachers' supervision, and evidence of home training. Many children were rated by more than one teacher. Those ratings were averaged to provide a score for each child in the sample. The mean scores for children from homes with employed mothers and from those with full-time homemakers were computed for each area. Scores for children six to eleven were analyzed separately from the twelve and over age grouping because the type of instruction was different.

The results revealed few differences among children. For the younger children, there were no statistically significant differences (Table 8.1). Among the older age group, children whose mothers were employed scored slightly higher in academic achievement and acceptance by peers than children from homes with full-time homemakers. These data failed to support the supposition that maternal employment is detrimental to children. However, these conclusions are tentative, and much more research is needed to reach an adequate understanding of the effects of the mother's employment. Social class and mothers' education were not controlled in this study because the number of cases was too small. New studies should include a sample large enough to make possible a detailed analysis of many variables thought to be related to parent-child relationships.

Chapter Nine

Personalities of Children and Child-Rearing Attitudes of Mothers*

KATHRYN S. POWELL

STUDENTS of the family are finding an increasing need for additional information concerning the relationship between maternal employment and (a) characteristics of children and (b) maternal attitudes which might affect children.

The present investigation sought to obtain from longitudinal data information concerning the relationship between maternal employment and characteristics of children over a period of years. Cross-sectional data were used to obtain, at three stages of the family life cycle, measures of maternal attitudes toward child-rearing practices and the relationship between maternal employment and maternal attitudes.

MATERNAL EMPLOYMENT AND STRENGTH OF MOTIVES OF CHILDREN

While a relationship between maternal employment and emotional maladjustment of children is frequently implied, evidence which supports this assumption is limited. This study is the first longitudinal analysis of the relationship as measured by projective tests to be reported. The Children's Appreception Test (CAT) devised by Bellak (3) for children from three to ten, and the Thematic Appreception Test (TAT) for children over ten

---

* The dissertation on which this paper is based was directed by Dr. James Walters, Professor of Home and Family Life, School of Home Economics, Florida State University, 1960.

were used in the present study. They measure the strength of the motives of *achievement, affiliation,* and *power.* Nolan (11) found many individual differences from one age level to the next in children from three to ten and some reversals at different levels. Analyzing the relation between the strength of these three motives and maternal employment might help explain these individual variations because the mother's employment status also fluctuates. In terms of the projective tests, the motives were generally defined as follows:

1. *Achievement:* The story makes some reference to an achievement goal in terms of success in competition, unique accomplishment, or long-term involvement.

2. *Affiliation:* The story contains some evidence of concern in one or more of the characters about establishing, maintaining, or restoring a positive affective relationship with another person.

3. *Power:* The story makes some reference to the thoughts, feelings, and actions of one of the characters which indicates concern over the control or the means of influencing a person.[1]

If gainful employment of mothers reflects their concern for the families' "getting ahead," it might be hypothesized that this attitude would be reflected among their children, and that these children would develop stronger achievement and power motives than would those of full-time homemakers. On the other hand, it might be hypothesized that a negative relationship would exist between the gainful employment of mothers and the development in children of affiliation motives which reflect their need to establish, maintain, or restore positive affective relationships with others. Theorists frequently view maternal employment as depriving children of maternal affection, a situation which may result in emotional apathy of the children, characterized by lack of concern for others, or an excessive, neurotic dependence on others.

The subjects for the study of the relationship between maternal employment and the motives of children as measured by projective tests were twenty-seven mothers and their adolescent children who had been enrolled in the nursery schools of the Institute of Human Development of the Florida State University. The mothers were all white, American-born, urban, middle-class, and of intact families. Socio-economic status was determined by the short form of the McGuire-White Index of Social Status (10).

In order to obtain information concerning the strength of the motives of the children, the Children's Apperception Test (CAT) was administered yearly when the adolescents were at ages five, six, seven, nine, ten, and eleven. The Thematic Apperception Test (TAT) was administered to the

---

[1] Motives summarized from Atkinson (1).

same adolescents at age twelve. However, the strength of the motives was not sufficiently apparent to merit statistical analysis until the age of nine. The tests were scored by a qualified psychologist of the Institute of Human Development at the Florida State University for the motives of achievement, affiliation, and power following the system outlined in Atkinson (1).

The Mann-Whitney U test was computed to determine the relationship of maternal employment and the strength of the motives of achievement, affiliation, and power at the ages of nine, ten, and eleven on the CAT and at the age of twelve on the TAT. The values of U and resulting z-scores are shown in Table 9.1. Employment histories of the mothers were

TABLE 9.1 *Relationship between Employment Status of Mothers and Achievement, Affiliation, and Power Motives of their Children*

AGE	INSTRUMENT USED	MOTIVES						NUMBER
		ACHIEVEMENT		AFFILIATION		POWER		
		U	z-score	U	z-score	U	z-score	
9	CAT	57.00	3.05*	24.0	1.71	31.5	1.61	27
10	CAT	55.50	.54	51.5	.796	25.5	1.21	27
11	CAT	59.16	.172	38.5	1.23	49.0	.367	24
12	TAT	69.50	1.13	73.0	.91	66.0	1.26	27

* Statistically significant.

used to determine the maternal employment status at the time when the data on the children had been collected.

The highest relationship between maternal employment and strength of motives was between maternal employment and the achievement motives; children of employed mothers showed stronger achievement motives than those of non-employed mothers. The relationship at age nine was significant. There were no significant relationships between maternal employment and the motives of affiliation or power.

The findings of stronger achievement motives in children of employed mothers were in the expected direction. Hartley (7, 8, 9) concluded from sex-role studies that self-concept implications could be derived from her data: namely, that working mothers' daughters tended to perceive women as freer to move more widely, to behave more vigorously, and to achieve more freely than did their opposite numbers with non-working mothers. The present evidence of the relation between achievement motives in the child and maternal employment implies one aspect of the relationship between personality development of children and maternal employment.

The absence of a significant relationship between maternal employment and affiliation motives in children fails to support the findings of Essig and Morgan (5) and Rouman (14) which pointed toward a trend for children of employed mothers to be more lacking in cordial relationships with others and in feelings of love and understanding. It should be pointed out that the subjects in this study were from the same social class and represented a homogeneous group of school children; whereas, in the Essig and Morgan study (5), social class was not controlled, and in the Rouman study (14), children with problems in school were involved.

Evidence offered by this investigation and other studies herein reviewed (6, Chapter Ten) fails to support the belief that maternal employment has deleterious effects on the personality development of middle-class children.

MATERNAL EMPLOYMENT AND MATERNAL ATTITUDES

Increasing evidence points to the importance of maternal attitudes in the personality development of children. Radke (13) reviewed many of the earlier studies which have given rise to the current interest in the influence of the parent-child relationship upon the personality development of the child. In a study focused upon parental attitudes, Burchinal and Lovell (4) sought to determine attitudinal differences among mothers classified according to their employment status. Although these researchers found, in using the Parent Attitude Research Instrument, no significant differences between employed mothers and non-employed mothers, they concluded from the non-significant differences that employed mothers tended to: (a) be less likely to foster dependency in their children, (b) endorse harsh punishment more frequently, (c) minimize outside influences more, and (d) be more irritable over parent-child relations.

The subjects for this study of maternal attitudes were mothers whose children were enrolled in the laboratory schools of the Institute of Human Development or the University School of the Florida State University or the University Heights Nursery School and Kindergarten, a private school. The last school, adjacent to the University campus, was selected because an evaluation of the enrollments of all of the private schools in Tallahassee by a specialist in child development indicated that the family backgrounds of the children in this school were more similar to those of the children enrolled in the nursery school and kindergarten at the university than were those in other schools.

The questionnaires were mailed to: (a) all of the mothers of children enrolled in the Human Development nursery school and kindergarten at the Florida State University, in the University Heights Nursery School and Kindergarten, and in grades nine and ten of the University School at the Florida State University, and (b) to a random sample of sixty mothers of children in grades two, three, four, five, and six at the University School of the Florida State University.

The criteria for selection were: white, American-born, urban, middle-class, of intact families. Socio-economic status was determined by the short form of the McGuire-White Index of Social Status (10). Those mothers who did not meet the foregoing criteria as indicated by the school records were eliminated before the instruments were administered. All the mothers who returned the questionnaires and who satisfied the criteria were used as subjects.

The stage in the family life cycle was determined by the age of the oldest child. The three stages used were when the oldest child was: (a) of preschool age, (b) of elementary school age, and (c) of adolescent age. The grade level criteria for the age groups were (a) preschool children enrolled in nursery school or kindergarten, ranging from three to six, (b) elementary school age children in grades two, three, four, five, or six, ranging from seven to twelve, and (c) adolescents in grades nine and ten, aged thirteen or above.

Each age group was subsequently divided into "employed" or "non-employed" groupings, according to the mother's present employment status. A mother was classified "employed" if she worked sixteen hours a week or more in gainful employment outside the home.

Inspection of the employment histories of the forty-four gainfully employed mothers in all three groups revealed that:

1. Thirteen (29 per cent) had worked for the entire lifetime of the oldest child.
2. Four (9 per cent) had worked all but one year of the lifetime of the oldest child.
3. Seven (16 per cent) had worked all but three years of the lifetime of the oldest child.
4. Twenty (45 per cent) had worked less than one-third of the lifetime of the oldest child.

Among the 130 mothers included in the present investigation were 42 mothers whose oldest children were of preschool age, 41 whose oldest children were of elementary school age, and 47 whose oldest children were adolescents.

In the total preschool group of forty-two subjects, there were twelve employed mothers and thirty non-employed mothers. In this group, 83 per cent returned the questionnaire which was sent initially, but the number of employed mothers was too small to permit a statistical analysis. To secure responses from more employed mothers, questionnaires were mailed to mothers of children enrolled in the University Heights Kindergarten and Nursery School.

For the elementary school age group, the 82 per cent return of the questionnaire yielded usable responses from fourteen employed and twenty-seven non-employed mothers. For each grade, questionnaires were mailed to twelve mothers randomly selected from those who met the criteria. Of this total of forty-one, the grade distribution on the basis of grade of oldest child was: ten in the second grade, nine in the third grade, seven in the fourth grade, eight in the fifth grade, and seven in the sixth grade.

For the adolescent age group, eighteen employed and twenty-nine non-employed mothers, or a total of forty-seven, comprised the subjects used in the present analyses. Eighty-one per cent of the group of mothers whose oldest child was an adolescent returned questionnaires. This group consisted of thirty-one mothers having adolescents enrolled in grades nine and ten at the University School and sixteen mothers of adolescents in the Tallahassee public schools for whom longitudinal data were available in the Institute of Human Development at the Florida State University.

To measure attitudes of mothers toward children, a subscale, General Home Standards, was selected from Wiley's (16) Child Guidance Scale. Utilizing the responses of 172 subjects, Wiley (16) found a reliability coefficient higher than .80 on this subscale. A measure of validity of the instrument was obtained by making clinical judgments concerning the "sophistication" of the groups taking the test. For example, it was believed to be valid if persons who had had counseling or special instruction in child development were more likely to express attitudes which were favorable than were those who had had little experience with children. A detailed description of the measures of reliability and validity obtained has been presented by Wiley (15). The questions in the Wiley scale were concerned with attitudes that reflect respect for the welfare of the child as an individual as opposed to attitudes that reflect concern for adhering to standards imposed by comparison with what the parent did as a child, with what the friends, neighbors, or relatives think, or with perfection. This instrument was among the least age-oriented of the available scales for measuring attitudes toward child-rearing and therefore appeared to be the most appropriate for mothers in three different stages of the family life cycle.

Scores ranging from 23 to 115 were possible on the subscale, General Home Standards, of the Child Guidance Survey, the lower scores reflecting more favorable attitudes toward child-rearing. The scores for the 130 subjects ranged from 40 to 80 with the exception of one score of 25. A comparison of the median score of the instrument measuring attitudes toward child-rearing for each age group indicated a trend toward attitudes that were more favorable to the welfare of the child as an individual for the mothers with youngest children. The median score was 61 for the mothers whose oldest children were adolescents; 59.5 for the mothers whose oldest children were of elementary school age; 53.5 for mothers of preschool children. There

TABLE 9.2 *Maternal Attitudes toward Child-Rearing: Median Scores and Percentage of Employed and Non-Employed Mothers above Medians by Age Groups*

AGE GROUPS	MEDIAN SCORE ON GENERAL HOME STANDARDS	SUBJECTS ABOVE MEDIAN			
		MOTHER EMPLOYED		MOTHER NOT EMPLOYED	
		Per Cent	*Number*	*Per Cent*	*Number*
Preschool	53.5	50	12	50	30
Elementary school	59.5	57	14	44	27
Adolescent	61.0	55	18	48	29

was also a consistent trend for the non-employed mothers to have more favorable attitudes than the employed mothers.

In relation to the null hypothesis tested, there were no significant relationships between maternal employment and attitudes of mothers toward child-rearing at any of the three stages of the family life cycle studied, as shown in Table 9.2. These findings support the evidence presented by Burchinal and Lovell (4), and lend support to Bartemeier's (2) hypothesis that the growth and development of the personalities of children are part of an intricate complex of influences and experiences that are operative whether the mother is employed outside the home or remains at home.

The scores of the mothers in the present investigation may have been influenced to some extent by a number who did not mark maximum agreement or disagreement because they felt the need to qualify the statement. Further analysis of the respondents' reactions to this instrument would be helpful in construction of a revised instrument for measuring maternal attitudes toward child-rearing. Consideration is needed of the development of a measure of attitudes appropriate for mothers of children of varying age levels. In the present study, the mothers in the youngest stage of the family life cycle reflected the most favorable attitudes—though this finding may possibly result from a weakness of the instrument.

A need is indicated to consider controlling of parental attitudes in parent-child studies which seek to isolate the effects of specific techniques or conditions, such as maternal employment. As increasing evidence points to the importance of maternal attitudes in the personality development of children (13), support is lent to treating parental attitudes as a variable— to avoid the possibility that relationships between children's personality and a variable such as maternal employment may actually reflect a third variable, parental attitudes.

REFERENCES

1. Atkinson, J. W., ed. *Motives in Fantasy, Action, and Society.* Princeton, N. J.: Van Nostrand, 1958.

2. Bartemeier, L. "The Children of Working Mothers: A Psychiatrist's View." In National Manpower Council. *Work in the Lives of Married Women.* New York: Columbia University Press, 1958, pp. 173–83.

3. Bellak, Leopold. *The Thematic Apperception Test and the Children's Apperception Test in Clinical Use.* New York: Grune & Stratton, 1954.

4. Burchinal, Lee G., and Lovell, Lloyd. "Relation of Employment Status of Mothers to Children's Anxiety, Parental Personality and PARI Scores." Unpublished Manuscript No. 1425, Agricultural and Home Economics Experiment Station. Ames, Iowa: Iowa State University, 1959.

5. Essig, Mary, and Morgan, D. H. "Adjustment of Adolescent Daughters of Employed Mothers to Family Life," *Journal of Educational Psychology,* XXXVII (April, 1945), 219–33.

6. Hand, Horace G. "Working Mothers and Maladjusted Children," *Journal of Educational Sociology,* XXX (January, 1957), 245–46.

7. Hartley, Ruth E. "Children's Concepts of Male and Female Roles," *Merrill-Palmer Quarterly,* VI (January, 1960), 83–91.

8. ————. "Sex-Roles and Urban Youth: Some Developmental Perspectives," *Bulletin of Family Development,* II (Spring, 1961), 1–12.

9. ————. "Current Patterns in Sex-Roles: Children's Perspectives," *Journal of National Association of Women Deans and Counselors,* XXV (October, 1961), 3–13.

10. McGuire, C., and White, G. D. "The Measurement of Social Status." Unpublished paper, Research in Human Development No. 3, University of Texas, 1955.

11. Nolan, R. D. "A Longitudinal Comparison of Motives in Children's Fantasy Stories as Revealed by the Children's Apperception Test." Unpublished Ph.D. dissertation, Florida State University, 1959.

12. Nye, F. Ivan. "Employment Status of Mothers and Adjustment of Adolescent Children," *Marriage and Family Living,* XXI (August, 1959), 240–44. Reprinted as Chapter Ten of the present book.

13. Radke, Marian J. "Relation of Parental Authority to Children's Behavior and Attitudes." University of Minnesota Institute of Child Welfare Monograph No. 22, 1946.

14. Rouman, J. "School Children's Problems as Related to Parental Factors," *Journal of Educational Research,* L (October, 1956), 105–12.

15. Wiley, J. H. "A Scale to Measure Parental Attitudes toward Certain Aspects of Children's Behavior." Unpublished Ph.D. dissertation, University of Southern California, Los Angeles, 1950.

16. ————. "A Scale to Measure Parental Attitudes toward Certain Aspects of Children's Behavior," *Journal of Speech and Hearing Disorders,* XX (September, 1955), 284–90.

Chapter Ten

The Adjustment of Adolescent Children*

F. IVAN NYE

ALTHOUGH there is little empirical research on the effects of maternal employment on children, fairly comprehensive statements have been made by Bossard and Komarovsky. Bossard (1, pp. 282–86) feels that children of employed mothers have the following problems:

The mother is physically exhausted.

The child is lonely.

The child feels neglected and rationalizes his own anti-social behavior.

Children exploit lack of maternal control.

Mother is unable to render detailed services to the child.

Mother neglects supervision and training of the child.

All of these suggest serious adjustment problems for children of employed mothers.

Komarovsky (2, chap. 5) has enumerated conditions conducive to the welfare of the families of employed mothers. These include:

The father approves of the mother's employment.

The mother works short hours for high pay.

A suitable mother substitute is available.

Provided these conditions are present, Komarovsky sees no reason why the employment of the mother should necessarily adversely affect the children.

Present data cannot test all of these ideas in detail. They do make it

* Adapted from "Maternal Employment and the Adjustment of Adolescent Children," *Marriage and Family Living,* XXI (August, 1959), 240–44, by permission of the publisher. It is a partial report of a larger study of adolescent behavior supported, in part, by grants from the College Committee on Research of Washington State University.

possible, however, to determine whether adolescent children of employed mothers are more delinquent, show more psychosomatic symptoms, or are more likely to perform poorly in school. Bossard's position would suggest "yes" to each statement, whereas Komarovsky's position suggests that children of women working short hours for high pay should suffer little, if at all, from the employment of their mothers.

THE DATA

Respondents were 2,350 students of both sexes in grades nine-twelve of three small cities in Washington, hereafter referred to as the "Tri-Cities." This constituted a 75 per cent systematic sample initiated randomly.[1] Anonymous questionnaires were administered in the classroom under the general supervision of the writer and immediate supervision of classroom teachers. All questionnaires were returned, but for a variety of reasons approximately 1 per cent were considered invalid and not included in the analysis.

These communities differ in several respects from the state averages. They experienced more rapid growth in the decade 1940–50; there is a smaller proportion of people aged sixty-five or older; the population has been more spatially mobile; and the income level is above the state average. Probably the one difference related to the present investigation is income level.

Of more importance to the present investigation is the proportion of women employed. It would seem probable that communities in which higher proportions of women are employed would provide a more favorable public opinion toward employed mothers. Likewise, such communities might provide better facilities for the care or supervision of children. Table 10.1 shows that the Tri-Cities are near the average of urban areas of Washington and the United States with respect to the proportion of women employed. The proportion is also close to that of Washington cities of similar size (10,000 to 100,000). These cities are not atypical in respect to the proportion of women in the labor force.

Since the effect of employment might well be different in different social environments, present analyses are made separately in three socioeconomic categories, three categories by family size, three by education of the mother, by rural-urban residence, and by sex of the adolescent, making a total of thirteen subsamples. The analysis is restricted to unbroken homes.

---

[1] Four questionnaires were employed, each with a 25 per cent systematic sample. Items utilized in the present analysis were included in three of the four questionnaires.

TABLE 10.1 *Proportion of Women Fourteen and Older Employed in Washington (Urban), United States (Urban), and Washington Cities of 10,000 or More Population*

United States (Urban)	33.2
Washington (Urban)	31.6
Wenatchee	38.8
Pullman	38.7
Seattle	36.4
Olympia	33.8
Yakima	32.2
Walla Walla	32.2
"Tri-Cities"	32.1
Hoquiam	31.9
Spokane	31.5
Vancouver	31.4
Aberdeen	30.0
Tacoma	29.5
Port Angeles	28.9
Everett	28.7
Longview	28.7
Puyallup	27.6
Bremerton	26.9
Bellingham	26.7
Renton	25.1

A preliminary investigation of the adjustment of adolescents in families where mothers were employed part- or full-time revealed sufficient similarity to justify combining the two categories, which has been done in the present analysis.

EQUIVALENCE OF EMPLOYMENT CATEGORIES

Thirty background factors were checked to determine whether differences related to the employment status of the mother might affect the adjustment of the child. Of these, it was found that larger proportions of employed mothers have high school or college education, have husbands in lower socio-economic categories, have been widowed or divorced and have not remarried, have smaller families, and have urban residence (Table 10.2).

Do mothers take employment because they are uninterested in or hostile toward their children? If this were the case, children would suffer because of this fact rather than from anything connected with the employment of the mother. A Guttman-type child-rejection scale was constructed to measure the child's perception of the mother's attitude toward him.[2]

---

[2] Scale items and other detailed information are described in F. Ivan Nye (5, chap. 8).

TABLE 10.2 *Employment Status of Mothers and Selected Social Characteristics of their Families (Unbroken Families)*

SAMPLE CHARACTERISTICS	NOT EMPLOYED		PART-TIME EMPLOYED		FULL-TIME EMPLOYED	
	No.	Per Cent[1]	No.	Per Cent	No.	Per Cent
Mother. has College Education	227	17.0	51	16.9	155	25.9
Rural Residence	237	18.5	50	17.0	66	11.3
5 or more Children	370	27.4	70	22.8	70	11.6
Solo Parent (Mother)	14	1.1	14	4.7	79	13.2
Low Soc-Ec Status	447	43.8	112	50.5	193	44.8

[1] Percentages are based on different totals because of differing numbers of non-respondents by item.

Present evidence indicates that attitudes toward children exist on a continuum; but for convenience of analysis, scale scores were trichotomized. It appears from Table 10.3 that there probably is some relationship between

TABLE 10.3 *Employment Status of Mothers and Adolescents' Perception of Mothers' Attitudes toward Them**

PERCEIVED ATTITUDE OF MOTHER	NOT EMPLOYED		PART-TIME EMPLOYED		FULL-TIME EMPLOYED	
	No.	Per Cent	No.	Per Cent	No.	Per Cent
"Fully" Accepting	154	34	41	41	76	39
"Generally" Accepting	156	34	35	35	43	22
Intermediate to Rejecting	143	32	24	24	74	38
Total	453	100	100	100	193	99

* The relationship is statistically significant.

the employment status of mothers and attitudes toward children, but the data do not support the idea that working mothers are less interested in their children. Rather, the distribution shows a bimodal tendency. If the criteria were dichotomized instead of trichotomized, the relationship would disappear. It appears, therefore, that differential distribution of attitudes toward children as a variable is unlikely systematically to bias an analysis based on significance of differences between means.

EDUCATIONAL ACHIEVEMENT

Bossard's formulation would anticipate that children of employed mothers would achieve lower grades in high school than those whose mothers were not employed and therefore had more time to help them. If non-employed mothers do help with and/or supervise homework more than employed mothers, the latter must in some way compensate for it. Of the thirteen comparisons made of grade point average, none was significant at the 5 per cent level.[3] Actually, a majority of the non-significant differences favor the children of employed mothers.

Whether these or other variables are involved, the data do not support the common-sense idea that children of employed mothers have lower achievement levels in academic work.

NEUROTIC SYMPTOMS

Bossard asserts that the child of the employed mother is lonely and feels neglected. In statements made to the writer, both mothers and children have expressed the feeling that children hated to come home to an empty house. Of course children of non-employed mothers also sometimes come home to empty houses and feel lonely and neglected. The "empty house" would seem more characteristic of families in which the mother is employed, but children in these families do not feel particularly neglected (Table 10.3). There may be some security in (more) money from two incomes.

A psychosomatic symptoms scale was constructed from the items employed by social scientists in screening psychoneurotics in World War II (8, chap. 13). Two Guttman-type scales were created by selecting items from this list and subjecting them to image analysis: a nine-item scale for girls and a seven-item scale for boys (6).

The data show that anxiety taking the form of psychosomatic symptoms appears unrelated to the employed status of the mother. Of thirteen subsamples analyzed, only one (the urban sample) showed a significant relationship between the two variables. Since it is possible to obtain an occasional "significant" difference by chance when large numbers of tests are made, little significance is attached to one difference in thirteen tests.

AFFECTIONAL ATTITUDE TOWARD MOTHER

From Bossard's formulation, one would anticipate more hostility and less affection toward parents among children whose mothers are employed. Some ten years ago the writer analyzed data from a predominantly rural sample, finding a slight advantage in families in which the mother was

---

[3] For economy of space, all values in the following analyses except school grades were converted to T scores, thus normalizing distributions, and significance of differences between means were tested by computing standard scores (z). School grades approximate a normal distribution, although there is some skewness to the right.

employed part-time (4). As indicated in Table 10.3, children of employed mothers show a slight tendency to feel more fully accepted or more completely rejected than those of mothers who are not employed. Children of mothers employed part-time are least likely to feel rejected.

Data from thirteen subsamples, however, failed to reveal any significant association or consistent direction of differences between employment status of mothers and affectional attitude of adolescents toward them.

DELINQUENT BEHAVIOR

Bossard suggests that children of employed mothers seize on their mother's employment to rationalize their own misbehavior. In addition,

TABLE 10.4 *Employment Status of Mothers and Delinquent Behavior*[1]

| | EMPLOYMENT STATUS | | | |
SOCIAL VARIABLES	EMPLOYED *Delinquency Score*	NOT EMPLOYED *Delinquency Score*	CRITICAL RATIO	SUB-CATEGORY N
Socio-Economic Status				
High Soc-Ec Status	49.5	48.4	.8	160
Medium Soc-Ec Status	51.4	48.4*	4.8	1,036
Low Soc-Ec Status	51.2	50.5	.4	173
Family Size				
Large Families (5–9 Children)	51.7	49.4*	2.0	410
Medium Families (2–4 Children)	51.1	48.8*	4.0	1,236
Only Child	50.6	47.9*	2.0	182
Education of Mother				
College (1 year or more)	50.1	48.1*	2.2	355
High School (Grade 10–12)	50.9	48.5*	3.9	1,065
Junior High or Less	52.7	49.6*	2.8	385
Rural and Urban Residence				
Rural	54.5	46.9*	6.2	293
Urban	51.0	48.9*	4.0	1,457
Child Adjustment by Sex				
Male	50.5	48.6*	3.0	992
Female	51.7	48.7*	4.8	907

[1] Delinquency scores were converted to T scores to normalize distribution, thereby permitting the use of tests of differences between means. High scores indicate more serious and frequent delinquent behavior.

* Statistically significant difference.

employed mothers presumably experience more difficulty in exercising direct control and supervision of children, particularly in the "after school" period. Although there are numerous other controls which can inhibit delinquent impulses, it seemed logical to anticipate more delinquent behavior among the children of employed mothers.

The delinquency measure employed is the Guttman-type delinquency scale developed by Nye and Short.[4] The scale items include petty theft, truancy, ungovernability, vandalism, driving without a license, and alcholic and sexual offenses.

Eleven of thirteen tests found significant differences, with all (including those non-significant) showing somewhat more delinquent behavior among children of employed mothers. Although these differences are greater in some subcategories than others (notably rural), they are consistent throughout the analyses as shown in Table 10.4.

A final analysis was made controlling family size, socio-economic status, rural-urban residence, and sex of the adolescent (broken homes had been eliminated earlier). When these variables were controlled and the criterion dichotomized (as was done in the writer's recent book (5)), the differences became non-significant; however, when the criterion is trichotomized, they are significant. In neither case are the differences large; in both analyses the direction of differences is toward higher delinquency in the employed mother sample.

BROKEN HOMES

The preceding analysis was limited to children in unbroken homes. It cannot be assumed that the findings necessarily apply to broken homes. A separate analysis was undertaken, therefore, of children in broken homes in which mothers were or were not employed.

Of the 272 broken homes in which the parent had remarried, the mother was employed full- or part-time in 121, or 45 per cent. Differences between the children in the two samples (mother employed or not employed) were non-significant by each of the four criteria: school grades, psychosomatic symptoms, delinquent behavior, and affectional relationship to mother.

Of the 107 families in which the child was living with the mother only, 93 of the mothers were employed full- or part-time. No considerable differences were found by the criteria of delinquent behavior or school grades. Fewer psychosomatic symptoms and a closer affectional relationship to mother are, however, characteristic of the children of the employed

---

[4] Validity and reliability of the criteria are described in F. Ivan Nye and James F. Short, Jr. (7).

solo mothers. This does not appear unreasonable since financial problems and insecurities might be considerable in families in which there is no employed adult. This finding should be considered tentative, however, because of the small size of the sample.

SUMMARY AND DISCUSSION

The evidence appears to show that if Bossard's concept of the neglected, maladjusted child of the employed mother has any validity, the effects involved are small. School performance, psychosomatic symptoms, and affectional relationship to the mother appear unrelated to employment status of the mother. A small association appears to be present between employment status and delinquent behavior.

The parallel analysis employing a sample of broken homes reveals, in general, the same pattern of findings with the exception that no association was found between delinquent behavior and employment status of the mother. In the small sample of children living with mothers only, children appear somewhat better adjusted where the mother is employed.

Present data do not allow an adequate test of Komarovsky's formulation. High pay would be related to high educational level; however, professional occupations are not ordinarily characterized by short working hours.

LIMITATIONS

This analysis has employed samples of adolescent children. Bossard's conception of children of employed mothers might be more nearly correct if younger children were sampled. Additional research with younger children will be needed to determine this.

In the evaluation of past, present, and future research dealing with employed mothers, it must be considered that this constitutes a new combination of roles. Bossard's conception of the problems of children of employed mothers may have been more nearly correct a decade ago than it is today. The numbers of employed mothers, their social characteristics, and the attitudes of the society toward them have changed in the past decade and are likely to do so in the next. Household equipment will continue to improve, and it is extremely probable that the trend shifting economic production to factory and service establishments will continue. The working day may become shorter. Congruence of the roles of mother and employee may be achieved with some rapidity with the result that the effects of maternal employment on family members may change considerably within the *next* decade.

REFERENCES

1. Bossard, James H. S. *The Sociology of Child Development*. New York: Harper, 1954.
2. Komarovsky, Mirra. *Women in the Modern World*. Boston: Little, Brown, 1953.
3. National Manpower Council. *Womanpower*. New York: Columbia University Press, 1957.
4. Nye, F. Ivan. "Adolescent-Parent Adjustment: Age, Sex, Sibling Number, Broken Homes, and Employed Mothers as Variables," *Marriage and Family Living*, XIV (November, 1952), 327–32.
5. ————. *Family Relationships and Delinquent Behavior*. New York: John Wiley, 1958.
6. ————. "Some Family Attitudes and Psychosomatic Symptoms in Adolescents," *Coordinator*, VI (December, 1957), 22–26.
7. ———— and Short, James F., Jr. "Scaling Delinquent Behavior," *American Sociological Review*, XXII (June, 1957), 327.
8. Stouffer, Samuel A., and others. *Studies in Social Psychology in World War II: Measurement and Prediction*, Vol. IV. Princeton: Princeton University Press, 1950.

Chapter Eleven

Employment and the Adolescent*

ELIZABETH DOUVAN

FOR forty years or more the working mother has walked in our world like a lady in a fun house of mirrors, watching one or another of her features now exaggerated, now diminished, nearly always distorted. Even now, when it is clear that maternal employment is a permanent feature of our world, popular discourse about the issue carries the heady tone of a good fight. On a popular level, this kind of involvement is not to be decried. But passion serves poorly as the muse of science, and unfortunately in the past research has on occasion been all too close to the heat of debate.

More recently, as our editors indicate, social scientists have returned to the problem in a more dispassionate mood, raising more sophisticated, more disinterested questions about the impact of maternal employment on family life or child development in various settings, under various conditions. We seem at last on the way to a clarification of the issue.

We are not yet very far on the way, however. And it is this fact that justifies including the present chapter in a book on the issue. The data on which the chapter is based were not originally gathered for a systematic analysis of maternal employment. They suffer the usual limitation of such data: the crucial measure is unrefined because the variable it seeks to measure was not a central concept in the design of the study. Nonetheless, where knowledge is scarce, even fragments may be useful.

THE DATA

Our data are seriously limited in that we gathered no information (from adolescent subjects) about the length of time the mothers worked.

---

*Adapted from a book which the author is preparing in collaboration with Joseph Adelson (2).

142

We asked only whether the mother was currently employed and whether she worked full- or part-time. This obviously is a crucial problem, one which bars us from critical tests of many aspects of the theory of maternal employment. Nonetheless, we can report some interesting findings about the relationship between the mother's employment and adolescent development, and can suggest a theoretical scheme to account for the findings, one which knits them into a coherent pattern.

Our data come from two large national sample interview studies of adolescent boys and girls. The studies, conducted at the Survey Research Center of the University of Michigan, were sponsored by the Boy Scouts of America and the Girl Scouts of the U.S.A.

Respondents were selected in a multi-stage probability sampling (1) and represent school children of eleven through eighteen years for the girl sample and of fourteen through sixteen for boys. Each subject was interviewed at his school by a member of the Center's field staff; interviews followed a fixed schedule and lasted from one to four hours. For details about the studies and copies of the complete questionnaire readers may refer to the basic reports (3, 4).

PRELIMINARY FINDINGS

The analysis we report is limited to youngsters from intact families in which the father is employed. Two preliminary findings about the distribution of working mothers in major population groups should be stated at the outset since they affect the validity of all of our interpretations. We do not, to begin with, find any consistent or striking relationship between the social class position of the family (gauged by father's occupation) and the likelihood that the mother works outside the home. Except in farm families, where only about 15 per cent of all the mothers work, the proportion ranges between 32 and 45 per cent for all status groups in both of our samples.[1]

---

[1] In the girls' sample, the range is 33 to 41 per cent, and the direction of difference is not the same as we move down the ladder of skills represented by the father's occupation. So the figures are: 33 per cent for the wives of professionals and business executives; 41 per cent among wives of white-collar, sales, and clerical workers; 38 per cent for the skilled and semi-skilled blue-collar class; and 41 per cent in the families whose heads are unskilled workers. In the boys' sample, we find the highest proportion of working mothers in the professional class (45 per cent), and the lowest proportion outside the farm group in the skilled and semi-skilled blue-collar group (32 per cent). All other status groups are practically identical in the proportions of working and non-working mothers (38 per cent of wives of business executives, 40 per cent in the white-collar group, and 38 per cent in the unskilled blue-collar group). The largest difference in the analysis—between the professional and skilled worker groups in the boys' sample—is in the direction opposite from that one would predict on the basis of economic necessity.

The second finding concerns the relationship between mother's employment and the age of the child, and it also is a negative finding: That is, there is no relationship between the age of the child and the likelihood that his mother works outside the home. We know that there is a significant association between these variables in studies of younger children, but apparently within the adolescent range it breaks down.[2]

Most women probably make the commitment to return to work when the child enters school. By the time the child is eleven the mother is no longer delaying her return because of the child's age. A woman may delay the decision beyond this point for other reasons—including the fact that she has other younger children—but these delays will not bear any significant relationship to the age of our subjects.

These two findings reduce the need to exercise special controls in the analysis of the mother's employment. Yet we were interested in making separate analyses for the two major social classes on the grounds that the meaning of maternal employment must be quite different when the general economic position of the family is good or poor. We shall discuss the results of this controlled analysis after a description of our basic findings. We shall describe the results from the study of girls first, since girls seem most crucially affected by the mother's employment.

FINDINGS: ADOLESCENT ACTIVITIES AND EMPLOYMENT

On the basis of previous research (see Chapter Ten) and our own analysis of adolescent activity patterns, we developed certain conceptions about the meaning of full-time and part-time maternal employment—its impact on family life, the motivational factors that underlie the mother's work, and the significance of these factors for performance of the maternal role, particularly in relation to adolescent children. We looked at data on adolescent development and family life for tests of some of these derivations.

The analysis of adolescent activities that led to our formulations about full-time and part-time maternal employment can be summarized briefly.[3] Both groups of working-mother daughters are active in some sense—daughters of non-working mothers are never the most active on any index in our study—but the spheres of their activity are quite different. The single area

---

[2] Since the entry of mothers into the labor market has been shown to have multiple sources—economic necessity and the woman's desire to absorb increasing leisure are among the more critical factors—one might expect the child's age to have a greater effect in higher social classes where, presumably, the mother has a choice between working and not working and where simple economic pressure is not so decisive a force. When we analyze maternal employment in relation to the child's age in the higher social strata, however, we again find no relationship.

[3] The findings from this analysis are summarized in Table 11.1.

TABLE 11.1 *Maternal Employment Related to Activities of Adolescent Girls*

| ADOLESCENT ACTIVITY | MATERNAL EMPLOYMENT | | |
| | FULL-TIME (N = 235) | PART-TIME (N = 158) | NONE (N = 769) |
		Per Cent	
Household Responsibility			
Major	22	17	5
Moderate	30	36	30
Light or none	42	43	59
Work			
Holds a part-time job	81	74	70
Dating			
At age 13 or under			
Goes steady	5	1	—
Dates	17	22	14
Doesn't date	78	77	86
At age 14 to 16			
Goes steady	18	10	12
Dates	54	64	55
Doesn't date	26	26	32
At age 17 or 18			
Goes steady	45	38	27
Dates	50	61	65
Doesn't date	5	—	8
Group Membership			
None	30	16	25
Belongs to 1 or 2 groups	48	55	52
Belongs to 3 or more groups	21	29	23
Leisure Activities			
Low	27	14	14
Medium	48	37	47
High	35	49	39
Suggest Other Activities			
Yes	27	42	34
No	72	57	66
Leisure Reading			
None	16	4	10
Spend Leisure			
Alone	12	2	6
With friend(s)	46	41	42
With family	38	52	47

Note: Data in this and subsequent tables apply only to non-farm subjects. However, a separate analysis of farm subjects produced similar results where numbers were large enough to permit any reliable analysis.
— Less than half of 1 per cent.

they share—and in which they contrast with girls whose mothers do not work —is household responsibility: the proportion of girls who carry major responsibilities at home is larger where the mother works either full-time (22 per cent) or part-time (17 per cent) than in homes where the mother is not employed (5 per cent). Girls whose mothers do not work most often report that they do token jobs or none at all (59 per cent, compared to 43 per cent of girls whose mothers work part-time and 42 per cent of girls whose mothers work full-time).

Daughters of women who are employed full-time most often work hard at home, carry some kind of paying job, and date actively; in particular, they go steady more often than other girls at each age level. On the other hand, they report very few of the kinds of engagements we conventionally think of as "healthful leisure activities." They do not as commonly belong to clubs or other organized social groups, nor do they have as many group attachments as girls whose mothers work part-time or not at all. They have tried significantly fewer of the leisure activities suggested in a fixed list (compared to girls in the other two groups), and they have less interest in trying new sports, games, or hobbies. Fewer of these girls report any leisure reading. One gains the impression that the daughters of women who hold full-time jobs are active girls, but that their activity has a serious character. They work hard and their social life consists primarily of dating. They begin dating earlier than girls whose mothers are at home part- or full-time, and they go steady earlier and more commonly than other girls. Even in leisure they seem bent on early assumption of adult-like patterns.

Daughters of women who work part-time are outstandingly active girls, no matter what measure we employ. They are almost as responsible for home tasks as the girls whose mothers work full-time, and they often have jobs outside the home—not, again, as frequently as the full-time group, but more than girls whose mothers do not work. Practically all girls in this group have some formal group affiliation, and they belong to a larger number of clubs and organizations than girls in the other two categories. They date early and actively; they date as much as girls whose mothers work full-time, but they do *not* as often go steady. At each age level girls in the part-time group are less likely to go steady than are girls in the full-time category. Only after sixteen do they approach the full-time group in this regard.

The part-time group also has the largest number of specific leisure activities. They are enthusiastic about sports, games, and hobbies already experienced (compared to girls in either of the other categories), and they suggest a greater number of other activities they would like to try. In short, the daughters of women who work part-time are active in every sphere. They are different from the girls whose mothers work full-time in that they have a broader range of social and leisure activities.

One other difference among our groups in the area of leisure commitment: girls whose mothers work full-time spend relatively little leisure time with the family. They, more often than other girls, spend time "alone," and they share leisure activities with a friend more often than with family members. Girls from families in which the mother works part-time most often report that they spend their leisure with their families—more, even, than do the girls whose mothers do not work. Girls in the non-working-mother group fall between the other two groups on the distribution of time spent with family and with friends.

From their daughters' activities, we can infer something about the mothers who work full-time: they do not apparently spend much time with their daughters or take a highly active role in promoting and supervising a varied program of leisure activities for their children. The out-of-school activities which their girls most often report—part-time jobs and dating—do not make as many demands on parents as some other activities. They require no special parent involvement—as a child's group memberships often do—and they require no special facilities or equipment as many leisure sports and hobbies do. Both part-time working and dating can be carried on outside the parents' sphere. We may have in the daughters of full-time working women a precocious separation of the child from the family. Their early and frequent steady dating and the fact that they spend little time with the family suggest that they have shifted some major portion of their emotional involvement away from the home. One might suggest further that they form these extra-family involvements in order to supply emotional needs which have not been met at home, perhaps because their mothers are overextended in their own commitments outside the home. In short, we thought that a pattern of neglect might mark the families of women who carry full-time jobs.

PART-TIME GROUP

The activities of girls whose mothers work part-time suggest quite a different family pattern. Specifically we get the impression of active parents who participate energetically in the child's life. They spend a good deal of time with their children—according to girls' reports—and their children's pattern of leisure engagement is one which implies parent involvement.

The fact that a mother works part-time in itself implies certain things about her psychological make-up—more, it seems, than can be inferred from a full-time job commitment. Economic factors do not, we suspect, contribute as simply or forcefully to the decision to work in the case of part-time work. Very likely all women who look for employment are motivated by economic desires of some order—either they must supplement the husband's income to make ends meet at all, or they choose to work in order to increase the family's level of living and enlarge the number of luxuries the family can enjoy. We suspect that women who work part-time are less often directed by economic interests of a bare subsistence kind. Since full-time jobs are generally easier to find than part-time, we assign relatively greater weight to personal motivation as a determinant of this choice, and assume that the women themselves limit their work commitment. We suggest that these are women who, while they want to contribute to the family's economic well-being, are at the same time bound by a sense of responsibility to reserve their major emotional investment for direct care of the family.

This group may also include a relatively large proportion of women who seek in work some measure of personal fulfillment. Again, assuming that they are less economically pressed, and considering that it takes a degree of initiative to find part-time jobs, we might expect these women to be active and energetic, the kind of women who need some individual fulfillment beyond that provided in the roles of wife-homemaker and mother.

If these speculations are correct—and the high energy level of mothers in this group gains some support from the data on girls' activities—we might expect the part-time working mother to feel split loyalties and to have a rather complex personal integration based on a high level of energy and on a personal goal system in which one seeks challenges in the environment and takes pleasure in mastering them.

Women of this type would be similar to the "guilt motivated" working mothers that Lois Hoffman has described in her study of younger children reported in Chapter Six; these are women who enjoy their outside jobs and feel·some measure of guilt because they choose to spend part of their time away from the family in a personally gratifying activity. To reduce the guilt over what they conceive to be a self-indulgence, women of this type show a pattern of overprotective concern for their children, tend to demand less from them and to provide few opportunities for the child to learn through doing or meeting challenges unaided; they tend, in other words, to supply the child's needs too readily and completely through their own activity. Their children show the effects of maternal overprotection in dependency and an impaired capacity for individual problem-solving.

Our adolescent girls whose mothers work part-time do not look over-protected. They are highly active youngsters. Their activities are too many and too varied to permit any conclusion except that they have a great deal of initiative and responsibility. Yet for several reasons we cling to the view that the part-time working mother is like Hoffman's guilt-motivated mother at least in her high activity level, her strong sense of responsibility, and in the fact that she works primarily because she wants to work and enjoys the work role. We could explain the difference in effects on the child—between our subjects and Hoffman's—largely on the basis of the age difference in the two groups. Many of our working mothers may have returned to work only when their children approached adolescence. Even women who work while their children are young may feel less guilt as the children gain maturity and self-sufficiency, so that by the time their children reach adolescence, most working mothers may be more realistic and less selfless in their expectations *vis à vis* the child. The active woman who overprotects a younger child may become a model of activity for the older one.

The girls in our sample whose mothers work part-time certainly seem to be using some high energy model. From the fact that they spend a good deal of time with their families, and from the parent-involving activities they engage in, we ventured the not very radical speculation that the mother is the model they use. If this is the case, and if modeling is the process involved, we would expect these girls to be independent and responsible as well as energetic.

Our data generally support these speculations about the girls whose mothers work part-time. They are unusually developed in the area of autonomy. They show an independence of thought and values generally rare among girls, and their autonomy is apparently permitted and encouraged by the parents. Altogether this group can be said to show a pattern of development more common to boys than to girls in our culture (Table 11.2).

Their independence shows itself in many forms. For one, they have more open disagreements with their parents than girls in either of the other groups; they name more disagreements in answer to the general question, and in each of the specific areas probed—clothes, dating, hours, driving, friends, ideas—this group is consistently lowest in the proportion who say that the particular issue is not a source of disagreement between them and their parents. They are particularly likely—compared to the girls whose mothers work full-time or not at all—to say they disagree with their parents about ideas. In a series of picture-story questions, girls in this group think the heroine would question a parental restriction more than other girls do. In all, we get a picture of considerable verbal discussion and argument in the home. And this pattern is apparently accepted and stimulated by the parents: according to girls' reports, parents of this group frequently expect their daughters to be self-reliant and independent at the same time that they stress good manners and ladylike deportment. They allow their daughters a share in rule-making more often than other parents, at the same time that they maintain a clear and strong personal authority. The girls in this group picture parents as "strict and reasonable" in their exercise of authority more than girls in the other groups. They less often see their parents as lenient.

Another fact also leads to the conclusion that their self-assertion is encouraged: although these girls argue and assert themselves with the parents, they apparently have close and happy relationships with them. They

TABLE 11.2 *Maternal Employment Related to Features of Adolescent Development and Family Life*

ITEM	MATERNAL EMPLOYMENT		
	FULL-TIME (N = 235)	PART-TIME (N = 158) Per Cent	NONE (N = 769)
Disagreement with Parents			
Reports no disagreement	27	11	21
Disagreement with Parents on Issues			
Dating	26	35	30
Lipstick	16	21	20
Clothing	46	52	44
Cars, driving	30	37	35
Friends	40	44	35
Ideas	22	41	29
Index of Disagreement			
High (3 or more issues)	24	39	28
Response to Parents' Restriction (Projective)			
Questions restriction	2	13	8
Parents' Expectations of R			
Self-reliance	12	17	3
Good manners	48	59	50
Obedience, respect for authority	25	23	33
Part in Rule-Making			
R shares in rule-making	61	68	53
Parents' Strictness (Projective)			
Strict	16	15	15
Strict but reasonable	16	27	20
Lenient	58	46	52
Very lenient	8	9	11
Adult Ideal			
Mother	42	43	31
Father	1	6	—
All in-family choices	67	53	55
Intimacy of Friendship			
Can be as close as family tie	34	51	44
Cannot be as close as family tie	41	33	37
Response to Lonely Mother			
Return home	49	36	38

TABLE 11.2 *Maternal Employment Related to Features of Adolescent Development and Family Life*

ITEM	MATERNAL EMPLOYMENT		
	FULL-TIME (N = 235)	PART-TIME (N = 158) Per Cent	NONE (N = 769)
Choice of Confidante			
Mother	51	49	37
Friend	22	31	33
No one	12	3	5
Friendship Development Index			
High	10	27	18
Low	23	5	12
Expectations about Friendship			
Stress mutuality, relationship	22	38	33
Index of Traditional Femininity			
High	19	15	27
Low	23	26	18
Job Aspirations			
Choice of traditional masculine job	4	12	7
Mobility Aspirations			
Upward mobile	20	28	16
Index of Internalization			
High	21	34	23
Low	24	15	28
Response to Peer Pressure to Break Promise to Parents			
Resists pressure, sense of trust	16	28	13
Tell Parents of Misdeed			
Yes	45	58	40
Characteristics of Future Husband			
Ego skills	37	40	31
Family attitudes	24	37	27
Nature of Punishment			
Physical	13	9	12
Deprivational	69	69	65
Psychological	17	20	21
Attitude toward Authority			
Relies heavily on adults	30	33	40
Relies moderately on adults	59	47	49
Tends to reject adult authority	6	16	5

spend a good deal of time with their families, we recall, and they show both love and respect for the parents. Girls in this group very often choose their own mothers as an adult ideal. Both groups of girls who have working mothers choose the mother more often than do daughters of non-working women, but in the part-time group this looks less like a dependency sign than in the full-time group. These girls do *not* choose other relatives very often—their choices are not narrowly restricted to the family group. And they show other signs of independence from the family: they think a friend can be as close as a relative more than girls in either of the other groups, and they are least likely of any group to say (in response to a projective question) that a girl should leaye a good job to return home to her lonely mother. They try most often to work out some alternative solution to this problem. In light of their general autonomy—in these instances and in the apparent ease with which they disagree with their parents—we take the choice of the mother as a model to indicate uncomplicated respect and affection.

Two other series of findings fill out our picture of girls with part-time working mothers. They are, in the first place, highly developed and mature in their ideas about friendship. For all their warm and apparently satisfying relationship within the family, they are not retarded in friendship development.

The other set of finding relates to something we mentioned earlier—that the girls in the part-time working mother group may be developing an integration which does not adhere closely to traditional concepts of femininity. They score relatively low on an Index of Traditional Femininity—as do all of the girls whose mothers work. But this group shows certain other signs of a non-feminine orientation: they choose traditionally masculine occupational goals more than other girls do. In line with this last finding—although not the same finding, since it is based on the jobs they want their future husbands to hold—girls in this group aspire to upward social mobility more often than other girls. They choose their fathers as adult models somewhat more often (although still infrequently), and they show some signs of moral development that are more characteristic of our boy sample than of the general population of girls.

They are slightly higher on an index of internalization, and markedly different on responses to two individual questions in the index: the daughters of part-time working women more often say that the girl in the projective picture-stories would obey her parents because she had promised, because of a sense of trust, and they are much more likely than other girls to feel that if the girl *did* break her promise to her parents, she would tell them of her misdeed later. They show, in our view, a sense of commitment to the promise they have made—more than do girls in other categories.

These findings can be interpreted in light of our earlier speculations about the part-time working mother and her relationship to her adolescent children. We suggested on the basis of the adolescents' activity patterns that family relationships in these cases were strong and actively cultivated by energetic mothers. We find the daughters of these women to be, on one hand, warmly related to their families and apparently strongly identified with active mother-models. On the other hand, they show a degree of autonomy in relation to the family which is rare indeed among girls in our sample. The modeling concept forms the theoretical bridge between these two findings: the girls have warm and close ties to families which provide them a feminine model of unusual energy, independence, and responsibility. In modeling themselves after their mothers, they develop an autonomy which seems at first glance to contradict their close family ties. But this autonomy grows out of an identification with an independent mother and is encouraged by the parents. It implies not a rejection of the parents, but rather an internalization of their values.

The part-time working mothers apparently offer a model of integration that is not primarily based on traditional concepts of femininity and the feminine role. Daughters of women in this group express somewhat masculine predispositions in their occupational aspirations, their independence, their desire for social mobility. Girls in this group not only aspire to social mobility more than other girls, but they more often fit the pattern we designated a masculine mobility model: that is, they expect to acquire high status at least in part through their own efforts to achieve high prestige positions. They apparently conceive future achievement as a family enterprise which they will share with ambitious husbands.[4]

FULL-TIME GROUP

We can turn at this point to the other working mother group—i.e., to those girls whose mothers hold full-time jobs outside the home. We speculated, on the basis of the activity pattern that characterizes this group, that the girls whose mothers work full-time receive somewhat inadequate attention and companionship from their families and that they turn to friends and boyfriends for the warmth and closeness they fail to find at home. Our findings in this case are not, however, consistent or strongly supportive of the initial hypotheses. We find no indication that parents in the full-time

---

[4] Another finding fits this general interpretation: when asked what kind of man they hope to marry, girls in the group whose mothers work part-time tend to stress ego skills *and* family values. They would like the men they marry to have talent and drive and also strong family values: to like children, enjoy family life, spend time with the family.

working mother group neglect their children or deny them emotional support. We have suggested that they do not enter very actively into their children's leisure lives, but, apart from this, they apparently fulfill their obligations very much as other parents do.

We expected, for example, that signs of parental neglect might show up on measures of discipline and strictness, or in the attitudes adolescents express toward their parents. But we find no evidence of peculiar harshness or of rejection, no signs of excessive family conflict among girls whose mothers work full-time. In fact, they tend to disagree with their parents somewhat less than other girls do. They show no special resentment toward their parents, nor do they express an unusually strong desire for a closer relationship with their parents (on a projective question about a girl who would like her parents to be different). Girls in this group admire and respect their mothers more than the daughters of non-working women: they choose their mothers as models more frequently than do the girls whose mothers are not employed and about as often as girls in the part-time group. They think of their mothers in the role of confidante more than other girls do, and they are more tied to the mother emotionally if we can judge from their answers to the situation in which a girl is asked by her lonely mother to return home. They more often say the girl should go home than do girls in either of the other patterns.

The daughters of full-time working women show a mixed pattern of developed autonomy and unresolved dependency. The only interpretation which seems to lend any coherence to the findings is this: these girls are developed in ego skills which equip them for managing practical aspects of reality well and with ease, but emotionally their major commitment is still to the family. In this latter regard (i.e., emotional dependency) they appear to be less autonomous than other girls in this age group.

We have seen evidence of their autonomy in practical affairs in the unusual work load they manage. They share in rule-making at home more than girls whose mothers do not work, and about as often as those whose mothers work part-time. Their parents expect them to be independent and self-reliant, and they are least likely of all three groups to rely heavily on adult authority.

With respect to emotional dependence on the family, girls in the full-time working mother group distinguish themselves on a number of items. In addition to their responses to the question about the lonely mother who asks her daughter to return home, daughters of full-time working women choose their adult models exclusively from within the family more than girls in either of the other groups. They have fewer conflicts with their parents than the part-time group, and are similar in this regard to the non-working group. They also are less likely than the daughters of part-time working women to think that friendship can be as close as a family relationship. When we ask them to think of the person to whom a girl might confide a misdeed, these girls most often think of the mother.

IMPACT OF EMPLOYMENT BY SOCIAL CLASS

This peculiar combination of ego autonomy and affective dependence—and it is peculiar in that ordinarily we find adolescents moving toward independence at about the same pace in the two areas—leads into our second analysis, of the differential impact of maternal employment in the two major social classes. It seemed highly probable to us that the meaning of maternal employment would be different in the two classes, and, in the case of the full-time working mother, this is borne out in the analysis. A part-time work commitment has a relatively stable meaning and implication in both the middle and working classes, but full-time maternal employment apparently depends upon different motivational sources in the two groups, and has distinct meanings for family interaction. The findings we have reported for this group represent a combination of two quite different patterns.

MIDDLE CLASS

In the middle class the girls of full-time working women look more like those whose mothers work part-time: they are relatively active, autonomous girls who admire their mothers but are not unusually closely tied to the family. They have a high rate of participation in leisure activities and in organized groups—higher than either working-class girls whose mothers work full-time or middle-class girls whose mothers do not work. They do not have as active leisure lives as girls in the middle-class part-time group, but the differences between the two patterns are not large on our measures of leisure activity.

The serious and adult-like activities decrease in this group when we factor out class: middle-class girls in the full-time pattern do not have as much responsibility at home, and they do not hold part-time jobs as often as girls in the working class whose mothers work full-time. They date just as actively, but again look more like other girls of their class level whose mothers work part-time: they do not go steady as often as their counterparts in the working class. They spend more time with their families than the daughters of full-time working women in the lower class, and their relationships within the family look like those we have described for the part-time working mother pattern. Their parents expect them to be self-reliant, give them a share in rule-making, and apparently permit discussion and open disagreement. In all these respects, girls in the middle-class full-time group are more like those in the part-time patterns and different from girls in the working class whose mothers work full-time. They choose their mothers as ideals more than daughters of non-working women—this holds for all the working mother groups at both class levels—but they do *not* choose in-family models as exclusively as do their working-class counterparts. They think of the mother as confidante, but they also think that a friend can be as close to one as a family member. They do not characteristically think that a girl should yield personal work interests to return home to a lonely mother.

WORKING CLASS

The dependency which distinguished the total group of girls whose mothers hold full-time jobs is primarily a feature of working-class girls in the pattern. Here we find both a strong positive affection for the mother and a strong dependency component. The working-class girls in families where the mother works full-time show the primary characteristics of premature seriousness, deprivation in social and leisure activities, and emotional dependency. Compared to other working-class girls or to middle-class daughters of full-time working women, they have fewer group memberships and leisure activities, and they are more often responsible for major housekeeping tasks and part-time jobs. They are not striving toward emotional independence,

TABLE 11.3 *Full-Time Maternal Employment in Relation to Girls' Activities and Attitudes in the Middle- and Working-Class Groups*[1]

ITEM: ADOLESCENT GIRLS' BEHAVIOR, ATTITUDES	FULL-TIME MATERNAL EMPLOYMENT	
	MIDDLE CLASS (N = 104)	WORKING CLASS (N = 131)
	Per Cent	
Leisure Activities		
Low	18	34
Medium	42	51
High	40	15
Group Membership		
None	21	34
Belongs to 1 or 2 groups	54	49
Belongs to 3 or more groups	25	17
Household Responsibilities		
Major	15	27
Moderate	32	28
Light or none	47	39
Work		
Holds job	74	86

TABLE 11.3 (Cont.) *Full-Time Maternal Employment in Relation to Girls' Activities and Attitudes in the Middle- and Working-Class Groups[1]*

ITEM: ADOLESCENT GIRLS' BEHAVIOR, ATTITUDES	FULL-TIME MATERNAL EMPLOYMENT	
	MIDDLE CLASS (N = 104)	WORKING CLASS (N = 131)
	Per Cent	
Dating[2]		
Goes steady	5	16
Dates	49	33
Doesn't date	45	51
Spends Leisure Time		
Alone	5	17
With friend(s)	43	48
With family	47	32
Parents' Expectations		
Self-reliance	19	5
Good manners	54	43
Obedience	21	28
Part in Rule-Making		
R shares in rule-making	71	57
Disagreement with Parents		
Reports no disagreement	15	36
Index of Disagreement (specific issues)		
Disagrees with parents on 3 issues or more	43	28
Adult Ideal		
Mother	40	43
Father	1	1
All in-family choices	55	76
Intimacy of Friendship		
Can be as close as family tie	46	25
Choice of Confidante		
Mother	60	44
Friend	28	18
No one	7	16
Response to Lonely Mother		
Return home	37	56

[1] Middle-class status was assigned whenever the father's job was a professional, managerial, or white-collar one. The working class category includes all girls whose fathers hold manual jobs.
[2] Analysis of dating patterns with age and class both controlled reduced numbers severely. In the interest of reliability, we have run the analysis for all age groups. The class groups did not differ significantly in age, in any case.

nor are they encouraged by their parents to be self-reliant. In this regard they look most like girls whose mothers do not work and differ from all of the other working mother groups.

Compared to any other group in this analysis, the working-class girls whose mothers work full-time have strong emotional ties to the family: they admire and feel close to their mothers, and seem psychologically highly dependent on the family. In choosing an adult ideal, girls in this group name their mothers as often as girls in other working mother categories, and when we consider all in-family choices, they are far and away the group most family-oriented (76 per cent of this group name an ideal from the family group, compared to 60 per cent of the working-class non-working mother group, the second highest of all categories in this regard). They have fewer disagreements with their parents than any other group of girls, and they more often reject the notion that friendship can be as close as kinship. On the question about the lonely mother who wants her daughter to come to live with her, girls in this group give the traditional response of loyalty to the mother more than girls from any other constellation. The contrast is again a striking one—56 per cent of this group think the girl should return, compared to 42 per cent of the next highest group.

On the other hand, these girls do not spend a great deal of time with their families; they are more likely than other girls to say they spend most of their free time alone or with a friend. In many cases, this friend may be a steady boyfriend, since a large proportion of these girls go steady. If we take steady dating to indicate a transfer of emotionality from the family, then we are faced with the paradoxical fact that girls in this pattern are both very tied to their families and at the same time more likely to have shifted the focus of their emotional lives. One other indication that at least in some spheres they do not in fact rely on their mothers as much as one might think from their attitudes toward family relationships: they do not think of the mother as confidante as often as girls in the other working mother groups.

PATTERNS OF EFFECTS

The analysis of maternal employment within social classes has distinguished two patterns of effects that may accompany a mother's full-time work commitment. The patterns break on class lines in the following manner: in the middle class the effect of the mother's working full-time appears to be similar to the effects of a partial work commitment in either class group—family interaction is high and is geared to training children toward autonomy and self-reliance. Girls in such families are active in both organized and non-organized leisure activity, spend a good deal of time with their families, and are relatively autonomous in issues of judgment and authority. They admire their mothers, but do not seem particularly dependent on them.

The lower-class girl whose mother works full-time is not like other daughters of working women. The girls in this pattern come closest to our original conception of the girl who is neglected and suffers a serious loss in family life because her mother is overextended in her commitments, harassed, perhaps resentful. Here we find girls who carry very heavy responsibilities, lack normal leisure commitments, and apparently find in extra-family relationships (i.e., the steady dating relationship) the secure and stable companionship which they do not find at home. Though in fact they share very little time with their families, the girls in this group have a strong and sentimental conception of the importance of family ties, and continue to be emotionally dependent on the family at an age when other girls have begun to break their ties of dependency. This last set of findings does not, we think, contradict our original notion that full-time maternal employment might imply neglect: one reason girls from such families might be sentimental about the family and more dependent on it is that their needs for family-based security have never been adequately met. At the same time that girls with such backgrounds take unusual responsibility for daily realities, they may continue to yearn for the closeness and security of more normal family interaction.

EXPLANATION

Why should full-time maternal employment have such different effects in the two status groups? The simplest hypothesis relies on economic factors: the middle-class mother who works either part- or full-time very likely has some degree of choice in the matter. In the working class the two commitments may reflect quite different degrees of personal choice and financial press—the lower-class woman who works full-time may be responding to a much simpler and more imposing condition of economic need. Two minor findings from our study support this suggestion. When we asked girls to think of ways in which a girl might like her parents to be different, the girls in our working-class full-time group differed clearly from the other three working mother groups in one respect: while the other three groups all stand out for their reference to the parents' life style ("she'd like them to have a nicer home, go out, entertain more"), the working-class full-time group rarely gives such answers. On the other hand, the working-class full-time group gives economic *problems* as a source of worry for girls much more than any of the other working mother groups.

If in fact this is the case—that the working-class full-time pattern is the only one of our four working mother groups that represents serious economic deprivation—then we can make some ordered interpretations of our findings. The mother who works because of serious economic need is not necessarily one whose psychological make-up prepares her for the dual roles of homemaker and worker. She may feel herself taxed by the demands of a life complication which she did not choose and does not feel up to. Sheer economic deprivation adds a further burden of concern, and in many cases we might expect to find such women both harried and resentful or passively resigned to an unsatisfying and burdensome life situation. The pattern is similar to the one Lois Hoffman has characterized as guilt-free (4). Pressed themselves, such women feel no special obligation to their families. They expect to get their children to take a good deal of responsibility at home; they spend very little time and energy in managing or sharing their children's leisure affairs; and they engender in their children a strong sympathy and sentimental loyalty.

One is reminded of the mothers who so regularly appear in the short stories of Frank O'Connor and other Irish authors: the strong and stable support in a family whose father deals primarily in alcoholic charm and irresponsibility. The key for such a woman is to convert the children to her side, as emotional suppliers and supporters in the real problems of life. She inspires her children with both the strength to cope with reality and also the dependency that assures her some emotional gratification in an otherwise bleak life. To be sure this fictional Irish mother is an exaggerated form, but we suspect that some such pattern is the paradigm for understanding the emotional nexus that dominates many lower-status families in which the mother's employment is a condition for family survival.

We have already described the motivational pattern that we think underpins part-time maternal employment. The distinctive features here are that the woman herself chooses to work and that she maintains a vivid sense of obligation and responsibility toward her family. She chooses a complex rather than a simple life pattern, but the conditions of the pattern are set by her primary commitment to her family role. We see this as a pattern requiring unusual energy and one which results in a high degree of family interaction. Derivative effects of the pattern we note in the degree of parent participation in the leisure lives of their adolescent children and in the energy, autonomy, and responsibility that characterize girls from this family setting. These psychological features of the girls develop, we suggest, from a modeling process in which the girls identify with and draw their ideals from their own active and autonomous mothers.

The only pattern remaining to be accounted for is the middle-class mother who works full-time. We found this group of girls to be indistinguishable in most critical respects from the daughters of women who work part-time. We must now ask how a full-time work commitment might for a middle-class woman be the same—have the same meaning—as part-time employment. One suspects that economic need alone does not distinguish the two kinds of employment for middle-class women, and the woman of higher social status who works full-time does so, at least in part, because of personal choice.

MATERNAL EMPLOYMENT AND ADOLESCENT BOYS

One would expect—from the findings in the girls' study—that maternal employment might be a less important factor in the life of the adolescent boy. If we are right in our view that much of the influence of maternal employment comes about through a modeling process in which the girl fashions her ego-ideals and activities in keeping with the pattern set by her mother, then we can expect that this pattern will be less effective in predicting the boy's developing integration. For the boy, the model provided by his father will be the key to ego development, and the mother's activity or employment should be a comparatively minor factor.

Our interpretations of the meaning of work to mothers in the part-time and full-time patterns gain some general support from our data on boys. Here again we find that the lower-class family in which the mother works full-time has more pressing financial troubles—or, at least, that financial problems come through to the children more clearly. Boys in this group think of financial problems as a source of worry and also as something they would like to change about their own lives more often than do boys in any of the other working mother patterns, and often more than those whose mothers do not work at all. The other three types of working mother (i.e., higher-status women who work full-time and women of either high or low status who hold part-time jobs) again seem to be women who are unusually conscientious, active mothers. Their sons, like their daughters, report sharing leisure activities with their parents more than other boys do, and they have a larger number of leisure activities of the kind that imply parental involvement (i.e., membership in organized groups and active sports and hobbies).

Beyond these few findings, the working mother variable shows relatively little power to predict the boy's activities and psychological characteristics. When the mother's work stems from personal choice—or so we infer, at least—the boy has a relatively high leisure activity index, but he differs in no other area from boys whose mothers do not work. He is no more likely to work or date; he shows no signs of unusual achievement striving,[5] of

---

[5] When we consider only urban boys from lower-middle and upper-middle working-class homes, we do find a relationship between the boys' mobility aspirations and maternal employment. Boys who aspire to upward mobility more often report that their mothers work part-time than do boys whose orientation is non-mobile or downwardly mobile. While maternal employment is generally a less imposing force in the life of the boy, this finding suggests that in certain cultural settings, the fact that a boy has an ambitious mother may crucially affect the direction of his development. Kahl's work (5) supports this suggestion.

TABLE 11.4 *Working-Class Boys with Full-Time Working Mothers Compared to Other Boys on Selected Measures of Activity, Ego Development*

ITEM: BOYS' ATTITUDES, BEHAVIOR	MATERNAL EMPLOYMENT	
	FULL-TIME WORKING CLASS (N = 71)	ALL OTHER PATTERNS (N = 631)
	Per Cent	
Adult Ideals		
Father	12	27
No ideal	15	6
In-family models (including father)	45	41
Time Perspective		
Extended	32	45
Restricted	12	5
Dating		
Date	68	53
Doesn't date	32	47
Group Membership		
None	43	26
Belongs to 1 or 2 groups	48	53
Belongs to 3 or more groups	9	21
Leisure Activities		
Low	33	18
Medium	38	45
High	29	37
Work		
Holds a job	51	47
Intimacy of Friendship		
Can be as close as family relationship	46	41
Cannot be as close	52	56
Reliance on Parents: Advice on Issues		
Relies heavily on parents	40	44
Relies somewhat on parents	47	45
Does not rely on parents	13	10

special forms of ego development, or of precocious loosening of dependency ties.

The boys from families in which the mother's work is the product of economic necessity (i.e., lower-status women who work full-time) do differ from other boys in some respects, and this seems to us interesting in light of the fact that this is the one case in which maternal employment implies something about the father as a model. The fact that a mother "must" work —irrespective of her personal wishes—does not speak well for the father's capacity as a provider. Considering the importance of economic prowess in the American definition and evaluation of the male, a father who cannot or does not support his family adequately can hardly serve as an effective ideal for his son. And it is in the area of modeling that the boys differ most clearly from their age mates. They choose their own fathers significantly less often than other boys do, and they more frequently say that they have no adult ideals. Beyond this we find that boys in this group are somewhat rebellious in response to adult authority, and that they show signs of a poor ego integration. They have a relatively short time perspective and a low level of general activity. Only in dating are they especially active. They do not have part-time jobs as often as other boys; they have very few organizational ties and active leisure engagements. Our information on their family attitudes is limited: we did not ask boys as many questions in this area as we did girls. But boys in the lower-class full-time group do not seem to be emotionally dependent on the family in any way that compares with our findings for girls from similar family backgrounds. They do not think that family ties are always closer than friendships, and they do not rely heavily on parental advice or on in-family models more than other boys do. We would very much like to have information on the boy's relationship to his mother distinguished from his attitude toward his father, but in this our data on boys are specifically lacking.

We can say, by way of a general conclusion, that the effect of maternal employment in the boy's development is significant only when it serves to inform us about general features of family integration and, specifically, about the relationship between the boy and his father. When the mother's work rests to any significant degree on factors of personal choice—when, that is, it reflects qualities and motives of the mother but does not yield specific information about the father—it fails to predict a unique pattern of adjustment in the boy, although it appears to be an important force in the girl's integration. This difference in the findings for boys and girls supports our earlier view that the kind of woman who assumes an occupational role through a desire for some self-realization exerts an influence on her daughter's development through a modeling process in which the girl identifies with and incorporates many of her mother's ego characteristics.

REFERENCES

1. Bergsten, Jane W. "A Nationwide Sample of Girls from School Lists," *Journal of Experimental Education*, XXVI (March, 1958), 197–208.

2. Douvan, Elizabeth, and Adelson, Joseph. *Themes in American Adolescence.* Unpublished manuscript in preparation.
3. Douvan, Elizabeth, and Kaye, Carol. *Adolescent Girls.* Ann Arbor, Mich.: Survey Research Center, University of Michigan, 1956.
4. Douvan, Elizabeth, and Withey, S. B. *A Study of Adolescent Boys.* Ann Arbor, Mich.: Survey Research Center, University of Michigan, 1955.
5. Kahl, J. A. "Educational and Occupational Aspirations of 'Common Man' Boys," *Harvard Education Review,* XXIII (Spring, 1953), 186–203.

Chapter Twelve

Adolescent Roles: Rural-Urban Differentials*

PRODIPTO ROY

... IN THE spring of 1958, a study was conducted in a rural county in Washington, designated by the Secretary of Agriculture as an area with a "moderate" problem of low income in agriculture (3, p. 7). The nation as a whole was in an economic recession, and this chronically low-income county was affected in that the job situation was considered poor by its adults (9, p. 7). The present study concerning the effect of maternal employment on the family roles in this situation should not be considered exceptional. There are, at present, about 210 counties in the Rural Resource Development Program that may be theoretically viewed as chronically low-income rural counties (7, p. 5). In a society where the rural-urban mobility is still in process, the effect of maternal employment on family roles in rural areas such as these is germane to the general problem and may provide insights that contrast with the urban patterns.

1. FRAMEWORK OF ANALYSIS

The nuclear family may be viewed as a social system with four structurally related social positions—husband-father, wife-mother, son-brother, and daughter-sister (1). All four social positions, particularly the last two, have differential patterns varying with age. The role expectations of each family member have changed over the years in the American family, and

* Adapted from *Marriage and Family Living*, XXIII (November, 1961), 340–49 by permission of the author and the publisher. The research was conducted under Projects 1364 and 1415 of the Agricultural Experiment Station of the Washington State University and is known as Scientific Paper 2059.

they have varied with factors such as ethnic origin, occupation, education and residence.

A social position in a social system consists of a number of role expectations for that position. In the traditional wife-mother position the following may be considered the role expectations: mother of siblings, spouse of father, teacher, disciplinarian, playmate, housekeeper, etc. Into this social position is being squeezed a new role expectation—"supplemental earner."

The general hypothesis being tested in this study is that the addition of this new role to the wife-mother position affects the roles of the children. Owing to the difference between rural and urban sub-cultural patterns . . . the employment of the mother should affect rural and urban families in different ways. *The four-fold analysis attempted in this paper is designed to manifest the effects of employment of the mother, and of residence, on certain roles played by the teen-age son and daughter.*

Several rational and "common sense" fears are engendered in the minds of people whenever any institutionalized social positions are altered. Some of these fears relative to maternal employment, spelled out by Bossard (2, pp. 282–86) and tested by Nye (Chapter Ten), are:

> The child feels lonely. The child feels neglected . . .
> Children exploit lack of maternal control . . . (the child) rationalizes his own antisocial behavior.
> The mother is unable to render detailed services to the child.
> Supervision and training of the child are neglected.

Nye found little evidence to support Bossard's conception of the neglected, maladjusted child. There are several other effects on the social positions of the son and daughter that may be related to the employment of the mother. First, the employment of the mother might increase the amount of work that the son and daughter do at home and consequently cut down on work they do outside. Another consequence of the increased work at home might be a tendency to cut down on participation in school activities, out-of-school social activities, dating, and the amount of spare time. Employment of the mother, resulting in lack of supervision and training in regular study habits, might tend to lower the academic performance of children and possibly affect academic aspirations.

The general consequences of the disruptive forces in the traditional social position of the mother who has "abandoned her hearth" should manifest themselves in more delinquent behavior, less affection as perceived by the children, and probably less fairness of discipline. On the other hand, the employment of the mother may contribute to more democracy and cooperation in the family because of the greater sharing of work and decisions. Some may feel that there will be less democracy and cooperation in families with employed mothers. The hypotheses being tested in this study, stated in null form, are:

(1) That the employment of the mother does not affect the amount of household work done by the adolescent daughter and son.

(2) That the employment of the mother does not reduce the social activities of the daughter or son.

(3) That the employment of the mother does not lower the academic performance or aspirations of the daughter or son.

(4) That the employment of the mother does not affect the amount of delinquency, the affection, the fairness of discipline, the democracy, or cooperation in a family.

The statement of the above hypotheses is made in null form because there is not much empirical evidence to predict the outcome of the test in either direction. However, in both the frame of analysis and some of the literature cited there is one major underlying dysfunctional hypothesis—that is, the employment of the mother will result in undesirable effects in the children. Many of the subsequent tests were applied to prove or disprove this general dysfunctional hypothesis. Hence, the research hypotheses in reality have a direction of prediction.

2. METHOD

This study was conducted in two counties in the northeastern section of Washington. The data were gathered on a questionnaire which was filled out by high school pupils in Stevens County on March 10–12, 1958; the questionnaire was administered to all students in grades 9 to 12 who were present in school. In Ferry County, the questionnaires were administered to all students from the seventh to the twelfth grades during May, 1959. Totals of 1,086 and 257 questionnaires were obtained from Stevens and Ferry Counties respectively.

The residential classification was based on two questions asked of the respondents—(a) Do you live on a farm? and (b) Do you live out of town but not on a farm? If the answer was "no" to both questions, the respondent was classified as "town." These two counties are rural counties with only one population center of about 4,000 which would be classified under the census as "urban." The respondents' definition of "town" consisted of incorporated or unincorporated places with a population of about 200 or more people. The rural-town analysis used here is not the same as the rural-urban dichotomy used by the Census of Population. It was not felt that the cutting of the rural-urban continuum farther along the rural end of the scale was a violation of the principle of rural-urban analysis. In addition, the self-conception of an adolescent as a "town" resident adds social-psychological weight to the present classification.

One condition that Mirra Komarovsky suggests as conducive to family welfare in families with employed mothers is, "The mother works short hours . . ." (4, chap. 5). Three categories of employment were obtained from the data—"fully employed," "partly employed" and "not employed." Since Komarovsky raises the question that short hours may not really affect family structure, it was decided to exclude the "partly employed" group from analysis because of the logically inconclusive effect in the criterion variable. No validation was made of the children's statement regarding the employment status of their mothers, and no further questions were asked as to the number of hours worked, so that some objective cutting point may be made. It was assumed that boys or girls thirteen years or older knew the meaning of being employed "full-time."

There is evidence to show that employed mothers are better educated, that they more often belong to broken families, that they have fewer children and have husbands with higher prestige occupations (see Chapter One). Since some of these background factors may be related to the variables being tested, it was felt that sub-sampling would be necessary to control the variation caused by these background factors.

TABLE 12.1 *Social Characteristics Controlled by Matched Sub-Samples of Fully-Employed and Non-Employed Mothers*

	ORIGINAL SAMPLE		MATCHED SUB-SAMPLE	
	Employed Full Time	*Non-Employed*	*Employed Full Time*	*Non-Employed*
Per cent of parents living together	70.0	84.5	100.0	100.0
Median years of school—mother	12.2	11.6	12.8	12.8
Median number of siblings	2.2	3.5	2.8	2.8
Median age of Mother	43.8	41.6	43.9	42.9
Per cent of fathers in white collar occupations	27.1	18.3	29.6	37.2
Number of respondents	194	934	128	175

First, it was found that a higher proportion of the children of employed mothers did not live with their natural fathers and mothers. Since, in many cases, employment of the mother is necessitated by the breaking of the family, it was felt that only complete families in which both parents were living together should be included in the analysis. Further, this study is an analysis of the normative family to test the effect of the employment of the mother on the changes of roles of adolescent sons and daughters. Hence, so far as possible, all four social positions should be structurally operative. The analysis of factors such as divorce, no father, or step-father could be undertaken separately.

The other background factors of age and education of mother, number of siblings and occupation of father were controlled so that the employed and the unemployed families had similar proportions of each in the samples. Table 12.1 presents a comparison of the samples before and after subsampling.

3. RESULTS

HYPOTHESIS 1. HOUSEHOLD CHORES

In order to find out whether or not a higher proportion of boys and girls of fully employed mothers were performing the household tasks, a list of household chores was provided, and each boy or girl was asked to check, "What chores do you do at home? Regularly—occasionally." Twenty-one household chores were listed, with a place left for others. A chore score was computed by summing a 2–1–0 rating for each chore performed regularly, occasionally, or not checked. Table 12.2 shows the median chore scores for boys and girls by residence, comparing the families with employed mothers and families with non-employed mothers. There was a consistent trend manifesting that both boys and girls of employed mothers did slightly more housework. The differences observed were statistically significant in two out of the four samples. In total, the girls seemed to do more housework than boys. There was not much difference between the rural and town samples, the slight differences seeming to suggest that town boys did slightly more housework than rural boys.

A second way in which the differences between families of employed and non-employed mothers could be tested, would be a simple application of the Sign Test (10). A listing was made of the 21 chores with the proportion of boys and girls performing each chore regularly or occasionally. The hypothesis was that a higher proportion of the children of employed mothers would perform each household task; hence the sign of the difference should be positive in each case.

The rural girls did not provide consistent predictions in either direction (10 plus and 11 minus). The predictions for the town girls were in the ex-

TABLE 12.2　*Median Chore Scores and Work for Pay of Children of Employed and Non-Employed Mothers by Residence*

	RURAL			TOWN		
	Employed	Non-Employed	Sign	Employed	Non-Employed	Sign
Boys						
Median chore score	11.1	9.4	+*	14.8	12.6	+
Per cent worked for pay last year	90.3	94.4	—	91.9	95.1	—
Per cent worked for pay during summer	77.4	77.8	—	76.3	78.0	—
Per cent that have a job now	29.0	46.3	—	43.2	48.8	—
Average number of hours worked per week	2.8	7.9	—	4.8	5.7	—
N	31	53		36	40	
Girls						
Median chore score	25.3	24.7	+	26.4	19.8	+*
Per cent worked for pay last year	78.6	73.1	+	100.0	85.7	+
Per cent worked for pay during summer	42.9	34.6	+	50.0	50.0	
Per cent that have a job now	35.7	15.7	+	36.7	25.0	+
Average number of hours worked per week	3.3	2.4	+	7.1	3.5	+
N	27	52		29	27	

* Statistically significant.

pected direction in 17 out of the 21 cases, which is significantly different.

Data for the boys show that the predictions were in the expected direction in both sub-samples: the rural boys showed differences in the expected direction in 16 out of 21 cases and the town boys showed correct predictions in 14 out of 20 cases. The first is significant, the second approaches significance.[1] In the more womanly roles, the tasks expected of the mother, the expected predictions were more consistent. In other words, it seems that the sons of employed mothers were performing household tasks normally assigned to the expected home-maker position of mother. However, the differences were not large, and hence it should not be inferred that any radical role changes are taking place.

Corollary—Work for Pay.　One consequence of doing more household

[1] The more powerful extension of the Sign Test, the Wilcoxon Signed-Ranks test, would give statistically significant results.

work would be that the girls or boys would be prevented from doing work outside for pay and earning a little money of their own. Four questions were asked to test this corollary. The answers to these questions are tabulated in Table 12.2.

The pattern of response for the boys showed results in the expected direction: that is, that boys of employed mothers do less outside work for pay than boys of non-employed mothers. A lower proportion of employed mothers' sons worked for pay last year, a lower proportion worked for pay last summer, a lower proportion have jobs now, and the mean number of hours worked was lower. Both the rural and town samples showed consistent predictions. The differences were greater in the rural sample with respect to the proportion of boys that have a job now and the average hours worked.

The pattern of responses for the girls was consistently *opposite* to the predicted direction. A higher proportion of the employed mothers' daughters worked for pay last year, or worked for pay during the last summer. A higher proportion of the employed mothers' daughters have a job now, and on the average they work more hours per week. Both the rural and town samples were consistent in their predictions. It seems that the mother's example of working may have some direct influence on the daughter's following her example. A further hypothesis that arises out of this finding is that perhaps the breaking of the traditional feminine role by the mother makes it easier for daughters to break the traditional feminine role.

The null hypothsis may therefore be rejected and it may be concluded that, in general, a higher proportion of the children of employed mothers perform household tasks than the children of non-employed mothers. The pattern of behavior for the town boys and girls and the rural boys showed that the children of employed mothers performed household chores more often than the children of non-employed mothers. The rural girl sample was an exception to this finding: the differences observed between the employed and non-employed rural families were not statistically significant, and the patterns did not consistently support the above conclusion.

A corollary derived from the above hypothesis was that as a consequence of doing more work at home, the children would be able to do less work for pay outside the home. The sons of employed mothers consistently showed that they did less work outside the home for pay. The daughters of employed mothers, however, consistently showed the reverse; that is, a higher proportion of them worked, and for longer hours, than the daughters of non-employed mothers.

HYPOTHESIS 2. SOCIAL ACTIVITIES
The second hypothesis being tested is one that logically follows the first. If mothers are employed and the children have to do more of the household

chores, it follows that they should have less time of their own for social activities. This lack of time may be manifest in such behavior as less dating, less participation in school activities, and fewer hours of spare time.

The question was asked "How often do you date?" with answer categories "frequently," "occasionally," "seldom," and "never." The percentage of respondents that checked "seldom" or "never" date, are presented in Table 12.3. The results show no consistent pattern of responses—the boys' predictions would support the hypothesis for the rural sample and reject it for the town sample, and the girls' data would reject it for the rural sample and support it for the town sample. It seems that other factors more important than the employment of the mother govern dating behavior.

TABLE 12.3 *Social Activities of Children with Employed and Non-Employed Mothers by Residence*

| | RURAL | | | TOWN | | |
	Employed	Non-Employed	Sign	Employed	Non-Employed	Sign
Boys						
Per cent that seldom or never date	54.9	44.4	+	18.4	48.8	−
Median no. of school activities	2.6	2.0	+	2.6	2.6	+
Median SPI for school activities[1]	5.3	4.5	+	5.8	5.5	+
Median no. of out of school activities	2.2	1.7	+	1.9	2.4	−
Median SPI for out of school activities[1]	4.3	3.3	+	4.8	5.5	−
Median hours of spare time	18.8	15.4	+	19.3	14.7	+
Girls						
Per cent that seldom or never date	22.6	42.0	−	17.2	10.7	+
Median no. of school activities	1.9	2.5	−	3.2	3.4	−
Median SPI for school activities[1]	4.5	4.9	−	7.0	6.6	+
Median no. of out of school activities	2.2	1.9	+	2.2	2.6	−
Median SPI for out of school activities[1]	4.8	4.2	+	4.6	6.2	−
Median hours of spare time	17.5	15.00	+	13.0	19.3	−

[1] SPI is the Social Participation Index equivalent to a sum of a 3–2–1–0 rating on a list of activities or organizations.

Social participation was divided into school activities and out-of-school activities. Each type of social participation was measured by number of organizations to which the person belonged and the social participation index. The social participation index was a sum of 3–2–1–0 rating on a list of activities or organizations which were checked as "very active," "fairly active," "not very active," and not checked, respectively.

With respect to school activities, the sons of employed mothers seem to participate more than the sons of non-employed mothers, and the daughters of employed mothers seem to participate less than the daughters of non-employed mothers. The differences were not very great, particularly for the town sample. In the out-of-school activities, the rural samples of both boys and girls indicated that children of employed mothers participated *more* than the children of non-employed mothers, but the town sample of both boys and girls indicated that children of employed mothers participated *less* than the children of non-employed mothers.

The respondents were asked to report the number of hours they had free to spend as they wished last week. The medians were computed and recorded. Three out of the four test groups showed results opposite to the predicted direction; that is, children of employed mothers did not have less spare time than children of non-employed mothers.

The null hypothesis cannot be rejected from these data. Children of employed mothers seemed to have as much social life and spare time as children of non-employed mothers. The data suggest that rural employed mothers' children may participate more and town employed mothers' children may participate less in out-of-school activities. Further research will be needed to substantiate this rural-town differential.

HYPOTHESIS 3. ACADEMIC PERFORMANCE

The theoretical framework of analysis suggests that through lack of supervision of study hours or actual help with homework, resulting from the employment of the mother, the children of employed mothers should not perform as well in school as the children of non-employed mothers. Low academic performance may also be a function of more household chores.

One manifestation of performance is the grade point obtained. The question was asked in this way: "On your last report card, did you get mostly: —A's, —B's, —C's, —D's and —F's?" More than one place could be checked. The categories and sub-categories were arrayed in order from the highest to the lowest and a median grade point computed. (See Table 12.4.) Three out of four of the predictions were in the expected direction, but in only one were the differences observed statistically significant. The sons of employed mothers showed lower grade-point medians than the sons of non-employed mothers; differences observed for the town sample were statistically significant. The daughters of rural employed mothers showed a slightly higher median grade point than the daughters of non-employed mothers, but the town sample showed the opposite result. Neither of the differences was statistically significant.

It was further hypothesized that poor school performance may logically result in a low aspiration to continue studies into the college level. The results show that a higher percentage of the children of rural employed mothers plan to go to college than the children of non-employed mothers. A lower proportion of the children of employed town mothers planned to go to college than the children of non-employed town mothers.

An overview of Table 12.4 seems to suggest more consistency in the rural-town dichotomy than the boy-girl dichotomy. The town sample seemed consistently to support the hypothesis—that is, the children of employed mothers had a lower academic performance and aspiration. The rural sample, on the other hand, seemed to refute the hypothesis—a higher proportion of the children of employed mothers planned to go to college and the girls had a slightly higher grade-point average.

TABLE 12.4 *Academic Performance and Aspiration of Children of Employed and Non-Employed Mothers by Residence*

| | RURAL | | | TOWN | | |
	Employed	Non-Employed	Sign	Employed	Non-Employed	Sign
Boys						
Median grade point	2.1	2.2	—	2.1	3.0	—
Per cent that plan to go to college	41.9	37.7	+	64.9	70.0	—
Girls						
Median grade point	3.1	3.0	+	2.9	3.2	—
Per cent that plan to go to college	59.3	39.2	+	55.2	57.1	—

The null hypothesis in general cannot be rejected from the analyses of these data. The results seem to suggest that the employment of town mothers may lower the performance and aspirations of their children, but that the employment of rural mothers may raise their academic performance and aspirations. More research will be needed to substantiate these findings.

HYPOTHESIS 4. DISINTEGRATION OF FAMILY VALUES

The general hypothesis being tested is that a change in the normative role of the mother in the form of full employment will result in various dysfunctional manifestations. The first and most visible manifestation would be an increase in delinquency. The Bossard statements about the child's feeling lonely or neglected should manifest themselves in less affection between the mother and the child. Due to the time and energy expended in the new role of outside employment, the mother's understanding and disciplining of her children should suffer. Following the general dysfunctional hypothesis, there should also be less democracy and cooperation in the families with employed mothers.

Delinquency was measured by a checklist of delinquent-type behavior. The percentages of boys and girls who stated they had committed each delinquent act are shown in Table 12.5. If the hypothesis were true, that children of employed mothers are more delinquent than the children of normative non-employed mothers, then the direction of the signs in the table should be consistently positive. The rural boys show a 7:3 ratio against the hypothesis and the town boys show a 5:5 ratio. The rural girls show a 7:2 ratio against the hypothesis and the town girls show a 5:5 ratio. None of these four samples showed statistically significant differences under the Sign Test.

Therefore, the null hypothesis cannot be rejected from these data. The employment of the mother does not increase the delinquent behavior of either the sons or the daughters. If the rural boys and girls are viewed as one group, it will be seen from the table that in 14 out of 19 cases of delinquent behavior, the children of employed mothers showed less delinquency than children of the . . . non-employed mothers. Differences are statistically significant. The urban children showed random differences. This would suggest that possibly as a consequence of the mother's working out and the children's doing more household chores, there is *less* delinquency among rural adolescents. This finding will need to be retested for confirmation.

A second way in which the delinquency hypothesis was tested was through the construction of a unidimensional scale to measure delinquency. A Guttman-type scale was constructed and five items (marked with a ([1]) on Table 12.5) manifested unidimensionality with a coefficient of reproducibility of over 90 per cent for both the boys and the girls. These items were originally taken from a scale developed by Nye and Short (6). In the construction of the scale, the answer "no" to an item was rated positively, and consequently a high delinquency scale score means less delinquency. All scales were scored so that they were positively functional with regard to the family system. Therefore, the general dysfunctional hypothesis would predict the families with employed mothers to have lower scale scores than the families with non-employed mothers, and the difference should show a negative sign.

TABLE 12.5 *Delinquent Behavior of Children with Employed and Non-Employed Mothers by Residence*

| | RURAL | | | TOWN | | |
	Employed	Non-Employed	Sign	Employed	Non-Employed	Sign
Boys						
Skipped school (without excuse)[1]	53.3	53.7	—	51.4	51.2	+
Driven without driver's license	86.7	88.9	—	75.7	70.7	+
Ever disobeyed your parents	96.8	96.3	+	94.6	95.1	—
Ever told a lie	90.3	94.4	—	97.3	97.6	—
Refused to do as you were told[1]	54.8	55.6	—	48.6	55.0	—
Taken things that did not belong to you[1]	48.4	46.3	+	54.1	56.1	—
Taken part in gang fights	12.9	24.1	—	29.7	9.8	+
Drank beer, wine or liquor[1]	74.2	70.4	+	83.8	65.9	+
Purposely damaged property[1]	25.8	38.9	—	40.5	26.8	+
Have you ever been arrested	9.7	11.1	—	21.6	24.4	—
N	32	54		38	41	
Girls						
Skipped school (without excuse)[1]	46.4	57.7	—	56.7	42.9	+
Driven without driver's license	53.6	78.8	—	83.3	75.0	+
Ever disobeyed your parents	88.9	98.1	—	93.3	89.3	+
Ever told a lie	92.9	98.1	—	93.3	96.4	—
Refused to do as you were told[1]	44.4	44.2	+	43.3	42.9	+
Taken things that did not belong to you[1]	17.9	28.8	—	58.6	28.6	+
Taken part in gang fights	14.3	5.8	+	3.3	11.1	—
Drank beer, wine or liquor[1]	50.0	55.8	—	58.6	60.7	—
Purposely damaged property[1]	0.0	13.7	—	3.4	17.9	—
Have you ever been arrested	0.0	0.0		3.4	3.7	—
N	28	52		30	28	

[1] Items used in the Guttman scale.

The median scale scores are presented in Table 12.6. The medians of the delinquency scale score showed that the rural samples for both boys and girls refuted the hypothesis, whereas the urban samples for both boys and girls supported the hypothesis. Because of the contradictory results, the null hypothesis cannot be rejected; employment of the mother does not affect the amount of delinquency for boys or for girls.

A second scale was designed to measure the dimension of "affection" in the family. This scale and subsequent three scales were constructed by Walter Slocum and Carol Stone (10).[2] The scale scores indicated that the rural boys with employed and non-employed mothers rated their families equally on affection; the sons of urban employed mothers considered their families a little more affectionate than did the non-employed mothers' families. The rural sample for the girls favored the families of employed mothers, and the urban sample for girls favored the families with non-employed mothers. The results showed differences that were not consistent in any direction. Therefore, the null hypothesis cannot be rejected; the employment of the mother does not affect the amount of affection in a family as perceived by the sons or daughters.

A third scale was an attempt to measure a dimension called "fairness of discipline."[3] In three out of the four samples, the median scale scores provide results that are contrary to the hypothesis, and only in the town sample for boys did the results support the hypothesis. Therefore, the dysfunctional hypothesis can be rejected: that is, there is no association between the employment of mothers and unfair punishment practices.

A fourth scale was an attempt to measure the dimension of "democracy" in the family.[4] The medians computed from the scale score refuted the dysfunctional hypothesis in three out of the four samples. Only the town sample for girls supported the hypothesis. The hypothesis that employment of mothers would lower the amount of democracy in the family can be rejected from these data.

---

[2] The scale included eight items: parents dislike children—no; parents are hateful—no; children are ashamed of parents—no; parents show real love and affection for children—yes; children feel "close" to parents—yes; home life is very happy —yes; parents are generous with praise—yes; and rating of family on affection—very affectionate.

[3] The scale included six items: children are punished more severely than children in other families—no; children are disciplined when they don't need it—no; rating of family on fairness of discipline—discipline very fair or quite fair; some children in the family are punished more severely than others—no; parents get all the facts before punishing—yes; and enforcement of rules is not consistent—sometimes harsh, sometimes not—no.

[4] The items that constituted the scale were: rating of family on control by parents—very democratic or fairly democratic; parents listen to suggestions made by their children—yes; children are encouraged to make most of their own decisions— yes; and parents almost always respect children's opinions and judgment—yes.

The final scale constructed was designed to measure the dimension of "cooperation" in the family.[5] The median scale scores computed from the data seem to be contradictory on both the boy-girl dichotomy and the rural-town dichotomy. The rural sample for boys and the town sample for girls supported the hypothesis, and the town sample of boys and the

TABLE 12.6 *Median Scale Scores for Delinquency, Affection, Discipline, Democracy and Cooperation of Children of Employed and Non-Employed Mothers by Residence*

	RURAL			TOWN		
	Employed	Non-Employed	Sign	Employed	Non-Employed	Sign
Boys						
Median Delinquency Scale Score	2.94	2.70	+	2.61	2.79	—
Median Affection Scale Score	6.50	6.50		6.25	6.15	+
Median Discipline Scale Score	4.83	4.38	+	4.00	4.75	—
Median Democracy Scale Score	3.00	2.88	+	3.14	2.83	+
Median Cooperation Scale Score	2.86	3.29	—	3.75	2.80	+
Girls						
Median Delinquency Scale Score	4.00	3.53	+	3.21	3.78	—
Median Affection Scale Score	6.70	6.38	+	6.33	6.58	—
Median Discipline Scale Score	5.25	4.42	+	5.09	4.57	+
Median Democracy Scale Score	3.80	2.46	+	2.64	3.33	—
Median Cooperation Scale Score	3.00	2.31	+	2.13	3.70	—

rural sample of girls refuted the hypothesis. The null hypothesis therefore cannot be rejected from these data; the employment of the mother does not affect the amount of cooperation in a family.

From an overview of Table 12.6, it would seem that the rural families,

---

[5] There were five items that constituted the scale: parents help with homework when asked—yes; quarreling between parents and children is frequent—no; parents do not understand children—no; there is bickering and quarreling in the home—no; and the rating of family on cooperation—much cooperation within the family.

in general, consistently refuted the hypothesis that the children of employed mothers would manifest dysfunctional tendencies. The data consistently show, in eight out of the nine cases, that families with employed mothers actually scored better than families with non-employed mothers on the variables for which scales were constructed. The urban sample in general did not show any consistent trends.

4. CONCLUSIONS AND IMPLICATIONS FOR FUTURE RESEARCH

1. The children of employed mothers seem to do more household chores than the children of non-employed mothers; the pattern for the rural girls sample was not consistent and may well be an exception.

The corollary that because of increased work at home fewer children would work for pay outside the home was substantiated for the son but not for the daughter.

2. The employment of the mother does not seem to have any adverse effect on the social activities of the children. There may be a rural-urban difference with respect to out-of-school activities—showing that more children of rural employed mothers participate, and fewer urban employed mothers' children, than their counterparts with non-employed mothers.

3. The employment of the mother does not generally lower the academic performance or aspirations of the children. The results suggest a residential differential: the employment of town mothers was associated with lower academic performance and aspiration of their children, and the employment of rural mothers was associated with higher academic performance and aspiration of their children.

4. The general fear that delinquency would increase because of the employment of the mother was not substantiated. The results indicated that rural children of employed mothers seemed to manifest less delinquency than those of mothers not employed. The other scales were devised to measure affection, fairness of discipline, democracy, and cooperation as perceived by sons and daughters in the family. The results suggest that rural families in general benefited from the employment of the mother, in that the girls and, in part, the boys, showed less delinquency, more affection, more fairness of discipline, more democracy, and more cooperation in their families.

Certain general implications for further research can be made as a result of this study. *First,* the research design for any study attempting to test the influence of employment of the normative social positions of the family must carefully control the background factors. This was possible in the present study because of the fortuitous presence of a large number of respondents in the control group with which the experimental group could be matched. This was a fortunate coincidence because this research design was not specifically set up to study the effect of maternal employment on adolescent roles.

Second, the results of maternal employment indicate that differences between rural and town sub-cultures exist and need further investigation; perhaps the inclusion of a metropolitan sample would heighten the contrast. Traditional rural values of thrift and hard work, per se, may have some bearing on the theoretical framework and the hypotheses that logically follow. Since earning money and hard work are "good," then changes in family structure and "sacrifices" made by other members when the mother is fully employed are viewed favorably and may be functional.

Third, the effects of maternal employment on the role of the son seem to be different from the effects on the role of the daughter, and these role differentiations need to be studied separately.

Finally, the definition of the criterion variable of maternal employment should be more carefully treated in a restudy: (a) the hours of work performed should be specified; (b) the regularity of work in months per year should be stipulated; and (c) the duration of the employment in the number of years should be stated *to ensure that the experimental variable has been operative for a reasonable amount of time to manifest effects* in the test variables.

The hypotheses for further research should therefore be more specific and take into consideration sexual role differentiation and residence. Research hypotheses suggested from the results of this study may be stated thus:

1. That maternal employment results in less outside remunerative employment for the adolescent son and more for the daughter in both rural and urban families.
2. That maternal employment in rural areas raises the academic performance and aspiration of the son and daughter, but in towns it lowers academic performance and aspiration for both the son and the daughter.
3. That rural families show beneficial effects owing to maternal employment in that there is less delinquency, more affection, more fairness of discipline, more democracy, and more cooperation in the family.

REFERENCES

1. Bates, Frederick L. "Position, Role and Status: A Reformulation of Concepts," *Social Forces,* XXXIV (May, 1956), 313–21.
2. Bossard, James H. S. *The Sociology of Child Development.* New York: Harper, 1954.

3. *Development of Agriculture's Human Resources.* United States Department of Agriculture. Washington, D.C.: Government Printing Office, April, 1955.

4. Komarovsky, Mirra. *Women in the Modern World.* Boston: Little, Brown, 1953.

5. "Marital and Family Characteristics of Workers: March, 1958," *Current Population Reports.* Department of Commerce, Bureau of the Census, Series P-50, No. 87. Washington, D.C.: Government Printing Office, 1959. Other results of earlier surveys on this subject may be found in other reports in this series Nos. 5, 11, 22, 29, 44, 50, 62, 73, 76, and 81.

6. Nye, F. Ivan, and Short, James F., Jr. "Scaling Delinquent Behavior," *American Sociological Review,* XXXII (June, 1957), 326–31.

7. *Rural Development Program.* United States Department of Agriculture. Washington, D.C.: Government Printing Office, September, 1960.

8. Siegel, Sidney. *Nonparametric Statistics for the Behavioral Sciences.* New York: McGraw-Hill, 1956.

9. Slocum, Walter L. "Community Development Needs Perceived by Stevens County Adults and Teenagers," *Human Resources in Stevens Country—An Appraisal.* Pullman: Washington State University, September, 1959.

10. ————, and Stone, Carol, L. "A Method for Measuring Family Images Held by Teenagers," *Marriage and Family Living,* XXI (August, 1959), 245–50.

Chapter Thirteen

Mother Substitutes*

JOSEPH B. PERRY, JR.

A PART of the general movement of women into the labor force of the United States has been the tendency for increasing numbers of mothers of preschool children to work outside the home. See Chapter One. In families in which the mothers are employed away from the home, the "mother substitute"[1] is important in the socialization of the children. Relatively little attention has been given directly to these mother substitutes (1; 2; 3; 4, pp. 212–13; 5; 6). This paper is a discussion of some of the characteristics and attitudes of mother substitutes of employed mothers of pre-school children.

The paper is based upon data taken from interviews, held in the spring of 1958 in Spokane, Washington, with 104 employed mothers and 82 of their mother substitutes.[2]

THE FINDINGS

The employed mothers were asked to describe the characteristics of a desirable mother substitute. Since they often mentioned more than one characteristic, the following list includes only items considered important

* Adapted from "The Mother Substitutes of Employed Mothers: An Exploratory Inquiry," *Marriage and Family Living*, XXIII (November, 1961), 362–67, by permission of the author and the publisher.

This study was supported by a grant from the National Institute of Mental Health.

[1] The term "mother substitute" rather than "babysitter" is used to avoid the connotation of a high school girl watching children while the parents are out for the evening.

[2] See Chapter Five for a description of the methodology of the study.

by five or more employed mothers. The characteristics, in order of frequency mentioned, were that the mother substitute should: (1) like children, (2) be able to control them, (3) have good character—be dependable, responsible, trustworthy, conscientious, (4) have high moral standards, (5) understand children's thinking—get down to their level, (6) be able to care for the child's bodily needs, (7) be a mature person, (8) be intelligent and imaginative, (9) maintain a helpful relationship with the child, and (10) have experience with children.

One employed mother, in response to this question, said:

> She must be of good character and very honest, conscientious. Good at supervising children and make them mind. She should be kind and a mother type. She must know how to cook and see that the children are well fed. She must be alert and be sure she knows where the children are.

While these characteristics are not very precise, the employed mothers do have a set of standards by which they judge mother substitutes. The question of how well the mother substitute actually meet these criteria is considered below in terms of: (1) how the mother substitutes were hired, (2) the training and experience of the mother substitutes, (3) the mother substitutes' attitudes toward their work, (4) selected characteristics of the relationships between the employed mothers and mother substitutes, (5) a comparison of the mother substitutes' and employed mothers' attitudes toward the children, and (6) the reasons employed mothers changed mother substitutes.

The process through which mother substitutes obtained their positions was generally informal. Only four out of the 82 obtained their jobs with the aid of an employment agency. The remainder were hired through hearing from friends that a particular mother needed someone to care for her children, a mother's learning that a particular person was looking for children to care for, or the parents knowing the mother substitute and asking her to take the job.

The informality of the hiring process may be illustrated with the comment of a mother substitute who, when asked how she got her job, said:

> I was staying in the next block with an elderly lady. While there I got acquainted with a teacher who told me Mrs. ———— was looking for someone, so we got together.

In another case the mother substitute said:

> I made a chance remark to a friend that maybe I'd take a child to care for and in a day or two here comes Mrs. ———— and

asks me to care for her girl. My friend had told a sister of Mrs. _____ about me.

This informal procedure may have helped place the employed mother-mother substitute relationship on a friendship basis with two possible important consequences for the children. The first is that the more relaxed informal situation might permit the employed mother to ascertain better if the mother substitute possessed the desired characteristics. The second possible consequence is based upon the view that members of the nuclear family are often considered and treated as a single unit. Initial friendly relations toward one member of a family might then be diffused to all members of the family. A mother substitute who had established the basis for an informal friendship relation with an employed mother might be expected to behave in the same way toward the child or children in her care from the same family.

The mother substitutes largely lacked formal experience with children, as seventy-nine per cent had no formal institutional work experience with children, such as elementary school, nursery school, or kindergarten teaching. The other twenty-one per cent had worked with children in such capacities as Sunday school teachers, public school teachers, playground directors, and nurses. Also, thirty per cent of the mother substitutes had taken courses in child development, home economics, and nursing.

The mother substitutes did not have extensive experience in their jobs. Fifty-four per cent had been doing child-care work for two to four years, and an additional twenty per cent for four or more years.

Although the mother substitutes' formal training and work experience suggest that the majority were not well trained, almost all had some experience with children. Eighty-two per cent of the mother substitutes had children of their own. Furthermore, in this sample, twelve per cent of the children were cared for at home by their fathers, and twenty-eight per cent by some other relative. By way of comparison,[3] in the United States in 1959, 14.7 per cent of the children under six of employed mothers were in the care of their fathers, and 42.2 per cent were in the care of other relatives (5).

The mother substitutes were asked: "In general, if you had a choice, would you prefer to take care of children or engage in some other job or pursuit?" Forty-seven of the mother substitutes had no preference. Thirty-three said they would rather be doing something else.

Reasons given by the mother substitutes for prefering to care for

---

[3] These data are not directly comparable because the material in Lajewsky's *Child Care Arrangements of Full-Time Working Mothers* (5) refers to children under six years of age, while the children in the Spokane study were between three to five years of age.

children were: (1) it permitted the mother substitute to remain at home with her own children, (2) it provided their children or themselves with companionship, (3) it was easier than other jobs, and (4) a general liking for children or those in their care.

Those who wished to be doing something else gave the following reasons: (1) feeling that some other job would be easier, (2) wanting a career, (3) wanting a change and to meet people, (4) a desire to make more money. Six gave reasons for preferring another job which seemed to indicate a negative attitude toward children.

Another indication of the mother substitutes' feelings about their work was provided by their responses to the question: "How long do you plan to work at taking care of children?" Forty said they would care for children as long as they could, and another fourteen said they would continue as long as they were needed by the employed mother. Two said they would continue until they had children of their own, and two others said they would work until eligible for social security. The work was viewed as temporary by twenty-one who expected to be doing something else within a year and as semi-permanent by three others who did not expect to continue longer than five more years. That a majority of the mother substitutes viewed their work as permanent or semi-permanent might be taken as evidence for the tentative judgment that the employed mother-mother substitute relationships were relatively stable and mutually satisfactory.

An indication of the employed mothers' confidence in the mother substitutes came from their responses to the question: "Do you give instructions on matters like discipline, feeding, naps, etc., to the baby sitter, or do you leave such matters to the judgment of the baby sitter?" Thirty-three per cent of the employed mothers reported giving no instructions regarding child care to the mother substitutes, fifty-one per cent generally left matters to the judgment of the mother substitutes, but gave "some" instructions at special times, as when the child was sick.

This matter was perceived differently by the mother substitutes of whom sixty-eight per cent said they received no instructions from the child's parents. There were twenty-eight per cent who said they received "some" instructions. Several of the mother substitutes said they were given instructions on child care when they first began work, but that they were discontinued after a short time.

While there were differences, these findings suggest that many of the employed mothers leave child care activities to the judgment of the mother substitutes.

There was little disagreement between the employed mothers and the mothers substitutes on procedures of child care. Eighty-seven per cent of the mother substitutes stated that there had been no disagreements with the parents on such problems. Disagreements on problems such as eating habits, sleeping, toilet training, discipline, and table manners had occurred between fifteen mother substitutes and parents.

An indication of the confidence that the employed mothers placed in the mother substitutes is provided by their responses to the question: "What worries, if any, do you have about how your child is getting along with the person who is caring for him?" Eighty-three per cent of the mothers said they had no worries about how the child was getting along, while five per cent expressed concern about the mother substitute's care of the child in regard to problems of feeding and discipline. Other things which concerned the employed mothers were: (1) the possibility that the child might want to be home with his mother, (2) the possibility of illness and accidents, (3) the child's behavior with the mother substitute, and (4) in two cases a fear that the youth of the mother substitute might lead to difficulties.

The number of children cared for at the same time by mother substitutes ranged from seventeen who cared for only one child to one who operated a nursery with eight or more children in attendance. Generally, the number of children in the care of mother substitutes was small, with seventy-three per cent caring for four or less children at the same time. In those cases in which the mother substitute came to the employed mother's home, twenty-one per cent did not perform any duties other than caring for the child or children. However, thirty-seven per cent were expected to work at light household duties such as washing dishes, vacuuming, and "keeping things tidy," twenty-six per cent were expected to do a combination of light and heavy household work, and twelve per cent performed extra household duties without being asked to do so by the employed mother. This suggests that the mother substitutes were not so busy with household duties or burdened with so many children that they found it difficult to give attention to the children in their care.

The employed mothers were asked to express their judgment of the mother substitute's attitude toward children. Seventy-seven per cent said that the mother substitute liked or loved children. Another twenty-two per cent believed the mother substitutes' attitude toward the children was good, but with qualifications, such as thinking the mother substitute was too strict, too passive, too lenient and indulgent with the children, or favored one child over another. One per cent said their mother substitutes appeared to be uninterested in and indifferent toward the child.

The employed mothers and mother substitutes were asked: "What, if anything, does (the child) do that annoys or irks you?" There was a significant difference which showed, on this measure, the mother substitutes to be more favorable in their attitudes toward the children in their care than were the employed mothers of the children (Table 13.1).

TABLE 13.1 *What Does the Child Do That Annoys or Irks You?**

ITEMS OF BEHAVIOR MENTIONED	EMPLOYED MOTHERS Per Cent	MOTHER SUBSTITUTES Per Cent	NUMBER
No items of behavior	8	39	40
One item of behavior	73	50	117
Two or more items of behavior	19	10	28
Total	100	99	185

* The relationship is statistically significant.

The employed mothers and mother substitutes were also asked: "Does he (the child) ever do anything which seems deliberately designed to get on your nerves?" There was no significant difference, which suggests that, on this measure, the attitudes of the employed mothers and their mother substitutes were similar (Table 13.2).

TABLE 13.2 *Does He Ever Do Anything Which Seems Deliberately Designed to Get on your Nerves?**

ITEMS OF BEHAVIOR MENTIONED	EMPLOYED MOTHERS Per Cent	MOTHER SUBSTITUTES Per Cent	NUMBER
No items of behavior	69	77	135
One or more items of behavior	30	24	50
Total	99	101	185

* The relationship is not statistically significant.

The mother substitutes and employed mothers were asked: "What things about him, if any, do you find enjoyable?" In answering this question no mother substitute said, "nothing," but higher percentages of employed mothers mentioned three or four items of behavior than did the mother substitutes (Table 13.3). There was very little difference between the employed mothers and mother substitutes who said, "everything" or gave some other all inclusive response.

The responses of the employed mothers and mother substitutes to the items discussed above show that, in general, the attitudes of the mother substitutes on these measures were just as favorable, and in some cases, more favorable toward the child than were those of the mothers. No mother substitute, for example, said she found nothing enjoyable about the child in her care, but two per cent of the employed mothers said that they found nothing enjoyable about their children.

TABLE 13.3 *What Things about Him, If Any, Do You Find Most Enjoyable?*

ITEMS OF BEHAVIOR MENTIONED	EMPLOYED MOTHERS Per Cent	MOTHER SUBSTITUTES Per Cent
No items of behavior	2	0
One item of behavior	19	39
Two items of behavior	35	40
Three items of behavior	20	10
Four or more items of behavior	12	2
"Everything" or some other inclusive response	11	9
No response	2	1
Total	101	101

That the mother substitute arrangements of the employed mothers had been relatively stable and permanent over time is indicated by the fact that seventy-one per cent of the children had been in the care of only one mother substitute while their mothers had been working. Twenty-nine per cent of the children had been in the care of three or more mother substitutes during the period of their mothers' employment, but of these only two had been in the care of over five mother substitutes.

Of the over 115 changes of mother substitutes, which had been made by the employed mothers in this sample, only fifteen had occurred because the employed mothers felt that the mother substitute's work was unsatisfactory or the circumstances of the situation were unfavorable for the child.

The most common reasons for changing were because the employed mother or mother substitute moved, the parents wanted a sitter closer to home, or the mother remained at home for a time with a new baby and hired a different mother substitute when she returned to work. There were changes because the mother substitute had been hired on a temporary basis and because the mother substitute felt the pay was inadequate.

The small number of changes as a result of dissatisfaction with the mother substitute's work suggests that generally the employed mothers are satisfied with the persons they select to care for their children. Usually the relationship is severed for reasons other than because the mothers believe the mother substitutes are damaging the children.

CONCLUSION

Many sociologists argue that family structure in the United States has changed greatly in the last seventy-five to one hundred years. Economic and social activities which were once a part of family life now take place in other institutional structures. Among the activities still remaining in the family is said to be the early socialization of children. Yet the entrance into the labor force of a large number of mothers of pre-school children clearly suggests further changes in the family in that a new agent of socialization, the mother substitute, has become a part of the family social structure.

It is too soon and there is too little evidence to be able to say what the consequences of this change will be. However, it is doubtful that an employed mother, in the time she has for her children, can completely alter the influence of the mother substitute who cares for the children most of the day (4, p. 213). The employed mothers interviewed in this study were at least implicitly aware of this. Their descriptions of the "ideal" mother substitute may have been similar to their views of the "ideal" mother, even a reflection of their views of themselves as mothers.

These data indicate that the employed mothers were fairly successful in finding and keeping the kind of mother substitute they wanted, and that the treatment of the children was not radically different from that which they would have received from their mothers, had they not been working.

It must be emphasized that these concluding comments are speculative and are based upon data limited in their generality. Less tentative conclusions await further research designed to provide empirical answers to problems raised here.

REFERENCES

1. Bowen, Jessie. "Child Care Arrangements of Experienced Working Mothers," *Smith College Studies in Social Work,* XIV (December, 1943), 259–60.
2. Gray, Barbara. "The Child Care Problems of Forty-Six Working Mothers," *Smith College Studies in Social Work,* XIV (December, 1943), 261–62.
3. Herzog, Elizabeth. *Children of Working Mothers.* United States Department of Health, Education, and Welfare, Children's Bureau Publication, No. 382. Washington, D.C.: Government Printing Office, 1960.
4. Jones, Eve. *Natural Child Rearing.* Glencoe, Ill.: Free Press, 1959.
5. Lajewski, Henry C. *Child Care Arrangements of Full-Time Working Mothers.* United States Department of Health, Education, and Welfare. Washington, D.C.: Government Printing Office, 1959.
6. Stolz, Lois Meek. "Effects of Maternal Employment on Children: Evidence from Research," *Child Development,* XXXI (December, 1960), 749–82.

Chapter Fourteen

Effects on Children: Summary and Discussion

LOIS WLADIS HOFFMAN

THE researches reported in Part II of this book constitute the bulk of those that deal specifically with the effects of maternal employment on the child. Other relevant studies—such as those which greatly overlap these in subject matter, unpublished doctoral dissertations, preliminary research reports, and studies having only incidental relevance to the topic—have not been included. Data from these studies, as well as the data from the foregoing chapters, will be considered here, however, since one of the major aims of the chapter is to describe our present state of knowledge about the effects of maternal employment on the child.

Well-designed research on this topic was remarkably slow in coming, perhaps because of a tendency on the part of social scientists to shy away from social problem areas at a time when social science was just beginning to come of age. Like the *nouveaux riches,* anxious to disassociate themselves totally from the social class they have just left, social science was anxious to disassociate itself from social reform. Perhaps the renewed interest by social scientists in social problem areas reflects the security of having their field accepted as a science. Now they dare to renew old friends. This new research on maternal employment, however, is very different from that which was done earlier (3, 12, 13, 15). It reflects the increased methodological sophistication of the social scientists: the employment of modern techniques of sampling and design, the use of control variables, and the examination of data for knowledge rather than for argument.

Research on maternal employment has increased greatly in recent years. One of the first studies in this area to utilize a modern approach with controls on important variables, notably socio-economic status and broken homes, was reported by Nye in 1952 (18). Nye reported, among other things, that adolescent children of part-time working mothers had better relationships with their parents than children of either full-time working mothers or mothers who did not work at all. The differences between the full-time working and non-working groups were found to be statistically non-significant. In the middle of 1957, the Gluecks' well-publicized article appeared which reported an extensive examination of the relationship between maternal employment and juvenile delinquency in a sample of lower-class boys (4). The over-all finding was that maternal employment was not related to juvenile delinquency; and where there was such a relationship (for the "occasionally" working mothers), the data seemed to indicate it was not the employment that was important but the existence of an erratic household. Maternal employment seemed to be a *dependent* variable, like delinquency, rather than an independent variable.

In these two studies, the fallacy of many previous notions about maternal employment was exposed. As we have pointed out in Chapter Two, the relationship between maternal employment and presumed dependent variables can be examined only when the researcher controls other factors. When these factors are controlled, the correlates of maternal employment seem to disappear. But our present research has also taught us something else: that maternal employment is not so potent a variable that it can be used without further specification and without examination of the data separately within different subgroups. None of the studies done thus far has found meaningful differences between the children of working mothers in general and the children of non-working mothers. The few significant differences that have been reported can probably be attributed to chance variations, since they constitute a small proportion of the tests made and have not been replicated. When differences are studied separately within certain subgroups, however, the children of working mothers are different from the children of non-working mothers. An examination of the various studies indicates that the following categories have been effectively used as the basis of these subgroups:

1. social class
2. full-time versus part-time maternal employment
3. age of child
4. sex of child
5. mother's attitude toward employment

Other categories are suggested—such as the adequacy of substitute supervision (Chapter Five), the duration of the mother's employment (Chapter Seven), and the rural-town-urban distinction (Chapter Twelve); and still others might be used—e.g., the particular hours the mother is away, the attitudes of the community, the response of the father, the nature of the mother's work. The former five categories, however, are the main ones that have already been found to be important, and they will be used in this chapter in the attempt to order and integrate the existing data on the effects of maternal employment on the child.

MATERNAL EMPLOYMENT, JUVENILE DELINQUENCY, AND SOCIAL CLASS

The studies of maternal employment and juvenile delinquency illustrate well how the examination of a relationship separately for different subgroups can highlight empirical relationships that are otherwise obscured. In the case of maternal employment and juvenile delinquency, subgroups based on social class are particularly useful in helping to clarify some apparent discrepancies in existing data.

The question of whether or not maternal employment is related to juvenile delinquency has aroused a great deal of interest. To obtain the answer we look to three studies, one by Nye (Chapter Ten), the previously mentioned study by Glueck and Glueck (4), and a study we will discuss shortly by Gold (5). In general, Nye's results suggest there is such a relationship, while Glueck and Glueck's suggest there is not.

To review briefly the relevant findings of the study by Glueck and Glueck, they found no difference between regularly employed working mothers and non-working mothers with respect to the delinquency of their sons, but they did find that women who are employed "occasionally" are more likely to have delinquent sons than either group. In their discussion

TABLE 14.1   *Father's Work Habits, Mother's Employment Status, and Delinquency*[1]

	WORK HABITS OF FATHER NOT GOOD					
	DELINQUENTS		NON-DELINQUENTS		DIFFERENCE	
	Number	*Per Cent*	*Number*	*Per Cent*	*Number*	*Per Cent*
Housewife	*139*	57.0	*81*	25.8	*58*	31.2
Regularly employed	*57*	62.6	*29*	39.2	*28*	23.4
Occasionally employed	*86*	73.5	*22*	31.9	*64*	41.6
Total	*282*	62.4	*132*	28.9	*150*	33.5

Note: The only significant difference reported in this table is between housewife and occasionally employed in the delinquent group. That is, the delinquent boys whose mothers are occasionally employed are significantly more likely to have fathers with poor work habits than are the delinquent boys whose mothers are housewives. (No statistical comparisons were made between delinquent and non-delinquent groups.)

[1] Data reproduced with permission from a study by Glueck and Glueck (4, p. 341, Table IX).

TABLE 14.2 *Father's Emotional State, Mother's Employment Status, and Delinquency*[1]

| | FATHER EMOTIONALLY DISTURBED | | | | | |
| | DELINQUENTS | | NON-DELINQUENTS | | DIFFERENCE | |
	Number	*Per Cent*	*Number*	*Per Cent*	*Number*	*Per Cent*
Housewife	*100*	38.0	*49*	14.7	*51*	23.3
Regularly employed	*48*	47.5	*25*	27.5	*23*	20.0
Occasionally employed	*71*	53.8	*16*	21.9	*55*	31.9
Total	*219*	44.2	*90*	18.1	*129*	26.1

Note: The only significant difference reported in this table is between housewife and occasionally employed in the delinquent group. That is, the delinquent boys whose mothers are occasionally employed are significantly more likely to have fathers who are emotionally disturbed than are the delinquent boys whose mothers are housewives. (No statistical comparisons were made between delinquent and non-delinquent groups.)

[1] Data reproduced with permission from a study by Glueck and Glueck (4, p. 343, Table XI).

they see the occasionally employed mother as working out of caprice to escape "household drudgery and parental responsibility." Their data indicate that the families in which the mother works "only occasionally" are indeed more unstable than those in which the mother works regularly or not at all, but it appears that their instability is due mainly to problems stemming from the father rather than rejection by the mother. Reproduced here are two tables from this study which show that families in which the mother is occasionally employed are more likely to have husbands with poor work habits and emotional disturbances (See Tables 14.1 and 14.2). These data provoke questions about why these women *resist* regular employment rather than why they *seek* occasional employment. The more parsimonious interpretation would be to assume that, since they have no steady income from their husbands, their employment is not an escape but is motivated by financial need and, further, that the delinquency of their sons results from an inadequate father model and a generally disorganized home life, rather than from maternal rejection.

In any case, the over-all pattern of their data indicates that no relationship exists between maternal employment and delinquency. This conclusion is further strengthened by the fact that their sample includes broken homes, a variable known to relate to both delinquency and maternal employment (see Table 14.3).

How can Nye's results be reconciled with those obtained by Glueck and Glueck? Nye found that the children of working mothers were more likely to be delinquent than the children of non-working mothers.

There are two essential differences between these studies: the socio-

TABLE 14.3 *Broken Homes, Mother's Employment Status and Delinquency*[1]

| | BOYS REARED IN BROKEN HOMES | | | | | |
| | DELINQUENTS | | NON-DELINQUENTS | | DIFFERENCE | |
	Number	Per Cent	Number	Per Cent	Number	Per Cent
Housewife	133	50.6	102	30.6	31	20.0
Regularly employed	74	73.2	41	45.1	33	28.1
Occasionally employed	92	69.7	26	35.6	66	34.1
Total	299	60.3	169	34.0	130	26.3

Note: The only significant differences reported in this table are between housewife and regularly employed in the delinquent group and between housewife and occasionally employed in the delinquent group. That is, the delinquent boys whose mothers are regularly employed and those whose mothers are occasionally employed are each significantly more likely to be from broken homes than are the delinquent boys whose mothers are housewives. (No statistical comparisons were made between delinquent and non-delinquent groups in the original table. However, the percentage of broken homes in the delinquent group, 60.3 per cent, is significantly greater than the percentage in the non-delinquent group, 34 per cent.)

[1] Data reproduced with permission from a study by Glueck and Glueck (4, p. 342, Table X).

economic composition of the samples and the measure of delinquency (questionnaire versus police contact). Focussing first on social class, the Glueck sample is entirely lower-class, whereas Nye's sample is predominantly middle-class, although it also includes subjects in the upper and lower classes. If we re-examine Nye's findings reported in Chapter Ten, Table 10.4, we discover that only in the "medium socio-economic status" group are the children of working mothers significantly more delinquent than the children of non-working mothers. Since the entire Glueck sample can be classified as "low socio-economic status" and since Nye's critical ratio for this group is only .4, far below the level required for statistical significance, the data in the two studies are not at all contradictory. They only appear to be contradictory because of the different socio-economic make-up of the samples.

To further demonstrate this point, and also to show that it was not the difference in the measures that produced the seeming discrepancy between the two investigations, we turn to a study by Gold (5). Gold's measure of delinquency is similar to the Gluecks', but since his sample is not exclusively lower class, he has been able to examine the maternal employment-juvenile delinquency relationship separately for each social class. These data are reported in Table 14.4. The group designated by Gold as "white collar" is the same as that designated by Nye as "medium socio-economic status,"[1] and his findings are the same: maternal employment and

[1] The coding used by Nye to ascertain social class is described elsewhere (19).

TABLE 14.4   *Social Class, Mother's Employment Status and Delinquency*[1]

SOCIAL CLASS	MOTHER'S EMPLOYMENT STATUS				
	NON-EMPLOYED	PART-TIME EMPLOYED	FULL-TIME EMPLOYED	NON-ASCER-TAINED	TOTAL
	Per Cent				Number
*White-Collar** Repeated					
delinquents	28	16	44	11	*18*
Non-delinquents	74	5	20	—	*19*
Skilled (Blue-Collar) Repeated					
delinquents	48	4	48	—	*23*
Non-delinquents	58	—	35	8	*26*
Unskilled (Blue-Collar) Repeated					
delinquents	54	5	37	5	*41*
Non-delinquents	50	7	41	2	*44*

* Non-employed vs. part-time or full-time is statistically significant (Sign test).
Note: Working wives of white-collar men are significantly more likely to have repeated delinquent sons than are non-working wives; this is not true in the other socio-economic categories.
[1] Data reproduced with permission from a study by Gold (5, p. 238, Table 40).

juvenile delinquency are related in the white-collar group, but not in the blue-collar groups. Thus, whether juvenile delinquency is measured by questionnaire or by police contact, the pattern is the same and the results of all three studies are completely consistent.

The relationship between maternal employment and juvenile delinquency provides an excellent example of the double function of using adequate controls in research. Early studies suggested a relationship between these two variables, but this relationship was shown to be a spurious one which appeared because of the failure to control on social class and broken homes. Once these controls were instituted, the relationship seemed to be lost. When these variables are controlled, however, not only by holding them constant but also by examining the data separately within each group, the relationship appears again, but only in the middle class. Thus, control variables may serve to highlight relationships that might otherwise be obscured, as well as to eliminate relationships that are spurious.

The empirical generalization that maternal employment and juvenile delinquency are positively related only in the middle class should be taken as a starting point for further research. Why does this relationship exist in one group and not the other? Juvenile delinquency, like maternal employment is a complex variable. Each includes several kinds of behaviors and the paths leading to each are different. Is the delinquency of middle-class children different from that of lower-class children? Are the causal factors different for each? Or is maternal employment different in the' two classes? The motivations for maternal employment, the nature of the work, and the attitudes of the mother and other members of the family may all be different in the two classes. New studies will have to consider these factors and specify further the independent and the dependent variables. Only then will it be possible to interpret adequately the relationship between maternal employment and delinquency.

FULL-TIME VERSUS PART-TIME EMPLOYMENT

There are three studies indicating that part-time employment by the mother has a positive effect on the adolescent child. Nye reports such a relationship in this volume (See Chapter Ten, Table 10.3) and also in an earlier study (18). Douvan (Chapter Eleven) also reports a similar pattern. Her interpretation is that part-time employment reflects choice by the mother rather than economic coercion; under these conditions, the mother is more likely to compensate for her employment and to provide a positive model. In contrast, she suggests that full-time employment, especially in the lower class, is involuntary; the mother feels burdened and harried, and she neglects and overburdens the child.

There is some support for Douvan's assumption that part-time employment involves choice. Motz (17) reports a study in which wives working full-time expressed a preference for a more traditional family role structure, i.e., one in which the man supports the family and the woman does the household tasks, thus suggesting that their employment status was involuntary. The part-time working women, on the other hand, preferred a more diffuse sex role distinction, indicating that they wanted to work. In this study all the respondents were wives of college students. Since their economic circumstances were so similar, it is unlikely that choice differentiated the two groups originally. It seems more likely that the working experience itself made the part-time working wives more positive in their attitude toward work. Whether or not part-time employment reflects choice at the start, the ultimate effects may be the same since the mother is less likely to feel as harassed as the full-time working mother, and she has more time and energy available for her role as mother.

If the part-time working mother does find her employment gratifying, the question is raised as to whether she feels guilty about working, as the results obtained by Hoffman (Chapter Six) might imply. Douvan, in comparing her results to Hoffman's, finds no evidence of guilt and attributes this to the fact that there is less public censure when mothers of adolescent children work than when the children are younger. It is also possible, however, that part-time employment is *less* conducive to guilt feelings than full-time employment simply because it interferes less with the mothering role.

One other advantage of part-time employment over full-time is that part-time employment is less likely to communicate to the family that the father is a failure. When the mother works only part-time, the father is usually thought of as the major breadwinner—if not currently, at least in the near future.

In addition to having the above advantages over full-time employment, part-time employment shares with full-time employment certain advantages over non-employment. For one thing, there is considerable evidence that the employed mother provides a more positive model for her daughter than the non-employed mother. The finding that daughters of working mothers are more likely to choose their mothers as models or to want to work themselves when they grow up has been reported with elementary school children (7)[2] and adolescents (20, Chapter Eleven). The working mother may have higher status in the family and represent to her daughter a person who has achieved success in areas that are, in some respects, more salient to a growing girl than household skills.

Furthermore, particularly for the mother of adolescents, working may provide an enrichment of her life that enables her to perform her maternal functions in a more wholesome manner. In Chapter Two and elsewhere (11) we have outlined some of the frustrations the non-working mother faces when her children are all in school and no longer absorb her full energy. She may feel that her most important functions are over and as a result be loathe to release her hold on the children.

Adolescence is a time when children need a comfortable balance between warmth and guidance on the one hand and autonomy on the other. The mother who has given her children warmth and guidance may find it difficult to give them the needed autonomy, particularly at that time when she feels her major contribution to the family will soon be over. Von Mering (16) has reported that professionally active mothers indicated in an interview that they stressed independence training, while mothers who were exclusively involved in mothering emphasized the protective functions and emotional security. Yarrow (24) also found working mothers were

---

[2] The elementary school children described in Chapter Six were asked "If you could be someone else right now, who would you like to be?" Daughters of working mothers were slightly but not significantly more likely to say "mother" than were their matched "non-working" counterparts.

more likely to stress independence training although she found this working–non-working difference only among non-college women (p. 20). Both studies, however, support the present view that the working mother is more likely to encourage independence in the child.

Thus, part-time employment may help the mother of an adolescent to move from the role of protector and nurturer to that of independence trainer, thus enabling both mother and child to adapt more easily to this period of transition before the child leaves the family for adult status. Part-time employment is a less abrupt change for both than full-time employment. And it may be less of a change psychologically for the mother than non-employment since it enables her to fill the void and retain a feeling of contribution to the family.

AGE OF CHILD

The positive relationship between part-time employment and parent-child adjustment discussed above has only been found with adolescents and as yet cannot be generalized to younger children.

It seems likely that the age of the child at the time the mother is employed would be an important factor in the relationship between maternal employment and child adjustment. Although there is no research evidence for this, most psychologists feel that the child needs his mother at home most during the first five years of life. Popular sentiment is also in accord with this view, and it is therefore likely that working mothers of very young children are more concerned and even more likely to feel guilty than the working mothers of older children.[3] This inference is supported by the fact that it is the employed mothers of preschool children who seem most motivated by economic necessity rather than choice (See Chapter One, Table 1.4 and Chapter Two, p. 21). It is also borne out by a comparison of the findings reported by Hoffman (Chapter Six) and Douvan (Chapter Eleven). Thus, when those mothers who seem to like working are considered, the study with younger children suggests that the mothers respond with guilt and over-reaction, while the study with adolescent children suggests that the mothers' response is a more appropriate compensation for the fact of employment. In addition, Douvan finds, as does Roy (Chapter Twelve), that working mothers' adolescent children help

---

[3] Feld (Chapter Twenty-Three) reports that mothers of preschool children report feeling inadequate as parents more than mothers of older children do, and although the N is small, the working mothers of preschool children report such feelings more than any other group (Table 23.4, p. 343).

more around the house. Hoffman, however, finds this relationship with elementary children only when the working mother dislikes her work. For the working mother group as a whole (10) and especially for those who like work (Chapter Six), the opposite tendency was observed: working mothers' children help less than non-working mothers' children.

Apart from the psychological importance of the mother's presence for the young child, it is apparent that the mother of young children will be particularly harassed by employment. The younger child needs a great deal of care and supervision, and sheer physical safety requires that a mother substitute be provided. The effects of maternal employment should therefore be more dramatic, possibly more detrimental, but certainly different when there are young children in the family.

The logical argument seems reasonable, but most of the data do not support it. Rouman (21) studied public school children who were referred for guidance. His data do suggest that the younger children were somewhat more adversely affected by maternal employment. However, in Chapters Four and Five of this volume, the comparisons between the preschool children of working and non-working mothers revealed few significant differences. The chapters by Powell (Nine) and Burchinal (Seven) are even more to the point. Both of these studies deal with children of different ages whose mothers worked at different points in their lives. Neither study reports any sizable or meaningfully patterned differences. The Burchinal study presents well-controlled data separately for boys and girls and separately for pre-adolescents and adolescents. The mother's work history during the child's lifetime is carefully delineated. The dependent variables are well chosen and adequately measured. Yet a careful examination of the tables confirms Burchinal's conclusions that maternal employment during the child's preschool years appears to have no observable effects at later ages.

The Burchinal data are also important for questions concerning the continuity of the mother's employment. For example, it has been suggested that the child whose mother has worked almost continuously since his birth will be less distressed than the child who has grown accustomed to having his mother at home before "losing" her to the occupational world.[4] Burchinal's breakdown of the mother's employment history is particularly well suited to such analyses, but again the results do not support the view that maternal work continuity is an important variable in predicting child adjustment. The only data that support this view do so indirectly. In Chapter

---

[4] This idea was first suggested to the author by Dr. Cynthia Deutsch in personal conversation.

Twenty-Four, Nye indicates that the longer the mother has been employed, the better she adjusts to the child. Presumably the mother's adjustment in turn affects the child.[5]

To summarize, no one study alone provides evidence for the expectation that maternal employment affects children differentially depending on their age. It is only when we compare different studies in which the subjects vary in age that we find such evidence. Thus the positive effects of part-time employment have been found only with adolescents; the guilt reaction on the part of working mothers appears to be more pronounced with younger children; and having the child help in household tasks has been more consistently observed with older children. In addition, as will be discussed later, withdrawal symptoms have been found in sons of working mothers, mainly among the younger children.[6] These findings are suggestive but the definitive study in this important area is yet to be done.

SEX OF CHILD

Ruth Hartley has observed that one experience common to all children of working mothers is that they "are exposed to a female parent who implements a social role not implemented by the female parents of other children" (8, p. 42). One implication of this point is that since the child learns sex roles from observations of his parents, maternal employment influences the child's concept of the female role. Further, and more importantly, since one of the earliest statuses assigned to the child is that of sex, maternal employment presumably affects the female child's concept of herself and of the behavior expected of her.

There is an impressive array of data to support this theory. Hartley's own findings indicate that daughters of working mothers, in comparison to daughters of non-working mothers, are more likely to say that *both* men and women typically engage in each of several specified adult activities and that women *liked* to engage in various household, work, and recreational activ-

---

[5] The findings of the study by Glueck and Glueck (4) might be interpreted to mean that continuous employment has certain advantages over "occasional employment," but the extreme instability of the families included in the group classified as "occasionally employed" makes it impossible to ascertain the effects of the employment pattern per se.

[6] The study by Rouman (21) is one which suggests that withdrawal symptoms in the child are associated with maternal employment. Unfortunately this study does not indicate whether or not this association holds for both boys and girls and for both, younger and older children. However, since his sample is three-fourths male and his working mother group includes more younger children, it is likely that this relationship does particularly characterize the younger boys. The other studies, reported in Chapters Four and Six, studied only younger children and found the relationship only for boys.

ities. They were also more likely to see women as less restricted to their homes (8, p. 43). Both Mathews (15) and Duvall (2) found that children of working mothers, boys and girls, were more likely to approve of maternal employment than children of non-working mothers.

Hartley has also reported (7) that the daughters of working mothers are more likely to want to work themselves when they are older and when they have their own children; Peterson (20) reports the same findings with adolescent girls; and Douvan (Chapter Eleven) and Roy (Chapter Twelve) report that adolescent daughters of working mothers are, in fact, more likely to be currently employed. Douvan, who also stresses the modeling theory as the important link between the mother's employment status and the child's personality, finds that the daughters of working mothers score low on an index of "traditional femininity."

Another relevant finding reported by Douvan indicates that adolescent daughters of working mothers are more likely to name their mothers as the person they most admire. Girls want to do well in activities outside the home —in school, in recreational activities, and in social relations. The traditional role of the woman, the role communicated by the non-working mother, is not as consistent with these values as is the role communicated by the working mother, and, therefore, is less likely to represent the skills and qualities desired by the daughter. Thus, not only is the role represented by the working mother different in context than the role represented by the non-working mother, but the motivation to model the working mother appears to be stronger.

When the effects of maternal employment are considered in this light, it is clear that they must be different for boys and girls. For one thing, although maternal employment might affect all children's concepts of the woman's role, it should affect only the girls' self-concept—*unless the mother's working also reflects something about the father*. In Chapter Eleven, the finding is reported that lower-class boys whose mothers work full-time are *least* likely to name their father as the person they most admire. It is in such families that the mother's employment is most apt to reflect the fact, or the belief, that the father is an economic failure. Maternal employment even in these families does not necessarily *cause* the son to lose esteem for the father but may simply reflect or emphasize the conditions that do so.

To summarize thus far, for girls, maternal employment may contribute to a greater admiration of the mother, a concept of the female role which includes less restriction and a wider range of activities, and a self-concept which incorporates these aspects of the female role. For boys, maternal employment might influence their concept of the female role, but what the effects will be on their attitudes toward their father and themselves depends very much on the circumstances surrounding the mother's employment. This orientation may help in the interpretation of the research findings indicating that maternal employment has different effects on girls than on boys.

Relevant to this point are the findings reported in Chapter Four. This study by Seigel, Stolz, Hitchcock, and Adamson is a carefully controlled and well-executed study, and the paucity of significant relationships found justi-fies the authors' conclusions that there appear to be no differences between the children of working and non-working mothers. On the other hand, an examination of the findings (summarized in Table 4.2) reveals some inter-esting trends which are only briefly discussed. The sex differences are striking. The young sons of working mothers appear to be generally more dependent; they are more obedient, less self-reliant, less sociable, and more likely to seek succorance from adults. The young daughters, on the other hand, appear to be aggressive, dominant, disobedient, and independent. Despite the lack of statistical significance, the pattern of the findings presents a provocative picture, particularly since there are other studies which also suggest that the sons of working mothers are withdrawn and overly dependent. For example, in Chapter Six, an unexpected finding was that the sons of working mothers were more dependent on the teacher than the matched sons of non-working mothers. (This was the only finding in the study where differences in direc-tion made it impossible to combine boys and girls into one group.) Further-more, a study by Rouman, already mentioned, found that the children of working mothers were more likely to be sent to the guidance department for withdrawal problems than for any other kind of problem. While Rouman did not separate his subjects by sex, he did report that three quarters of his sample were boys, so it is likely that this finding applies mainly to boys.

If the above pattern of relationships should eventually be confirmed, it would not necessarily mean that the father in working mother families provides a weak model for boys. Dependency and withdrawal are symptoms associated with maternal deprivation, and it is possible that these sex dif-ferences in the effects of maternal employment are more complex than a simple modeling theory would suggest. It may be, for example, that any detrimental effects that maternal employment might exert on the child are counterbalanced for girls by the more positive model presented by the work-ing mother. This suggests that maternal employment has a more negative effect on boys than on girls, an interpretation which receives some support from a study by Hand (6) using elementary school children. He found that the sons of working mothers were more likely to fall in the group classified as maladjusted, while the daughters were more likely to fall in the group classified as well-adjusted. These results, however, were not statistically significant.

The confusing picture presented by the various studies dealing with maternal employment and the child's academic achievement might possibly be clarified if researchers made it a rule to analyze their data separately by sex. In summarizing some of these studies Stolz (23) attempted to reconcile the finding by Hoffman (Chapter Six) that maternal employment relates negatively to school performance and I.Q. with the findings by Nye (Chapter Ten) and Hitchcock (9) that there is no significant relationship between these variables. Stolz interpreted this discrepancy by pointing out that the Hoffman study used teacher ratings which might be biased against the children of employed mothers. This explanation is inadequate, however; first, because there is no evidence that this is a salient teacher prejudice; second, because the teachers did not know the researchers were interested in maternal employment; and third, because it does not explain why this presumed prejudice did not affect the other variables rated by teachers or why the more objective I.Q. scores were also lower for the children of the working mothers who liked work.

To add to the confusion, additional studies not considered by Stolz have also found inconsistent results. Thus, Burchinal (Chapter Seven) found his eleventh grade sons of working mothers to have significantly lower school grades even after socio-economic level was controlled; Nolan (Chapter Eight) found differences which favor the children of working mothers; and Roy (Chapter Twelve) found differences which favor the daughters of working mothers in his rural sample and the children of the non-working mothers in his town sample; and Powell (Chapter Nine) found the children of working mothers to have higher achievement *motives*.

These findings might be capable of order if the results were reported separately by sex. In light of the above discussion about sex differences, a reasonable hypothesis would be that maternal employment is negatively related to achievement for boys, but for girls there might be no relationship or even a positive one. Four of the studies reported in this section, Chapters Six (Hoffman), Eight (Nolan), Nine (Powell), and Ten (Nye), have not reported their data separately for each sex, and therefore it is impossible to ascertain the extent to which one sex is carrying the direction and significance level of the relationship. In most studies data are examined separately by sex and combined only if the directions are the same. However, when both sexes are combined, the significance or non-significance of the relationship may still be carried more by one sex group than the other; and the results in different studies can be compared accurately only when the samples are similar or made so by subgroup analysis. While this section raises sex as the basis for such subgroup comparisons, other bases are possible, and the Roy data (Chapter Twelve) specifically indicate the usefulness of the town-rural distinction. Thus, it is possible that if all of these conflicting studies reported data separately for each relevant subgroup, the relationship between maternal employment and academic achievement would be the same across studies but different within the different subgroups.

MOTHER'S ATTITUDE TOWARD EMPLOYMENT

Two of the chapters in this section, Six and Eleven, were concerned with the mother's attitude toward employment as a factor which affects the impact of maternal employment on the child. In Chapter Six, the mother's attitude was measured directly; in Chapter Eleven, it was inferred from a combination of social class position and whether the mother's employment was full- or part-time. Both studies indicate that the mother's attitude is an important variable to be considered, and both suggest similar results. When the mother's employment is gratifying to her, the mother-child relationship is a warm one; with the younger children it seems to be too warm, suggesting the possibility of a guilt reaction on the part of the mother. When the mother's employment is not satisfying, the mother-child relationship is almost the opposite. There seems to be less interaction and there are also indications that the child may be heavily burdened with household tasks. The fact that working–non-working differences are so divergent when the mother's attitude is considered indicates the fruitfulness of this approach.

Other social scientists have also come to view the working mother's attitude as an important variable. Siegel (22), in a theoretical paper, and Yarrow (24), in a preliminary research report, have expressed an interest in subdividing both the working mothers and the non-working mothers according to their satisfactions in their respective roles. Yarrow's data are based on a sample of 100 middle- and upper-middle-class, white, intact families with at least one child in elementary school. The mothers were first divided into four groups: working mothers who preferred to work, working mothers who preferred not to work, non-working mothers who preferred to work, and non-working mothers who preferred not to work. These groups were compared in various combinations with respect to their positions on a " 'good' mothering scale." Actually few of the comparisons were significant, and the only difference worthy of note is that the dissatisfied non-working mothers scored predominantly at the low end of the scale. Mothers were also grouped according to the personal goals that were being met by working or not working. Four groups were again set up: mothers working for self-fulfillment, mothers working for family benefits, non-working mothers who saw mothering as a duty, non-working mothers who loved mothering. Several aspects of mothering behavior were considered, but all differences reported were *within* employment categories. Whether these data did not highlight any working–non-working differences or whether they were not examined for this purpose, is not clear from the report.

The third basis for subgroup analysis used by Yarrow is the mother's education. This variable clearly highlighted working–non-working differences which were otherwise obscured. Working–non-working comparisons among college women indicated that the working women were less sensitive to their children's needs but that both they and their husbands engaged in more planned activities with their children. These differences were not found among non-college women. In the non-college group, on the other hand, the working women were more likely than the non-working women to stress independence training and to give over to their husbands the disciplining of the child. Neither of these differences was found for the college group.

Yarrow's findings are preliminary and the report is therefore too incomplete for us to attempt to reconcile certain inconsistencies. It would appear, for example, that the failure to find employed college women stressing independence training is inconsistent with the results reported by von Mering (16). It is also difficult to understand the broader conceptual significance that education has in her study. Since the sample is relatively homogeneous, it presumably does not represent social class. It might represent achievement strivings, as Yarrow assumes, or some other attitude or personality trait of the mother; it might even represent simply being better informed. In any case, her data do indicate the value of analyzing working–non-working differences separately for different subgroups based on the mothers' individual characteristics.[7]

Another empirical study which considers the mother's attitude toward work is reported by Peterson (20). He used as his major dependent variables the mother's "interest" and "control" as perceived by the adolescent daughter. "Interest" is defined as the number of the daughter's "behavioral areas" in which the mother is interested. "Control" refers to the extent to which the mother attempts to control her daughter's behavior according to some predetermined standard of conduct. Peterson found no relationship between the mother's employment status and either of these variables. However, he also tested to see whether several maternal attitude variables related to interest and control. Unfortunately, from the standpoint of this chapter, he did not introduce the attitude variables as test variables, i.e., he did not use them as the basis for subgroups within which employment differences were examined. They were employed only as independent variables. For the total group, ignoring the mother's employment status, Peterson tested to see whether the mother's attitude toward the feminine role, the extent of her non-familial

---

[7] This discussion of Yarrow's data is based on a report presented at the 1961 meeting of the Society for Research in Child Development (24). A revision of this report has since been published (25).

interests, and her emphasis on children as the major aspect of marriage were related to interest and control. Within the employed group only, he tested to see whether motivations for employment, enjoyment of work, and femininity of the specific occupation were related to the same two dependent variables. Within the non-employed group only, he tested to see whether the willingness to go to work in the future was related to interest or control. The results of these tests were inconclusive since very few significant differences were found and no coherent pattern emerged.

INTERPRETATION OF RESULTS BASED ON SUBGROUP ANALYSIS

We have, in essence, suggested that the relationship between maternal employment and some child-relevant variable, such as mothering behavior or a characteristic of the child, be re-examined within subgroups. The composition of the subgroups depends on a third variable believed to be of possible importance in the original relationship. We have suggested several such variables: social class, full-time versus part-time employment, age of child, sex of child, and mother's attitude toward work. Variables used in the manner suggested here are referred to as "test variables" by Lazarsfeld (14), who discusses the interpretation of this kind of analysis in some detail. Lazarsfeld points out that when test variables are introduced they may have any of the following statistical effects: the relationships obtained in each subgroup may be greater than the original one; they may all be smaller than the original one; the relationship in one subgroup may be greater while the relationship in another is smaller; and, finally, counter trends which were concealed in the original findings may be brought to light. By careful consideration of what the test variable does to the original relationship and what the time sequence of the three variables probably is, the researcher can determine the theoretical role of this third variable, the test variable.

Lazarsfeld describes four test variable patterns. Two of these, one in which the test variable is a "condition" and the other in which it is a "contingency," specify the circumstances under which the original relationship holds true more strongly. The two differ in time sequence: the "condition" exists, in the case of maternal employment, prior to the employment and influences the effects that employment will have. The mother's need for achievement might be such a variable. The "contingency" variable is one that intervenes between the independent and dependent variables. Job satisfaction, as used in Chapter Six, is a contingency variable. Had guilt over working been measured in that study, it also would have been a contingency variable.

The third type Lazarsfeld calls an "explanation." This refers to the discovery that the original relationship obtained between the independent and dependent variables was spurious. In the case of maternal employment and juvenile delinquency, father-absence might be thought of as an example of this type of test variable. Father-absence precedes (and relates to) both employment and delinquency. If the relationship between maternal employment and delinquency were examined separately for families having fathers and families not having fathers and the original relationship were lost in both cases, then father-absence would be, in Lazarsfeld's terms, an "explanation."

For the fourth type Lazarsfeld uses the term "interpretation." This too applies where the original relationship disappears in each subgroup analysis, but here, the test variable intervenes between the independent and dependent variables. The number of hours the mother is away while the child is at home might be seen as an example of an "interpretation." Suppose it were found that the number of hours the mother is away related to the child variable in the same way, whether or not the mother worked, and also that maternal employment did not relate to the child variable when the number of hours the mother is away was held constant. We would then have to conclude that it was not the mother's working per se which had the effect, but the sheer time she spent away from home. Her employment becomes, in a sense, irrelevant if the effect is the same whether she works or spends the same amount of time playing bridge or in charitable activities. Its only relevance is as one cause of the mother's absence from home; i.e., other things equal, employed mothers are away longer than non-employed ones.[8]

The Lazarsfeld presentation, which we have oversimplified for clarity, can be very helpful in formalizing the method of introducing test variables and making appropriate interpretations, but the researcher's job does not end here. The introduction of test variables, which is essentially what has been referred to in this paper as subgroup analysis, clarifies the relationship between the variables. But in so doing, it may also raise new and more sophisticated questions than could have been anticipated. An example is the Gold finding presented in Table 14.4, which throws light on the maternal employment-delinquency relationship by suggesting that social class is a "condition" of this relationship. The new challenge raised by this finding is that of understanding the processes by which this condition operates. Why are maternal employment and juvenile delinquency related in the middle class and not in the lower class? Only further research and the introduction of new test variables can answer this provocative question.

An additional problem not covered in the Lazarsfeld formulation is that of time sequence. For expediting his discussion, Lazarsfeld assumes the time

---

[8] This example, as all of the others in this section except for the example from Chapter Six, is not taken from any empirical research. Whether these examples are really the type of test variables suggested here depends ultimately on research findings.

sequence of the variables is known. This is often the case simply by reasoning. For example, if the father's occupation is used as the index of social class, it is reasonable to assume .that class precedes maternal employment. This assumption would obviously not be sound, however, if total family income were used as the index of class. Often, the time sequence is much more difficult to ascertain. Consider mother's job satisfaction, for example, which was mentioned earlier as intervening between the mother's employment and her child-rearing behavior. This sequence may appear to be a safe assumption since one cannot be satisfied with a job before one has it and since it seems more reasonable to suppose that job attitudes affect child-rearing practices than the reverse. Yet this assumption can be challenged. For example, the possibility is raised in Chapter Six that the attitude toward work and the attitude toward the child might both result from some characteristic predisposition of the mother, and thus the real variable that job attitude stands for (e.g., a positive outlook on life) might be prior to both maternal employment and child-rearing behavior. A second such consideration is the possibility that the mother's job attitude might be partly influenced by the kind of child she has. Non-assertive children, for example, are easier to cope with than rebellious children; the mothers who like work might therefore do so because they have non-assertive children and this makes the work situation less stressful. In this case, maternal employment, child behavior—and possibly child-rearing behavior—might all be prior to job attitude.

Such problems of time sequence (actually they are questions of cause and effect) continually plague the social science researcher. Fortunately, there are ways of making these problems less serious. One is to examine the logic of the argument more carefully in the light of all the data available. This was done in Chapter Six by the indication that the mother's characteristic predisposition could not account for the findings since it was not consistent with all the data—i.e., *both* groups of working mother children showed signs of maladjustment. To answer the second point, that work attitude might be a function of the child's personality, additional data were presented to show that work attitude depended on the kind of job the mother held. Another way of handling questions of time sequence, then, is by tying the variable in question to other aspects of the situation which are more sharply fixed with respect to sequence. Often, however, as in this example, some doubt remains, and the final demonstration awaits further research which focuses on these issues.

THE NEGLECTED POPULATION

To eliminate extraneous variables, only intact, white families have usually been studied. Certainly, for most research purposes the non-intact family and the Negro family should be studied separately, but the fact is, they are not being studied at all. When we consider that 19 per cent of the full-time working mothers with children under twelve are not living with their husbands, and that 14 per cent of the full-time working mothers with children under twelve are non-white (1, p. 7), we see that two large segments of the working mother population have been ignored.

An exception is the Peterson study already mentioned (20). Although the major part of Peterson's report deals with intact families, he does analyze some of the data for the non-intact families. In his sample of intact families he found no working–non-working differences with respect to his two dependent variables, interest and control, but among his non-intact families, working mothers were significantly lower than non-working on control and slightly higher on interest. It is difficult to evaluate these findings or even compare them with Peterson's own data on intact families, because he did not control on social class in his analyses of the non-intact family. Furthermore, his definition of a non-intact family[9] is broad, including all families in which the child does not live with both *biological* parents. Nye (Chapter Ten) also analyzes his data separately for the non-intact families, and he does differentiate those in which the mother has remarried from those in which there is no father at all. In the families without fathers, however, Nye found so few non-working mothers that he was unable to make meaningful working–non-working comparisons.

We have found no studies on the effects of maternal employment on the child among Negroes. It seems reasonable to assume that the effects of maternal employment for Negroes are different from the effects for whites. For one thing, maternal employment has a longer history among Negroes and, according to a theory outlined by Siegel (22), this should mean that it exerts less stress. A related difference is that among Negroes, because of racial discrimination, males have often been more handicapped than females in obtaining work; the women have at least had domestic employment open to them. This situation should also contribute to the meaning that maternal employment has in the family. For example, even when the mother works out of economic necessity, it should be less likely to symbolize the father's *personal* failure. In addition, there are Negro-white differences in family structure, subjective (as well as objective) social class, child-rearing patterns, and other relevant behaviors and attitudes. It is because of these differences that researchers have omitted Negroes from the maternal employment studies which focus on whites, but these very differences make them an important group to study for theoretical purposes. The sheer numbers of Negro working mothers make them a socially important group to study.

---

[9] Peterson uses the term "broken family."

IMPLICATIONS

Until recently the general view was that maternal employment had a great many effects on the child—all of them bad. Since 1952, however, research findings have challenged this view. But the pendulum has perhaps swung too far in the opposite direction and the new outlook seems to be that maternal employment has no effects at all. Throughout this chapter there has been an underlying assumption that maternal employment does affect the child. The effects may be good, bad, or incapable of evaluation; and they may depend on a multitude of other considerations; but until considerably more research is done, we are not prepared to concede that maternal employment has no effects. This orientation has led us to try in this chapter to make some order out of current research findings and to suggest an approach for future work.

We have not tried to summarize all of the relevant findings. The preceding chapters in this section will provide the reader with a rather thorough knowledge of the current data, and we have supplemented this with summaries here of studies which are not reported separately.[10] On the whole, however, findings have been discussed mainly as illustrations of the major point of this chapter. This is that maternal employment by itself is too broad a concept to be used fruitfully in parent-child studies and that, in future work, test variables should be introduced to make this concept more psychologically meaningful.

Because of our focus on the independent variable, maternal employment, we have given little attention to the dependent variables chosen for study, but a similar point could be made about them. That is, they are often not conceptualized in the most theoretically meaningful way. Perhaps because of the social-problem aspects of maternal employment, the dependent variables often seem to have been selected because of their evaluative properties rather than their theoretical relevance. Furthermore, even the evaluation may be inaccurate because of the failure to take into account certain properties of these variables. For example, most child development variables are curvilinear in their implications for health. Negative evaluations may therefore be more appropriate when the behavior or attitude is extreme in *either* direction. The high point on a scale of maternal control may be overcontrol; the low point on a scale of child aggressiveness may be timidity.

Maternal employment is an area rich in both theoretical significance and importance as a social problem. These qualities are intimately linked. Useful social action requires that we understand precisely what aspects of

---

[10] The article by Lois Meek Stolz (23), referred to elsewhere in this chapter, is a scholarly summary of research findings on the effects of maternal employment on the child.

maternal employment are important, what its specific effects on the child are, and the process by means of which these effects take place. The aim of this chapter is to stimulate research that will help us achieve this state of knowledge.

REFERENCES

1. *Child Care Arrangements of Full-time Working Mothers.* United States Department of Health, Education, and Welfare, Children's Bureau, Publication No. 378. Washington, D.C.: Government Printing Office, 1959.

2. Duvall, Elise B. "Conceptions of Mother Roles by Five and Six Year Old Children of Working and Non-Working Mothers." Unpublished Ph.D. dissertation, Florida State University, 1955.

3. Essig, Mary, and Morgan, D. H. "Adjustment of Adolescent Daughters of Employed Mothers to Family Life, *Journal of Educational Psychology,* XXXVII (April, 1946), 219–33.

4. Glueck, Sheldon, and Glueck, Eleanor. "Working Mothers and Delinquency," *Mental Hygiene,* XLI (July, 1957), 327–52.

5. Gold, M. *A Social-Psychology of Delinquent Boys.* Ann Arbor, Mich.: Institute for Social Research, 1961.

6. Hand, Horace. "Working Mothers and Maladjusted Children," *Journal of Educational Sociology,* XXX (January, 1957), 245–46.

7. Hartley, Ruth E. "Children's Concepts of Male and Female Roles," *Merrill-Palmer Quarterly,* VI (January, 1959–60), 83–91.

8. ————. "What Aspects of Child Behavior Should be Studied in Relation to Maternal Employment?" In Alberta Engvall Siegel, ed. *Research Issues Related to the Effects of Maternal Employment on Children.* University Park, Penna.: Social Science Research Center, 1961, pp. 41–50.

9. Hitchcock, Ethel Alice. "Relation of Maternal Employment to School Behavior and Achievement of Intermediate Grade Boys." Unpublished manuscript, 1959.

10. Hoffman, Lois Wladis. "Some Effects of the Employment of Mothers on Family Structure." Unpublished Ph.D. dissertation, University of Michigan, 1958, available on microfilm.

11. ———— and Wyatt, F. "Social Change and Motivations for Having Larger Families: Some Theoretical Considerations," *Merrill-Palmer Quarterly,* VI (July, 1960), 235–44.

12. Kasmar, Ruth A. "Employed Mothers of Children in the A.D.C. Program; Cook County Bureau of Public Welfare," *Social Service Review,* XIX (March, 1945), 96–110.

13. LaFollette, Cecile Tipton. *A Study of the Problems of 652 Gainfully*

Employed Married Women Homemakers. New York: Teachers College, Columbia University, 1934.

14. Lazarsfeld, Paul F. "Interpretation of Statistical Relations as a Research Operation." In Paul F. Lazarsfeld and Morris Rosenberg, eds. *The Language of Social Research.* Glencoe, Ill.: Free Press, 1955, pp. 115–25.

15. Mathews, Selma M. "The Effects of Mothers' Out-of-Home Employment upon Children's Ideas and Attitudes," *Journal of Applied Psychology,* XVIII (February, 1934), 116–36.

16. Mering, Faye Higier von. "Professional and Non-Professional Women as Mothers," *Journal of Social Psychology,* XLII (August, 1955), 21–34.

17. Motz, Annabelle Bender. "Conceptions of Marital Roles by Status Groups," *Marriage and Family Living,* XII (Fall, 1950), 136–62.

18. Nye, F. Ivan. "Adolescent-Parent Adjustment: Age, Sex, Sibling Number, Broken Homes, and Employed Mothers as Variables," *Marriage and Family Living,* XIV (November, 1952), 327–32.

19. ————. *Family Relationships and Delinquent Behavior.* New York: John Wiley, 1958.

20. Peterson, E. T. "The Impact of Maternal Employment on the Mother-Daughter Relationship and on the Daughter's Role Orientation." Unpublished Ph.D. dissertation, University of Michigan, 1958, available on microfilm.

21. Rouman, J. "School Children's Problems as Related to Parental Factors," *Journal of Educational Research,* L (October, 1956), 105–12.

22. Siegel, Alberta Engvall. "Characteristics of the Mother Related to the Impact of Maternal Employment or Non-Employment." In Alberta Engvall Siegel, ed. *Research Issues Related to the Effects of Maternal Employment on Children.* University Park, Penna.: Social Science Research Center, 1961, pp. 29–36.

23. Stolz, Lois Meek. "Effects of Maternal Employment on Children: Evidence from Research," *Child Development,* XXXI (December, 1960), 749–82.

24. Yarrow, Marian Radke. "Changes in Family Functioning as Intermediary Effects of Maternal Employment. In Alberta Engvall Siegel, ed. *Research Issues Related to the Effects of Maternal Employment on Children.* University Park, Penna.: Social Science Research Center, 1961, pp. 14–24.

25. ————. "Maternal Employment and Child Rearing," *Children,* VIII, (November-December, 1961), 223–28.

Part III

THE HUSBAND-WIFE RELATIONSHIP

Chapter Fifteen

Parental Power Relations and the Division of Household Tasks*

LOIS WLADIS HOFFMAN

THE employment of mothers may be seen as part of a general trend toward a decrease in the differentiation of sex roles. Other variables that might be included in this trend are: the increased participation of fathers in routine household tasks, a change in power relations from male dominance toward husband-wife equality, and corresponding changes in ideology about sex roles in the family.

Each of these variables can be seen as mutually reinforcing. For example, the mother's outside employment may exert a pressure toward the father's increased participation in household tasks. The increased participation of the father, on the other hand, makes the mother's employment more feasible by lessening the demands of her conventional homemaking role. In addition, the holding of a favorable ideology would seem to contribute to the occurrence of both events; while their occurrence, for whatever reason, should stimulate the development of a legitimizing ideology.

Husband-wife power relations might be similarly interrelated. Thus, it seems likely that employment would increase a woman's power vis-à-vis her husband because of the socially defined importance of the monetary con-

* Reprinted from *Marriage and Family Living,* XXII (February, 1960), 27–35, by permission of the publisher. This paper is based on a doctoral dissertation submitted to the University of Michigan in 1958. The data were collected as part of a larger project supported by the Foundation's Fund for Research in Psychiatry and supplemented by a grant from the National Institute of Mental Health. Some of the analyses reported here were made possible by a grant from the Horace H. Rackham Graduate Student Research Fund.

tribution; while a woman who already had high power would be more likely to go to work because of greater motivation, greater control over her own decisions, and greater success in obtaining her husband's participation in household tasks. Finally, the endorsement or rejection of a male dominance ideology might affect both the woman's employment and her power and be affected by each of these variables in turn.

These four variables, then, might be seen as a system in which a change in one effects change in the others. However, at any given time, and particularly in periods of rapid social change, they may exert counterpressures and work against each other, since each can be separately affected by variables external to the system. For example, a wife may be forced to seek employment even though her husband is dominant, takes no part in household tasks, and there is ideological support for both these conditions. While it is true that such a family might resist mother employment longer than other families, the monetary advantages might eventually override this resistance. What happens in this situation? Does the mother's employment exert changes in the family structure despite the existing ideology, or must the ideology be supportive for employment to have such an effect? This problem is the focus of the present study.

Treating the mother's employment as the independent variable, this study deals with its effects on the husband's and wife's household participation and on the husband-wife power relationship *when the relevant ideologies are held constant.* The question essentially is this: is the mother's employment, unabetted by ideology, sufficient to induce these changes in family structure? The specific hypotheses are as follows:

Hypothesis 1. The employment of the mother outside the home will function to decrease her participation in household tasks and to increase that of her husband.

Hypothesis 2. The employment of the mother outside the home will function to decrease her decision-making in household tasks (activity control) and to increase that of her husband.

Hypothesis 3. The employment of the mother outside the home will function to increase her power vis-à-vis her husband.

The assumption behind the first hypothesis is simply that the stress of working, in terms of the time and effort it takes on the part of the mother, makes it necessary for the husband to take over some of her household tasks in order to maintain the smooth functioning of the household. Of the three hypotheses, this one would appear to be the most mechanical and direct in nature.

The second hypothesis is closely related to the first. Most houshold decisions are rather trivial and are usually made routinely by the person who performs the activity in question, e.g., what will be made for supper is apt to be decided by the person who cooks. It follows that if the mother's employment brings about a decrease in her household task participation and an increase in that of her husband (as stated in Hypothesis 1), there should be corresponding changes in household decision-making or activity control. Further, it seems likely that the working mother would be more willing to relinquish her activity control, not only in order to gain her husband's help with tasks, but also because of the alternative gratification she may receive from having one sphere, her outside job, which is her own.

The third hypothesis deals with the power aspect of the husband-wife relationship. Power is quite different from activity control. Whereas the latter concerns the sheer volume of decisions made, most of which are of relatively little concern to other persons, power involves decisions which may have important effects on others. As a simple approximation of "importance," power will be considered here as the extent to which one person decides over the other's behavior. The prediction that the mother's employment will function to increase her power vis-à-vis her husband is based on three assumptions: (a) money is an important basis of power so that the control of money leads to the possession of power; (b) a person has more control over the money he earns himself than other persons have; (c) the role of wage-earner in our society carries with it greater opportunities for developing feelings of achievement, competence, and contribution than does the role of housewife. The theory is that by her employment the mother obtains control of a certain amount of money, thus gaining greater control over financial decisions. This financial control may also enable her to gain more extensive familial power. Furthermore, because she is working and earning money, she gains a new concept of her own worth and thus becomes more assertive. In short, both the husband and the wife are more likely to accept the legitimacy of the working woman's claim to power.

It can be seen that the hypothesis regarding power is more complex than the others since it involves intervening ideational processes between the mother's employment and the dependent variable.

METHOD

SAMPLE

The total sample included 324 intact families with at least one child in the third through sixth grades of three elementary schools in Detroit, Michigan. The schools were selected so that the sample drawn would represent Detroit socio-economically, but would be relatively homogeneous with respect to ethnic factors, excluding Negroes and families living in neighborhoods associated with particuar ethnic groups.

Within this sample were 89 families with working mothers and 89 families with non-working mothers who were closely matched to them with respect to those characteristics, both ideological and situational, which seemed most likely to relate to the independent and dependent variables. *The matched sample was used to test the three hypotheses presented earlier;* i.e., scores obtained by the "working" families on the dependent variables were compared with those obtained by the matched "non-working" families.

The total sample of 324 families was used initially to assess the importance of the ideology controls. It was then kept in reserve for purposes of making *post hoc* analyses should the hypotheses not be confirmed, and it therefore become necessary to ascertain which of the matching controls were responsible for nullifying relationships.

CONTROL ON IDEOLOGY

Two ideological variables were used in matching the respondents: ·
1. Mother's attitude about the extent to which men should not participate in household tasks—to be called *traditional sex role ideology.*
2. Mother's attitude about the extent to which men should hold superordinate positions over women—to be called *male dominance ideology.*

Endorsement of the traditional sex role and male dominance ideologies was expected to relate to low household participation by the husband and to husband dominance, respectively. Such endorsement was also expected to be negatively related to the mother's employment as discussed earlier; i.e., the ideologies and the behavioral patterns they imply would operate against her employment. Therefore, if these ideologies were not controlled, any relationship found between mother employment and family structure might be the spurious result of ideology and the corresponding behavior patterns existing before employment, instead of reflecting a true effect of employment. By controlling these variables, then, they can be eliminated as selective factors, and any differences found between the working and non-working families can more readily be attributed to the independent operation of the employment variable. It should be pointed out, however, that instituting these controls makes for a strict test of the hypotheses, because any changes in ideology *and the corresponding behavior patterns* that might have resulted from mother employment by the time the data were collected would also be eliminated.[1]

SITUATIONAL CONTROLS

Matching, with respect to situational factors, was greatly facilitated by the homogeneity of the total sample. Thus, as already indicated, it was

---

[1] This is particularly true since matching on ideology was precise; i.e., actual scores were used rather than general high-low distinctions.

possible to remove the following extraneous factors: absence of a parent; rural and ethnic factors; and, to some extent, stage in the family cycle. In addition, three situational variables were used in setting up the 89 matched pairs: husband's occupation, number of children under thirteen years of age, and age of oldest child. Husband's occupation and age and number of children are known to be related to women's employment status (4). Age and number of children, in addition, seemed likely to affect the division of labor in that having many young children should increase the work load; while having one's oldest child near maturity would provide potential assistance with the housework. Furthermore, by controlling on both of these variables, the control on family cycle—felt to be potentially related to power—is more effective than merely relying on the presence of an elementary school child. Finally, the husband's occupation also seemed likely to relate to both dependent variables—division of labor and power.[2]

MEASURES

Data reported here were gathered from two sources: paper and pencil interviews with the children and mailed questionnaires answered by the mothers. The children's interviews were used for measuring the dependent variables, while the mothers' questionnaires were used for measuring the independent and control variables.

The questions used in the child interview were similar in form to those developed by Herbst (3). There were 33 paired items in all, the child being asked in each case which family members *do* a particular routine household activity and which members *decide* about that activity. For example, one item pair was as follows:

Who cooks the evening meal?

Who decides what to cook for the evening meal?

These questions were read to the child, who indicated his response by *encircling* or *underlining* the appropriate answers from a list of household persons. Circles were used to designate major actors, and underlines to designate minor ones. It was clearly indicated that the interviewer was interested in the child's particular family rather than general social norms.

Task Participation. The task participation scores were computed for mothers and for fathers by scoring two points when the parent was reported to have a major role in *doing* a given household activity, one point when he was reported to have a minor role, and zero when he was reported to have

---

[2] After the data were collected it was discovered that a number of families included persons who were not members of the conjugal family. Such persons were disproportionately represented in the families with working mothers (p $<$ .05). Accordingly, as a final control all such families were excluded from the analyses dealing with the division of labor and activity control.

no role. Each parent was thus given a total activity participation score based on the child's responses to all the 33 *doing* questions. In addition subscores were computed. For example, each parent was given a score for participation in Mother's Household Area. This was based only on those items which asked about activities that are conventionally done by mothers. Similarly, task participation scores were computed for Father's Household Area, Common Household Area, and Child Care Area, the last being differentiated not by the conventional performer of the role but by the content of the activity itself.[3]

Activity Control.   Whereas the measure of task participation used only the *doing* questions in the child interview, the measurement of decision-making participation or activity control used only the *deciding* questions. Each family was assigned two activity control scores, each based on the total 33 items. One score represented the mother's activity control and the other, the father's. In addition to differentiating major from minor actors (as in the task participation measure), these scores took into account the exclusiveness of the deciding role.

Power Relationship.   In using the child interview responses to measure the power relationship between the mother and father, both the *doing* and *deciding* questions were used, a pair of questions constituting the coding unit. In assigning weights to these responses in order to yield a measure of power, the assumption was made that when the child reports that one parent performs an act and the *other* parent makes the decision about the act, he is telling something about the power relationship between his parents. Underlying this assumption are the notions that (a) power is expressed in the extent to which one parent decides over the other's behavior; (b) when a child gives such a response, he may or may not be reporting the actual situation regarding that particular act, but his over-all pattern of responses to the total set of questions reflects his general picture of the mother-father relationship. Thus, for example, a child who responded to all the items by indicating that his father alone did all of the tasks but that his mother alone did all of the deciding about these tasks, would have a general picture of his father as being low-powered in relation to the mother. Finally, it is felt that (c) the child is an observer of the family scene, and, while a given child may perceptually distort the picture somewhat, the scores in the aggregate are valid.

To state the operational definition of power simply: power is the extent to which one parent decides over the other parent's behavior more than the other decides over his behavior. The specific weighting system is reported

---

[3] The total participation score is more than the sum of the four subscores because some of the 33 items did not fit the four household area categories.

in Table 15.1. Since only the over-all scores are seen as valid indicators of power, as indicated above, it was felt that small differences in scores should not be stressed. Therefore, the distribution of power scores was split at the midpoint for purposes of making statistical tests.

TABLE 15.1 *Scoring System for Parental Power Measure*

CHILD'S RESPONSE	WEIGHT
Mother decides, father does	3
Mother decides, both do	2
Both decide, father does	1
Mother decides, mother does; father decides, father does; both decide, both do; neither parent decides, neither parent does	0
Both decide, mother does	−1
Father decides, both do	−2
Father decides, mother does	−3

Traditional Sex Role Ideology. The scores used in matching on sex role ideology were based on the degree of agreement the mothers indicated with the following items:

1. Raising children is much more a mother's job than a father's.
2. Except in special cases, the wife should do the cooking and house cleaning and the husband should provide the family with money.
3. If the man is working to support the family, his wife has no right to expect him to work when he's at home.
4. A man who helps around the kitchen is doing more than should be expected.
5. A man ought to feel free to relax when he gets home from work.

All items were answered on a four-point scale: *agree a lot, agree, disagree, disagree a lot.* The greater the agreement, the greater the endorsement of traditional sex role ideology.

To assess the importance of sex role ideology as a control, the scores on this measure for the total sample were related to the father's participation in Mother's Household Area and in Total Activities. Both of these relationships were significant, endorsement of traditional sex role ideology being associated with low father participation in Mother's Household Area and with low father participation in Total Activities. Traditional sex role ideology also related significantly to mother's working status; non-working women being more likely to endorse it than working women. Thus, it would appear that sex role ideology is an important variable to control in studying mother employment and the division of labor in the home.

Male Dominance Ideology.   The scores used in matching on male dominance ideology were based on the degree of agreement mothers indicated with the following items:

1. Some equality in marriage is a good thing, but by and large the husband ought to have the main say-so in family matters.
2. It goes against human nature to place women in positions of authority over men.
3. A wife does better to vote the way her husband does, because he probably knows more about such things.
4. Men should make the really important decisions in the family.

Items were answered and scored in the same way as the sex role items.[4]

It was found that scores on this measure for the total sample did not relate to the power scores nor to mother's working status. Further analysis, however, revealed that although the expected relationship did not exist for the working group, endorsement of male dominance was associated with low mother power for the non-working group (p. < .10).[5] These findings seem to suggest the possibility of some unanticipated interaction between male dominance ideology and mother's working status. This point will be taken up in more detail in the discussion of the power findings.

RESULTS AND DISCUSSION

HYPOTHESIS 1—TASK PARTICIPATION

Significance tests were made comparing the matched pairs on father's participation and mother's participation, in each of the four household areas and in the total activities. The results are reported in Table 15.2.

It can be seen that all results are in the predicted direction, with employed mothers participating less and their husbands participating more in all areas. The findings are significant for the mother's participation in Mother's, Father's, and Common Household Areas. This pattern is unchanged when full-time workers are differentiated from part-time workers. The significant differences in father's participation involve the Common Household Area, Total Activities, and, when the comparison is made between families with full-time working mothers and matched families with nonworking mothers, the Mother's Household and Child Care Areas.

---

[4] Ideology questionnaires were also answered separately by fathers. The correlations between mothers' and fathers' scores on traditional sex role ideology and male dominance ideology were .32 and .36 respectively, both being significant at better than the .01 level. Only the mother's ideology was used in the present study.

[5] This finding also occurred with fathers' responses. Endorsement of male dominance by the father is significantly associated with low mother power in the nonworking mother families (p < .05), but not in families where the mother works.

TABLE 15.2 *Mother's Working Status and Household Task Participation of Mother and Father*

HOUSEHOLD AREA	DIRECTION OF RELA- TIONSHIP
Mother's Participation	
Mother's	W < NW*[1]
Father's	W < NW*
Common	W < NW*
Child-care	W < NW
Total activities	W < NW
Father's Participation	
Mother's	W > NW
	(FT > NW)*[2]
Father's	W > NW
Common	W > NW*
Child-care	W > NW
	(FT > NW)*
Total activities	W > NW*

° Statistically significant.
Note: N = 75 matched pairs. This includes only families which do not have servants or outside relatives as regular household participants.
[1] W = working; NW = non-working.
[2] Refers to comparisons which included only full-time working mothers (FT) and the non-working mothers matched to them, 45 pairs in all.

If one views the mother and father participation scores as complements of one another, the over-all pattern of the data clearly supports the hypothesis that the employment of mothers functions to decrease their participation in household tasks and to increase that of the fathers.

It should be noted that when these same comparisons were made using the total sample, all differences except one were significant. The single exception, father's participation in Father's Household Area, may have resulted from the low ceiling of the particular measure; that is, most fathers had maximum participation scores in Father's Household Area.[6]

HYPOTHESIS 2—ACTIVITY CONTROL

Hypothesis 2 receives strong support from the data. Working mothers have significantly less activity control than non-working mothers, and their husbands have significantly more, thus confirming the hypothesis.

---

[6] Although not germane to the present analysis, it is interesting to note that maximum effects occur when ideology and employment operate in the same direction. That is, the husband's participation is highest when the wife is employed and the ideology is non-traditional, lowest when neither of these conditions exist, and in-between when only one of them exists.

HYPOTHESIS 3—POWER

Hypothesis 3 was tested by comparing power scores for the matched pairs of working and non-working women. *No difference was found.* When the *total* sample was examined, however, it was found that working mothers did have more power than non-working mothers (p < .06).[7] *This difference was apparently completely washed out by the matching.*

Matching on male dominance ideology alone, however, cannot account for the washing out of the relationship, since, as already noted, endorsement of this ideology relates to high mother power only in the non-working group. It will be recalled, however, that the two groups were also matched on husband's occupation, number of children under thirteen years of age, and age of oldest child. To throw further light on the relationship between mother's employment status and power, the total sample was examined to see how much each of the ideological and situational control variables, alone and in various combinations, related to employment status and to power.

The results of these analyses showed that the most effective controls were (a) husband's occupation and (b) the other two situational controls —number of children under thirteen and age of oldest child—which, acting in combination, resulted in a control on having only one child. Where the husbands had low income occupations, the wives were more likely to be employed (p < .05)[8] and also to have high power (p < .15).[9] This means that in the total sample the working group included relatively more women from lower income families, and, since in lower income families the woman's power is higher, the correlation between the woman's employment and power was thereby heightened. Women with only one child were significantly more likely to be employed than other women (p < .01) and somewhat more likely to have high power (p < .01).[10] This means that in the total

---

[7] The small size of the relationship between mother employment and power is probably due partly to the homogeneity of the total sample. The Detroit Area Study (University of Michigan), which used a more heterogeneous sample, found a much stronger relationship. But when a sample similar in makeup to the one used here was pulled out, the relationship obtained was comparable to that found here.

[8] This probability and all that follow are based on the two-tailed test.

[9] The positive association between social status of husband's occupation and his dominance has also been reported by Gold (1) and Heer (2). It is interesting that although the present study shows this same pattern, it also shows high social status of father's occupation to be associated with rejection of male dominance ideology by both mothers (p < .05) and fathers (p < .01).

[10] The Detroit Area Study found similarly that mothers of only one child were more active than other mothers in making important family decisions. The relationship was not continuous, there being no further differences as the number of children increased beyond one. Heer (2), using only actively affiliated Catholics as subjects, found a continuous relationship, the mother's power varying inversely with the number of her children. He also reported that standardizing scores for number of children diminished but did not eliminate power differences between working and non-working wives. (See Chapter Eighteen.)

sample the working group included more women with only one child than the non-working group—actually 25 per cent as compared to 7 per cent; and since having only one child relates positively to a mother's power, the correlation between mother's employment and power was heightened.

If the correlation obtained between working and power in the total sample was thus affected by the relationship of each of these variables to husband's occupation and family composition, it would seem to follow that a relationship between mother employment and mother power found in the total sample here, as well as in other studies, is merely the spurious result of failing to institute the necessary controls. Yet, there is considerable theoretical basis for assuming that outside employment does exert a pressure toward increasing a woman's power. At least four general theories predicting this can be inferred from the existing literature.

1. The person who receives wages in exchange for services has more control over this money than other family members; and this control can be used, implicitly or explicitly, to wield power in the family.

2. Society attaches greater value to the role of wage-earner than to that of housewife and thus legitimizes for both parents the notion that the former should have more power.

3. An independent supply of money enables the working woman to exert her influence to a greater extent because she is less dependent on her husband and could, if necessary, support herself in the event of the dissolution of the marriage.

4. Working outside the home provides more social interaction than being a housewife. This interaction has been seen as leading to an increase in the wife's power because of: (a) the development of social skills which are useful in influencing her husband; (b) the development of self-confidence; (c) the greater knowledge of alternative situations that exist in other families; and (d) the more frequent interaction with men, which may result in the feeling that remarriage is feasible.

Certain of these theories appear to be somewhat limited. For example, "3" as well as "4d" assume a rather tenuous marriage. Furthermore, it may be argued that the assumption underlying "4a"—that the development of social skills is important—implies that family decisions are based on arguing and wit rather than on the simple assertion of power, as may often be the case.

Theories "1," "2," and "4b" are those which provide the theoretical basis presented earlier for the hypothesis that the mothers outside employment increases her power. These particular theories in combination seem too sound to be readily dismissed despite the fact that the analysis thus far raises serious doubt about the existence of a relationship between employment and power. Because of the face validity of these theories, and because of the sheer predominance of theories predicting a relationship between the mother's employment and power, further examination of the relationship was undertaken.

Employment, Ideology, and Power. A possible explanation for the discrepancy found between theory and data is as follows: the mother's employment does exert a force in the direction of increasing her power in the home, but there is a counterforce that prevents the effects from taking place in a simple one-to-one fashion. Such a counterforce might be the prevailing male dominance ideology. Perhaps the notion that men should be dominant is so deeply ingrained that any threat to the asymmetric balance of power in the marriage relationship is warded off because a certain amount of husband dominance is essential for the wife to feel adequately feminine, for her husband to feel adequately masculine, and for the integrity of the marriage.[11]

To explore this idea further, the relationship between a mother's working status and parental power was analyzed within ideology groups. It was found (Table 15.3) that women who endorsed male dominance, as well

TABLE 15.3 *Mother's Male Dominance Ideology and the Relationship between Mother's Working Status and Parental Power —Total Sample*

MOTHER'S POSITION ON MALE DOMINANCE IDEOLOGY SCALE	RELATIONSHIP FOUND BETWEEN WORKING STATUS AND MOTHER'S POWER	N
Endorsement of male dominance (top half)	Working mothers have MORE power than nonworking mothers*	179
Reserved rejection of male dominance (third quartile)	Working mothers have LESS power than nonworking mothers*	78
Complete rejection of male dominance (fourth quartile)	Working mothers have MORE power than nonworking mothers*	67

* p < .05; two-tailed test.

as those who completely rejected it, showed the originally hypothesized positive relationship between the mother's working status and power. However, women who indicated reserved rejection of male dominance, i.e., those who rejected it but not completely or consistently, showed an inverse rela-

---

[11] The implication here that wife dominance is dysfunctional to the marriage relationship is borne out by data reported by Wolfe (5). Wolfe reports that wives in wife-dominant families are less likely to indicate marital satisfaction than are wives in either husband-dominant or equalitarian families.

tionship. For this group, mother's employment is associated with having low power.

The matched sample showed a similar pattern (Table 15.4), although for purposes of the statistical analysis it was necessary to combine the "endorsement" and "complete rejection" groups.[12] To see further if this pattern resulted from spurious factors, the "reserved rejection" group was compared with the other two on all of the control variables as well as education of parents, duration of mother's employment, and whether the mother worked part or full time. The "reserved rejection" group did not differ from the others on any of these characteristics.

TABLE 15.4 *Mother's Male Dominance Ideology and the Relationship between Mother's Working Status and Parental Power—Matched Sample*

MOTHER'S POSITION ON MALE DOMINANCE IDEOLOGY SCALE	RELATIONSHIP FOUND BETWEEN WORKING STATUS AND MOTHER'S POWER	NO. OF PAIRS[1]
Endorsement of male dominance; and	Working mothers have MORE power than non-working mothers*	49
Complete rejection of male dominance		14
Reserved rejection of male dominance	Working mothers have LESS power than non-working mothers*	21

* p < .10; two tailed test.
[1] The number of pairs does not total 89 because 5 pairs of respondents were dropped when both respondents did not fall within the same ideology grouping.

Since the pattern reported in Tables 15.3 and 15.4 does not appear to be spurious, it provides interesting material for *post hoc* speculation and has implications for further research. Possibly the male dominance ideology is so deeply imbedded in American culture and personality structure, that *unless strongly rejected,* it operates as a counterforce to the pressure exerted by the mother's working. It is possible that the mother's employment not only exerts pressure toward increasing her power through giving her greater monetary control, a more legitimized claim to power, and greater self-confidence; but that her employment in and of itself may be a threat to the status

---

[12] Combining was necessary because the "complete rejection" group in the matched sample included so few subjects that the expected frequency of the cells was less than required. It was warranted because the expected as well as the obtained direction of the relationship was the same in the two groups.

quo of the marriage relationship. *Thus, whereas working may exert a pressure toward her increased power in the family, the male dominance ideology might lead her to become actually less dominant than before in order to compensate for the threat offered by the sheer fact of her employment.* To restore the former asymmetric balance the wife may be compelled to express less power in direct interaction than before she went to work.

The relationships found for the "reserved rejection" and "complete rejection" groups may be understood in these terms. That is, in the latter group there is no counterforce and the effect of employment can operate unabated; whereas in the former group the working women respond to the threat of their employment by becoming less dominant than before in interacting with their husbands.[13]

If this explanation is accepted, however, the group *endorsing* male dominance needs further consideration, since the working women in this group do have more power. Three alternative explanations are here set forth that attempt to explain why these women may exempt their own husbands from the right to deference which they accord men in general.

1. When women who endorse male dominance go to work, it is more likely to be out of economic necessity. Going to work under these conditions may lead them to perceive their husbands as failures and, therefore, undeserving of the deference due men in general.

2. Even if women endorsing male dominance do not go to work out of economic necessity, they may be more likely than other women to consider the economic role as the legitimate basis of power, since this is in keeping with a male dominance ideology. If this were true, the fact of their working, for whatever reason, would lead them to exempt their own situation from that which they consider generally appropriate.

3. Women who endorse male dominance may have a perception of masculinity which is so exaggerated that their husbands must fall short of this ideal. When they go to work, the counteracting force of the ideology is negated and does not block the power increments that result from employment. The counterforce is negated because these women consider their own husbands as inadequate compared to their ideal of masculinity and, hence, not deserving of deference. Neither do they feel their femininity threatened by employment, because, compared to their conceptions of masculinity, they are quite feminine.

Adequate tests of these *post hoc* hypotheses could not be made with the data at hand. However, two inferences drawn from the first hypothesis

---

[13] This same theory, and the unusual interaction between male dominance ideology, employment, and power, explain the failure, reported earlier, to find a relationship between endorsement of male dominance and low mother power for the working women.

were tested using interview data obtained from the mothers. The first inference is that women who report they are working because of economic necessity will have more power than women who report they are working for other reasons. This was tested and confirmed ($p < .05$). The second inference is that women who endorse male dominance should be more likely to report that they are working because of economic necessity than women who reject male dominance. This was tested, but the data indicated no such tendency. An inference from the second hypothesis that women endorsing male dominance would consider earning money as the main basis of power, was not supported by the interview data. These women were no more likely than others to consider earning money as the basis of power in the home. None of the available data had a bearing on the third hypothesis. The lack of any test is unfortunate, because this hypothesis might not only explain the pattern of findings under discussion but is particularly rich in implications for the study of male-female interaction in general.[14]

SUMMARY AND CONCLUSIONS

This study investigated the effects of the mother's outside employment on task participation, routine decision making (activity control), and power structure in the family. The total sample included 324 intact Detroit families having at least one child in elementary school. To highlight mother's employment as the independent variable, 89 of the working women in this group were matched to 89 non-working women on ideologies about sex roles and male dominance, husband's occupation, number of children under thirteen years of age, and age of oldest child. These 89 matched pairs were used to test the hypotheses.

The results were as follows:

1. Working mothers participated less than non-working mothers in household tasks, and their husbands participated more.

2. Working mothers made fewer decisions about routine household matters than non-working mothers, and their husbands made more.

3. There was no difference in husband-wife power between working and non-working women in the matched sample, although in the total

---

[14] It is possible that certain of the employment-power theories listed earlier are more valid for one ideology group than another. For example, one of these theories holds that the mother's wish to be more assertive is restrained only by the fear that doing so might lead to the dissolution of the marriage, and, further, that the economic security resulting from her employment is sufficient to permit the expression of assertiveness. This theory assumes a minimum of affectional ties between husband and wife; therefore, it would be more applicable to the women endorsing male dominance, if these women do, in fact, have greater marital dissatisfaction as suggested in this chapter.

sample working women did have more power than non-working. Analysis suggested that controls on husband's occupation and on age and number of children accounted for the washing out of the relationship when the matched groups were compared. Further subgroup analyses found the expected positive relationship between employment and power among women who endorsed the male dominance ideology and among women who consistently rejected it; the opposite relationship held for women who showed a reserved rejection of this ideology. This pattern was found both for matched groups and for the total sample. *Post hoc* hypotheses were advanced to account for it.

It may be concluded that a mother's employment leads her husband to assume some of her former household tasks and to become more active in making the corresponding decisions even when ideology is held constant.

The results also suggest that women's employment does not affect family power structure directly but only in interaction with the pre-existing ideologies and personalities of the actors. It seems that power relationships, unlike division of labor, are either too deeply interwined with psychological needs to respond readily to an outside stimulus, or that mother's employment is too weak a stimulus. The several recent attempts to show the presence or absence of a relationship between mother employment and husband-wife power, therefore, seem to be oversimplifications of what should be studied as a complex and multivariate phenomenon.

REFERENCES

1. Gold, Martin, and Slater, C. R. "Office, Factory, Store—and Family: A Study of Integration Setting," *American Sociological Review,* XXIII (February, 1958), 64–74.
2. Heer, David M. "Dominance and the Working Wife," *Social Forces,* XXVI (May, 1958), 341–47. Reprinted as Chapter Eighteen of the present book.
3. Herbst, P. G. "The Measurement of Family Relationships," *Human Relations,* V, No. 1 (1952), 3–30.
4. National Manpower Council. *Womanpower.* New York: Columbia University Press, 1957.
5. Wolfe, Donald M. "Power and Authority in the Family." In D. Cartwright, ed. *Studies in Social Power.* Ann Arbor, Mich.: Institute for Social Research, 1959.

Chapter Sixteen

Family Variables*

KATHRYN S. POWELL

MATERNAL employment is composed of many different psychological factors according to Yarrow (13), who suggests that these various elements be disentangled.

The present investigation seeks information concerning the relationship between maternal employment and (a) mothers' perceptions of their marital adjustment, (b) mothers' rejection of the homemaking role, and (c) the performance of household activities by family members—at three stages of the family life cycle. The stages of the family life cycle and the subjects used in this study were described in Chapter Nine.

MARITAL ADJUSTMENT

Few studies have been made of the marital adjustment of employed mothers. However, several studies have compared the marital adjustment of employed and non-employed wives. The findings of Locke and Mackeprang (7), for example, indicate that no relationship exists between the employment status of women and marital satisfaction. Havemann and West (3), on the other hand, conclude that employed women have a higher divorce rate than non-employed women.

In another study, Nye (9) collected data from 1,993 mothers of children in grades one and ten in three Washington towns. Using a Guttman type scale to measure marital conflict, permanence, happiness, and satis-

* The dissertation on which this paper is based was directed by Dr. James Walters, Professor of Home and Family Life, School of Home Economics, Florida State University, 1960.

faction, as reported by the mother, Nye compared the marital conflict of employed and non-employed mothers. These significant differences were found: where the mother was employed, quarreling was found to be more frequent, and marital adjustment scores more frequently showed unhappiness and dissatisfaction (Chapter Nineteen).

In the present study, to obtain information regarding the marital adjustment of the subjects, the Marital-Adjustment Test devised by Locke and Wallace (8) was chosen. Concerning the validity of this short form of 15 questions, the test differentiated between persons who were judged by friends to have good marital adjustment and those who had sought divorce or professional help with marital problems. A reliability coefficient, computed by the split-half technique and corrected by the Spearman-Brown formula, was .90. On the basis of a comparison of the mean of 135.9 for the adjusted with a mean of 71.7 for the maladjusted, a critical ratio of 17.5 was obtained, which is highly significant. Furthermore, use of a test with a relatively small number of items, all of which have been found to be discriminatory, is desirable in a study such as this which includes comparisons of several characteristics of family living.

The instrument used, Locke and Wallace's Marital-Adjustment Test, yields scores ranging from 2–158 points, the higher scores reflecting a more satisfactory adjustment (8). The scores for the 130 subjects in this study ranged from 23 to 158. Locke and Wallace found that for the 236 subjects used to establish the validity of the test, 96 per cent of the well-adjusted group achieved scores of 100 or more; whereas only 17 per cent of the maladjusted group achieved adjustment scores of 100 or higher.

Among the 130 subjects studied in the present investigation, 120 (92 per cent) had scores of 100 or more. This suggests that in the group there were relatively few mothers who perceived themselves as being poorly adjusted in marriage. A comparison of the marital adjustment scores of mothers who were gainfully employed with those of mothers who were full-time homemakers in each of the three stages in the family life cycle revealed one significant relationship between maternal employment and marital adjustment. The employed mothers of adolescents scored significantly lower on marital adjustment than did the non-employed mothers of this age group.

The range of scores of mothers of adolescents was 23–154. There were six mothers who scored lower than 100; all but one of them were employed. About 28 per cent of the employed mothers scored above the median for the total group, while 62 per cent of the full-time homemakers' scores were above the median (see Table 16.1).

The 47 mothers whose oldest children were in elementary school had

TABLE 16.1 *Marital Adjustment and Maternal Rejection of the Homemaking Role: Median Scores of Mothers*

| MEASURE | MEDIAN SCORES OF MOTHERS | | |
	Preschool[1] Group	Elementary[1] Group	Adolescent[1] Group
Marital Adjustment	133.5	133.5	129
Rejection Homemaking Role	12.5	11.5	11.5

[1] Age of Oldest Child.

scores ranging from 78 to 158, with 3 scoring under 100. Eight (57 per cent) of the 14 employed mothers scored above the median for the group.

The scores of the 42 mothers whose oldest children were of preschool age ranged from 78 to 158 also, but only 1 scored below 100. One-half of the employed mothers in this group scored above the median for the entire sample.

Specifically, there were no significant relationships between marital adjustment and employment status for mothers whose oldest child was of preschool or elementary school age. The relationship between marital adjustment and employment status of mothers whose oldest child was an adolescent was significant, with the employed mothers reflecting poorer marital adjustment than the non-employed mothers.

The present investigation supports previous studies which have indicated a relationship between maternal employment and marital adjustment and identifies the employed mothers who are low in marital adjustment as those with adolescent children.

ANALYSIS OF MARITAL ADJUSTMENT SCORES

The statistically significant relationship between marital adjustment and employment status of mothers whose oldest child was an adolescent suggested further analyses of the findings. One analysis was a study of the relationship between maternal employment and the performance of household tasks by various members of the household.

The employed mothers of adolescents performed as many household tasks as did the non-employed mothers of adolescents, while the employed mothers of elementary school or preschool age children did not perform as many household tasks as did the non-employed mothers. This suggested that marital adjustment may be the function of the relationship between the employment of the mother and the wife role.

When the wife enters gainful employment, her role in the family changes to some extent. Are there concomitant changes in the performance of household tasks by various family members? Performance of household tasks by various family members, as reported in the present study, is shown in Table 16.3. In the families with adolescents, the husbands whose wives were employed performed fewer household tasks than the husbands whose wives were not employed; while the employed wives performed practically the same number of household tasks as the non-employed wives. Since this was not true of the families of preschool and elementary school age children, it poses the possibility that the lower marital adjustment scores of mothers of adolescents may be explained in part by the lower performance of household tasks by various family members.

The rank-order correlation of marital adjustment scores and performance of household tasks by fathers was determined for each of the three stages in the family life cycle as follows:

(a) for families of preschool age children $r_s = -.05$

(b) for families of elementary school age children $r_s = .15$

(c) for families of adolescent age children $r_s = .51$

The above findings indicate the need for a more complex analysis of the husband-wife relationship of employed wives. Where satisfactory marital adjustment exists for families where the mother is employed, what, if any, changes are there in roles of family members? The present evidence suggests that younger families may be more flexible in their roles, and that this flexibility may contribute to a more satisfying marital adjustment for women.

MATERNAL REJECTION OF THE HOMEMAKING ROLE

It is increasingly recognized that women's continued employment can no longer be attributed solely to the need for money or to current labor demands. Based on reported interviews, Lloyd-Jones (6) concluded that the entry of women into gainful employment is evidence that "women quite obviously are responding to some powerfully controlling new conditions but without much, if any, consolidated understanding on the part of society of these conditions." Feldman (2) observed that many married women who feel the need for achievement in a field other than the home may be seeking satisfaction in paid work.

Recognition of the importance of the homemaker's attitude toward her role is evidenced by Schaefer and Bell (12) in the development of a scale to measure such an attitude. Included in the Parent Attitude Research Instrument (PARI) is a subscale, Rejection of the Homemaking Role, which contains items designed to measure dissatisfaction with the duties of caring for the home and children. Burchinal and Lovell (1), using the PARI, found no relationship between maternal employment and the rejection of the homemaking role. Further evidence is lacking concerning a relationship between the employment status of mothers and their rejection of the homemaking role in spite of the concept in the literature that women are entering the labor force in increasing numbers because they are dissatisfied with the traditional homemaking role.

To measure the dissatisfaction of the mothers with the duties of caring for the home and children, the Rejection of the Homemaking Role subscale from the PARI was used. Rejection of the homemaking role is indicated by a possible score of 20, and non-rejection, by a minimum score of 5. The scores of subjects of this study covered the entire range from 5 to 20. The median score obtained for the preschool group was 12.5 and the medians for the elementary school age group and the adolescent group were 11.5 for each group (Table 16.2). Thus mothers of preschool children who were full-time homemakers showed a slightly greater tendency than other mothers to reject the homemaking role.

No significant relationship between maternal employment and the mother's rejection of the homemaking role was found at any of the three stages of the family life cycle studied (Table 16.1). There was a trend toward greater rejection of the homemaking role by mothers who were full-time homemakers and whose oldest child was of preschool age. Rejection of the homemaking role is more prevalent under conditions that "tie-

TABLE 16.2 *Marital Adjustment and Maternal Rejection of the Homemaking Role: Percentage of Employed and Non-Employed Mothers above Median Scores*

| MEASURE | PERCENTAGE OF MOTHERS ABOVE MEDIANS | | | | | |
| | Preschool[1] | | Elementary[1] | | Adolescent[1] | |
	Employed	Non-Employed	Employed	Non-Employed	Employed	Non-Employed
Marital Adjustment	50	50	57	48	28*	62*
Rejection, Homemaking Role	50	50	36	56	67	45
Number	*12*	*30*	*14*	*27*	*18*	*29*

* Difference is statistically significant.
[1] Age of oldest child.

down" a mother; namely, those conditions prevailing for mothers of pre-school children.

PERFORMANCE OF HOUSEHOLD TASKS BY MEMBERS
OF THE HOUSEHOLD

Students of the family have assumed that adding the role of employee to the woman's roles of wife and mother often necessitates a redefinition of the roles of family members in terms of duties and responsibilities. See the foregoing discussion of the comparison of the performance of household tasks by various members of the households of employed and non-employed mothers.

Knowledge concerning the manner in which household routines are managed by families in which the mother is or is not gainfully employed is practically non-existent. The extent to which traditional roles are modified as the result of the mother's prolonged daily absence from home has not been studied sufficiently. Facts are few.

A few studies indicate that in families of employed mothers more household duties are performed by other family members than in families of non-employed mothers. Hoffman (4) found in a study of 324 Detroit families who had at least one child in the third through sixth grades, that in families of employed mothers, more household tasks were performed by the fathers and fewer by the mothers than in families where the mothers were not employed. Although there was no difference statistically, Powell (11) found in a study of 170 children in grades three through seven that there was a tendency for children of employed mothers to perform more home tasks than those of non-employed mothers. In a study of family responsibilities and social stratification, Olsen (10) found no significant differences in the division of household tasks between families of gainfully employed wives and families of non-employed wives. Joint husband-wife assumption of responsibility was found to be negatively correlated with the age of the couple, the older couples jointly assuming responsibilities less often than the younger couples.

The number of home activities performed by the father, mother, children, maid, and other adults were computed from responses to the instrument adapted from Johannis' instrument (5). The differences between mean responses of families in each of the three stages of the family life cycle where the mother was employed and where the mother was a full-time homemaker were determined. The performance of home activities by father, mother, children, maid or servant, and other adults was analyzed by computing for each member of the household a gross score which represented the number of home activities which that person performed. The resulting mean number of activities for each age group in families where the mother was employed and in those where the mother was not employed are shown in Table 16.3.

In families where the oldest child was of preschool age there were statistically significant differences between the number of activities of persons in homes where the mother was gainfully employed and in homes where the mother was a full-time homemaker. As might be expected, the families of full-time homemakers had fewer activities performed by maids or other adults than did families of employed mothers (Table 16.3). In families of preschool children where the mother was gainfully employed, the mean number of tasks was smaller for mothers and larger for fathers than in families where the mother was a full-time homemaker, although the differences were not significant statistically.

Where the oldest child was of elementary school age, the mean number of tasks performed by employed mothers was 29; for those who were not employed, the mean was 34.6. In families of employed mothers, maids performed a mean of 7.52 tasks as compared with a mean of 1.55 in families of full-time homemakers. Although the differences were not statistically significant, in families where the mother was gainfully employed, the mean number of tasks performed by the fathers was more, and by the children, less than in families of full-time homemakers.

Similarly, Hoffman (4) found for families in this stage of the family life cycle that working mothers participated less than non-working mothers in household tasks and that their husbands participated more—when the families included only members of the conjugal family.

In families where the oldest child was an adolescent, there were no significant differences between the number of activities of persons in homes where the mother was gainfully employed and in homes where the mother was a full-time homemaker. The means shown in Table 16.3 indicate that a similar number of home activities were performed by the various members of the household in families where the mother was a full-time homemaker and where the mother was employed. At this stage in the family life cycle, the subjects reported performance of fewer home activities by fathers when the mother was gainfully employed than when the mother was a full-time homemaker.

The present multiphasic analysis of the relationship between maternal employment and family life indicates a need to analyze further the relationship between marital adjustment and maternal employment. Evidence of a relationship between marital adjustment and performance of household tasks by husbands suggests that greater flexibility in husband-wife

TABLE 16.3 *Mean Scores on Home Activities for Families of Employed and Non-Employed Mothers*

MEAN SCORES ON HOME ACTIVITIES

| HOME ACTIVITIES PERFORMED BY | PRESCHOOL[1] | | ELEMENTARY[1] | | ADOLESCENT[1] | |
	Employed (N = 12)	Non-Employed (N = 30)	Employed (N = 14)	Non-Employed (N = 27)	Employed (N = 18)	Non-Employed (N = 29)
Father	18.40	15.10	19.00	18.33	16.80	18.34
Mother	30.75	33.00	29.00	34.60*	32.90	33.00
Children	2.83	1.36	3.64	4.37	10.10	9.30
Maid	5.50	1.83*	7.42	1.55*	1.83	1.58
Other adults	1.58	.36*	—[2]	—[2]	—[2]	—[2]

[1] Age of oldest child.
[2] Too few to warrant comparison.
* Statistically significant difference (.01 level).

roles may contribute to a more satisfying marital adjustment for younger women. Performance of household tasks may be a variable that should be held constant in studies of the relationship between marital adjustment and factors such as maternal employment. There is, further, an indication that insights into family life may be gained by studying families in the various stages of the family life cycle.

REFERENCES

1. Burchinal, Lee G., and Lovell, Lloyd L. "Relation of Employment Status of Mothers to Children's Anxiety, Parental Personality and PARI Scores." Unpublished manuscript No. 1425, Agricultural and Home Economics Experiment Station. Ames, Iowa: Iowa State University, 1959.

2. Feldman, Frances L. "Supplementary Income Earned by Married Women." In National Manpower Council. *Work in the Lives of Married Women.* New York: Columbia University Press, 1958, pp. 93–129.

3. Havemann, Ernest, and West, Patricia S. *They Went to College.* New York: Harcourt, Brace, 1952.

4. Hoffman, Lois Wladis. "Effects of the Employment of Mothers on Parental Power Relations and the Division of Household Tasks," *Marriage and Family Living,* XXII (February, 1960), 22–35. Reprinted as Chapter Fifteen of the present book.

5. Johannis, T. B., Jr. "The Adolescent's View of Father Roles in Relation to Socio-economic Class." Unpublished Ph.D. dissertation, Florida State University, 1955.

6. Lloyd-Jones, Esther. "Education for Re-entry into the Labor Force." In National Manpower Council. *Work in the Lives of Married Women.* New York: Columbia University Press, 1958, pp. 27–40.

7. Locke, Harvey J., and Mackeprang, Muriel. "Marital Adjustment of the Employed Wife," *American Journal of Sociology,* LIV (May, 1949), 536–39.

8. Locke, Harvey J., and Wallace, K. M. "Short Marital-Adjustment and Prediction Tests: Their Reliability and Validity," *Marriage and Family Living,* XXI (August, 1959), 251–55.

9. Nye, F. Ivan. "Employment Status of Mothers and Adjustment of Adolescent Children," *Marriage and Family Living,* XXI (August, 1959), 240–44. Reprinted as Chapter Ten of the present book.

10. Olsen, M. E. "Distribution of Family Responsibilities and Social Stratification," *Marriage and Family Living,* XXII (February, 1960), 60–65.

11. Powell, Kathryn S. "Home Tasks of a Selected Group of Children in Middle and Late Childhood." Unpublished Master's thesis, Florida State University, 1954.

12. Shaefer, E. S., and Bell, R. Q. "Development of a Parental Attitude Research Instrument," *Child Development,* XXIX (September, 1958), 339–61.

13. Yarrow, Leon J. "Maternal Deprivation: Toward an Empirical and Conceptual Re-evaluation," *Psychological Bulletin,* LVIII (November, 1961), 459–90.

Chapter Seventeen

Rural Employment and Husbands and Wives*

FRANCENA L. NOLAN

THE percentage of women employed outside the home has been lower in rural than in urban areas. In 1958 the proportions of all women fourteen and over in the labor force was: urban, 38.7 per cent; rural non-farm, 30.1 per cent; and rural farm, 24.4 per cent (3). Although these data were for all women, one might expect the percentage of married women employed outside of the home to follow a similar pattern.

One reason for the differential between rural and urban employment is the relative scarcity of opportunities for work for women in rural areas. Recently, better transportation and the location of industry in outlying areas have tended to equalize opportunities in some areas. However, the traditional definition of the wife's role may still discourage the acceptance of outside employment. In the past, family roles were defined within an agrarian context. One would expect, therefore, to find a greater tendency toward the maintenance of traditional role expectations among those people experiencing the least shift from the agricultural way of life. The farm family remains close to the soil and may therefore be more likely to continue those activities associated with home production of foods, such as gardening, canning, preserving. The extent to which these activities con-

---

* Expanded from Francena L. Nolan and Dawn H. Tuttle, *Certain Practices, Satisfactions and Difficulties in Families with Employed Homemakers,* Bulletin 655, Pennsylvania Agricultural Experiment Station, 1959. This was a report of a study conducted by the Department of Home Management, Housing and Home Art, College of Home Economics and Department of Agricultural Economics and Rural Sociology, Pennsylvania Agricultural Experiment Station, Project 1259. Project Leader, Francena L. Nolan.

241

tinue to be defined as necessary parts of the homemaker role may give the farm wife a work load which precludes acceptance of outside employment.

In addition to the amount of work, attitudes and values epitomized by the phrase "a woman's place is in the home" may obstruct the employment of women—married women in particular. Supporters of this definition of the woman's role are not limited to rural areas. In fact, the vast majority of married women are not gainfully employed (70 per cent of married women living with their husbands are full-time homemakers (3)). The normative pattern is for the wife to be a full-time homemaker. However, the number of married women employed and seeking employment has steadily increased since 1940. The question here is discovery of the extent to which the background and living situation of rural women may serve as greater deterrents to employment than those of urban women.

Since industrialization has penetrated rural life less than it has urban, employment opportunities for rural women have been slow to develop. The newness of the situation may create attitudinal barriers that serve as deterrents to the employment of married women. However, as homemaking chores are lightened, more and more functions in the socialization of children are performed outside of the home; and as farming becomes mechanized and specialized and outside work opportunities increase, rural women may follow their city sisters to stores, offices, and factories.

STATEMENT OF THE PROBLEM

The focus of this chapter is on the changes in family roles associated with maternal employment in a rural community and the impact of these on housekeeping practices, supervision of the children, participation in community activities, and satisfaction with the living situation.

METHODOLOGY

A farm trade center offering some diversity in employment opportunities for women was selected for study. Full-time homemakers and employed homemakers were compared so that changes related to employment could be differentiated from changes associated with technological innovations which penetrate all families—but at different rates. The full-time homemakers were subdivided into farm and non-farm groups to ascertain the differential impact of change in varying environments.

The sample was limited to those families consisting of a husband, wife, and at least one child of eighteen or under, where maternal employment is most likely to interfere with basic familial functions. Only those women who worked 30 or more hours a week were considered in the employed category. Women employed part-time were not included in the study.

In spring of 1956, trained interviewers using a prepared schedule interviewed both the husband and wife in 59 families with employed homemakers and the wife in 69 farm families and 168 non-farm families with full-time homemakers.

DESCRIPTION OF SAMPLE

In spite of the attempt to minimize basic characteristics by holding family types constant, employed homemakers were slightly older (37.2 mean years compared with 36.6 farm and 32.1 non-farm full-time homemakers), had husbands who were older (41.0 mean years compared with 39.0 farm and 34.7 non-farm full-time homemakers), and were slightly better educated (11.2 mean years compared with 9.9 farm and 11.0 non-farm), had children who were older (10.9 mean years compared with 9.6 and 7.2), and had somewhat fewer of them (2.0 compared with 2.7 and 2.3) than both groups of families with full-time homemakers. Husbands with employed wives were more likely to be in white-collar or service occupations and less likely to be farmers than those with full-time homemakers (Table 17.1).

TABLE 17.1 *Occupations of Husbands in Families with Employed and with Non-Employed Homemakers*

HUSBAND'S OCCUPATION	EMPLOYED HOMEMAKERS (N = 59)	FULL-TIME HOMEMAKERS (N = 236)
	Per Cent	
White-Collar (*total*)	31	19
Professional	10	7
Manager	14	7
Clerical	5	2
Sales	2	3
Craft-Operatives (*total*)	32	39
Craftsmen	19	25
Operative	13	14
Service	20	3
Laborer	7	12
Farm	8	25
Farm Laborer	2	2
Total	100	100

For the most part, the employed women worked as operatives (31 per cent) in the two local factories, or in service occupations (39 per cent)— as waitresses, maintenance workers, attendants at a nearby state institution, or cafeteria workers at school; 12 per cent were in clerical positions; 10 per cent, professional; 3 per cent each, in management and in sales; and 2 per cent, in private households. Several of the employed women helped their husbands in family businesses.

FINDINGS

DIVISION OF HOUSEHOLD TASKS

One measure of change in role definition was the participation of different family members in household activities. Data were obtained concerning family members' performing or helping with 19 common household tasks. The average number of tasks performed by the wife, husband, and children six and older revealed that all homemakers, regardless of their situation, assumed the major responsibility for household tasks, although employed homemakers performed slightly fewer (17.20) than full-time homemakers (17.74 farm and 18.30 non-farm). Husbands with employed wives helped with considerably more tasks (3.95) than other husbands (1.14 farm, 1.83 non-farm). As might be expected, children in farm families with full-time homemakers performed the largest number of tasks (6.39 compared with 5.28 for employed and 4.18 for non-farm with full-time mothers). Farm families apparently have diverged least from the traditional role definition of housework for women and children.

Further evidence of the change in role definition of family members was revealed in data concerning the kinds of household activities family members and others performed (Table 17.2). Husbands with employed wives were more likely than other husbands to help with meal preparation, dishes, and entertaining. These data suggest that the change in definition did not occur to the same extent in all aspects of the role. Differences within a rural community between farm and non-farm segments appear to be similar to the differences found by Blood (1) between farm and city people, suggesting that role definition may be associated with occupational differences rather than place of residence.

The children's participation in household tasks differed significantly for five tasks. In three, emptying the garbage, ironing, and polishing the furniture, farm children were more likely to help than children in the other two categories. Children in non-farm, full-time homemaker families were least likely to help in all five of those activities. Apparently the definition of the child's role is dependent upon the family's circumstances. If the child's help is needed, he participates.

TABLE 17.2 *Help Received from Family Members with Selected Housekeeping Tasks*

HELP RECEIVED FROM:	EMPLOYED HOMEMAKERS	FULL-TIME HOMEMAKERS	
		FARM	NON-FARM
		Per Cent	
Husbands	*(N = 59)*	*(N = 69)*	*(N = 168)*
Shop	53	42	55
Prepare meals*	47	14	19
Wash dishes*	42	9	20
Empty garbage*	36	14	36
Bake	7	—	4
Wash	14	1	5
Iron	14	—	—
Dust	10	—	1
Wash windows*	17	1	11
Pick up	24	14	20
Clean bath	2	—	—
Clean floors	19	—	5
Make beds	19	—	3
Change beds	8	—	2
Entertain*	36	12	24
Children, 6 Years of Age or Older	*(N = 54)*	*(N = 53)*	*(N = 98)*
Shop	9	9	5
Prepare meals	30	40	26
Wash dishes	72	72	60
Empty garbage*	41	53	35
Bake	24	40	30
Wash*	20	28	8
Iron*	31	43	20
Dust	46	57	40
Wash windows	20	21	16
Pick up	54	55	47
Clean bath	22	21	12
Clean floors*	31	34	19
Make beds	35	40	33
Change beds	11	13	10
Entertain	33	45	33
Preserve	4	—	—
Clean refrigerator	11	15	4
Clean oven	2	6	3
Polish furniture*	19	30	9

* Difference is statistically significant.

The majority of families in all three situations had apparently adapted to their individual circumstances. In spite of differences in help received, approximately two-thirds of all homemakers thought family members helped as much as they should.

DIFFICULTIES IN HOUSEKEEPING

One of the problems for employed homemakers as seen by 233 full-time homemakers was the difficulty of combining two jobs—housekeeping and outside employment. Nearly 75 per cent thought it would be difficult; only 7 per cent felt sure it would be done successfully; and 12 per cent thought it possible under some conditions. However, when respondents were asked whether it was a problem to do their housework, 66 per cent of employed homemakers compared with 48 per cent of full-time homemakers said, "No problem" or "Hardly any." This was contrary to expectations. A possible explanation was the presence of more young children in the families with full-time homemakers than in those in the employed category. Children can make housework seem interminable.

Another possible explanation may be the way in which the housework was approached. Three-fourths of the employed homemakers indicated that they had changed their housekeeping practices. Their comments included such statements as:

"Yes, you cut corners."

"I learned to do it at a certain time, to be well organized."

"Now I keep three machines going—washer, iron, and sewing machine."

Additional evidence of the ability of the employed wives to cope successfully with housework came from their husbands. Sixty-eight per cent of the husbands reported no difficulty for their wives; 18 per cent said the wives had help; and 4 per cent made other comments; only 10 per cent said their wives had trouble in completing the housework. Demands from an outside job may motivate the employed homemaker toward efficiency at home; whereas the full-time homemakers may be less pressed for time and therefore have less reason to change work habits.

Again, there appeared to be little support for the concern expressed by full-time homemakers over the difficulty of combining homemaking and an outside job. These employed homemakers were doing it successfully—at least by their own standards and those of their husbands.

USE OF HOME AND COMMERCIAL PRODUCTS

In addition to a different division of labor among family members, some tasks which formerly had to be done at home can now be done commercially. As a result, a change in the definition of the wife's housekeeper role can come about by her decision to use commercially prepared goods.

These data indicated that most homemakers baked pies, cakes, and cookies, and did some canning and pickling, but that farm full-time homemakers were more likely than other wives to "bake a lot," "bake bread," freeze foods, and sew clothing (Table 17.3). With the exception of sewing, employed homemakers and non-farm full-time homemakers performed similar tasks. Although all used mixes to the same extent, farm homemakers were least likely to use commercially frozen foods, as might be expected, because many froze their own.

TABLE 17.3 *Housekeeping Practices by Employment Status of the Mother*

PRACTICES	EMPLOYED HOMEMAKERS	FULL-TIME HOMEMAKERS FARM	NON-FARM
		Per Cent	
Bake a lot*	43	59	35
Bake cakes, cookies	97	97	95
Bake pies, tarts	86	93	83
Bake bread*	31	62	31
Preserve a lot*	58	93	67
Can	88	100	89
Freeze	49	84	55
Make pickles, etc.*	80	97	81
Sew clothing*	25	67	44
Use mixes in baking	88	77	81
Use commercially frozen foods*	66	43	64

* Difference is statistically significant.

SUPERVISION OF CHILDREN

Another area in which to examine role definition is the supervision of children. Two activities—assistance with school lessons and help at bedtime for children under twelve—were selected. In both, the farmers were less likely to participate than other husbands (Table 17.4). Farm mothers were more likely than others to assume complete responsibility for the children. Again, the difference appeared to be associated more with occupational variance than with a change in roles brought about by the employment of the wife. It does appear that husbands with employed wives were more likely to assume total responsibility for assistance with lessons than those in non-farm, full-time homemakers' families. This may be because the educational level of husbands with employed wives is higher and labor is divided according to competence and is not a necessity created by the mother's employment.

TABLE 17.4 *Help Given Children with Lessons and at Bedtime by Employment Status of the Mother*

HELPERS	EMPLOYED HOMEMAKERS	FULL-TIME HOMEMAKERS FARM	NON-FARM
		Per Cent	
*Assistance with Lessons**	(N = 51)	(N = 46)	(N = 84)
Wife	35	54	39
Both	31	28	42
Husband	26	11	8
Children or other	8	7	11
Total	100	100	100
*Help Given at Bedtime**	(N = 41)	(N = 51)	(N = 157)
Wife	56	88	57
Both	27	4	35
Husband	10	0	4
Children or other	7	8	4
Total	100	100	100

° Difference is statistically significant.

From these data, the traditional role definition appears to be more prevalent in farm families than in other types. This is no doubt associated with the demands of an agrarian way of life rather than an adherence to tradition for tradition's sake. In some cases, the definitions of family roles have changed to the greatest degree in families with employed homemakers. However, certain changes among non-farm, full-time homemakers also seemed to indicate a general acceptance of increased participation in home-making activities by the husband and the use of commercial services by the wife.

PARTICIPATION IN COMMUNITY ACTIVITIES

Employment of the wife is often cited as undesirable because it takes women away from volunteer organizations and community activities. Such participation is considered vital to the accomplishment of essential community work.

Information concerning formal participation of both the husband and wife was obtained. Scores for each organization were assigned by the following system: one point for membership, two for attendance, three for paying dues, four for being a committee member, and five for holding office within the past two years. The maximum score for one organization was fifteen points (2). The sum of the scores for each organization was used as the individual's formal participation score.

Formal participation scores of husbands in employed homemaker families were significantly greater than those of husbands in full-time homemaker families (17.6 for employed compared with 10.4 farm and 10.4 non-farm full-time homemaker). The difference may be related to the greater number of white-collar workers among husbands of employed homemakers than among those of full-time homemakers. Although the formal participation scores were not statistically different for the wives, there seemed to be an indication of a somewhat higher level among employed homemakers (15.8 for employed compared to 10.8 for farm and 11.8 for non-farm full-time homemakers).

SATISFACTION WITH LIVING SITUATION

The satisfaction with the living situation was measured through a composite score derived from attitudes of respondents concerning the specific situations under investigation.

Data were summarized under two general categories: (1) answers reflecting success in coping with the problems of daily living, such as unfinished tasks, fatigue, time pressures and (2) answers reflecting attitudes about the respondent's own situation as a full-time or employed homemaker.[1] Mean scores for ability to cope ranged from 3.2 for the employed homemakers and their husbands to 3.0 for the farm, full-time homemakers. Apparently all of these families, regardless of employment status, were able to handle the daily living problems with aplomb. In addition, they apparently were able to derive satisfaction within the framework of their own situation. Mean scores for satisfaction ranged from 3.3 for the non-farm, full-time homemaker to 3.1 for the husbands of employed homemakers.

Additional indication of the ability of families with employed homemakers to adjust to the situation was reflected in plans for the future. Slightly over 66 per cent of the employed homemakers planned to continue working, and 90 per cent of the husbands said it was worthwhile for their wives to work.

SUMMARY AND CONCLUSIONS

Data used to measure the impact of maternal employment on the family and the community failed to support strong negative attitudes about the

---

[1] For each category, answers to specific questions were scored using the following scale:

    4—well satisfied, approve
    3—fairly well satisfied
    2—both satisfied and dissatisfied
    1—somewhat dissatisfied
    0—not satisfied, disapprove

consequences of the employment of mothers. Families with employed home-makers appeared to be able to redistribute the homemaker's work load in such a way that, at least for those areas measured, the mother was not failing in her obligations to her children, her house, or her community. Although much more research is needed on the impact of maternal employment, at present there appears little support for the assumption of an inherent incompatibility between the wife and mother roles and the worker role. The families in this rural community were managing their homemaking responsibilities and apparently doing so quite satisfactorily to them, even in situations where the wife performed dual roles.

Family role definition did differ somewhat among these families. In some areas, the tendency toward a sharing of household responsibilities between husband and wife was most pronounced in the employed homemakers' families. However, role definitions in non-farm, full-time homemakers' families indicated a more general acceptance of increased participation in homemaking by husbands. Farm families adhered more closely than other families to the traditional role definition for husband and wife.

The attempt to measure the impact of maternal employment on the children, the housekeeping, community participation, and the general level of satisfaction, failed to reveal adverse effects. Children of employed mothers were receiving supervision. Housekeeping tasks were dispatched to the satisfaction of the families involved. Community participation was not neglected. Families with employed homemakers expressed feelings of success in coping with problems of daily living and reflected satisfaction with their own situation to the same extent as those with full-time homemakers.

REFERENCES

1. Blood, Robert O., Jr. "The Division of Labor in City and Farm Families," *Marriage and Family Living,* XX (May, 1958), 170–74.
2. Chapin, F. S. "The Measurement of Sociality and Socio-Economic Status," *Sociology and Social Research,* XII (1927–1928), 208–17.
3. *Development of Agricultural Human Resources, A Report on Problems of Low-Income Farmers.* United States Department of Agriculture. Washington, D.C.: Government Printing Office, 1955.
4. "Marital and Family Characteristics of Workers." In *Current Population Report.* United States Department of Commerce, Bureau of the Census, Series P-50, No. 87. Washington, D.C.: Government Printing Office, 1959, pp. 1–2.

Chapter Eighteen

Dominance and the Working Wife*

DAVID M. HEER

MOST of the existing studies on the effects of the working wife on family life have been based on predominantly middle-class cases. The dearth of studies of the effects on family life of the working-class working wife is unfortunate because a larger proportion of working-class families have working wives than do middle-class families. Therefore, it was decided that in the present study explicit attention would be given to comparing the effect of the working wife on family decision-making in the working class with its effect in the middle class.

The existing literature contains three previous studies which have dealt with the effect of the wife's working on family decision-making. Kligler (5), in a predominantly middle-class sample of respondents from the New York area, showed that the working mother influenced family decisions on major purchases, loans, savings, and investments to a greater extent than did the nonworking mother. This difference was statistically significant at beyond the .05 level.

Fougeyrollas (2), in a study of respondents in a suburb of Paris, France, demonstrated that the working wife had greater authority in making decisions in a variety of areas. The sample contained respondents from all social classes but results were not published showing the effect on decision-making of the wife's working for different social classes separately.

The third existing study relating the effect of the wife's work status to family decision-making came to publication when the present study was in

* Adapted from *Social Forces,* XXXVI (May, 1958), 341–47, by permission of the author and the publisher. Copyright © 1958, The University of North Carolina Press.

progress. In a reanalysis of their data comparing 500 delinquents with 500 matched nondelinquents, Sheldon and Eleanor Glueck show that for both the delinquent and nondelinquent samples, the working mother is more apt to dominate family affairs than the nonworking mother (4, pp. 327 ff.). The Gluecks do not explain how they decided that either the mother or the father dominated family affairs. Apparently this was determined from the coding of unstructured interviews usually with the mother alone, sometimes with the father, with both parents, or with one of the boy's older siblings or a relative. We are also told that "we had the judgment of the psychiatrist which was made following his interview with the boy" (3, pp. 41–52, 112).

THE STUDY

The data for the present study were gathered from the answers to 138 oral interviews with respondent couples living in the Greater Boston area. In all cases both husband and wife were interviewed together. Of the total families interviewed, approximately one-quarter were working-class families in which the wife was working, one-quarter were working-class families in which the wife did not work, one-quarter were middle-class families in which the wife was working, and one-quarter were middle-class families in which the wife did not work. All families had at least one child of elementary-school age and a father in the age range from 26 to 46. In order to compare middle class and working class without simultaneously being compelled to hold constant religious and ethnic differences, it was decided to interview only Roman-Catholic families of Irish descent. Thus, any speculative generalizations to the broader American scene of the data here presented must take into account the special peculiarities in these families engendered by their adherence to the Catholic faith and by their Irish cultural background.

The names of the respondents were selected in collaboration with the parish pastor and/or parochial school principal in 11 parishes in the Greater Boston area. The great majority of respondents were from the city of Boston. In 10 of the 11 parishes, the respondents were selected from a list of families having children in the parochial school. In all, there was only one family out of the 138 in which no child attended a parochial elementary school. In all cases both partners in the marriage were Roman Catholic.

For purposes of this study, middle-class families were differentiated from working-class families by a classification of the husband's occupation. The classification employed was that contained in the 1950 Census of Population publication, *Alphabetical Index of Occupations and Industries*. Families where the husband's occupation was classified as being professional manager, proprietor, official, sales or clerical worker were deemed to be middle-class. Families where the husband's occupation was craftsman, foreman, operative, service worker, or laborer were defined as working class.

A working-wife family was defined as one where the wife was currently gainfully employed for at least ten hours a week and either had worked for two years or planned to remain in the labor force for a total of at least two years. In no case was a family interviewed unless the husband was also gainfully employed for at least two years prior to the interview. A nonworking-wife family was defined as one where the wife had not been gainfully employed for at least two years prior to the interview. In almost all cases she had not been employed since the birth of her first child.

Interviewing in low-income parishes was restricted to working-class families. In relatively high-income parishes interviewing was limited to middle-class families. In the parishes of middle income or of varied income, interviewing included both middle- and working-class respondents. Thus, an attempt was made to secure middle-class respondents from middle-class neighborhoods and working-class respondents from working-class neighborhoods.

In each parish, the names were requested of all Irish families where the mother was working which met the other requirements. In addition, an approximately equal number of names of families was wanted where the wife did not work. In about half the cases, the selection of the nonworking-wife families was made by the writer by a random-number process or under his direct observation with instruction to pick names in a successive sample. In the other half, it was made by the nun or priest in the researcher's absence after he had given instructions that the names were to be picked at random.

Prior to the interview a letter was sent to each prospective respondent couple. The letter informed them that their name had been given the researcher through the cooperation of their local pastor and that when he came to call he would carry a letter from their pastor asking for their cooperation in the project.

The interview refusal rate was approximately one-third. However, it was approximately the same in the working-wife and the nonworking-wife groups. Probably the major reason for the high refusal rate was the stipulation that the husband and wife were to be seen together. In addition, some of the families feared that it was another Kinsey report and that the questions would be more intimate than they actually were.

A comparison of the four major subgroups on various demographic variables reveals that the groups are quite comparable on all but one variable: the number of children. The average number of children in the working-class working-wife group was approximately $2\frac{1}{2}$, in the working-class housewife group about 4, in the middle-class working-wife groups around 3, and finally in the middle-class housewife group $4\frac{1}{2}$. It is incidentally interesting that the middle-class families in both working-wife and housewife groups have more children than their working-class counterparts.

TABLE 18.1 *Who Usually Wins Out If There Is Disagreement in Family Decision-Making*

GROUP	BOTH PARTNERS AGREE THAT HUSBAND USUALLY WINS OUT	ONE PARTNER SAYS HUSBAND USUALLY WINS, OTHER PARTNER SAYS DECISIONS ARE MUTUAL	BOTH PARTNERS SAY DECISIONS ARE MUTUAL; OR EACH SAYS THE OTHER WINS OUT	ONE PARTNER SAYS WIFE USUALLY WINS, OTHER PARTNER SAYS DECISIONS ARE MUTUAL	BOTH PARTNERS AGREE THAT WIFE USUALLY WINS OUT	TOTAL ANSWERING	MEAN SCORE FOR GROUP OF HUSBAND'S RELATIVE INFLUENCE[1]
	Per cent	*Per cent*	*Per cent*	*Per cent*	*Per cent*		
Working class, working wife	15	09	37	18	21	33	−.21
Working class, housewife	28	02	63	00	07	40	.43
Middle class, working wife	28	06	47	10	09	32	.34
Middle class, housewife	50	03	34	13	00	32	.91

RESULTS OF ANALYSIS OF VARIANCE

SOURCE	F
Difference between working-wife and housewife groups	10.99*
Difference between working and middle class	8.49*
Interaction	0.03

[1] A plus score indicates greater influence of husband.
* Statistically significant.

The present study tried to answer several questions relative to the effect of the working on family decision-making. First, there was an interest in establishing whether or not the increased influence of the working wife in family decision-making would exist separately in both the middle and the working class. Secondly, there was an interest in finding out whether or not the working-class working wife would have more to say about family decisions than the middle-class working wife. It was hypothesized that since the earnings of the working-class working wife would more nearly approximate those of her husband than those of the middle-class working wife, she would have more say in family decision-making than her middle-class counterpart. Finally, there was a desire to try to answer the question: Is the presumed association between the working-wife family and increased feminine influence in family decision-making a real cause-and-effect relationship or is it due to other factors associated both with the wife's working and feminine predominance in decision-making.

Husband and wife sitting down together were asked the following question: "Now I would like to know something about decisions in your family. When there's a really important decision on which you two are likely to disagree, who usually wins out?" The opinions of each spouse were then coded. The results are presented in Table 18.1. A mean score on relative influence in family decision-making was constructed in the following way. If both husband and wife agreed that the husband usually won out, the couple received a score of plus 2. If one spouse said the husband usually won out but the other said the decisions were equal, a score of plus 1 was given. If both spouses agreed that neither won out more than the other or if each claimed the other to win out more, a score of 0 was given. Similarly, if one spouse thought the wife won out while the other claimed decisions were mutual, a score of —1 was given. If both spouses agreed that the wife won out usually, a score of —2 was assigned.

For lack of a nonparametric substitute, two-way analysis of variance was used to test the two effects of work status of wife and social class upon influence in family decision-making. A glance at Table 18.1 will show that interaction is extremely small and that both the wife's work status and social class are significantly related to family decision-making.[1]

---

[1] It may be worthwhile to speculate whether any difference in results would have occurred had the question on decision-making been asked of husband and wife separately rather than jointly. There is a plausible argument that bias would be lessened if the husband and wife were asked separately rather than together. If interviewed jointly, the partner who is actually more dominant might cause the submissive partner to agree that the two have equal influence. In some cases this may have occurred. However, it is equally plausible that asking the question of the spouses jointly reduces an element of bias operative when each is interviewed alone. In our culture equality between the partners is preferred to marked dominance by one. When questioned

TABLE 18.2 *Questions Measuring The Personality Trait of Dominance in Nonmarital Roles*

---

1. Do you usually try to convince other people to do things your way?

   Yes   No   ?

2. Does your shyness ever keep you from doing things you would otherwise like to do?

   Yes   No   ?

3. At a social gathering do you take the responsibility of introducing people to the other persons they do not know?

   Yes   No   ?

4. If you are interested in buying some article you saw for sale in the classified columns of the newspaper do you frequently try to bargain down the price before you buy?

   Yes   No   ?

5. Do you suffer from feelings of inferiority?

   Yes   No   ?

6. Have you ever been responsible for the organization of any clubs, teams, or other groups?

   Yes   No   ?

7. Do you feel ill-at-ease when you have to strike up conversation with strangers?

   Yes   No   ?

8. When a waitress brings you a dish at a restaurant that is not prepared the way you ordered, do you ask her to take it back rather than accept it the way it is?

   Yes   No   ?

The finding that the working-class working wife has more say in family decision-making than the middle-class working wife was hypothesized. However, adequate thought had not been given in advance to the decision-making process in the nonworking-wife families. Post hoc we may speculate that the difference is due to the following: In any serious period of crisis in family decision-making during which the wife might threaten to seek a legal separation, the consequences, both socially and economically, of carrying through that threat would probably be greater for the middle-class than for the working-class wife.

---

alone, therefore, the dominating partner is tempted to deny greater influence, whereas in a joint interview the other partner can contradict him. I noted several instances in which a respondent who at first claimed that he did not have the greater influence admitted this fact after his spouse had pointed out examples. Thus, it would appear that, although questioning spouses together may in some cases introduce bias, in other cases it acts to eliminate bias. Further research is necessary to determine which situation produces less bias.

TABLE 18.3   *Results of the Eight-Item Personality Test of Dominance in Nonmarital Roles*

GROUP	MEAN SCORE OF WIVES	MEAN SCORE OF HUSBANDS	MEAN HUSBAND-WIFE DIFFERENCE	NUMBER OF CASES
Working class, working wife	7.48	8.33	.85	33
Working class, housewife	6.98	8.65	1.67	40
Middle class, working wife	7.91	11.18	3.27	33
Middle class, housewife	7.66	10.09	2.43	32

RESULTS OF ANALYSIS OF VARIANCE

SOURCE	F
I. Scores of wives	
Working vs. nonworking wife	0.56
Working class vs. middle class	1.17
Interaction	0.06
II. Scores of husbands	
Working vs. nonworking wife	0.48
Working class vs. middle class	14.60*
Interaction	1.58
III. Mean husband-wife difference scores	
Working vs. nonworking wife	0.00
Working class vs. middle class	4.05*
Interaction	1.11

* Statistically significant.

A third question which the present study hoped to help answer was whether the association of feminine predominance in family decision-making with the working-wife family is a mere chance coincidence or a cause-and-effect relationship. This writer's hypothesis was that it was such a cause-and-effect relationship. To prove this one way or the other is very difficult, but perhaps this study will at least shed some light on the problem. For instance, it could plausibly be argued that the relationship is a mere association due to the fact that a woman who goes out of the home to take a job is by nature more dominant in her dealings with other individuals than is her husband.

Therefore, any differences found between working and nonworking wives in their relative degree of power in family decision-making could be explained entirely on the basis of personality differences between the two groups.

To test this possibility, it was decided to devise a short test of dominance in general interpersonal relations but excluding the marriage relation. An original set of eight items was correlated, on a sample of 50 women from Boston settlement house mothers' clubs, with the Bernreuter Personality Inventory Test of Dominance (1). After this pretesting of items, a revised set of eight questions was obtained and again correlated with the Bernreuter test of dominance on an additional group of 101 women also from settlement house mothers' clubs. A coefficient of .79 resulted.

The eight questions are shown in Table 18.2. They were presented to the respondents on a sheet of paper and each spouse wrote out his answers on this sheet privately.

For each of the four groups, the mean score for husbands, the mean score for wives, and the mean husband-wife score difference is shown in Table 18.3. As might be expected, the working women in both middle and working class score higher than their nonworking counterparts. It is surprising to note, however, that the husbands of middle-class working wives score higher than the husbands of middle-class nonworking wives. The only statistically significant differences in this table, however, are those occurring for the scores of husbands and for the husband-wife difference scores between the working and the middle-class. Thus we see that there are no large differences between working-wife and housewife families in their scores in the personality trait of dominance as here measured.

What happens to the relationship between work status and decision-making when we try to hold constant the husband-wife difference in general personality dominance? Let us subdivide each of our four groups on the basis of this latter variable. By this procedure we have held constant most, if not all, of the variation between the four groups in the husband-wife difference scores. The results are shown in Table 18.4. We see there that for both working class and middle class, the differences in family decision-making dependent on the work status of the wife still remain. In the case of the working class, the difference between working-wife and nonworking-wife groups is significant. In the case of the middle class, this difference approaches statistical significance.

The major variable in which the working-wife subgroups of the sample differed from the housewife subgroups was the number of children. Somewhat unexpectedly, it was discovered that in every subgroup there was a positive association between the number of children in the family and the influence of the husband in decision-making. It was therefore decided to compute the degree of association between the number of children and the

TABLE 18.4 Mean Scores on Husband's Relative Influence in Family Decision-Making, by Wife's Work Status, Social Class, and Husband-Wife Difference in a Personality Test of Nonmarital Dominance

	RANGE OF HUSBAND-WIFE DIFFERENCES IN PERSONALITY TEST SCORES		MEAN HUSBAND-WIFE DIFFERENCE ON PERSONALITY TEST	MEAN SCORE OF HUSBAND'S INFLUENCE IN DECISION-MAKING[1]	NUMBER OF CASES
Working class, working-wife group	From 3 to	10	6.27	−.27	11
	From −1 to	2	0.58	−.83	12
	From −12 to	−2	−4.80	.60	10
Working class, housewife group	From 3 to	11	6.00	.27	15
	From −2 to	2	0.32	.47	19
	From −8 to	−3	−4.83	.67	6
Middle class, working-wife group	From 1 to	11	5.59	.27	22
	From −5 to	0	−1.50	.50	10
Middle class, housewife group	From 3 to	12	6.06	1.06	17
	From −7 to	2	−1.67	.73	15

RESULTS OF ANALYSIS OF VARIANCE

SOURCE	F
I. Working Class	
Husband-wife personality difference	2.76
Working vs. nonworking wife	7.23*
Interaction	0.92
II. Middle Class	
Husband-wife personality difference	0.51
Working vs. nonworking wife	3.30*
Interaction	0.74

[1] A plus score indicates greater influence of husband.
* Statistically significant.

influence of the husband in decision-making for all four subgroups combined. In computing this association, differences in decision-making due to social class and wife's work status were held constant. The individual scores on family decision-making were each subtracted from the mean score of their subgroup. Kendall's Tau was then computed from the rankings of these deviates and the rankings of each couple on the number of their children. The resultant value for Tau was .114, which is significant. Thus, holding constant both social class and wife's work status, a statistically significant positive association between the influence of the father in family decision-making and the number of children in the family was found.

To determine if the number of children could account for the association between wife's work status and the relative influence of each spouse in decision-making, the mean scores of the husband's relative influence in decision-making for each of the subgroups were recomputed after the cases in each subgroup had been standardized for the number of children.[2] Both the standardized and the unstandardized results are shown in Table 18.5. It will be seen that the previous differences both by wife's work status and by social class remain. However, the magnitude of the difference dependent on the wife's work status has been reduced considerably, particularly so in the case of the middle-class subgroups.

What are the possible conclusions that can be drawn from these results?

TABLE 18.5 *Mean Influence of Husband in Decision-Making by Wife's Work Status and by Social Class, Standardized for Number of Children in Family, and Unstandardized[1]*

	STANDARDIZED FOR NUMBER OF CHILDREN	UNSTANDARDIZED	NUMBER OF CASES
Working class, working wife	—.16	—.21	33
Working class, housewife	.33	.43	40
Middle class, working wife	.39	.34	32
Middle class, housewife	.62	.91	32

[1] A plus score indicates greater influence of husband.

[2] The component proportions for this standardization were the following five groups of families: (1) with one child, (2) with two children, (3) with three children, (4) with four children, (5) with five children or more.

First it seems likely that the differential incidence of a generalized trait of personality dominance cannot account for the fact that working wives have more influence in family decision-making than housewives (although to rule out this factor entirely might be presumptuous in view of the possibilities for error in the present rather rough attempt to assess the personality trait of dominance).

Secondly, the association found between the number of children in the family and the husband's influence in decision-making raises an interesting possibility: Not only may the work status of the wife affect the degree of her influence in family decision-making, but conversely, at least for this sample of Roman Catholics, her relative influence may also indirectly affect her work status. We may first presume that among principled Roman Catholics the teachings of the Church concerning birth control are faithfully followed. This fact would imply that the only means of birth limitation available to these couples is that which can be obtained through the "rhythm method." If the periodic sexual abstinence required by the rhythm method is more irksome to the husband than to the wife, then it should follow that the requisite restraint in sexual relations might be most likely to occur in those families where the wife in general had the greater influence in family decision-making. Therefore, families in which the wife had the greater influence would tend to have the fewer number of children. Having fewer children, the wife could more easily enter the labor force. Thus, not only would the wife's work status exert an effect on her relative influence in decision-making but the reverse chain of causation would exist as well. Further research is needed to continue the exploration of these possibilities.

SUMMARY

In a sample of Irish Roman Catholic families with at least one child of elementary-school age we have shown that both in the working class and in the middle class the working wife exerts more influence in decision-making than the nonworking wife. We have also shown that whether they are employed or not, wives in working-class families have more say in family decision-making than wives in middle-class families. We have also tested the hypothesis that this correlation between the wife's work status and influence in family decision-making could be accounted for by an association between the wife's work status and a husband-wife difference in the personality trait of dominance in nonmarital roles. The present results indicate that this hypothesis is false. An unexpected by-product of the study was a statistically significant positive association between the number of children in the family and the influence of the husband in decision-making. Holding constant the number of children, the association between the wife's work status and the relative influence of each spouse in decision-making was maintained, but in reduced magnitude.

REFERENCES

1. Bernreuter, Robert G. "The Theory and Construction of the Personality Inventory," *Journal of Social Psychology,* IV (November, 1933), 387 ff.
2. Fougeyrollas, Pierre. "Prédominance du Mari ou de la Femme dans le Menage," *Population,* VI (January–March, 1951), 83 ff.
3. Glueck, Sheldon, and Glueck, Eleanor. *Unraveling Juvenile Delinquency.* New York: Commonwealth Fund, 1950.
4. ————. "Working Mothers and Delinquency," *Mental Hygiene,* XLI (July, 1957), 327–52.
5. Kligler, Deborah H. "The Effects of the Employment of Married Women on Husband and Wife Roles." Unpublished Ph.D. dissertation, Yale University, 1954.

Chapter Nineteen

Marital Interaction*

F. IVAN NYE

LITTLE previous research or theory bears directly on the marital adjustment of employed mothers. Locke and Mackeprang reported no difference in the marital adjustment of employed and non-employed wives (8). The employed wives were not, however, all mothers. Haveman and West, analyzing data from college graduates gathered in 1947, concluded that employed women (not all of whom were mothers) had smaller families and a higher divorce rate (3). Komarovsky later hypothesized conditions under which mothers could be employed without adversely affecting marital or parent-child adjustments (5). Parsons brushed the question aside as of little importance because the occupations and positions taken over by married women do not often compete in status terms with those occupied by husbands (10). (For concurrent research, see other chapters in Part III of this book.)

Two ideas stemming from role theory appear to be particularly illuminating. First, major role innovations are accompanied by conflict as new definitions differ from the old ones (1); and, second, the present housekeeper and related roles of the full-time housewife are not completely satisfying to many women if 40 per cent of those with school-age children have taken employment.

---

* Revision of "Employment Status of Mothers and Marital Conflict, Permanence, and Happiness," *Social Problems,* VI (Winter, 1958–1959), 260–67, section from F. Ivan Nye and Evelyn MacDougall, "The Dependent Variable in Marital Research," *Pacific Sociological Review,* II (Fall, 1959), 67–70 and revision of F. Ivan Nye, "Maternal Employment and Marital Interaction: Some Contingent Conditions," *Social Forces,* XL (December, 1961), 113–19 by permission of the publishers.

The preceding ideas suggest that the employment of mothers may be differentially related to various criteria of marital success, such as the following:

(a) *Conflict.* Conflicting definitions of the mother's roles will result in more arguments and quarrels in families in which the mother is employed. Hypothesis: Conflict is more frequent among couples in which the mother is employed full-time than among those in which she is not employed.

(b) *Permanence.* Arguments and quarrels, together with the knowledge that mothers can support themselves, will result in more separations and thoughts of divorce among employed mothers. Hypothesis: Separations and divorce are more characteristic of couples in which the mother is employed.

(c) *Happiness and satisfaction.* Employment increases the family level of living, the prestige of the mother, the appreciation of her by her husband, and the amount of democratic decision-making in the family; moreover, she enjoys some of the social contacts connected with her job. Hypothesis: Marital happiness and satisfaction are greater among full-time employed mothers than among mothers not employed.[1]

SOCIAL-PSYCHOLOGICAL EQUIVALENCE

A comparison of subsamples of employed and non-employed mothers implies that the samples were equivalent before employment and that differences found were the result of employment. Ideally, attitude and behavior data on socio-psychological equivalence should be collected at the instant just prior to the beginning of the woman's employment. For several reasons this is impracticable. It was possible, however, to collect such data from women college seniors just prior to graduation. It is believed that attitudes and behavior patterns are sufficiently formed by the age of twenty-one or twenty-two years to provide some evidence concerning equivalence. It is

---

[1] The logic of characterizing a group of marriages at the same time by high conflict and high happiness might be questioned. These characteristics have not, however, been generally accepted as antitheses. One school of thought in sociology and psychiatry has held that open conflict in marriage is beneficial in that it results in problem-solving and release of tensions and frustrations.

At the time the study was planned, it appeared to the writer that the economic, social, and psychological advantages of employment might more than offset the anticipated conflicts. Additional research by the writer and Evelyn McDougall now incorporated in this report has shown that marital happiness and absence of marital conflict will scale on the same dimension (9). This makes the above hypothesis untenable. The writer prefers, however, to present this untenable hypothesis and refute it rather than to eliminate it in the light of now available knowledge.

recognized that circumstances in marriage will alter the preferred pattern, but attitude and behavior differences should be maximized between those who want or do not want to combine motherhood and an occupation.

Data were gathered from 211 female seniors graduating from the State College of Washington in June of 1957. The group was divided into those favorable and those unfavorable to employment after marriage. A woman was classified as favorable to such employment if she indicated that she would prefer to return to work at any time after the birth of her children. If she indicated that she would work only under special circumstances and/ or only until the birth of her first child, she was considered to have an unfavorable attitude toward employment after marriage.

The aspect of equivalence relevant to the present analysis is the attitude of women toward the opposite sex: do girls who prefer to combine marriage and a vocation have different attitudes toward the opposite sex than those who prefer the traditional role of wife and mother? Seven questions were asked to obtain information on this point: (a) present marital status, (b) frequency of dating, (c) feeling comfortable or (d) easy with men, (e) importance of marriage as a value, and (f) adjustment to and (g) frequency of quarreling with father. It was assumed that girls who married or became engaged in college, dated frequently, felt comfortable and easy with men, and who had had little conflict with their fathers have favorable attitudes toward the opposite sex. In an initial analysis, two items distinguished significantly between women who do and do not want to combine marriage and a vocation, and five items did not. When those who were making little progress toward marriage (not married, engaged, pinned, or dating frequently) were removed, differences became non-significant. No present evidence, therefore, requires the rejection of the null hypothesis that women who combine motherhood and employment and those who do not are simple random samples from the same universe in terms of premarital attitudes toward the other sex. Present investigation on this point is not, however, conclusive, and more research on this matter would be desirable.

CRITERIA OF MARITAL SUCCESS

MEASUREMENT

Burgess and Wallin have shown that a number of measures of marital success have been developed and can be alternatively employed as the criterion (1). Landis recently found that a considerable proportion of divorces followed no prior warnings of marital conflict and unhappiness (6). In view of these findings, it was decided initially to employ multiple criteria rather than to attempt a composite measure of marital success. The criteria selected were conflict, permanence, happiness, and satisfaction as reported by the mothers.

As one measure of marital conflict, a number of items were devised to obtain frequency of arguments on children, finances, recreation, house and furniture, radio and T.V., and "other." It was presumed that inter-action in each area is essentially independent of other areas, although some interrelationship might be present. To determine whether some common dimension might be present which would justify employing a total score, the items were dichotomized and scaled employing the Guttman Cornell Technique. The analysis revealed a reproducibility coefficient of .92, sug-gesting a single dimension in spousal arguing. Since this finding was un-expected, a second sample was drawn and scaled with a resulting coefficient of .90. These findings seemed to justify the use of an "arguing scale" as one measure of marital conflict.

THE RESPONDENTS

As part of a larger study of the employment status of mothers, data were collected from 1,993 mothers in three Washington towns in the spring of 1957. The respondents were mothers of children in grades one and ten of the public and parochial schools in these communities. Names and addresses of mothers were obtained from school records of all public and parochial schools and data collected from them by mailed questionnaires, of which 78 per cent were returned. Bias from non-response was checked by comparing the returned questionnaires with those collected from 99 per cent of tenth grade students in the same schools (see Chapter Ten). The result of this check revealed no appreciable non-response bias by marital status, education of the mother, or employment status of the mother.

The small cities sampled had populations of 10,107; 10,228; and 21,809 in 1950. They experienced a rapid growth in the decade 1940 to 1950 and continued to grow in the 1950's. Related to this rapid growth is a dearth of retired people and high spatial mobility. The income level is higher than that of the state as a whole.

These differences, however, appear unrelated to the prevalence of women in employment. Presumably communities characterized by large pro-portions of employed mothers would be more tolerant and sympathetic toward them, which might, in turn, affect marital adjustment. To determine whether these communities had a higher than average proportion of em-ployed mothers a comparison was made between the occupational structure of the three towns and that of the State of Washington and the nation as a whole. The proportion of women employed in the three communities (32.1 per cent) is very near the state average (32.9 per cent) for cities 10,000 to 100,000. The proportion employed in all urban areas of Washington (31.6 per cent) is slightly lower than for the United States (33.2 per cent). Both "professional" and "clerical" categories of women workers are slightly higher for the three communities than for cities of comparable size in Washington. In other respects, these communities do not appear to be atypical with respect to the employment of women.

The sample is principally urban. A few farm families (53) in which children attended city schools were included initially but were dropped in the interests of homogeneity, restricting the respondents to the non-farm population. Families in which there was no male head (77) were likewise eliminated, as were the non-Caucasian families (7) in the sample. All families therefore, include father and mother (or step-parent), are non-farm, and Caucasian. Since it had been found in another sample (Chapter One) that employed mothers were more likely to be highly educated, have smaller families, fewer preschool children, to involve broken homes, and to be from low socio-economic levels, these variables were controlled by random subsampling (Table 19.1).

TABLE 19.1 *Social Characteristics of Mothers Employed Full-Time and Not Employed, and of Matched Samples of the Same Employment Categories*

	ORIGINAL SAMPLE		MATCHED SAMPLE	
SOCIAL CHARACTERISTICS[1]	*Employed Full-Time*	*Not Employed*	*Employed Full-Time*	*Not Employed*
Preschool children	23.3	64.8	29.1	30.3
Large families	27.3	45.8	27.6	27.7
Upper status	18.0	27.8	22.1	22.5
Low education	8.9	17.1	10.0	10.0
Remarriage	13.0	11.9	15.1	15.5

[1] Social Characteristics:
   Preschool children—one or more present in home.
   Large family—four or more children.
   Upper status—professional, semi-professional, and business other than family operated.
   Low education—grade or junior high school only.
   Remarriage—widowed or divorced and remarried.

FINDINGS

CONFLICT

With respect to arguments, the data provide support for the hypothesis that more marital conflict is present among couples in which the mother is employed (Table 19.2). It is true that couples who argue frequently on six or more subjects (scale type I) are about proportionately divided among the employment categories. Employed mothers are, however, considerably overrepresented in scale type II, in which they have frequent

TABLE 19.2 *Employment Status of Mother and Arguments with Spouse**

| ARGUMENTS SCALE TYPE[1] | MATERNAL EMPLOYMENT STATUS | | | |
| | NOT EMPLOYED | | EMPLOYED FULL-TIME | |
	Number	*Per Cent*	*Number*	*Per Cent*
1	9	2.3	4	2.1
2	18	4.6	16	8.2
3–6	274	69.4	145	74.7
7	94	23.8	29	14.9
Total	395	100.0	194	99.9

* Statistically significant.
[1] Scale Types:
  1: Arguments on all six subjects sometimes or oftener
  2: Arguments on children, money, recreation, house and furniture, and "Other" sometimes or oftener
  3: Arguments on children, money, recreation, and "Other" sometimes or oftener
  4: Arguments on children, money, and "Other" sometimes or oftener
  5: Arguments on children and money sometimes or oftener
  6: Arguments on children sometimes or oftener
  7: Arguments on no subject sometimes or oftener

TABLE 19.3 *Employment Status of Mother and Various Criteria of Marital Adjustment*

| CRITERIA OF MARITAL ADJUSTMENT[1] | NOT EMPLOYED (N = 400) | | EMPLOYED FULL-TIME (N = 199) | |
	Number	*Per Cent*	*Number*	*Per Cent*
Conflict				
Argued	183	45.8	103	51.6
Quarreled*	30	7.6	26	13.4
Permanence				
Lived apart*	46	11.6	33	16.7
Considered divorce*	178	46.6	133	60.1
Happiness				
"Was unhappy"	80	20.7	52	26.8
Satisfaction				
"Was dissatisfied"	110	28.9	56	28.3

[1] Categories presented are from the lower end of the marital success distribution.
  Arguing: sometimes or oftener in four or more areas
  Quarreling: fairly often or more frequently
  Lived apart: one or more times following a quarrel
  Considered divorce: all responses except never
  Happiness: partly unhappy, unhappy, and very unhappy
  Satisfaction: partly or less satisfied
* Statistically significant.

arguments on five subjects. At the other extreme, proportionately fewer employed mothers argue frequently on no topic (scale type VII). Quarreling is found to be more frequent also among couples in which the mother is employed full-time (Table 19.3). The difference is statistically significant.

Roughly equivalent data were collected from the adolescent children of employed and not employed mothers as part of another study. The adolescent perception of the quarreling and disagreement between parents agrees with that of the mothers themselves that there is more conflict between spouses in families in which the mother is employed. The accumulated data, therefore, provide some evidence supporting the hypothesis that there is more marital conflict among couples in which the mother is employed full-time.

PERMANENCE

Two items were included to secure some indication of the permanence of the marriage; these were living apart after a quarrel and whether or not the respondent had ever considered divorce (Table 19.3). Whether these experiences later do lead to divorce or permanent separation is not known. The data also show that a slightly larger proportion of employed mothers have at some time been divorced, but there is no information about whether the divorce occurred before or after employment. Since the data on living apart temporarily, considering divorce, and having been divorced, are all consistent, however, it provides limited support for the hypothesis that divorce and separation are more likely to occur among couples in which the mother is employed.

HAPPINESS

Mothers were asked to rate the happiness of the marriage: "Everything considered, how happy has your marriage been for you?" The findings (Table 19.3) do not support the hypothesis that employed women are happier in their marriages, since the differences are non-significant, and are in the opposite direction.

SATISFACTION

Satisfaction is thought to relate the actual situation to a level of expectation. It is possible that one may not be particularly happy in marriage and yet be satisfied. It may be a somewhat more inclusive concept, also, in that it may include elements of standard of living, prestige, vocational satisfactions, and perhaps even parent-child relations. As implied above, it was thought that the employment of the mother was favorable to some of these satisfactions and, therefore, that the employed mother would feel more satisfaction with her relationship to her husband. The data, however, indicate no significant relationship between the employment status of the mother and satisfaction with the marital relationship. If the five-fold classification of entirely dissatisfied, somewhat dissatisfied, fairly well satisfied, generally satisfied, and entirely satisfied is consulted, slightly more non-employed mothers are entirely dissatisfied and slightly fewer are entirely satisfied. More, however, are fairly well or generally satisfied, so that when the distribution is dichotomized, the categories are almost exactly balanced, as shown in Table 19.3.

A MARITAL ADJUSTMENT SCALE[2]

Following the analysis by multiple criteria it was decided to investigate the possibility of a single dimension in marital success. A preliminary analysis was made of the interrelationship of several criteria of marital adjustment, including happiness, satisfaction, quarreling frequency, confiding in husband, considering a divorce, and living apart following a quarrel. Significant interrelationships were found. Each item was also found to be related to arguing scale types.

The intercorrelations found suggested the possibility of a single dimension in marital adjustment. All of the items in the arguing scale, an item on the extent of confiding in the husband, and a trichotomization of the item on satisfaction with the relationship with the husband were included in the first scale. Several of the items from the arguing scale were dropped from the final analysis for the sake of brevity. Although the extent of confiding in the husband is significantly related to all other items on the scale, the coefficients of contingency suggested that the extent of confiding is relatively independent of the other items with the exception of happiness and satisfaction. This was borne out in attempts to scale it with other items, in that the error indicated that it may not be in the same dimension as the other items in the scale. The remaining nine items were scaled employing the Cornell technique (Table 19.4).

The scale derived fulfilled the criteria of a quasi-scale (9). Three general samples of 100 were employed to test scalability. These produced reproducibility coefficients of .86, .87, and .88. The Israel Gamma technique (Image Analysis) was employed with the result that reproducibility was raised to .97 or higher (9). The other prerequisites of a scale were generally fulfilled—that is, first, random error formed a "sort of gradient pattern," second, range of marginal frequencies was found, and, third, in no instance were there more errors in an item than in any one of its marginal frequencies. For a further description, see Nye and MacDougall (9).

---

[2] The following scale description is taken from F. Ivan Nye and Evelyn Mac-Dougall (9).

TABLE 19.4 *Scale Pattern of Marital Adjustment Items[1]*

SCALE TYPE	ITEMS									BEFORE IMAGE ANALYSIS[2]	AFTER IMAGE ANALYSIS
	1	*2*	*3*	*4*	*5*	*6*	*7*	*8*	*9*	*Per*	*Cent*
00	0	0	0	0	0	0	0	0	0	.53	.53
01	1	0	0	0	0	0	0	0	0	2.18	1.53
02	1	1	0	0	0	0	0	0	0	4.67	5.29
03	1	1	1	0	0	0	0	0	0	7.33	10.04
04	1	1	1	1	0	0	0	0	0	8.13	3.22
05	1	1	1	1	1	0	0	0	0	10.04	2.75
06	1	1	1	1	1	1	0	0	0	14.34	13.58
07	1	1	1	1	1	1	1	0	0	13.75	17.60
08	1	1	1	1	1	1	1	1	0	13.81	6.08
09	1	1	1	1	1	1	1	1	1	14.13	21.35
10	1	1	1	1	2	1	1	1	1	11.10	18.02
										100.01	99.99

[1] Thirteen samples of 100 were drawn, coefficients of reproducibility ranged from .978 to .994. Items are:
1. Ever lived apart after a quarrel? 0. Once or more often; 1. Never.
2. Argue about the use of the house and furniture? 0. Very often to sometimes; 1. Rarely or never.
3. Argue about recreation? 0. Very often to sometimes; 1. Rarely or never.
4. Satisfaction with relationship with husband. 0. Entirely dissatisfied to fairly well satisfied; 1. Entirely or generally satisfied.
5. Everything considered, how happy has your marriage been for you? 0. Decidedly unhappy to neither very happy nor unhappy; 1. Decidedly happy; 2. Extraordinarily.
6. Argue about money? 0. Very often to sometimes; 1. Rarely or never.
7. Have you ever considered separating from your husband? 0. Seriously to not seriously; 1. Rarely or never.
8. Frequency of quarreling. 0. Continuously to occasionally; 1. Rarely or never.
9. Argue about children? 0. Very often to sometimes; 1. Rarely or never.

[2] The table is based on 1,892 cases. A total of 99 respondents were lost—83 through being widowed or divorced and not remarried and 16 through excessive omission (more than 3).

After scalability was established on samples of 100 drawn from the entire group, other samples of 100 were drawn from those having junior high school educations or less, high school, or some college education; and those from groups which have children under twelve only or adolescent children only. Goodness of fit tests indicated that there were no significant differences between the distribution of scale types within any of these three groups.

A relationship is found between employment status and marital success when one employs the scale as the criterion. The relationship is low, since it reaches only the 5 per cent level of significance with a sample of almost 600, and $\bar{C}$ is only .17. The difference favors the non-employed mother. The distribution of scale types for the part-time employed mother is similar to that of the non-employed mother.

SUMMARY AND DISCUSSION

Present data support the idea that employment of mothers typically increased conflict in marital relationships. This is consistent with some aspects of role theory. It likewise seems clear that satisfaction and happiness in marriage are not significantly different by employment categories. This probably means that the more prevalent conflict in families where the mother is employed is counterbalanced by increased satisfactions for the mother. Some evidence supporting the latter idea is found in another part of the study which finds that employed mothers are better satisfied with their communities and with their daily work (Chapter Twenty-Two).

Concerning permanence, the interpretation of the data may be debated. Clearly more employed mothers have considered divorce. If we dichotomize marital status into unbroken and broken homes, the differences are significant. It is extremely probable, however, that many women enter employment as a *result* of the break. If we look only at broken homes in which remarriage has occurred (thereby relieving the pressure on the woman to earn money), the differences are less than 2 per cent between employment categories; that is, 13.0 per cent of women employed full-time are remarried compared to 11.9 per cent of women who are not employed. A similar slight difference was found among mothers of high school students in another study. These differences are statistically non-significant.

Employment of mothers might be expected to precipitate some divorces. If conflict related to the employee role is added to family interaction already characterized by conflict and dissatisfaction, divorce or other dissolution might result in some families which otherwise might continue a precarious existence. In more strongly integrated families, conflict related to employment and the greater financial independence of the mother may result in thoughts of divorce, but present data give some reasons to think that such thoughts are infrequently transmitted into action.

CONTINGENT CONDITIONS AND TEST VARIABLES

To this point the analysis has dealt with the general relationship of maternal employment to marital interaction. The purpose of the following analysis is to determine whether any of several related variables or conditions modifies the low negative association found earlier between employment and marital success.

There is considerable justification for employing socio-economic status as a test variable. Komarovsky has stated that material adjustment of employed wives should be better in instances in which the wife's salary is high, her work challenging, and the hours short (5). Landis sees employment as a challenge.

a prestige-gaining device, and an outlet for skills and talents (7). Komarovsky's conditions maximize the personal satisfactions of the wife with a minimum disruption of family routine and services. Landis' conditions would most frequently be met at the higher educational and occupational level. Employment would seem, therefore, to be more likely to lead to the achievement of personal goals and satisfactions when it occurs in the professional and upper white-collar jobs.

If the employment of the wife occurs in a family in which the income of the husband is low, the economic contribution of the wife provides a relatively larger increase in the family level of living. It may, however, equal or exceed that of the husband, or, for some periods, it may be the only or principal income. If the latter conditions are present, which are contrary to the norms, the mother's employment may become a cause of conflict because of her superior economic position. In the light of these considerations, it might be expected that the relationship between employment status and marital adjustment would be more favorable to employed mothers in the high, rather than the low, socio-economic categories.

Certain difficulties are encountered in testing these notions. Since non-employed mothers themselves have no occupational classification, no comparison of them by their occupational level is possible. Comparison can, however, be made between those employed part-time and full-time by the occupational level of the wife. The education level of the mothers and the occupational level of husbands are also available, and inferences of the occupational level of the mother are possible.

OCCUPATION OF THE HUSBAND

The analysis of employment status and marital adjustment was made separately within four broad occupational groups (of husbands): first, professional and managerial; second, clerical and sales; third, crafts and operative; and fourth, laborer and service. None of the analyses revealed significant differences. All sample differences favored the marital adjustment of the non-employed mother; however, the differences favoring her were least in the professional and managerial group. If these differences were present in the populations compared, one might conjecture marital adjustment was affected least adversely in the professional and managerial group. Since all differences involved are non-significant, however, this is little more than conjecture.

OCCUPATION OF THE MOTHER

A second series of analyses was made relating employment status to marital adjustment within broad occupational categories of part-time and full-time employed mothers. If the ideas discussed above are correct, the marital adjustment of mothers employed full-time in professional and managerial jobs should compare more favorably with part-time employed mothers in those categories than would the lower prestige occupations. The analysis within the four broad occupational categories described above revealed only non-significant differences between the marital adjustment of mothers employed full-time and part-time. The sample differences were not different within the professional and managerial categories.

EDUCATION LEVEL OF MOTHER

Finally, an analysis was made within the education levels of mothers with (a) junior high school or less, (b) some high school education, (c) high school graduates, and (d) at least some college education. In each analysis the relationship between employment status and marital adjustment was non-significant, and in each the difference favored the non-employed mother. Differences were least, however, between the employment categories in the college-educated category. The sample differences are quite large for the women with junior high or less education (Table 19.5). Table 19.5 shows almost no differences in marital adjustment by employment status within the college-educated category. It does show rather large (although non-significant) differences in marital adjustment by employment status among women with little education, notably *fewer employed* mothers having the best marital adjustment.

TABLE 19.5 *The Relationship of Employment Status to Marital Adjustment by Education Level of Mothers**

MARITAL ADJUSTMENT (BY SCALE TYPE)	SOME COLLEGE EDUCATION		NUMBER
	NOT EMPLOYED (N = 79)	EMPLOYED FULL-TIME (N = 50)	
	Per Cent		
0–4 (poor)	21.5	22.0	28
5–8 (intermediate)	39.2	46.0	54
9–10 (good)	39.2	32.0	47
	99.9	100.0	129
JUNIOR HIGH OR LESS EDUCATION			
	(N = 39)	(N = 19)	
0–4 (poor)	20.5	23.6	13
5–8 (intermediate)	30.8	52.6	22
9–10 (good)	48.7	21.1	23
	100.0	100.0	58

* Neither analysis reveals a statistically significant relationship.

INTERPRETATION

Employment of the test variable of socio-economic status fails to disclose any statistically significant relationships between employment status and marital adjustment. The non-significant differences are, however, generally consistent internally and with theoretical ideas. These ideas may now be restated for further examination. There is no evidence that full-time employment of mothers improves marital adjustment for any socio-economic category. All analyses produce non-significant differences, and all show a higher proportion of non-employed mothers with good marital adjustment. In the higher socio-economic categories, however, differences are slight, suggesting that confusion and conflicts associated with the new role combination are compensated by personal satisfaction derived from interpersonal relationships, professional achievement, and material gains associated with employment. These positive gains are complemented by the possession of more labor-saving equipment at home, hired assistance with housework, and more household tasks performed by agencies outside the home.

Central to this argument, also, is the thesis that the employment itself is comparatively satisfying for well-educated women working in professional and other high-status occupations. They are respected, well-paid, and have relatively responsible and challenging work. Their status positions in the occupational hierarchy are above those occupied by many men. Employment for these women more typically enhances self-respect and leads to interpersonal relationships which are relatively satisfying.

The data have consistently shown greater differences in marital adjustment between employed and non-employed women in the lower socio-economic categories. Since the economic need is probably greater and the economic contribution to the family level of living is greater, other factors must be considered. Such jobs as waitress, janitress, and housemaid are more tiring physically. Women in these occupations typically have fewer household conveniences and less hired help with housework. The nature of the work does not in itself enhance self-respect or respect from the public. By their occupation, they are at the bottom of the prestige scale in relationship to both sexes. Employment in itself tends to be tiring, boring, and probably unproductive of satisfying interpersonal relationships. The feelings directly or indirectly associated with employment probably negatively affect marital adjustment in the lower socio-economic families.

NUMBER AND AGE OF CHILDREN

It has been widely assumed that, as children grow older, the presence of the mother in the home during the day becomes less crucial. Children can presumably meet their own needs easier and require less supervision as they grow older. Some students of personality would take the position that personality is essentially formed in infancy and that unfavorable environmental change would have little adverse effect on children at older ages. Although the above assumptions are more directly related to children than to marital adjustment, the welfare of the children might be expected to affect marital adjustment.

Families were divided into three categories: those with adolescent children only, those with children from six to twelve only, and those who had preschool children in addition to other children (no family in this sample had preschool children only). The relationship of employment status to marital adjustment proved to be non-significant in each of the above categories. The non-significant differences were not in the expected direction. Therefore, insofar as marital adjustment is concerned, the age of the children does not appear to be an important variable.

For similar reasons, it would be anticipated that marital adjustment might be more adversely affected by employment of mothers of large rather than small families. This was tested by dividing families into small families (one to three children) and large ones (four or more children). No difference was found sufficient in size to warrant interpretation. Marital adjustment does not appear to be more adversely affected by employment of mothers of large rather than of small families.

DURATION OF EMPLOYMENT

The number of years the mother is employed could be expected to affect marital adjustment in two ways. The adjustment of personal habits and the development of family procedures to adjust to the employment of the mother should, over a period of time, reduce conflict and facilitate a more efficient performance of family functions.

The opposite effect might be anticipated from conflict and tension arising from employment. As these continue over a period of years, the frustrations and irritations may become aggravated. The basic question is, therefore, "Have families *themselves* been able to develop adjustive mechanisms which have reduced conflict and efficiently met family needs, or have such conflicts and tensions continued over the years?" This is a different question from whether society can and will develop *cultural* adaptations to the employment of mothers.

Present data give no support for the idea that marital adjustment will improve over a period of years during which the wife is employed. Marital adjustment of wives employed one, two or three, or four or more years does not differ significantly. The non-significant differences are, however, consistent, with the proportion of poorly adjusted marriages increasing with increased length of time in employment.

Although present evidence is not conclusive, it provides more support for the idea that individual families are not typically successful by their own action in resolving *marital* conflict and removing irritations and frustrations associated with employment. For example, an unresolved problem may be child care and supervision between 4:00 and 5:00 P.M. Because of the rigidity of the economic structure, the family cannot by its own action bring the mother home by 4:00.

MARITAL STATUS

The sample included women married to their original mates and women who had remarried following divorce, annulment, or widowhood. There is no compelling reason for anticipating a different relationship between employment and marital adjustment in these two subcategories. The findings reported below are therefore best described as an example of serendipity, although once the findings are known the rationalization of them is not difficult.

The analysis of employment status and marital adjustment was made within the original marriage and the remarriage samples. The effect of this

TABLE 19.6 *The Relationship of Employment Status to Marital Adjustment by Marital Status*

MARITAL ADJUSTMENT (BY SCALE TYPE)	ORIGINAL MATE*		TOTAL *Number*
	NOT EMPLOYED (N = 335)	FULL-TIME (N = 167)	
	Per Cent		
0–4 (poor)	20.6	25.7	*112*
5–8 (intermediate)	39.1	46.7	*209*
9–10 (good)	40.3	27.5	*181*
	100.0	99.9	*502*
	REMARRIAGE†		
	(N = 60)	(N = 30)	
0–4 (poor)	30.0	26.7	*26*
5–8 (intermediate)	35.0	40.0	*33*
9–10 (good)	35.0	33.3	*31*
	100.0	100.0	*90*

* Original mate analysis: Relationship is statistically significant.
† Remarriage analysis: Relationship is not statistically significant.

test variable is particularly illuminating. In the total sample, the relationship between employment and marital status is barely significant at the 5 per cent level. The separate analyses indicate a definite negative relationship in the original marriages and *total absence* of relationship in the remarriage category (Table 19.6). The specification of this contingent condition increases the association in the original marriage category *and eliminates it* in the remarriage category.

INTERPRETATION

Since these findings were not predicted on the basis of previous research or theory, how may they be rationalized?

Remarriages average older than original marriages. The woman is likely to have had more job experience and to be better able to handle her domestic roles and that of employee simultaneously. Since the roles of second wife and stepmother are not well defined or completely accepted in American society, a job may compensate for incomplete acceptance as wife and mother. Second marriages *may* be somewhat more utilitarian than first, thus a finaicial contribution to the family may serve as a concrete demonstration of the contribution of the wife. This line of reasoning cannot be extended too far, however, because the data show that employed and non-employed mothers average about the same in marital adjustment. This is in rather marked contrast, however, to the relationship in original marriages in which the differences are significant. It suggests that the compensations associated with employment balance the conflicts and frustrations for the remarriages. This does not appear to be true in the original marriages.

ATTITUDE OF WIFE TOWARD EMPLOYMENT

Mothers' attitudes toward employment vary greatly from those who wish to work regardless of the familial situation to those who do not contemplate it under any circumstance. It has been suggested that this is a crucial variable in the effect of employment on personal adjustment and social relationships. There is some inherent danger in this approach in that wanting to work may be a *product* of simultaneously successfully playing the employee and domestic roles, rather than a causal factor.

In an attempt to throw some light on this attitudinal variable, each woman was asked to complete one of four statements: (1) I am working and I'm glad because . . . , (2) I am working but wish I weren't because . . . , (3) I am not working and am glad I'm not because . . . , (4) I am not working but wish I were because. . . .

Of those employed, 80 per cent said they were glad they were working, 15 per cent wished they were not, and 5 per cent were so ambivalent that they could not be placed in either category. The analysis of attitude toward employment and marital adjustment proved non-significant; however, the sample differences were in the expected direction. Present data do not, therefore, support the idea that *attitude* toward employment is closely related to marital adjustment either as cause or effect.

Of those not employed, 74 per cent said that they were glad they were not working, 20 per cent wished they were, and 6 per cent were classified as ambivalent. There *is* an indication in the data that those *not working* but wishing they were working average significantly poorer marital adjustment.

INTERPRETATION

Although the data suggests some relationship among employed women's wanting to work and good marital adjustment, the association is not close and may be due to sample error. This suggests that wives do not generally associate their employment with their attitudes toward their husbands—that is, that it is necessary for them to work, not because the husband is lazy or incompetent, but because of the high cost of living or rising level of expectations. If there is an association between attitude toward working and marital adjustment, some part of it would also have to be considered effect rather than cause. That is, some women would wish they could stop working because it adversely affects their marriage.

For those not working but wishing to do so, there *is* evidence of poorer marital adjustment. This suggests a wish for escape or for compensating activity outside the family on the part of some non-working wives. In some cases, also, a frustrated wish to use time, talents, and training in employment may contribute to poor marital adjustment.

ATTITUDE OF HUSBAND TOWARD EMPLOYMENT

Present findings are consistent with those of Gianopulos and Mitchell (8). In families in which the wife is employed and the husband disapproves, marital adjustment averages poorer. *However*, in families in which the wife is not employed but the husband would approve of her entering the labor force, marital adjustment is poorer also.

The importance of these findings is limited by the fact that husbands of women employed full-time generally approve of the arrangement. Only one in nine did not; therefore, this group cannot affect the marital adjustment of the total group very much. To check this point further, however, employed women whose husbands approved of their working were compared with non-employed women whose husbands approved of their not working. A significant difference similar to those previously reported and favoring the non-employed was still present.

There is, not surprisingly, an association between the husband's approval of the wife's occupational role and her marital adjustment, *whether or not* the wife is employed.

It was suggested above that marital adjustment might be adversely affected if the wife earned more than the husband. In the present study, 298 employed women supplied information concerning both their own and their husband's incomes. Of these, 59 were earning as much as or more than their husbands. The marital adjustment of these wives was compared with that of women earning less than their husbands. The differences proved non-significant but in the expected direction. Since some of the differences may be related to lower socio-economic status rather than equal or superior earning power of the wife, the data suggest that the marital adjustment of the woman is not greatly affected. The adjustment of the husband might be affected more than that of the wife, but data to test this supposition are not presently available.

RÉSUMÉ

The relationship of employment status to marital adjustment was subjected to the test variables of socio-economic status, age and number of children in family, duration of employment, the contingent conditions of marital status, and attitude of both wife and husband toward her employment.

The data suggest that any net *adverse* effect of employment on marital adjustment is less in the higher socio-economic families than in the lower. The differences between employed and non-employed almost disappear in the higher occupational and educational categories. This is consistent with conjectures made by Komarovsky and Landis and suggests the utility of additional research by socio-economic status.

The test variables of family size and age of children and length of time the mother had been employed were unproductive. The relationship between employment and marital adjustment is not appreciably affected by these variables.

Dissatisfaction with the wife's occupational role by either the wife or the husband is related to poor marital adjustment. Some caution is necessary in evaluating this statistical association. The husband may be unhappy with his wife's employment because it has had an adverse effect on their marriage rather than the reverse; or, of course, both may be caused by some third variable.

An interesting and unanticipated finding was supplied by the employment of remarriage as a contingent condition. All differences in marital adjustment are accounted for by differences in the original-marriage category with no differences found in the remarriage groups.

REFERENCES

1. Burgess, Ernest W., and Wallin, Paul. *Engagement and Marriage.* New York: Lippincott, 1953.
2. Gianopulos, Artie, and Mitchell, Howard E. "Marital Disagreement in Working Wife Marriages as a Function of Husband's Attitude Toward Wife's Employment," *Marriage and Family Living,* XIX (November, 1957), 373–78.
3. Havemann, Ernest, and West, Patricia Salter. *They Went to College.* New York: Harcourt, Brace, 1952.
4. Kendall, Patricia L., and Lazarsfeld, Paul F. "Problems of Survey Analysis." In Robert K. Merton and Paul F. Lazarsfeld, eds., *Continuities in Social Research.* Glencoe, Ill.: Free Press, 1950, 148–58.
5. Komarovsky, Mirra. *Women in the Modern World.* Boston: Little, Brown, 1953.
6. Landis, Judson T. "The Trauma of Children in Divorce," *Marriage and Family Living,* XXII (February, 1960), 7–13.
7. Landis, Paul H. *Making the Most of Marriage.* New York: Appleton-Century-Crofts, 1955.
8. Locke, Harvey J., and Mackeprang, Muriel. "Marital Adjustment of the Employed Wife," *American Journal of Sociology,* LIV (May, 1949), 536–39.
9. Nye, F. Ivan, and MacDougall, Evelyn. "The Dependent Variable in Marital Research," *Pacific Sociological Review,* II (Fall, 1959), 67–70.
10. Parsons, Talcott, and Bales, Robert F. *Family Socialization and Interaction Process.* Glencoe, Ill.: Free Press, 1955.
11. Siegel, Sidney. *Nonparametric Statistics for the Behavioral Sciences.* New York: McGraw-Hill, 1956.

Chapter Twenty

The Husband-Wife Relationship

ROBERT O. BLOOD

THE annual increments in the percentage of married women working since the war make this one of the most rapid social changes ever to have occurred spontaneously during normal peace-time prosperity. The extent of the change involved when a wife's main working hours are removed from the home is overwhelming in magnitude. Both the speed and scope of this innovation command attention.

The purpose of this chapter is not to inquire into the causes of this change but to examine its consequences. Nor are we interested in the consequences for children, crucial as the socialization process is for the welfare of society. Rather, our concern is with the effects of the wife's employment on the husband-wife relationship.

Revision of the marital relationship is to be expected when the wife changes her role from housewife to working wife. Marriage roles are inevitably reciprocal. In terms of the basic necessities of family living, what one partner does not do, the other partner must do. We would expect, therefore, that the wife's removal from the domestic sphere for 40 hours a week will decrease the services which she can perform for her family and increase those which her husband must perform. At the same time, we would expect the influence patterns and emotional relationships of husband and wife to shift as their roles in the division of labor shift.

The consequences for marital roles of the wife's participation in the economic system have intrinsic interest. They should be seen, however, as part of a larger theoretical framework.

(a) Not only the wife but the husband participates in the economic system in varying degrees ranging from not at all (unemployment), to partial, to full-time, to excessive participation (overtime work in a single job or holding two jobs). The consequences of the wife's employment vary significantly not only by the amount of her own participation in the economic system but by the amount of her husband's.[1]

(b) When both partners are employed, the consequences for marriage differ according to the comparative resources derived by both partners from their work. In economic terms, the employed wife normally earns less than her husband. But some wives earn as much or more, raising specters of competitiveness and ego threat for the husband which deserve empirical testing. Moreover, dual-income families differ not only in relative incomes but in the comparative prestige of the two jobs. What happens to marriage when the husband of a famous movie star is regularly introduced by his wife's professional name? Finally, jobs differ in the demands they make on the worker, how much they exhaust him or stimulate him, how much they preoccupy him mentally during his off-duty hours.

(c) The consequences for marriage will also differ according to whether the wife works for her husband or for someone else. If she helps her husband, a wife spends an increased amount of time with him but plays a dependent role since he is the economic boss. A wife who works for someone else is taken away from contact with other family members and thereby achieves a more independent stance vis-á-vis them. Most contemporary discussions of working wives deal with the latter situation, which will be the focus of this chapter.[2]

(d) From a broader point of view, participation in the occupational system is simply one type of participation in various social systems external to the family. The non-monetary resources of knowledge, skill, and stimulus which the working wife acquires are also derivable from participation in formal organizations and voluntary community service. Likewise, varying amounts of the partners' time and energy are consumed by unpaid activities outside the home. The consequences for marriage may be quite similar when time is spent outside the home in either paid or unpaid activities. In any case, the wife's employment should be viewed in the larger context of participation external to the system of family roles which affects the perform-

---

[1] In the author's book, *Husbands and Wives* (4), he analyzes the effects on the husband-wife relationship of the "comparative work participation of husband and wife" in a six-fold classification depending on whether the wife is employed or not and whether the husband is employed over-time, full-time, or not at all.

[2] Nye (13), however, fails to discriminate between these two types of employment. "A mother is considered employed if she is paid for her labor *or if her labor directly adds to family income (such as working in husband's office)*" (italics added). Because collaborative wives are usually fewer in number than independently employed wives, Nye's article will nevertheless be viewed as presumably indicative of the latter situation.

ance of family roles. Not only does non-remunerative external participation provide a substitute for paid employment, but various combinations of the two types of external participation exist in particular marriages. For example, the dual-income marriage with a minimum of unpaid external participation allows more time for family role performance than the marriage where the couple works and carries on other outside activities as well.

These four variables suggest some of the complexity of the phenomenon of the wife's employment in itself, the independent variable with which we are concerned. For purposes of this chapter, most of this variability will be ignored and we will assume that employment is a unitary phenomenon. The progress of future research requires increased attention to particular types and circumstances of employment and their differential consequences for the marriage relationship.

However, there are other factors besides the nature of the partners' external participation which affect the marital impact. (a) One of these is the extent of need for the wife's income. Economic necessity is the chief reason for working given by working wives. However, "necessity" is a slippery term in an advertising-saturated culture. Nevertheless, in general, the lower the husband's income, the greater the necessity for the wife to supplement it. And the greater the necessity for her paid activity, the less resentment for the loss of her unpaid services at home. Although the husband's income is the most easily measured index of need, it is oversimplified, for it fails to take into account such complexities as number of children and extent of their need for college tuition, medical care, or other special expenses. Also, the capital assets of a newly-formed family (house, car, furniture, and appliances) cannot be inferred directly from the husband's current income.

(b) Since gains from the wife's income are offset by loss of her services at home, the need for income must be balanced against the need for these services. Perhaps even more than the need for extra income, the need for the wife's domestic services changes over time. It is closely geared to the stages in the family life cycle, measured not so much in the conventional terms of the age of the oldest child as in the age of the youngest. The younger he is, the greater his dependency needs and therefore the greater the need for the mother to stay home and care for him. Children who are frequently sick need a readily available nurse, as do many aged relatives. Sometimes the husband's occupation requires meals at irregular hours or someone at home to answer the telephone. These are illustrative situations which tend to keep the wife home in the first place and intensify the negative consequences of her removal if she does go to work.

Such complexities indicate that the wife's employment cannot be evaluated in dollars alone because her income sometimes has crucial and sometimes only marginal significance to the family. Nor can the loss of the wife's services be measured only in the number of hours she is away from home. The balance of such varied factors determines how much of a net gain or loss the husband and wife consider her employment to be.

The preceding discussion suggests how many factors must be considered in order to understand fully the impact of the wife's employment on the family role system. To date, very few of these factors have been investigated. Hence, this chapter will necessarily be limited to the wife's employment as an all-or-none phenomenon. The main findings of the relevant literature will be reviewed and special tabulations presented from the author's Detroit Area Study.[3] The effects of the wife's employment will be examined on (a) the division of labor in the home, (b) the marital power structure, (c) the leisure-time interaction of husband and wife, and (d) how they evaluate their marriage in general.

All of the relevant literature involves cross-sectional research designs. That is, employed women are treated as an "experimental" group to be compared with non-employed women as a "control" group. This design fails to secure "before" measures which would guarantee that the observed differences between the two "after" groups are truly consequences of employment rather than pre-existing selective differences. Hence, all the research findings to date must be accepted tentatively, pending the time when longitudinal research can observe marriages in the process of changing as the wife goes to work. Such follow-up research would need a control group of continuously non-working wives to rule out changes due to increasing length of marriage, to progress through the sequence of stages in the family life cycle, or to general historical forces.

THE DIVISION OF LABOR IN THE HOME

By definition, the wife's employment takes her out of the home, normally for 40 hours a week plus commuting time. These are usually the hours during which the housewife (i.e., non-working wife) does the bulk of her housework. The traditional division of labor gives the husband sole responsibility for earning the family income and the wife general responsibility for the housework. Only those tasks which are too heavy or too technical for the wife are performed by the husband.

The traditional division of labor is challenged by the wife's exodus from the house. Husband and wife then share the responsibility for earning money on a roughly equal basis. The average American husband works a 40-hour week and most wives do the same. Some married couples even share the

[3] These tabulations were made possible by a grant from the Board of Governors of the Horace H. Rackham Faculty Research Fund of the University of Michigan. They supplement the tables published by Blood and Wolfe.

same ride to work, so their departures and returns are simultaneous. Inso-far as husband and wife have equal time available, in the long run house-work should theoretically be shared equally.

Modification of the division of labor in the direction of equality is accelerated by the inability of working wives to complete their housework unaided. To be sure, increased income makes it possible to purchase labor-saving devices and the notorious TV dinners, to hire part-time maid service and utilize commercial services such as laundries and restaurants. Moreover, many wives who managed to keep reasonably well occupied when they spent full-time at home discover that they can accomplish a surprising amount in shorter periods if they have to. Both the wife and the members of her family may lower their standards of housekeeping under the new circumstances. Yet, despite all these shortcuts and the added non-family personnel, the chances are that the working wife is unable to get the housework done with-out her husband's cooperation. Provided he has no legitimate excuse (i.e., no counter-claims upon his time), he is likely to respond by increased par-ticipation in the domestic division of labor.[4]

Five research projects have tested the hypothesis that the wife's employ-ment increases the husband's share in the division of labor. In all five cases, the hypothesis is confirmed. Blood and Hamblin find that the median hus-band's share of the housework is 15 per cent when the wife does not work and 25 per cent when the wife is employed (3). This is not just a relative difference but an absolute increase in the number of hours per week which the husband spends in housework.

Using the child's report of whether household tasks are done by the father only, the mother only, or both parents, Hoffman finds that the work-ing wife does fewer tasks and her husband more in four different task areas: fathers', mothers', common, and child-care (Chapter Fifteen).

Nolan finds that employed wives shift the burden of housekeeping both onto their husbands and onto commercial services. The amount of time de-voted to household operations is reduced by decreasing home canning, freezing, and sewing, and increasing use of prepared mixes in baking. Hus-bands of working wives help out more in virtually all areas of feminine activity, including foods (meal preparation, baking, dish-washing), clothing (washing and ironing), and cleaning (dusting, picking up, cleaning floors and baths, making beds). Such husbands also help more with the children, both at bedtime and with homework (Chapter Eight and Seventeen).

Analogous to Nolan's finding that housekeeping is shifted to commercial resources is Powell's discovery that Florida working wives depend heavily on

---

[4] The author reports elsewhere that farmers have such a legitimate excuse in the accessibility of their farm chores evenings and weekends (1). This is presumably one of the reasons why farm wives are less apt to be employed. See Nolan (Chapters Eight and Seventeen).

paid housekeepers. The availability of Negro women as cheap labor in the Deep South reduces the impact of the wife's departure on the husband. Despite the employment of maids, husbands of working wives do more tasks in Powell's preschool and school-age samples, leaving only those in the adolescent stage of the family life cycle who fail to respond to the wife's need. The disappointment of their wives with this non-responsiveness is suggested in the poor marital adjustment of the adolescent group (14, see Chapter Sixteen). In other words, husbands who fail to respond to the employed wife's need for household assistance can expect to suffer the consequences. The statistically normal and morally normative impact of the wife's employment on the division of labor is for the husband's share to increase.

The dramatic impact of the wife's employment on the division of labor in the home can be seen in Table 20.1. These data are from a representative

TABLE 20.1 *Wife's Share of Household Tasks by Husband's Income and Wife's Employment Status*

WIFE'S SHARE OF HOUSEHOLD TASKS	HUSBAND'S INCOME UNDER $5,000		HUSBAND'S INCOME, $5,000 OR MORE	
	Wife Not Working	*Wife Working*	*Wife Not Working*	*Wife Working*
		Per Cent		
Very low	7	27	7	23
Low	29	39	32	46
Moderate	34	20	33	19
High	18	6	23	8
Not ascertained	11	8	5	4
Total	99	100	100	100
Number of families	*184*	*66*	*284*	*48*

sample of white married women in the Detroit Metropolitan Area.[5] The data represent a summary index of eight household tasks performed by the husband always, usually, or half the time, or by the wife usually or always. It will be noted that three times as many working wives fall at the "very low" end of the continuum, and three times as many housewives at the "high" end.

Detailed analysis shows that the wife's employment results in substantial increases in the number of husbands who assume all the responsibility for mowing the lawn and shoveling the sidewalk. It also results in substantial decreases in the number of wives who carry sole responsibilities for getting the husband's breakfast, doing the evening dishes, and straightening up the

---

[5] For details of methodology, see Blood and Wolfe (4, Appendix A).

living room when company is coming. Working wives also tend to do less household repairing and do less grocery shopping by themselves (especially in the lower income group where the main shift is to joint shopping). The only task which working wives maintain as active an interest in is the economic one of "keeping track of the money and bills." Here the wife's lessened time is offset by an increased sense of involvement in the family finances— so no significant change occurs.

The general result of the husband's increased responsibility for traditional masculine tasks and his increased sharing of the traditional feminine ones is an increase in the degree of conformity to the masculine role and a decrease in conformity to the feminine role in working-wife marriages. These complementary trends are expressed in Tables 20.2 and 20.3 where the masculine tasks include the sidewalk, lawn, and repairs, while the feminine

TABLE 20.2 *Conformity to Masculine Role in the Division of Labor by Husband's Income and Wife's Employment Status*

CONFORMITY TO MASCULINE ROLE	HUSBAND'S INCOME UNDER $5,000		HUSBAND'S INCOME, $5,000 OR MORE	
	Wife Not Working	Wife Working	Wife Not Working	Wife Working
		Per Cent		
Low	12	5	15	6
Moderate	16	18	21	13
High	25	21	23	19
Very high	40	53	37	63
Not ascertained	7	3	4	–
Total	100	100	100	101
Number of families	*184*	*66*	*284*	*48*

TABLE 20.3 *Conformity to Feminine Role in the Division of Labor, by Husband's Income and Wife's Employment Status*

CONFORMITY TO FEMININE ROLE	HUSBAND'S INCOME UNDER $5,000		HUSBAND'S INCOME, $5,000 OR MORE	
	Wife Not Working	Wife Working	Wife Not Working	Wife Working
		Per Cent		
Low	12	50	18	31
Moderate	33	26	31	27
High	24	12	27	25
Very high	26	8	21	13
Not ascertained	5	5	3	4
Total	100	101	100	100
Number of families	*184*	*66*	*284*	*48*

tasks are breakfast, the dishes, the living room, and the groceries. This state of affairs (which also appears in Hoffman's data) means that the wife's employment introduces greater flexibility into the handling of the traditional feminine tasks but *less* flexibility into the handling of masculine ones. Hence, it would be misleading to describe dual income families as involving more sharing of *all* household tasks. Only in the sense of a greater equalization of the *amount* of work done by husband and wife do such families experience more sharing in general.

To summarize, husbands of working wives usually do more housework, their wives less. The wife curtails her normal sharing in masculine tasks. On the other hand, the husband enters domains traditionally reserved to wives. Only household tasks so technical that the male partner cannot learn them or so closely linked to employment that the wife's entrance into the occupational world reinforces her participation in them resist the pressure to change created by the wife's exodus from the home.

That these shifts in the division of labor are not always accomplished smoothly is suggested by conflicts in working-wife families. Nye finds that dual-income couples quarrel more frequently than one-income couples. He also finds some tendency for the former group to argue about more topics, the chief difference significantly being in the area of "house and furniture" (Chapter Nineteen).

Gianopulos and Mitchell do not compare working wives as a whole with non-working wives in their analysis of cases from the files of the Marriage Council of Philadelphia (5). Their "finding" that husbands who disapprove of their wives' working have more marital conflict involves circular reasoning. However, the authors make a useful analysis of areas in which conflict occurs. When conflict occurs in working-wife families, it does not spread randomly over all aspects of marriage. For instance, there is no increase in difficulties over in-laws, friendships, or sexual or religious matters. Almost all the significant differences are concentrated in the "domestic-economic" field. Most revelant to the division of labor are conflicts focussed on household management (where wives are especially touchy), on the husband's work and children (sore points for the husbands), and on the wife's working and financial matters (which both partners report as trouble spots).

The Detroit Area Study provides further support to these tendencies (with the added value of an income control). Working-wife conflicts over financial matters are concentrated at low-income levels. When the husband earns less than $5,000 a year, 23 per cent of the working wives but only 17 per cent of the non-working wives report that money has been their chief area of disagreement.[6] Conversely, disagreements over marital roles are con-

---

[6] Although not significantly different within the rigorous . nits of the one chief area of disagreement, these data may reflect a significant ten ency for low-income working couples to disagree *more often* about money.

centrated in higher income brackets. Above $5,000, only 2 per cent of the non-working wives but 10 per cent (five times as many) of the working wives report that marital roles have been their chief bone of contention.

These three studies suggest that when the wife goes to work, new conflicts arise between husband and wife. However, these conflicts do not pervade all aspects of the marriage but reflect the stresses created by the wife's absence from the home. Cause-and-effect relationships can be assumed in the difficulties two-income couples have over household management, over whether the wife should work, and over children.[7] These difficulties reflect the obstacle which the wife's work places in the way of getting housework done and caring for the children.

By contrast, the higher incidence of conflicts over money and the husband's, work seem likely to be selective factors. Dual-income couples quarrel over money not because of the extra income but in spite of it. Indeed, it is because they have financial difficulties that the wife goes to work. Longitudinal research is needed to show how much financial conflicts are resolved by the extra income and how much they persist due to the working wife's greater involvement in financial decision-making. The husband's job, similarly, is likely to appear troublesome to working-wife couples primarily because it fails to provide an adequate income and thereby propels the wife into the labor market.

To conclude, the division of labor in the home is profoundly altered by the wife's daily departure from the home. Some couples make this transition smoothly but others experience difficulties along the way, difficulties which are concentrated around the reassignment of housekeeping and child-rearing tasks to fit changed family circumstances. The less the financial necessity for the wife to work, the less gracefully the husband takes on these added responsibilities at home. So, the need for the wife's employment significantly affects the stress resulting from changes in the division of labor in the home.

THE MARITAL POWER STRUCTURE

The effect of the wife's employment on the balance of power between husband and wife is less clear than the effect on the division of labor. The universal hypothesis has been that employment increases the wife's power. Certainly popular American opinion is to this effect.

The basis for this assumption is frequently economic. It is assumed that the working wife's paycheck represents a resource which she uses to bargain

---

[7] Because working wives are often childless, greater difficulties regarding children are revealed only when the presence of children is controlled in the analysis. In the Detroit Area Study this variable is uncontrolled with the result that fewer working wives report children as their chief disagreement.

with her husband. If he fails to knuckle under to her demands, she can withhold the check or quit work.

Regardless of the basis of her added power, it has also been assumed that it is manifested in every aspect of marriage. The working wife can supposedly use her influence to twist her husband's arm in any decision—financial, recreational, or whatever.

However, the complex changes in the division of labor should warn us that these are oversimplified interpretations of the causes and effects of changes in the wife's power. On the one hand, the significance of the wife's employment is more than economic; it is a form of external participation likely to have social and psychological consequences similar to participation in other external activities. Nevertheless, on the other hand, those aspects of marital influence most likely to be affected are the ones most clearly tied to the outside world. That is, the wife's employment is likely to increase her influence in external areas but to decrease her influence in internal areas. So, marital power cannot be treated as a unitary phenomenon.

Unfortunately, much of the research to date (especially this writer's!) has made a global approach to the problem. Moreover, every one of the six research projects to be discussed uses a different measure of marital power. Not only do these projects differ in the topical areas of influence studied, but they differ in the way in which influence is ascertained. Under the circumstances, it is not surprising that many studies appear to contradict each other. However, the theoretical urgency of the question of the effect of the wife's employment on the marital power structure requires detailed examination of these studies in order to solve the puzzle presented by their apparent contradictions.

Table 20.4 is an example of a global index of marital power. It shows

TABLE 20.4 *Marital Decision-Making Pattern by Husband's Income and Wife's Employment Status*

MARITAL DECISION-MAKING PATTERN	HUSBAND'S INCOME UNDER $5,000		HUSBAND'S INCOME, $5,000 OR MORE	
	Wife Not Working	*Wife Working*	*Wife Not Working*	*Wife Working*
		Per Cent		
Husband-dominant	21	9	31	10
Syncratic	24	21	23	31
Autonomic	23	26	27	27
Wife-dominant	21	30	13	19
Not ascertained	11	14	6	13
Total	100	100	100	100
Number of families	*184*	*66*	*284*	*48*

substantial decreases in the proportion of husband-dominant families when the wife goes to work. At low-income levels this results in an increased number of wife-dominant families. In high-income families, however, the increase is divided between wife-dominance and syncratic (shared-equal) decision-making. The most general conclusion to be drawn from this table is that the wife's employment increases her power either unilaterally or on a shared basis.

Yet three other studies find no difference in power between working and non-working wives. Can this contradiction be reconciled?

Our previous discussion suggested the desirability of discriminating between different areas in which marital power is exercised. Examination of the eight decisions summarized in Table 20.4 demonstrates the value of this approach. Four of the eight items involve significant decreases in the husband's power and increases in the working wife's: what car to buy, what house to choose, whether to buy insurance, and whether the wife should work. Decisions about where to spend summer vacations are more often made jointly in working-wife families (at the expense of wife-only decisions in low-income families and of husband-only decisions in high-income families). A shift toward joint decisions about how much money to spend on food also occurs in the low-income group (reminiscent of the shift toward joint-grocery shopping). Decisions about the husband's job are so unilateral in all groups that significant differences are impossible. However, the wife's power actually decreases in one area when she goes to work, namely in deciding what doctor to call when someone is sick. This is a decision correlated with the child-care responsibilities of the typical non-working wife and therefore operates in opposite fashion to the majority of items in the list.

The suggestion that the working wife's power decreases in areas associated with the role of housewife is confirmed by Hoffman's finding that working mothers have significantly less "activity control" than non-working mothers. The activities concerned are routine household activities, so this means that wives who go to work decrease their decision-making with reference to the domestic division of labor and their participation in the execution of those same household tasks. A housewife should be looked upon as a specialist in housework who not only does the housework herself but is her own boss. She normally decides autonomously which tasks to do next and how, while the husband concentrates on his own interests. To generalize, then, one of the effects of the wife's employment on the marital power structure is to decrease the wife's autonomy in the area of household tasks.

What, then, are the areas in which the working wife's power increases? The four items in the Detroit Area Study where this occurred—car, house, insurance, and the wife's employment—are major financial transactions, the first three major expenditures, the last a major source of income. They are also relatively infrequent decisions with persisting consequences, not choices which are made and remade every day. The amounts of money involved and the extent of the practical repercussions make these major decisions that affect the whole family. Perhaps, therefore, they can be described as *major economic decisions*.

First, the literature will be examined to see whether this emergent hypothesis is confirmed by other studies. Then the rationale for this relationship will be presented.

Heer asked his subjects (both husbands and wives) "who usually wins out" when the partners disagree about *"a really important decision"* (Chapter Eighteen). While the reference here is vague, it is at least possible that the respondents had decisions similar to our major economic ones in mind when they answered the question. If this assumption is correct, Heer's finding that working wives make significantly more "really important decisions" lends support to the hypothesis.

More specific is Kligler's finding that middle-class working mothers make significantly more decisions about "major purchases, loans, savings, and investments," items highly comparable to the Detroit Area Study ones (9).

Middleton and Putney used a quite different research technique, namely Strodtbeck's method of observing husband-wife resolution of revealed differences (11). Although many of the issues resolved refer to major decisions, the authors recognize that the experimental situation calls for comparatively insignificant decision-making in comparison with real life. Their research is therefore not a direct replication of the three previous ones which investigated how major decisions are made in actual practice.

Nevertheless, Middleton and Putney provide additional support to our hypothesis, for they find a significant difference between differing areas of decision-making. Decisions about child-rearing are correlated with the housewife role, confirming the Detroit Area Study finding on choice of doctor and Hoffman's finding on household "activity control." The same is true for recreational opinions and role attitudes. However, the area of "purchases and living standards" is not correlated with the housewife role. Although there is no difference between the proportion of decisions won by working and non-working wives in this area, the net effect of the wife's employment is to increase her power in this economic area *in comparison to* her power in other areas. Hence, we can assert that, relatively speaking, the wife's employment is associated in this study, too, with increased power in economic decision-making.

Blood and Hamblin's failure to distinguish between different areas of decision-making probably accounts for their failure to find a significant difference between working and non-working wives in family power structure. Although rated by judges as "important" decisions, less than half of the 18 items in the Blood-Hamblin power scale involve major economic decisions. The remaining items include several household-type decisions which other research suggests are correlated with the housewife role. Such an ambiguous scale cannot reveal the opposite effects which the wife's employment has on major economic as contrasted with minor household decisions.

Hoffman's failure to find a significant difference between power scores of working and non-working women refers to a quite different definition of power, namely the extent to which the husband carries out household tasks which the wife decides about, and vice versa. We have previously discussed Hoffman's findings that the working wife's (a) task participation decreases and (b) activity control also decreases. *If these two variables decrease at the same rate,* there is no difference between working wives and housewives in the extent to which they boss their husbands around in the house. In other words, even though the husband of an employed wife washes more dishes, it does not necessarily mean that his wife has explicitly ordered him to do so. Rather, he participates more actively in household decision-making as he engages in more household tasks.

This review of the literature suggests, therefore, that the wife's employment (a) decreases the decisions she makes in household task areas, (b) but increases her share in major economic decision-making, while (c) leaving unchanged the amount of influence of husband and wife *over* each other.

These conclusions are relevant to Blood and Wolfe's summary of their chapter on "The Power to Make Decisions" that "power in American marriages is not a matter of brute coercion and unwilling defeat so much as a mutual recognition of individual skills in particular areas of competence and of the partners' dual stake in areas of joint concern" (4, p. 45). The greater voice of working wives in economic decisions is not so much a result of greater bargaining power as of greater familiarity with economic matters. Participating in the occupational system gives them new experiences which increase their competence in making certain kinds of decisions. The fact that this is not a question of economic bargaining is suggested by Blood and Wolfe's report that the wife's voice in the same eight decisions also increases when she is an unpaid participant in church activities and other formal organizations.

So, a spontaneous reallocation of the balance of power occurs when the wife goes to work, increasing her power regarding decisions relevant to her new role, and decreasing it in decisions relevant to the housekeeping role she is partially forsaking. In neither case does the shift mean that one partner coerces the other. Americans are too equalitarian for that. Rather, the new power structure represents an appropriate adaptation to the revised division of labor inside and outside the home.

LEISURE-TIME INTERACTION OF HUSBAND AND WIFE

Family living has always involved keeping house and making decisions. However, the rise of civilization has increased the importance of leisure time. An increasingly salient reason for American marriages is desire of the partners to spend their leisure together.

Blood and Wolfe report that the most highly valued aspect of married life is precisely companionship in doing things together. Other valued types of leisure-time interaction are the expression of love and affection and the therapeutic relief of emotional problems (4).

Unfortunately, little research has been done on these newly significant aspects of marriage. Nevertheless, it does not seem likely that they will prove to be affected as directly by the wife's employment status as the power structure and the division of labor. Many of these leisure time pursuits are either quickly accomplished or occur at considerable intervals. Even rather busy couples can manage to find time for them if they wish to. Only those activities which require substantial amounts of time are likely to be interfered with by the hours the wife spends at work.

A second reason that these leisure-time pursuits are less likely to be affected is that they are largely qualitative matters and therefore less dependent on the amount of time available. There is a world of difference between a peck on the forehead and a "real kiss." Factors more subtle than the sheer absence of the wife from the home during the day operate as intervening variables in determining the meaning of their leisure-time interaction to the two partners. Nevertheless, secondary repercussions of the wife's employment may be discoverable.

COMPANIONSHIP

By companionship we mean the marriage partners' enjoyment of each other's company in leisure-time activities. Working-wife families have a considerable basis for companionship built into their structure. By definition, they share household tasks more as the husband moves into the wife's traditional spheres of activity. The Detroit Area Study shows (Table 20.5) that decision-making also shifts from sharing relatively few decisions toward more sharing. These structural characteristics mean that two-income families are apt to have a sense of companionship quite apart from the question of how they spend their leisure time.

Nevertheless, shared decision-making or shared dish-washing is not the

TABLE 20.5   *Sharing in Decision-Making by Husband's Income and Wife's Employment Status*

| NUMBER OF SHARED DECISIONS | HUSBAND'S INCOME UNDER $5,000 | | HUSBAND'S INCOME, $5,000 OR MORE | |
	Wife Not Working	Wife Working	Wife Not Working	Wife Working
		Per Cent		
Low (0–2)	42	35	36	25
Moderate (3–4)	27	23	38	35
High (5–8)	20	29	20	27
Not ascertained	11	14	6	13
Total	100	101	100	100
Number of families	*184*	*66*	*284*	*48*

heart of the matter. True companionship lies not in working together but in playing together. Here our information is spotty. None at all is available on what Blood and Wolfe call the purest form of companionship—going out together just to have a good time. Such "dating companionship" extends into marriage the activities preferred in dating and courtship: movies, meals out, and dancing. How may the wife's employment affect their frequency? Does extra income make a bigger recreational budget possible? Or does the extra strain of work and housework leave the wife (and perhaps the husband, also) too tired to leave home? Perhaps, also, the very fact that the wife has been away all day makes her no more anxious to go out in the evening than the proverbial husband, preferring an easy chair and slippers.

Although information on dating companionship is not available from the Detroit Area Study, a few tidbits partially fill the gap. One of these is what Blood and Wolfe call "informative companionship"—i.e., how often the husband tells the wife about things which happened during the day. The data show no differences between working and non-working wives in the frequency of receiving this kind of information from their husbands.

Whereas informative companionship requires little effort and takes place at home as a by-product of routine living, most forms of companionship require more activity. One of these is "colleague companionship," or getting together with either the husband's or wife's work-mates.

Table 20.6 shows that dual-income couples are more apt to engage in colleague companionship a few times a year and less apt never to do so. The reason for the difference may be that both partners have work-mates so there is a wider pool of potential friends to draw from. Obviously, the time consumed by the wife's work is not sufficient to prevent her from entertaining or being entertained at least every few months. However, it

TABLE 20.6 *Colleague Companionship by Husband's Income and Wife's Employment Status*

FREQUENCY COUPLE GETS TOGETHER WITH WORK-MATES	HUSBAND'S INCOME UNDER $5,000		HUSBAND'S INCOME, $5,000 OR MORE	
	Wife Not Working	*Wife Working*	*Wife Not Working*	*Wife Working*
		Per Cent		
Weekly	8	9	9	10
Monthly	15	15	22	13
A few times a year	12	23	24	40
Less often	11	11	11	10
Never	53	41	32	27
Not ascertained	1	2	2	–
Total	100	101	100	100
Number of families	*184*	*66*	*284*	*48*

may be no coincidence that this frequency corresponds roughly to the number of holidays from work which the wife has each year.

The most extensive colleague companionship, however, is not that of working wives but of high-income housewives, who more often entertain at least once a month than any other group of wives. This group includes wives of white-collar workers who help their husbands get ahead by throwing parties for the boss and prospective clients. Blood and Wolfe found that such "hostess-companions" have the highest sense of companionship with their husbands of any group of Detroit wives. However, some high-income housewives neither work nor carry any other significant economic role and feel very dissatisfied in the area of companionship.

Apparently dual involvement in the occupational world provides a certain minimal amount of auxiliary social participation. However, the working wife is just too busy to respond to the extra margin of entertaining and visiting which high-income husbands ordinarily require (7). So the pinch of working shows in this area of companionship at high-income levels.

Further evidence that dual-income couples are not satisfied just to sit at home and recuperate from their labors occurs in Gianopulos and Mitchell's finding that one of their few trouble spots which is neither domestic nor economic is recreational (5). The Detroit Area Study's income control confines this difficulty to the upper-income group. Disagreements about recreation are mentioned by 15 per cent of non-working and working low-income wives and by the same percentage of high-income housewives, but by 25 per cent of high-income working wives. Apparently these working wives

TABLE 20.7 *Wife's Satisfaction with Companionship by Husband's Income and Wife's Employment Status*

WIFE'S SATISFACTION WITH COMPANIONSHIP	HUSBAND'S INCOME UNDER $5,000		HUSBAND'S INCOME, $5,000 OR MORE	
	Wife Not Working	*Wife Working*	*Wife Not Working*	*Wife Working*
		Per Cent		
Enthusiastic	30	39	33	23
Quite satisfied	31	36	37	56
Can't complain	24	9	15	4
Nice to have more	8	11	11	10
Dissatisfied	4	–	3	6
Not ascertained	3	5	1	–
Total	100	100	100	99
Number of families	*184*	*66*	*284*	*48*

expect a lot of companionship and are unhappy when they do not get it. At least this interpretation is suggested by Table 20.7.

Two groups of wives are equally dissatisfied with their husbands' companionship. One is the low-income housewife who, according to our inferences, gets the least companionship of any of the four groups. Her family structure involves little built-in sharing, and her husband's income is too small to pay for nights out on the town. So she is the classic example of the lonely working-class housewife (15). The other is the working wife of a high-income man. Her income adds little to the ability of the family budget to support recreational activities. Rather, time is scarcer than money. And though she experiences more companionship than low-income housewives, she still does not have as much as high-income housewives enjoy. Since the latter is her relevant reference group, the comparison dims her enthusiasm.

Most companionable of all are the low-income dual-income marriages. Here the wife's income makes "all the difference in the world" between hard times and good times, and the couple shares more both in and outside of the home than their housewife reference group. Although Table 20.6 showed that the high-income housewives have the most colleague companionship, this doesn't necessarily mean they have more of other types of companionship. Their husbands are more occupationally involved than low-income husbands. As a result, they may engage in more occupationally-relevant companionship but in less frivolous dating. Research is needed to test this hypothesis. In any case, high-income housewives are moderately well satisfied with the companionship they get.

To summarize, the relationship between the wife's employment and marital companionship seems to run in opposite directions, depending on the husband's income. If his income is below average, the wife's work is tangibly rewarding and increases their ability to engage in enjoyable uses of leisure time together. If his income is above average, there is less need for the wife to work and a sense of deprivation arises from the impaired amount of leisure time available.

LOVE

If there is less need for the high-income man's wife to work and a correspondingly greater sense of deprivation connected with it, then why work? We have already noted that, percentage-wise, fewer wives do work under these circumstances. For those few who do, the suspicion arises that their employment is sometimes a result—not a cause—of their dissatisfaction with their husbands.

Table 20.8 shows that as far as love and affection are concerned,

TABLE 20.8 *Wife's Satisfaction with Husband's Love and Affection by Husband's Income and Wife's Employment Status*

WIFE'S SATISFACTION WITH HUSBAND'S LOVE AND AFFECTION	HUSBAND'S INCOME UNDER $5,000		HUSBAND'S INCOME, $5,000 OR MORE	
	Wife Not Working	*Wife Working*	*Wife Not Working*	*Wife Working*
	Per Cent			
Enthusiastic	25	38	37	25
Quite satisfied	41	38	44	52
Can't complain	22	15	12	13
Nice to have more	4	5	4	6
Dissatisfied	3	–	1	4
Not ascertained	5	5	1	–
Total	100	101	99	100
Number of families	*184*	*66*	*284*	*48*

Detroit wives feel the same way they do about companionship. Again the two most satisfied groups are the middle ones, and the least satisfied, the outside ones. Satisfaction is associated with working when extra income is needed, with staying home when it is not. Perhaps, high-income husbands resent their wives' employment and love them the less for it. Perhaps, also, as Gianopulos and Mitchell put it, "working is engaged in by the wife as a substitute source of gratification of personal needs that are not satisfied in the marital interaction." Only a before-and-after method of research could disentangle the time sequence here. All we can say conclusively is that the needfulness of the wife's employment seems to be crucial to whether or not the wife feels her husband loves her.

UNDERSTANDING

Although companionship and affection have been recognized for some years as aspects of urban marriage, it is only recently that Blood and Wolfe have explored the therapeutic role which marriage partners can play through understanding each other's problems and feelings. Assuming that every person experiences frustrating situations from time to time, the question is how often married individuals share their troubles with the spouse.

Table 20.9 shows that working wives in Detroit tell their troubles to

TABLE 20.9 *Therapeutic Utilization of Husband After a Bad Day by Husband's Income and Wife's Employment Status*

FREQUENCY WIFE TELLS HER TROUBLES AFTER A BAD DAY	HUSBAND'S INCOME UNDER $5,000		HUSBAND'S INCOME, $5,000 OR MORE	
	Wife Not Working	*Wife Working*	*Wife Not Working*	*Wife Working*
		Per Cent		
Always	21	32	19	25
Usually	22	20	26	19
Half the time	23	24	27	31
Seldom	16	12	19	15
Never	16	9	6	4
Not ascertained	2	3	2	6
Total	100	100	99	100
Number of families	*184*	*66*	*284*	*48*

their husbands more often than stay-at-home wives. There are several possible reasons for this. One is the equalitarian structure of their marriages which provides a framework within which sharing easily occurs. Washing dishes together is a natural setting for communication with a minimum of effort. Second is the companionship expectations which working wives seem to have, their greater stress on the desirability of togetherness in various areas. Third is the fact that insofar as the working wife's troubles arise on the job she can expect a more knowledgeable response from the husband than a housewife whose problems arise in a world apart. Troubles with the boss, with fellow workers, and with the job itself are the husband's meat, so he becomes a logical resource. Their common employment status also affects the nature of the husband's response (see Table 20.10).

TABLE 20.10 *Husband's Therapeutic Response by Husband's Income and Wife's Employment Status*

HUSBAND'S THERAPEUTIC RESPONSE	HUSBAND'S INCOME UNDER $5,000		HUSBAND'S INCOME, $5,000 OR MORE	
	Wife Not Working	*Wife Working*	*Wife Not Working*	*Wife Working*
		Per Cent		
Help toward solution	5	2	8	4
Help in withdrawing from situation	3	3	3	4
Sympathy, affection	26	30	30	29
Advice, discussion how wife can solve	14	30	18	25
Passive listening	18	11	18	15
Dismissal as unimportant	7	5	9	8
Criticism, rejection	8	8	5	6
Wife never tells her troubles	16	9	6	4
Not ascertained	4	3	2	4
Total	101	101	99	99
Number of families	*184*	*66*	*284*	*48*

Since he is an expert on the kinds of problems she has, he can advise her on how to cope with them. Knowing how to handle them, he less often feels paralyzed into non-responsiveness. Knowing personally the poignancy of the kinds of troubles she has, he is less tempted to dismiss them as unimportant. On the other hand, insofar as her problems occur at work rather than at home, he cannot pitch in and help directly with their solution the way the responsive husband of a housewife can take over the children or plunge into housework.

Only the increased advice is sizeable enough to be statistically significant, but the marginal differences in Table 20.10 show a common effect of the wife's entrance into the occupational system. Having entered a man's world, she now encounters masculine-type frustrations, and can expect a more expert commentary from her husband than wives with enigmatic domestic difficulties.

These shifts are larger in the low-income group, suggesting again that these husbands respond more positively than high-income ones to their wife's employment.

Thus, this exploration of the impact of the wife's employment on her leisure-time relationship to her husband shows a number of observable differences. Employed wives seem to expect more interaction with their husbands in these as well as in other aspects of their marriages. However, the quality of the relationship is affected by the extent of the need for her to assume such an unusual role. The greater the need (measured by the husband's income), the more positively the marriage is affected. The less the need, the less positive—or even the more negative—the effect. Hence it is difficult to generalize about the effects of employment, regardless of circumstances, and more rewarding to specify conditions which influence the effects.

MARITAL SATISFACTION

What has just been said about the importance of conditions applies with special force to attempts to summarize the impact of employment on the satisfactoriness, success, or happiness of marriages. The Detroit Area Study (4), Nye (Chapter Nineteen), and Locke and Mackeprang (10) all found no difference between conventional and two-income marriages as a whole in marital satisfaction or adjustment.[8] However, as would be expected from the preceding tables, the Detroit Area Study reveals small but suggestive differences when the income-condition is controlled (see Table 20.11).

Table 20.11 suggests tentatively that employment under conditions of need may enhance the satisfactoriness of the marriage for the wife.[9] On the other hand, unneeded employment may be either the cause or the result of dissatisfaction of the wife with her marriage.[10]

Since the differences in Table 20.11 are small and not statistically significant, they should be interpreted with caution. They point the way, however, to a more fruitful approach for future research, namely to specify more precisely conditions under which employment has positive effects and

_____

[8] Although Nye finds no difference in the wife's satisfaction, dual-income families in his sample have more conflicts, more separations and thoughts of divorce, and more unhappy wives than conventional marriages.

[9] Although students of social stratification normally treat income and occupation as indices of the same thing (i.e., social status), they apparently have opposite effects on marital satisfaction in relation to employment. We have suggested that low income produces a need to work and therefore greater satisfaction when the wife does work. Nye, on the other hand, finds that employment for wives of white-collar husbands produces less "marital maladjustment" than for wives of blue-collar husbands. To be sure, satisfaction and marital adjustment are not identical measures, but if we assume comparability, we might resolve the apparent contradiction by hypothesizing that need for the wife to work is greatest when white-collar husbands earn low incomes. Since such husbands have a high-income reference group, their wives may have the greatest sense of relative deprivation and the greatest need to close the gap between actual and expected income. Hence their work may be particularly appreciated by the family.

[10] Evidence for the latter is found by Nye: the 20 per cent of non-working wives in his sample who wished they were working had significantly poorer marital adjustment than those satisfied with their role. Only a longitudinal research design can discover the extent to which "unneeded" employment *causes* marital difficulty or *results from* marital dissatisfaction.

TABLE 20.11 *Wife's Marital Satisfaction by Husband's Income and Wife's Employment Status*

| | HUSBAND'S INCOME UNDER $5,000 | | HUSBAND'S INCOME, $5,000 OR MORE | |
| | Wife Not Working | Wife Working | Wife Not Working | Wife Working |
		Per Cent		
Wife's mean score on marital satisfaction Index	4.60	4.78	4.78	4.54
Number of families	*159*	*60*	*257*	*43*

Source: Blood and Wolfe (4, Table 38, p. 102). The index combines: (a) the wife's satisfaction with the standard of living provided by her husband's income, (b) her satisfaction with the companionship and affection derived from him (Tables 20.7 and 20.8 above), (c) his understanding of her problems and feelings, and (d) the congruence of her preferred and actual or expected number of children—all weighted by the relative importance attached to each aspect of marriage.

those where the effects are adverse. Better than focussing on global measurement of the subjective impact of employment on the partners is concentrating on the effects of employment in specific areas of marriage—as was done earlier in this chapter.

Even more important, when it comes to the subjective evaluation of the wife's employment, is the question of the husband's reaction. He is the one who loses a full-time household servant when the wife goes to work. He must increase his share of the housework by helping out with traditionally feminine jobs. The husband also loses status in the family as the balance of power shifts toward the wife in the crucial area of major economic decisions. His loss of power and of "face" is particularly great when his wife's income is greater than his own. (In 20 per cent of Nye's cases, the wife earned more than the husband, and marital adjustment was worse than usual for dual-income marriages.) If anyone is to feel dissatisfied with the wife's employment, we would expect it to be the husband. Unfortunately the three studies which have dealt with marital satisfaction (the Detroit Area Study, Nye, and Locke and Mackeprang) have not interviewed husbands. A forthcoming monograph by the author will provide cross-cultural data from a Japanese sample of both husbands and wives (2). Meanwhile, we can see only half the story of the effects of the wife's employment on husband-wife relationships when we see it through the wife's eyes alone.

SUMMARY

The structural impact of the wife's employment on marriage seems well established. (a) The wife decreases her housekeeping activities while the husband increases his by performing masculine tasks more unilaterally and by helping with feminine tasks. (b) In an appreciable number of families, the pressure for revising the division of labor results in conflict between husband and wife over marriage roles. (c) The power structure of marriage shifts in the direction of a greater voice for the wife in major economic decisions and a lesser voice in routine household decisions. Neither shift, however, means that one partner is pushed around by the other. Rather, decision-making roles adapt naturally to the new economic and housekeeping roles of the partners.

The impact of the wife's employment on the performance of family functions has been less thoroughly documented. Tentatively we may generalize that (a) dual-income couples expect more interaction and joint activity in their leisure time but that (b) reduction in the amount of leisure time available when housework must be confined to off-work hours interferes with the more time-consuming uses of leisure.

The impact of the wife's employment on the couples' evaluation of their marriage is least understood. Nothing is known yet about male evaluations. Employed wives as a whole do not differ appreciably from housewives in their evaluations of their marriages. However, there appear to be positive evaluations associated with work in low-income households and negative evaluations when the husband's income is high.

REFERENCES

1. Blood, Robert O., Jr. "The Division of Labor in City and Farm Families," *Marriage and Family Living,* XX (May, 1958), 170–74.
2. _____. *Love Match and Interview Marriage in Japan* (tentative title). To be published circa 1964.
3. _____, and Hamblin, Robert L. "The Effect of the Wife's Employment on the Family Power Structure," *Social Forces,* XXXVI (May, 1958), 347–52.
4. _____, and Wolfe, Donald M. *Husbands and Wives: The Dynamics of Married Living.* Glencoe, Ill.: Free Press, 1960.
5. Gianopulos, Artie, and Mitchell, Howard E. "Marital Disagreement in Working Wife Marriages as a Function of Husband's Attitude toward Wife's Employment," *Marriage and Family Living,* XIX (November, 1957), 373–78.
6. Heer, David M. "Dominance and the Working Wife," *Social Forces,* XXXVI (May, 1958), 341–47. Reprinted as Chapter Eighteen of the present book.
7. Helfrich, Margaret L. "The Generalized Role of the Executive's Wife," *Marriage and Family Living,* XXIII (November, 1961), 384–87.

8. Hoffman, Lois Wladis. "Effects of the Employment of Mothers on Parental Power Relations and the Division of Household Tasks," *Marriage and Family Living*, XXII (February, 1960), 27–35. Reprinted as Chapter Fifteen of the present book.

9. Kligler, Deborah H. "The Effects of the Employment of Married Women on Husband and Wife Roles." Unpublished Ph.D. dissertation, Yale University, 1954.

10. Locke, Harvey J., and Mackeprang, Muriel. "Marital Adjustment of the Employed Wife," *American Journal of Sociology*, LIV (May, 1949), 536–39.

11. Middleton, Russell, and Putney, Snell. "Dominance in Decisions in the Family: Race and Class Differences," *American Journal of Sociology*, LXV (May, 1960), 605–9.

12. Nolan, Francena L. See Chapters Eight and Seventeen of the present book.

13. Nye, F. Ivan. "Employment Status of Mothers and Marital Conflict, Permanence, and Happiness," *Social Problems*, VI (Winter, 1958–1959), 260–67. An extended version of this article appears as Chapter Nineteen of the present book.

14. Powell, Kathryn S. "Maternal Employment in Relation to Family Life," *Marriage and Family Living*, XXIII (November, 1961), 350–55.

15. Rainwater, Lee, and others. *Workingman's Wife*. New York: Oceana, 1959, esp. chaps. ii and iv.

PART IV

ADJUSTMENT OF THE MOTHER

Chapter Twenty-One

Maternal Mental Health

LAWRENCE J. SHARP AND F. IVAN NYE

THOUGH many writers have stressed the importance of the relationship between occupation and mental health (1, p. 44; 2; 5, chap. 8), few have offered more than speculation about relationships between mothers' employment and mental health (3; 4, chap. 9; 6; 7; 9, chap. 4; 11; 13, chap. 10; 16, pp. 13–16). But a variety of relevant ideas have been advanced.

For example, Lundberg and Farnham believe that the employee role is basically masculine and that the woman who is employed outside the home is placed in the impossible position of playing a masculine role during the day and a feminine one morning and evening (11). Parsons takes an opposing position (16, pp. 13–16). He states that the work done outside the home is little different from that done in the home. It is usually service work and is generally supportive or nurtural. Women are infrequently employed in executive positions in which they would be required to play roles associated with masculinity in our society. Komarovsky (8, chap. 8) and Landis (9, chap. 4) have pointed to the frustrations experienced by talented and ambitious women when marriage and parenthood prevent their participation in the occupational world. Myrdal and Klein believe that during most of her adult life, the roles of the non-employed married woman are not sufficiently productive to be satisfying to her (13, chap. 10).

The ideas advanced may be thus summarized: (a) some believe that employment of the mother places her in the impossible position of playing contradictory roles—contradictory roles which necessarily lead to increased anxiety, behavioral defenses by which this anxiety is controlled, and mental ill-health; (b) others hold that the employee role is not essentially different from the roles of wife and mother, may be successfully integrated, and results in no significant changes in mental health; (c) finally, some maintain that satisfaction gained from the employee role in terms of family goals may be such that real gains in personality fulfillment and mental health are made. For this latter position, see Sharp (18) and Nye (14).

Along with these three ideas about the direct relationship between mothers' employment and their mental health, other ideas from mental health etiology must be considered. Rather than a direct effect, it may be that employment has only a contingent effect upon the mother's mental health. Leavy and Freedman found that among employees in general, including both males and females, "Employment provided a demonstrable release for energies which were themselves directed by neurotic conflict." (10, p. 67) They concluded that economic on-the-job competition may act as a pathogenic agency in the development of psychoneurosis. That is, the cultural evaluation of work provides a screen of acceptability for compulsive overactivity, the neurotic nature of which may be evident only after the individual develops a disabling mental disorder. In an earlier study, it was found in a sample of mothers who had developed mental illnesses sufficient to require hospitalization, that those who were employed within one year of hospitalization were diagnosed psychoneurotic more frequently than non-employed mothers (18). It may be that among mothers with an already somewhat disorganized personality, employment temporarily serves as a release and control of conflicts which later result in major mental disorder. It is entirely possible that employment is a crucial factor for the mental health of mothers only in the contingency that the mother already possesses personality characteristics which are leading to mental ill-health.

Because of the possibility that mothers' employment may have either a direct effect or only a contingent effect upon their mental health, and since a long-range longitudinal study has been impossible up to this time, the analysis of the relationship between mental health and employment must be undertaken on two levels. First, evidences of mental health among employed and non-employed mothers in the general population must be considered. Second, evidences of the effect of employment upon those employed and non-employed mothers who have developed major mental health problems must be taken into account.

WOMEN IN THE GENERAL POPULATION

It was noted that mothers' employment has been viewed in three contrasting ways by other authors. Employment is viewed as (a) harmful, (b) non-significant, or (c) beneficial. These contradictory ideas suggest the suitability of the null hypothesis that: Employed mothers do not differ from non-employed mothers in anxiety level.

The women in this analysis were mothers of children in grades one and ten in three small Washington cities. All were Caucasian, non-farm, and all were living in families in which the husband was present. Working and non-working samples were matched by number of children in the family, presence of preschool children, socio-economic status, education level of wife, and marital status (original or remarriage). For a further description of the sample, see Chapter Nineteen.

THE ANXIETY CRITERION

Researchers have found psychosomatic symptoms a satisfactory device for the identification of psychoneurotics. The items employed here were selected from those employed to screen psychoneurotics during World War II and since employed as a criterion of anxiety in adolescents (15; 19, p. 499).

In the above cited research, psychosomatic symptoms were found to constitute a quasi-scale which was refined by the application of image analysis. Fifteen items were employed in this previous research. From these, the best ten items were included in the present project. One of these, "Do you ever bite fingernails now?" was dropped because of a high ratio of error. The other nine are included in the present measure.

One additional item not previously employed was added. This was having consulted a psychiatrist or having wanted to do so. This behavior is presumably indicative of anxiety. The items included in increasing order of affirmative responses are:

Have you ever consulted a psychiatrist in the past five years?
Have you ever been troubled with cold sweats?
Do your hands tremble enough to bother you?
Have you ever been bothered by shortness of breath when you were not exercising or working hard?
Are you ever bothered by nightmares?
Have you ever been bothered by your heart beating hard?
Have you ever been bothered by pressures or pains in the head?
Are you ever bothered by nervousness?
Do you have trouble in getting or staying asleep?
Have you ever had spells of dizziness?

These items were scaled employing the Cornell Technique and a reproducibility coefficient of .824 was found. From previous experience it is assumed that this can be increased to about .85 by varying the order of the respondents to minimize error.

A reproducibility coefficient of this size suggests a dominant dimension is present, even though some minor dimensions are probably also present. Image Analysis was applied, therefore, to suppress minor dimensions and reduce errors of unreliability. This reduced scale error to 2 per cent. The revised scale would estimate the scores that individuals would receive if only the dominant dimension (anxiety) was measured. A discussion of this rationale and technique of Image Analysis can be found in Riley, Riley, and Toby (17, pp. 396–409).

The validity of psychosomatic symptoms as indicators of anxiety has been generally recognized and will not be discussed at length. One check was made, however. Psychosomatic symptoms scale types were cross-tabulated with the item, "Have you seen or wanted to see a psychiatrist in the past five years?" The scale predicts visitation to a psychiatrist very well. No mother admitting less than six symptoms had visited or expressed a wish to visit one. It should be noted that the item, "consulted a psychiatrist," is included in the scale; however, it is represented only in scale type 00 and does not effect the distribution of the other scale types.

Since recall data are involved and definition of terms are not precise, some element of unreliability must be present. As Guttman has said, however, in a scale there can be little else than the dimension being measured (19, p. 499). Unreliable responses are recorded as errors in scale analysis, and if there are many such errors, the items will not scale. To test reliability, the split-half test was employed. The Spearman-Brown estimate of reliability for this scale is .96. This is a somewhat higher figure than would be anticipated and suggests that Image Analysis is an effective technique for reducing errors of reliability.

When all items were dichotomized, 11 scale types were created from those who admitted no symptoms to those who admitted nine and also indicated that they had seen a psychiatrist.

ANXIETY FINDINGS

An examination of the data shows little reason to reject the null hypothesis that employed mothers do not differ from non-employed mothers in anxiety level. Almost identical proportions of full-time, part-time, and non-employed mothers fall into the high, middle, and low psychosomatic terciles. Actually the small, non-significant differences favor the mothers employed full-time.

TEST VARIABLES IN ANXIETY FINDINGS

Although no relationship was found between employment status and anxiety as measured by psychosomatic symptoms in the sample as a whole, possible relationships in substrata of the sample might have been obscured. Accordingly, the relationship was studied by socio-economic level and several other test variables selected because of possible relationship to the analysis.

Socio-Economic Status. The relationship of employment status to anxiety was studied in four categories by the occupation of the husband.

These categories were: (a) professional and managerial, (b) clerical and sales, (c) craft and operative and (d) labor and service (there were no farmers in the sample).

The four analyses resulted in only one significant difference. Among wives of men in professional and managerial occupations, the employed mothers show a tendency toward a bimodal distribution.[1] Proportionately, they show fewer symptoms or more symptoms than do the non-employed mothers. In this group of well-educated, relatively prosperous women, employment would seem to increase or decrease anxiety depending on the presence or absence of additional variables.

Subsequent to this finding it was noted that Frumkin reported that males cite income as most important for occupational satisfaction, while females name job prestige (5). It was also noted that Joan W. Moore reported that participation in voluntary organizations for upper-class women is significant to the women's view of herself in the entire class (12). In other words, upper-class women join prestigeful voluntary associations earlier, enjoy greater gratification, and find their roles linked to family and class responsibilities. Wondering if this might also not be true for the employment of relatively prosperous mothers, the sub-hypothesis was advanced that: Mothers whose husbands are in the managerial or professional occupational category will show fewer anxiety symptoms when they are members of an occupational category similar in level to that of their husbands. This explained the previously noted bimodal distribution at a statistically significant level (Table 21.1). The sub-hypothesis was supported.

TABLE 21.1 *The Relationship of Status Equality of Husbands' and Wives' Occupations to Anxiety Scale Types*

OCCUPATION OF HUSBAND	WIFE'S OCCUPATION STATUS EQUAL TO OR GREATER THAN HUSBAND'S	WIFE'S OCCUPATION STATUS LESS THAN HUSBAND'S	TOTAL
	Per Cent		*Number*
Professional or managerial*	36.8	63.2	*68*
Clerical-sales	47.6	52.4	*164*
Crafts-operatives	41.7	58.3	*24*
Laborer-service	49.2	50.8	*59*

* Difference is statistically significant (above .05 level).

[1] It is recognized that in a series of tests, one "significant difference" may occur by chance; however, this one is consistent with some previous research reported here.

Educational Level. Since educational level brings mothers into differential contact with newer concepts of family life and child development, it seemed worth while to employ it as a test variable. The analysis by junior high, some high school, graduation from high school, and college revealed no significant differences or consistent minor differences. If education level has an effect on the relationship, it is offset by other variables associated with education.

Occupation of Mother. This test variable revealed no statistically significant differences. There are some rather sizable percentage differences, however, in the blue-collar groups. Women who are craftsmen, operatives, laborers, and service workers more often appear in the high anxiety category when employed full-time. The opposite trend is present in the white-collar female occupations. The numbers in these matched samples, however, are too small to make further analysis profitable. This might warrant additional specialized research.

Family Size and Stage of Development. Family size and stage of development were employed as test variables because the duties and responsibilities of the mother might be greater and more difficult in larger families and where preschool children are present. The analysis suggests that employed mothers of preschool children experience more anxiety than those not employed. Whereas in the general sample employed mothers showed slightly fewer symptoms, employed mothers with preschool children show more symptoms. Differences are mostly non-significant and may be due to sampling error. But they are consistent with the attitudes of the public and with statements made by mothers themselves.

There is an interesting sample difference in the opposite direction for older women with no children younger than the tenth year in school. At this family stage, a considerably larger proportion of employed (53 per cent) than non-employed (36 per cent) women are in the lowest category of psychosomatic symptoms. Although this would not necessarily have been anticipated, it may be rationalized that these women need an additional significant role. Their children are becoming more independent, and they can foresee both the termination of any important function as mother as well as the loss of physical attractiveness. Since the differences are not statistically significant, however, they are only suggestive.

Size of family as a test variable reveals no significant differences. There is no support at all for the idea that anxiety level should be higher for employed mothers with families of four or more children. In the sample, 14 per cent of employed mothers with large families are in the most psychosomatic category, compared to 24 per cent for mothers of large families who were not employed. Although it is possible to speculate, present information is insufficient to provide an adequate rationale for this difference.

Marital Status. Marital status proved a valuable test variable in the analysis of the relationship of employment status to marital adjustment (Chapter Nineteen). In the relationship of employment status to anxiety, however, it appears useless.

WOMEN IN THE MENTALLY ILL POPULATION

As was noted, earlier writers have found a difference in the motivations of men and women as to the satisfactions they gain from work. It was also noted that at least one report suggests employment may be a means whereby neurotic conflicts are temporarily controlled (10). An earlier report specifically concerned with employment of mothers tended to support this contention (18).

From these earlier works, it was concluded that mothers' employment may have only a contingent effect upon their mental health. That is, employment possibly becomes a crucial factor in mental health only when certain predisposing personality factors are operative. Accordingly, the hypothesis is advanced that if predisposing personality factors make employment one of many possible contingent factors leading to mental ill health, mentally ill employed mothers should show historical evidence of early personality instability.

Accordingly, a 40 per cent random sample, stratified by month of admission, of 525 native, white, female first-admissions was taken from the three state hospitals of Washington. All admissions took place between July 1, 1954, and June 30, 1957. Fifty-eight of the 210 cases so obtained were lost because of suspected inadequate reliability of case history information or subsampling for an equal number of employed and non-employed mothers. The final sample is composed of 76 mothers of children eighteen years of age or under who had never been employed prior to hospitalization for mental illness, and 76 mothers of such children who had been employed 24 or more hours per week within one year of hospitalization.

THE DATA AND MENTAL ILLNESS CRITERIA

The data collected about these 152 women came from their medical case histories. These case histories were compiled in the normal course of hospital routine by psychiatrists, psychologists, and social workers. Only those items of information which appeared to be most systematically gathered by all who made up the case histories were accepted for research purposes.

Ultimately, six variables from these case histories were accepted as meeting research criteria: (a) psychiatric diagnosis, (b) number of marriages of the wife, (c) expressions of guilt about role of mother by the patient, (d) expressions of acceptance or rejection of children by the patient, (e) expressions of acceptance or rejection of the husband's occupational status by the patient, and (f) mental illness onset.

Psychiatric diagnosis was accepted with full recognition of its limitations as an airtight classificatory scheme. Nevertheless, because it is widely used in mental health research, and because it is generally understood by interested persons, it was accepted.

The number of marriages of the wife was routinely recorded in the case histories with a high degree of reliability.

Expressions of guilt about the role of mother by the patient was found as part of a routine report by the social worker on family relationships of the patient. The presence or absence of such statements by the patient was specifically noted. The same is true of expressions of acceptance or rejection of children by the patient, and acceptance or rejection of the husband's vocational status. These three variables, especially when intense, were assumed to be indicative of personality instability.

Finally, mental illness onset was included in the case history as part of the psychiatric diagnosis. It was recorded as "chronic" or "acute," depending on whether or not the onset was of long historical duration, or relatively short in nature. This variable was assumed to be the most indicative of past-life personality instability.

DIAGNOSTIC FINDINGS

Forty-seven per cent of the employed mothers were diagnosed as psychoneurotic, while only 6 per cent of the non-employed mothers were so diagnosed (Table 21.2). Sixty-eight per cent of the non-employed mothers were diagnosed as psychotic, as compared with only 35 per cent of the employed mothers. The relationship between employment status and phychiatric diagnosis is significant. According to psychiatric diagnosis, it was found that

TABLE 21.2 *Diagnostic Categories Associated with Employment Status*

DIAGNOSTIC CATEGORIES OF DISORDERS	EMPLOYED MOTHERS		NON-EMPLOYED MOTHERS	
	Number	*Per Cent*	*Number*	*Per Cent*
Organic	6	7.8	11	14.5
Psychotic	27	35.5*	52	68.4*
Neurotic	36	47.4*	5	6.6*
Behavioral	7	9.2	8	10.5
Total	76	99.9	76	100.0

* Relationship is statistically significant.

mentally ill employed mothers do have different personality types than mentally ill non-employed mothers.

INSTABILITY AND EMPLOYMENT STATUS

To determine whether or not the past life histories of these women showed differentials in personality instability according to employment status the aforementioned variables were cross-tabulated with employment status.

Number of Marriages. More formerly employed mentally ill mothers (27.6 per cent) had multiple marriages than formerly non-employed mentally ill mothers (13.2 per cent). The relationship between employment status and number of marriages was statistically significant for these mothers.

Expressions of Guilt about the Mother Role. The relationship between expressions of guilt about the role of mother and employment status was not statistically significant, though it was in the direction hypothesized. The employed mothers (30.3 per cent) more often expressed such feelings than non-employed mothers (24.6 per cent).

Expressions of Acceptance of Children. This item was statistically non-significant in relation to employment status. Twenty per cent of the employed mothers and 17 per cent of the non-employed mothers stated some rejection, resentment, or conflict in their relationships with their children.

Expressions of Acceptance of Husband's Vocation. While non-significant, this item was in the direction hypothesized. Of the employed mothers, 38.8 per cent expressed dissatisfaction, rejection, or feelings of undesirability about their husband's vocational status. Of the non-employed mothers, 19.1 per cent made such statements. Very often these statements were in terms of the adequacy of the husband's income. Occasionally they reflected aspects of marital conflict, indicating dissatisfaction with the husband's ambition or vocational drive. A few were in terms of the effect of the particular occupation upon the husband. Because these women expressed satisfaction or dissatisfaction in so many ways, the significance of the direction of these responses as indications of personality instability is minimal.

Mental Illness Onset. The relationship between the onset of mental illness and employment status was statistically significant and in line with the hypothesis. Of the employed mothers, 30.9 per cent had chronic onsets. Only 20.1 per cent of the non-employed mothers had chronic onsets. Since the number of employed mothers diagnosed as neurotic is so much greater than the number of non-employed mothers, this may reflect the nature of neuroses and the symptoms by which they are diagnosed. Nevertheless, while the agreement between onset and diagnosis is not surprising, it is significant that employed mothers are more often classified as having exhibited symptoms of mental illness over a longer period of time. A greater proportion of mothers possessing personality factors predisposing them to mental illness were employed than not employed.

SUMMARY AND CONCLUSIONS

The primary analysis of the relationship between employment and anxiety symptoms failed to disclose that employed mothers in the general population had more psychosomatic symptoms than non-employed mothers. In general, it appears that the null hypothesis that employed mothers will not differ significantly from non-employed mothers in anxiety level is not refuted. This seems to fit the rationale that if playing competing roles simultaneously produces anxiety, then some aspect of the employee role also reduces anxiety. This rationale appears to be true for all but employed wives of husbands in professional or managerial occupations. Here, it was found that the status of the woman's occupation with reference to that of her husband is crucial. Apparently for the upper-income group mother, occupational prestige and social status are related to anxiety level. However, in view of these tentative findings, there may be other aspects of the upper-income group employed mother's occupation which are even more definitive for her mental health. Perhaps the differential between the husband's occupation and her occupation is indicative of educational, social, and background differences which are of key importance in any marriage relationship.

The deficiencies of case history data, the criticisms which can be leveled at psychiatric diagnostic categories make the findings presented here extremely tentative. Many related factors are involved when a woman who is also a mother and an employee develops a severe form of mental illness. As the data suggest, it may very well be that employment contributes to the mental health and well-being of some employed mothers, while it serves the opposite effect for other employed mothers, depending on contingent conditions yet unknown.

REFERENCES

1. Clark, Robert E. "Psychoses, Income and Occupational Prestige," *American Journal of Sociology,* LIV (March, 1949), 44.
2. _____. "The Relationship of Schizophrenia to Occupational Income and Occupational Prestige," *American Sociological Review,* XIV (June, 1948), 325–30.
3. Cottrell, Leonard S., Jr. "Roles and Marital Adjustment," *Publication of the American Sociological Society,* XXVII (June, 1933), 107–15.
4. Elliott, Mabel A., and Merrill, Francis E. *Social Disorganization.* 4th ed.; New York: Harper, 1961.

5. Frumkin, Robert M. "Occupation and Major Mental Disorder." In A. M. Rose, ed. *Mental Health and Mental Disorder.* New York: Norton, 1955, chap. 8.

6. Gianopulos, Artie, and Mitchell, Howard E. "Marital Disagreement in Working Wife Marriages as a Function of Husband's Attitude toward Wife's Employment," *Marriage and Family Living,* XIX (November, 1957), 373–78.

7. Kluckhohn, Florence R. "Cultural Factors in Social Work Practice and Education: The Female Role in the United States as an Example of a Particular Kind of Strain," *Social Service Review,* XXV (March, 1951), 45–47.

8. Komarovsky, Mirra. *Women in the Modern World.* Boston: Little, Brown, 1953.

9. Landis, Paul H. *Making the Most of Marriage.* New York: Appleton-Century-Crofts, 1955.

10. Leavy, Stanley A., and Freedman, Lawrence Z. "Psychoneurosis and Economic Life," *Social Problems,* IV (July, 1956), 55–67.

11. Lundberg, Ferdinand, and Farnham, Marynia F. *Modern Woman, The Lost Sex.* New York: Harper, 1947.

12. Moore, Joan W. "Patterns of Women's Participation in Voluntary Associations," *American Journal of Sociology,* LXIV (May, 1961), 592–98.

13. Myrdal, Alva, and Klein, Viola. *Women's Two Roles: Home and Work.* London: Routledge & Kegan Paul, 1956.

14. Nye, F. Ivan. "Social and Psychological Correlates of the Employment of Mothers." Paper read before the Northwest Council of Family Relations, Missoula, Montana, November, 1958.

15. _____. "Some Family Attitudes and Psychosomatic Symptoms in Adolescents," *Coordinator,* VI (December, 1957), 22–26.

16. Parsons, Talcott, and Bales, Robert F. *Family, Socialization and Interaction Process.* Glencoe, Ill.: Free Press, 1955.

17. Riley, Matilda White, Riley, John W., Jr., and Toby, Jackson. *Sociological Studies in Scales Analysis.* New Brunswick, N. J.: Rutgers University Press, 1954.

18. Sharp, Lawrence J. "Employment Status of Mothers and Some Aspects of Mental Illness," *American Sociological Review,* XXV (October, 1960), 714–17.

19. Stouffer, Samuel A., and others. *Measurement and Prediction.* Princeton, N. J.: Princeton University Press, 1950.

Chapter Twenty-Two

Personal Satisfactions

F. IVAN NYE

A NUMBER of previous studies have dealt with the relationship of maternal employment to some limited feeling or relationship of the mother. For example, Heer (Chapter Eighteen), Blood (2) and Hoffman (Chapter Fifteen) studied the decision-making process and the division of labor within the family. In previous papers, this writer has analyzed its relationship to marital satisfaction (6), to satisfaction with the maternal role (7), and to neurotic symptoms (Chapter Twenty-Two).

The purpose of the present report is to attempt an over-all estimate of the impact of employment on the mother's satisfaction with life. To accomplish this, some of the more specialized findings are incorporated, but the analysis is also extended to areas not previously covered. Finally, a number of contingent conditions will be introduced to determine whether or not a general relationship exists between maternal employment and generalized feelings of satisfaction and dissatisfaction.

THE RESPONDENTS

The sample and method for this study have been described elsewhere (Chapter Nineteen). There were 1,991 mothers of children in grades one and ten and 265 mothers who had a child who had married within the past two years. The former group is referred to as in the "active" parental period, the latter as in the "post" parental period. The respondents were not aware that they were participating in a study of employed mothers.

SATISFACTION: SINGLE OR MULTIPLE DIMENSIONS?

A sociological frame of reference suggests that one segment of an individual's relationships, such as his occupational life, might be satisfactory,

320

while some other area, such as his marital relationship, is not. One area of relationships, however, would be expected to influence behavior patterns and emotional tone in the second. Since the individual interacts in several roles with different individuals and groups, one would anticipate different degrees of success and various gratification levels. It would be expected that several somewhat interrelated dimensions would be involved. In contrast, a psychological orientation suggests basically similar levels of satisfaction in the several clusters of interrelationships, since the same personality is involved in each.

A check of the literature revealed no satisfactory measure of general satisfaction. A number of items were therefore devised to provide an indication of the level of satisfaction in the principal relationships in which the mother is a participant. The items and response categories were as follows.[1]

Please indicate degree of satisfaction or dissatisfaction in each of the following areas:

17. Your family income:
    (1) __entirely dissatisfied
    (2) __somewhat dissatisfied
    (3) __fairly well satisfied
    (4) __generally satisfied
    (5) __entirely satisfied

18. Your house and furniture:
    (1) __entirely satisfied
    (2) __mostly satisfied
    (3) __fairly well satisfied
    (4) __somewhat dissatisfied
    (5) __entirely dissatisfied

19. Your recreation (including visiting):
    (1) __entirely dissatisfied
    (2) __somewhat dissatisfied
    (3) __fairly well satisfied
    (4) __generally satisfied
    (5) __entirely satisfied

20. Your relationships to your children:
    (1) __entirely satisfied
    (2) __mostly satisfied
    (3) __fairly well satisfied
    (4) __somewhat dissatisfied
    (5) __entirely dissatisfied

21. Your relationship to your husband:
    (1) __entirely dissatisfied
    (2) __somewhat dissatisfied
    (3) __fairly well satisfied
    (4) __generally satisfied
    (5) __entirely satisfied

22. Your community as a place in which to live:
    (1) __entirely satisfied
    (2) __mostly satisfied
    (3) __fairly well satisfied
    (4) __somewhat dissatisfied
    (5) __entirely dissatisfied

23. Your daily work:
    (1) __entirely dissatisfied
    (2) __somewhat dissatisfied
    (3) __fairly well satisfied
    (4) __generally satisfied
    (5) __entirely satisfied

---

[1] These were listed as a continuation of the psychosomatic items on the questionnaire completed by 1,991 mothers. See Chapter Nineteen for sample description.

TABLE 22.1 The Interrelationship of Satisfaction Items ($\bar{C}$) [1]

ITEMS	Income	House and Furniture	Recreation	Children	Husband	Community	Work
				Correlation			
Income	1.00	.42	.35	.23	.47	.24	.39
House and furniture	.42	1.00	.30	.31	.31	.33	.39
Recreation	.35	.30	1.00	.33	.48	.28	.61
Children	.23	.31	.33	1.00	.45	.35	.39
Husband	.47	.31	.48	.45	1.00	.89	.79
Community	.24	.33	.28	.35	.89	1.00	.36
Work	.39	.39	.61	.39	.79	.36	1.00

[1] Your family income
Your house and furniture
Your recreation (including visiting)
Your relationship to your children
Your relationship to your husband
Your community as a place in which to live
Your daily work

To determine the interrelationships among the above areas, each satisfaction item was associated with every other item (Table 22.1). The associations proved significant in every instance, but covered a wide range of size from a low of .23 (income with children) to a high of .89 (husband with community).

The presence of a statistical interrelationship among items suggests a common element in the seven items which could be anticipated from either a sociological or psychological frame of reference. The varying sizes of the statistical relationships do not, however, provide a clear indication of whether the common element is dominant or not. Satisfaction with husband is closely related to both daily work and community, but the latter two are not closely related to each other (Table 22.1).

Scalability of the seven items was tested by the Cornell Technique with a resulting reproducibility coefficient of .83. This indicates a common dimension but also suggests minor dimensions or considerable idiosyncratic elements in the analysis. Image Analysis might have been employed to suppress minor dimensions and to minimize idiosyncratic responses. However, since a single dimension is not logical from a sociological frame of reference and the statistical relationship is equivocal, each item was treated separately and the composite was used as an index rather than a scale.

FINDINGS FOR ACTIVE FAMILY STAGE MOTHERS

SATISFACTION WITH DAILY WORK

Some women are attracted to employment, in part, because of a positive interest in a particular vocational activity; others like the stimulus of associating with the people they meet. Even so, only a minority of employed women have expressed such motivations as primary factors in their decision to enter employment. Both observers and employed women themselves have indicated that the combined duties of housewife and employee were burdensome and produced some feelings of anxiety, frustration, and fatigue.

Present data provide support for the position that women employed full-time find more satisfaction in their work than non-employed women find in housework. Those who are employed full-time are better satisfied with their work, also, than those with part-time employment. The part-time workers share the interests of outside work and interpersonal relationships, but they earn less and are less likely to hold professional or supervisory positions. Perhaps, therefore, their work is typically less interesting and less rewarding in terms of achievement or income.

SATISFACTION WITH COMMUNITY

The full-time employment of mothers reduces their participation in community affairs. If this represents a deprivation either in some particular kind of activity or in the interpersonal relationships sacrificed, it should produce dissatisfaction with the combined roles of employee and mother. The data do not support the idea that employed women feel deprived (Table 22.2). Sixty-two per cent of the employed mothers are well satisfied or completely satisfied with their communities compared to 52 per cent of those not employed. The best satisfied, however, are those employed part-time. Those who have the most time available for community activity (the non-employed) are, as a group, the most *dissatisfied* with their communities. This implies that a low level of satisfaction and/or a high level of frustration is involved in unpaid community work.

MARITAL SATISFACTION

This topic has been treated in more detail elsewhere and will only be summarized here. With a single item—satisfaction with relationship to the husband—employed as the criterion, no difference is found between the employed and not employed. But if a Guttman-type marital adjustment scale is employed, a significant difference indicates better marital adjustment for non-employed mothers. Presumably the scale is a more reliable criterion than the single item. The use of marital status as a test variable disclosed that the association was in the unbroken marriages with no association found within the remarriages (see Chapter Nineteen for a detailed discussion).

SATISFACTION WITH CHILDREN

This relationship has been treated in more detail in Chapter Twenty-Four and will be summarized only. The single general item dealing with satisfaction and children revealed no significant difference between working and non-working mothers. Sample differences favored the employed mothers by differences of from two to four percentage points. A quasi-scale showed similar small non-significant differences favoring the employed mother. Two significant items and a majority of non-significant items from the quasi-scale indicated better adjustment for the employed mothers. When the test variable of family size was introduced, the association became statistically significant *within the small family subsample*. It appears that small family size is a contingent condition for the positive association between employment of mothers and their satisfactions with the maternal role.

OTHER SATISFACTIONS

No significant differences were found among employment categories with respect to satisfaction with family income, house and furniture, or recreational life. The non-significant differences favor the employed mother on the first two and the non-employed mother on the last. It is interesting that although employed mothers say that they work for added income, they are no better satisfied with their income or standards of living than non-working mothers. It will be shown in Chapter Twenty-Five that employment appears to reduce formal entertaining and daytime visiting. This does not greatly decrease employed mothers' satisfaction with their recreational life but may account for the small differences observed in the samples, provided these are not due entirely to sample error. The data, however, indicate very little, if any, relationship between employment and satisfaction with income, housing, and recreation.

A SATISFACTION INDEX

As discussed above, interrelationship of responses to the seven satisfaction items was examined. Despite a significant association of each item with every other, it seemed unsatisfactory from either logical or statistical grounds to treat satisfaction as a single dimension. The items do satisfy the requirements of a quasi-scale. A total score was computed assigning one point for each item answered "generally" or "entirely satisfied." The distribution of satisfaction scores is from a low score of zero to a high score of seven (Table 22.2).

TABLE 22.2 *Employment Status of Mothers and Satisfaction Total Scores**

| SATISFACTION SCORES | NOT EMPLOYED | EMPLOYMENT STATUS | | TOTAL |
| | | PART-TIME | FULL-TIME | |
		Per Cent		*Number*
0–2 (low)	35.8	24.7	25.5	257
3–5	47.1	50.0	59.4	363
6–7 (high)	17.1	25.4	15.0	142
Total	100.0	100.1	99.9	762

* The relationship is statistically significant.

The association between employment and satisfaction total scores is significant. In general, the total scores favor the employed—particularly those employed part-time. Among the non-employed is a particularly large group of women who are generally dissatisfied with their lives. But both non-employed and full-time employed women include about equal proportions who are satisfied in all or all but one area. If the part-time employed are removed from the analysis, the relationship is still significant.

TEST VARIABLES

Some differences were found between not employed, part-time, and full-time employed mothers. Both part-time and full-time employed mothers were found to be somewhat better satisfied than those not employed. However, employment may be associated with satisfactions under some conditions and not under others; the association might even be reversed under some conditions.

FAMILY SIZE

Size of family is a less significant condition here than it would be in a special analysis of adjustment to children. The employed mothers are generally better satisfied whether the family is large or not. Interestingly, a tendency discernable in the total sample (Table 22.2) is increased in the subsample of larger families; that is, that differences in satisfactions are concentrated in the lower end of the distributions. More than a third of the non-employed mothers are distinctly dissatisfied with their lives (score 0–2 in Table 22.3) compared to a quarter of the employed. Full-time employed mothers tend to concentrate in the middle range (scores 3–5), not strongly dissatisfied but not "ecstatic" about their lives. In the subsample of mothers with four or more children, this tendency seems to increase. Over 40 per cent of the non-employed women with large families have satisfaction scores 0–2 compared to less than 30 per cent who are employed full-time, but the largest group of full-time employed mothers (over 60 per cent) falls in the intermediate group. In the best satisfied category (scores 6–7), there are more non-employed mothers than employed, although the difference is not significant. Among mothers with large families, those who are employed are intermediately satisfied and those who are non-employed tend to be least satisfied. The presence or absence of preschool children failed to have an appreciable effect as a test variable. Contrary to popular belief, the employed mothers of preschool children verbalize not less but *more* satisfaction with their daily lives than their non-employed counterparts.

EDUCATION OF THE MOTHER

Highly educated women command higher paid and higher prestige occupations. Their work is less tiring physically and their daily contacts are with men and women in the upper social echelons. It seems reasonable, therefore, that the highly educated working mother would combine much of the desirable in the occupational and familial worlds.

Present data suggest that education and related variables are relevant. Employed mothers with college educations show a considerably smaller proportion in the dissatisfied and a larger proportion in the highly satisfied categories (Table 22.3). In contrast, employed mothers with only high school educations are concentrated in the intermediate satisfaction category and are underrepresented in both the lowest and highest categories.

Table 22.3 *Employment Status and Satisfaction with Daily Living by Education of the Mother*

SATISFACTION SCORES	SOME COLLEGE EDUCATION			
	NOT EMPLOYED	PART-TIME	FULL-TIME	TOTAL
	Per Cent			*Number*
0–2 (low)	46.7	37.8	22.9	*39*
3–5	42.2	50.0	51.4	*55*
6–7 (high)	11.1	22.2	25.7	*22*
Total	99.9	100.0	100.0	*116*
	SOME HIGH SCHOOL*			
0–2 (low)	34.1	24.5	27.3	*132*
3–5	48.3	48.9	60.9	*225*
6–7 (high)	17.7	26.6	11.8	*79*
Total	100.1	100.0	100.0	*436*

* For high school women the relationship is statistically significant.

We cannot say that the relationship between employment status and satisfaction scores is contingent on the college education of women, but the direction appears to be clearer and more consistent in that category. The data on high-school–educated mothers suggest that employment is related to intermediate satisfactions rather than to the polar extremes. The subsample of mothers with less than some high school education was too small to warrant separate analysis.

It was presumed that the occupation of the husband would sort the mothers into socio-economic levels; however, its use as a test variable was unproductive.

MARITAL STATUS

Separate analyses within the categories of "remarried" and "living with original mate" disclosed no relationship materially different from that found in the total sample.

ADJUSTMENT IN THE "POST-PARENTAL" PERIOD

Previous analyses have studied employed mothers in the "active"' motherhood period—that is, those with minor children at home. In deciding to add a sample of mothers who had passed this stage, it was believed that employment might take on added significance as children left home and the roles of mothers lost much of their former significance.

The sample and method have been described elsewhere (1). These women had at least one child who had married within the previous two years. The largest proportion were between forty-five and fifty-five years of age. (While no specific definition of the "empty nest" period is entirely satisfactory, this sample was selected with that portion of the life cycle in mind.) Employed and non-employed mothers were compared for social differences. The result was that those employed were found to be younger and to have (or have had) fewer children. These variables and marital status were controlled.

FINDINGS

It was anticipated that women whose responsibilities as mothers were declining would require other significant roles from which to obtain social status and a sense of personal worth. The data, however, directly contradict this hypothesis. The non-employed are significantly *better* satisfied with their recreation and family income. Non-significant differences in satisfaction with the relationship to husband, with house and furniture, with daily work, and with children, all favor the non-employed mother at this stage (Table 22.4).

TABLE 22.4 *Employment Status and Satisfactions ("Post-Parental" Mothers)*

ITEM: SATISFACTIONS	DIRECTION FAVORS
Recreation	Non-employed*
Income	Non-employed*
Relationship to husband	Non-employed
House and furniture	Non-employed
Community	Employed
Daily work	Non-employed
Relationship to children	Non-employed

* Difference statistically significant.

Since these findings are totally unexpected, the best that can be offered is an *ad hoc* interpretation. The most obvious difference between the two samples is age. The "post-parental group" averaged eleven years older than the active, family-stage mothers. This may be important both physiologically and socially. The reduced energy output of more advanced years may make the time and energy demands of the job more difficult to meet. Socially, the quest for upward mobility may have run its course, so that the money added does not contribute to distant goals.

Two other differences connected with this older age sample may also be important in explaining their lack of satisfaction with employment. These older women have less education and thus less preparation for higher-level positions. Twenty-six per cent had no more than junior high school education—in contrast to 9 per cent among the younger mothers. These differences were reflected in the actual positions reported: 40 per cent were employed in craftsman, operative, service, and household work— contrasted with about half that proportion in these low status positions among the younger employed mothers.

Thus, the older women are typically working on less skilled jobs involving more tiring physical labor for lower pay. It may be recalled that when the test variable of education of the mother was employed above (Table 22.3) for those with less than college education, the direction of association between employment and verbalized satisfactions changed, revealing that employed mothers were concentrated in the medium satisfaction score category. The positive association suggested in the college-educated group was not, however, *reversed* in the high school group as was true for the older women as a group (Table 22.4).

Although, as previously mentioned, the findings oppose most speculation concerning this age period, they are congruent with a small recent empirical study by Gass (3). In a study of 85 middle-aged, upper-middle-class women, she found that many women were highly satisfied with having considerable time available for leisure and enjoyed the passive role of a "full-time housewife" with few duties and considerable help. "I enjoy my leisure time but waste a lot of it. However, I enjoy wasting it" (3, p. 485). Gass states that both the positive aspects of possessing leisure time and the "desire for passivity and their fear of competition and failure" help to keep this group out of employment and relatively satisfied with a housewife role (3, p. 485).

SUMMARY AND DISCUSSION

General satisfaction was found generally to favor the employed mother whether single items or a quasi-scale was employed as the criterion. The one exception is marital satisfaction.

The use of test variables suggests, however, that a linear relationship may be present only in the substratum of highly educated women. Employed women with only a high school education are concentrated in the middle satisfaction categories and are underrepresented in both the low and high satisfaction categories. The same tendency is seen for employed mothers with large families.

A subsequent analysis of mothers in or approaching the "empty nest" stage suggests that the opposite is true for older women—not necessarily because they are older *per se*—but perhaps because they are less well trained and hold inferior positions. Further research with larger samples of older women is needed to determine whether biological and social differences necessarily associated with age are involved or whether the relevant considerations are educational and occupational differences coincidental with age.

The above question appears to be important. If older employed mothers find less satisfaction in their work than younger mothers because they have less physical energy or because they lose some of their social ambitions, women and society are confronted with another dilemma. By the time the mother has completed her child-rearing responsibilities, she no longer has the physical energy or ambition to want to be both housekeeper and employee. However, if older employed women are less satisfied because of their lack of training for higher level positions, this problem will be resolved as older, well-trained women replace older, untrained women.

REFERENCES

1. Axelson, Leland J. "Personal Adjustment in the Postparental Period," *Marriage and Family Living,* XXII (February, 1960), 66–69.
2. Blood, Robert O. Jr., and Wolfe, Donald M. *Husbands and Wives: The Dynamics of Married Living.* Glencoe, Ill.: Free Press, 1960.
3. Gass, Gertrude Zemon. "Counseling Implications of Woman's Changing Role," *Personnel and Guidance Journal,* XXVII (March, 1959), 482–87.
4. Heer, David N. "Dominance and the Working Wife," *Social Forces,* XXXVI (May, 1958), 341–47. Reprinted as Chapter Eighteen of the present book.
5. Hoffman, Lois Wladis, "Effects of the Employment of Mothers on Parental Power Relations and the Division of Household Tasks," *Marriage and Family Living,* XXII (February, 1960), 27–35. Reprinted as Chapter Fifteen of the present book.
6. Nye, F. Ivan, "Employment Status of Mothers and Marital Conflict, Permanence, and Happiness," *Social Problems,* VI (Winter, 1959), 260–67.
7. ————. "Employment Status of Mothers and Adjustment to Children." Paper read before the American Sociological Society, Chicago, 1959. Reprinted as Chapter Twenty-Four of the present book.

Chapter Twenty-Three

Feelings of Adjustment*

SHEILA FELD

THE assessment of the mental health of any individual or group is a difficult problem; both the theoretical and empirical criteria used to evaluate mental health are diverse. In recent years, there has been increasing consensus that this diversity is necessary and that a multiple criterion approach to mental health would be most fruitful (1, 4, 8). In the present paper, such an approach is used to compare the feelings of adjustment or distress in a national representative sample of working mothers with those of a like group of non-working mothers.

A multiple criterion approach was used in a recent nationwide interview survey of the self-assessed mental health of the nation that was " . . . designed to investigate the level at which people are living with themselves—their fears and anxieties, their strengths and resources, the problems they face and the ways they cope with them" (2). The present paper is based upon data from that survey conducted by the Institute for Social Research of the University of Michigan. Information about different kinds of experiences of distress or satisfaction—unhappiness, the sense of inadequacy, tension in a marriage or with children, problems at work, constant worries, feelings of an impending nervous breakdown, etc.—were obtained during the interviews. All the data were self-reports.

* This work was carried out at the Survey Research Center of the University of Michigan and at Yale University. The author is presently on the staff of the Mental Health Study Center, National Institute of Mental Health.

Valuable consultations with Drs. Lois W. Hoffman, Gerald Gurin, and Joseph Veroff, and the statistical work of Mrs. Kathleen Goode and Miss Patricia Hatfield are gratefully acknowledged. Funds from the Joint Commission on Mental Illness and Health, the National Institute of Mental Health, and the Rackham School of Graduate Studies of the University of Michigan were utilized at various stages of this research.

331

Comparisons of groups differing on a variety of socially significant dimensions—education, income, occupation, status consistency, age, sex, religion, etc.—have already been reported (2, 3, 10). They indicate that subgroups differ largely in the way satisfactions or distress are experienced and the reasons for such feelings rather than that one group is more *generally* distressed or satisfied than another. Based on this background, the present analysis of feelings of adjustment among working and non-working mothers was undertaken with the expectation that comparisons between these two groups of women would be characterized by differences in the *kinds* of distress experienced rather than the over-all extent of distress experienced. The previous research in this area provided few clues about the specific kinds of differences that should be expected. The work of Nye (Chapter Nineteen) does suggest that marital difficulties should be greater for working women. And many have speculated that anxiety about the maternal role is generated by outside employment (see for example, 7, pp. 318–21).

Most of the previous research has focussed on the effects of maternal employment on the mental health of the children. Stoltz (9) has pointed out that many of these studies suffer from overconcern with the fact of employment itself and relative neglect of the interaction between employment status and the personal characteristics of mothers.

Knowledge of the psychological characteristics of working and non-working mothers is of interest both methodologically and theoretically. For instance, if, prior to employment, the working mother was more maladjusted than the non-working mother, it would be spurious to interpret a relationship between employment and the mental health of the children as due simply to maternal employment. On the other hand, if a psychological variable such as positiveness of attitudes toward children differentiated working and non-working mothers after employment—but not prior to it—it would be legitimate to speak of the effects of maternal employment on the psychic state of children. Theoretical insight into the mechanisms of such effects would also be possible.

Since the present study does not provide data from mothers both before and after they join the labor force, it does not permit differentiation between psychological conditions that lead to employment and those that result from employment. It can, however, provide a basis for delineating those aspects of maternal adjustment that demand further treatment along these lines.

SUBJECTS

A total of 2,460 adult respondents were interviewed for the major project upon which this study is based. The sample was selected by area sampling probability methods to constitute a representative cross-section of adults, twenty-one years of age or older, living in private households in the United States. Persons residing in military establishments, hospitals, religious and educational institutions, logging and lumber camps, penal institutions, hotels, and larger rooming houses are excluded, thereby underestimating the transient segment of the American population and that segment with severe "acting-out" behavioral symptoms. Another, and unknown, excluded segment is the approximately 8 per cent of those persons contacted who refused to be interviewed.[1]

The results reported in this paper are based on that portion of the total sample that meets the following criteria: Female, white, is currently married, has living children, either works full-time or is a full-time housewife. The subsample was further limited since only two-thirds of the total sample were asked all the questions forming the focus of this study. The resulting N is 438.[2]

PROCEDURE

The measures of experiences of distress used are based on some of the questions asked during an interview conducted in the homes of the S's in 1957. The interviews were from one to four hours long, and averaged a little under two hours. They were conducted by trained interviewers of the Survey Research Center of the University of Michigan.

Six areas of manifest content are covered by the indices of satisfactions and dissatisfactions: general feelings of satisfaction or distress (indices 1–4); attitudes toward the self (indices 5–8); marital adjustment (indices 9–11); adjustment as a parent (indices 12–14); and psychological and psychosomatic complaints (indices 15–18). The indices, the questions upon which they are based, and the categories of analysis, are listed below. The order in which the indices appear follows roughly their order in the interview.

1. *Worrying.* "Everybody has some things he worries about more or less. What kinds of things do you worry about most? Do you worry about such things a lot, or not very much?" (1) a lot, (2) sometimes, (3) never.

2. *Unhappiness.* "Taking things all together, how would you say things are these days—would you say you're (1) *very happy*, (2) *pretty happy*, or (3) *not too happy* these days?"[3]

---

[1] For a more detailed description of the sampling technique see Gurin *et al.* (2, Appendix II).

[2] The following statistics on the total sample of 1,383 women may be of interest: 25 per cent worked full time, 7 per cent worked part time, 64 per cent were full-time housewives, and 4 per cent were unclassified. For the total sample of 964 currently married women, the figures are 18, 9, 72, and 1 per cent, respectively.

[3] Here, and in other instances, numbers in parentheses were not used by the interviewer in asking the question.

3. *Future unhappiness.* "Compared to your life today, how do you think things will be 5 or 10 years from now—do you think things will be happier for you than they are now, not quite as happy, or what?" (1) unhappier, (2) about the same, (3) happier.

4. *Nervous breakdown.* "Have you ever felt that you were going to have a nervous breakdown?" (1) yes, (2) no.

5. *Lack of uniqueness of self.* "People are the same in many ways, but no two people are exactly alike. What are some of the ways in which you're different from most other people?" (1) some indication *S* thinks she is not different, (2) *S* mentions differences.

6. *Lack of self-acceptance.* Coder rating of differences mentioned in answer to questions used in index 5—obtained only for *S*'s who mention some way in which they are different from other people. (1) negative differences predominate, (2) ambivalent (differences are equally positive and negative), (3) neutral differences predominate, (4) positive differences predominate, (5) very positive differences predominate.

7. *Shortcomings in the self.* "Many people, when they think about their children, would like them to be different from themselves in some ways. If you had a daughter how would you like her to be different from you?" (1) mentions desired changes in child, (2) explicitly says does not want child to be different.

8. *Lack of strong points in the self.* "How about your strong points. What would you say were your strongest points?" (1) does not mention strong points, (2) mentions strong points.

9. *Marital inadequacy.* "Many women feel that they're not as good wives as they would like to be. Have you ever felt this way?" (If yes) "Do you feel this way a lot of times, or only once in a while?" (1) a lot of times, (2) once in a while, (3) never.

10. *Marital unhappiness.* "Taking things all together, how would you describe your marriage—would you say your marriage was (1) *very happy,* (2) *a little happier than average,* (3) *just about average,* or (4) *not too happy?*"

11. *Marriage problems.* "Even in cases where married people are happy there have often been times in the past when they weren't too happy— when they had problems getting along with each other. Has this been true for you?" (1) yes, (2) no.

12. *Negative orientation to children.* "And now I'd like to ask you some questions about having children. First, thinking about a woman's life, how is a woman's life changed by having children?" Coder rating of first-mentioned change. (1) negative, (2) neutral, (3) positive.

13. *Problems in raising children.* "Most parents have some problems

in raising their children. What are the main problems you've had in raising your children?" (1) mentions some problems, (2) never had problems.

14. *Inadequacy as parent.* "Many women feel that they're not as good mothers as they would like to be. Have you ever felt this way?" (If yes) "Have you felt this way a lot of times, or only once in a while?" (1) a lot of times, (2) once in a while, (3) never.

15. *Psychological anxiety.* "Do you have any trouble getting to sleep or staying asleep? Have you ever been bothered by nervousness, feeling fidgety and tense?—*nearly all the time, pretty often, not very much, never?*" Summation of replies yields scores from (1) most psychological anxiety—to—(6) least psychological anxiety.[4]

16. *Physical ill health.* "Do you feel you are bothered by all sorts of pains and ailments in different parts of your body?"—yes, no. "For the most part, do you feel healthy enough to carry out the things that you would like to do?"—yes, no. Summation of replies yields scores from (1) most ill health—to—(3) least ill health.

17. *Immobilization.* "Do you find it difficult to get up in the morning—*nearly all the time, pretty often, not very much, never?*" " Are you troubled by your hands sweating so that you feel damp and clammy—*many times, sometimes, hardly ever, never?*" Summation of replies yields scores from (1) most immobilization—to—(6) least immobilization.

18. *Physical anxiety.* "Have you ever been bothered by shortness of breath when you were not exercising or working hard? Have you ever been bothered by your heart beating hard?—*many times, sometimes, hardly ever, never?*" Summation of replies yields scores from (1) most physical anxiety—to—(6) least physical anxiety.

19. *MacMillan's summary of symptoms.* Summation of 16 items, used in the Stirling County community mental health study (6) that differentiated S's on the basis of psychiatrists' diagnoses of psychological difficulty yields scores from (1) most anxious—to—(5) least anxious.

Four factors emerged from a factor analysis of these 19 indices based on a sample of 542 married women with children (see 10). The following factor scores were computed by summating those indices that were strongly and uniquely loaded on each factor:

Factor 1. Felt psychological disturbance. Index 19—MacMillan's summary of symptoms.[5]

---

[4] Indices 15, 16, 17, and 18 are derived from a factor analysis of 20 items dealing with psychological, physical, or psychosomatic symptoms (2, chap. vii).

[5] Indices 15, 16, 17, and 18 are each strongly and uniquely loaded on factor 1, but they were not included in the factor score because index 19, a summation including those indices, has the highest loading on factor 1.

Factor 2. Unhappiness. Indices 2, 10, and 11—unhappiness, marital unhappiness, and marriage problems.

Factor 3. Lack of identity. Indices 5 and 8—lack of uniqueness of self, lack of strong points in the self.

Factor 4. Social inadequacy. Indices 7, 9, and 14—shortcomings in the self, marital inadequacy, and inadequacy as parent.

After a series of questions about their parental role, the following questions were asked to determine the work status of the S's.

"Now I'd like to talk to you about your work. What kind of work do you do?" (If housewife) "Do you do any part-time or full-time work for pay outside the home?" (If yes) "What kind of work do you do?"

DESIGN OF THE ANALYSIS

The major analysis is reported in terms of the tau beta rank order correlation (5) between the work–non-work dichotomy of employment status and the separate indices of feelings of adjustment. The reader should note that while the power efficiency of the rho and tau rank order correlations are the same, the numerical value of the tau coefficient is lower. Tau was preferred because it has been generalized to the case of the partial correlation coefficient.

For certain comparisons within selected groups percentage data will be presented. Table 23.1 provides estimates of the significance of differences between percentages in the present study.

While the cross-sectional character of the over-all study design does not allow us to distinguish the effects of the motivations for employment from the effects of employment itself, certain differences between working and non-working mothers can be controlled. Controls were achieved by eliminating certain groups from the analysis or partialling out the effect of certain variables from the correlations between employment status and the indices of feelings of adjustment.

DEMOGRAPHIC DIFFERENCES

Three groups were eliminated from the analysis: non-whites, women not currently married (the single, divorced, separated, or widowed women), and women who work part-time. For both non-whites and women who are not currently married, there is evidence that the incidence of and probably the motivation for work differ from the rest of the population of working mothers (7). Further, their patterns of self-evaluations of distress are different. Since neither group is large enough in the present sample to permit its use as a separate group, both were eliminated from consideration. The intermediate group that works part-time was not considered because of its small size.

TABLE 23.1 *Approximate Sampling Error Differences for Percentages from 35 to 65 Per Cent*

NUMBER	500	300	200	100	75	50	25
75	12.3–16.2	12.9–17.0	13.4–17.9	15.2–20.1	16.2–21.2		
50	14.8–19.2	15.4–19.7	15.8–20.7	17.3–22.4	18.2–23.5	20.0–25.7	
25	20.5–26.1	20.8–26.5	21.2–27.2	22.4–28.6	23.1–29.4	24.5–31.1	28.3–35.8

Note: The values shown are the differences required for significance (two standard errors) in comparisons of percentages derived from two different sub-groups of the current survey. Two values—low and high—are given for each cell. The lower estimates are based on simple random samples. The higher values are based on the computation of individual sampling errors carried out on the current study data, and allow for the departure from simple ran-dom sampling in the survey design such as stratification and clustering.

Another important variable known to relate to women's work status is their social class status—as reflected in their husband's occupation and income and in their own educational level. Data on husband's income are not available in the present study; only family income, a combination of the wages of both the working mothers and their husbands, was ascertained. The negative relationship between paternal income and maternal employment is not replicated when family income is used.

Of these available indices of social status, the education of the S is most consistently related to the indices of self-evaluations of distress. The relationship has been summarized in the following way:

> Two important themes run through the differential responses of persons at varying educational levels. First, people with more education seem to be more introspective about themselves, more concerned about the personal and interpersonal aspects of their lives. Secondly, more educated people seem to have . . . a greater sense of well-being and satisfaction.
>
> Their introspectiveness is reflected in . . . (1) feelings of inadequacy as a parent and as a husband or wife, (2) reports of both shortcomings and strongpoints in the self, and (3) more of the psychological immobilization symptoms. . . .
>
> [There is a] greater sense of well-being. . . . They are happier —in their over-all evaluations of their current happiness, in their marriages, . . . and are more optimistic about the future than less educated respondents. . . . these education differences are maintained even when income level is held constant. . . . (2, pp. 210–11).

Because of the relationship of education to both work status and self-evaluations of distress, educational level will be a primary control variable, and the first question to be dealt with is whether there are demographic differences between working and non-working women when education of the S is controlled. A three-way classification of education was employed. S's who had: zero to eight years of education were classed as *grade school*; at least some high school education and no college education, as *high school*; and some college education as *college*.

Working mothers are clearly different in several respects from mothers who are not employed. Working mothers are more likely: to be middle-aged (thirty-five to forty-nine) rather than very young or very old, not to have children of preschool age, and to have higher family incomes than housewives. In addition, working mothers seem to be more likely to (a) be from families who are not recent immigrants to the United States, (b) be residing in non-rural areas, and (c) have smaller families than mothers who are not employed. The occupations of the husbands of working mothers are not appreciably different from those of non-working mothers except that they are more likely to be in managerial occupations and less likely to be farmers. These occupational patterns could be as relevant to residence patterns as to status differences: working mothers are less likely to be from rural areas and their husbands are less likely to be farmers and more likely to be in the urban-type managerial occupations. In any event, these occupational differences are not major. These findings are, on the whole, consistent with other studies (7, Chapter Nineteen).

DEMOGRAPHIC VARIABLES AND DISTRESS

The above differences are relevant here only when the demographic variables are related to the indices of self-evaluations of distress. In those instances, we will statistically control on the demographic variables by the Kendall partial rank correlation. Unfortunately, the sampling distribution of this statistic is not yet known; thus no tests of significance are possible; the significance of the zero-order tau beta correlation will be used as a guidepost to approximate the significance of the partial correlation.

Family income is an important correlate of feelings of distress. It is more closely associated with feelings of satisfaction and certain symptom patterns than with introspectiveness. Thus, when education is controlled, women in high income groups give more positive evaluations of current happiness and marital happiness and show lower scores on the physical ill health and physical anxiety indices. But their feelings of inadequacy or self-perceptions do not differ from those of women from lower-income groups.

While the relationship between age of children and the self-evaluations of distress has not been systematically studied, maternal age, a closely related variable, has been shown to relate to many of the experiences of distress. Because many fewer women with young children work, the age of children will be controlled where appropriate. However, since the number of working mothers with children of preschool age is very small, this control will limit the discussion to women with school-age children.

The relationships previously reported between maternal age and feelings of adjustment are largely linear rather than curvilinear, as is the relationship between age and employment status. Older people tend to minimize self-doubts and the perception of problems more than younger people: they worry less often, have less frequent feelings of inadequacy in marriage, fewer problems in marriage and in rearing children, more positive self-images of their unique qualities, and fewer feelings of shortcomings. But they are not necessarily more gratified: they do have more positive orientations toward children, but they do not differ from younger women in marital happiness, and they feel less happy in their current life situations. Among older women, symptomatology is more common on the psychological anxiety, physical ill health, and physical anxiety indices, but less common on the immobilization index. Controls are necessary for relationships with variables described as significantly related to maternal age. But since the relationship between age and employment status is curvilinear, partial correlations are not the appropriate means of effecting them. Instead, working mothers and housewives will be compared within age categories whenever appropriate.

The other variables that may differentiate working and non-working mothers—immigrant status, place of residence, and size of family—are not important correlates of feelings of adjustment and will therefore not be considered in further analyses.

RESULTS

The correlations between the employment status of mothers and their reports of feelings of distress are presented in Table 23.2. There is considerable similarity in the self-evaluations of working and non-working mothers; the bulk of the correlations are not significantly different from zero (i.e., $p > .05$).

As anticipated, the differences that do occur between working mothers and housewives do not characterize one of these groups as generally more distressed than the other group. *Employed mothers show more self-acceptance and fewer physical symptoms of distress;* but in contrast, they report *more frequent doubts of their adequacy as mothers.*

In terms of the four factor scores previously derived from these 19 indices, only factor 4 (feelings of shortcomings, marital inadequacy, and parental inadequacy) is significantly related to maternal employment status. It is apparent from the individual correlations that the parental inadequacy index largely accounts for this positive relationship. The physical ill health scores and the physical anxiety scores are both highly loaded on factor 1 in the original factor analysis (10). The more psychological symptoms indexed in the psychological anxiety and immobilization scores are also loaded on this factor. Therefore the relatively high negative correlations between physical ill health symptoms and employment status are not strongly reflected in the factor 1 correlation with employment status.

The correlations between employment status and education have been included in Table 23.2 to define those indices which require controls for education and to provide a yardstick for evaluating the importance of employment status in predicting distress. It is clear from comparing these two sets of correlations that a mother's educational level is a much more important determinant of her feelings of distress than her employment status.

TABLE 23.2 *Tau Beta Correlations between Self-Evaluations of
Distress and Employment Status and Education of Mothers*

| INDICES OF DISTRESS | TAU BETA CORRELATIONS | | NUMBER[1] |
	EMPLOYMENT STATUS	EDUCATION	
Worrying	—.002	.044	422
Unhappiness	—.018	.212*	436
Future unhappiness	.009	.183*	374
Nervous breakdown	.048	.081*	438
Lack of uniqueness of self	.030	—.001	434
Lack of self-acceptance	—.074*	.017	349[2]
Shortcomings in the self	.012	—.126*	384
Lack of strong points	—.029	.036	434
Marital inadequacy	—.002	—.166*	423
Marital unhappiness	.039	.196*	438
Marriage problems	.017	—.019	437
Negative orientation to children	—.047	—.082*	433
Problems in raising children	.035	—.049	433
Inadequacy as parent	.090*	—.123*	424
Psychological anxiety	—.023	.101*	433
Physical ill health	—.153*	.199*	437
Immobilization	.015	—.108*	433
Physical anxiety	—.075*	.094*	433
Factor 1: Psychological disturbance	—.034	.169*	433
Factor 2: Unhappiness	.009	.168*	435
Factor 3: Lack of identity	.014	.020	430
Factor 4: Social inadequacy	.086*	—.179*	361

* Statistically significant.
[1] Minor variations in numbers are due to lack of response or uncodable responses.
[2] Includes only those persons who mention some way in which they are different from other people.
Note: Positive correlations occur when working women, or more educated women, are more likely to feel distress.

The four indices that show significant correlations with employment status will now be examined more closely in order to determine whether these differences are confounded by the demographic correlates of maternal employment.

Working mothers mention more positive and fewer negative qualities when they describe the ways in which they are different from other people than do mothers who are not employed.[6] Since the educational level of

---

[6] Examples of responses coded positive are: "I'm a happy-go-lucky person," "I'm the kind of person who works hard at everything I tackle." Negative responses included: "I guess I'm more nervous than a lot of women," "You might say I was lazy."

these mothers is unrelated to the lack of self-acceptance index, no education control is necessary. Maternal age, however, is significantly related to this index (Tau = .091); older women show less lack of self-acceptance. When the relationship between work status and the lack of self-acceptance index is examined within age level, the direction of the results is consistent with the over-all relationship only for the middle-aged mothers; 80 per cent of the employed mothers and only 65 per cent of the non-working mothers mention self characteristics that are predominantly positive; while the figures are 7 per cent and 17 per cent for predominantly negative characteristics. Because of the small number of working mothers in the younger (N=10) and older (N=6) age categories, the lack of relationship in those groups cannot be considered definitive. It seems warranted to conclude that the relationship between work status and lack of self-acceptance cannot clearly be interpreted as simply a reflection of age differences in the two groups of mothers.

Age of children is also related to lack of self-acceptance; mothers with children of preschool age have significantly more negative images of their unique qualities than women with older children (Tau = .094). Since housewives more frequently have very young children and also have more negative self-images than working mothers, the control on the age of the children reduces the correlation between employment status and lack of self-acceptance. The resulting partial correlation (Tau = −.056) is appreciably less than the zero order correlation (Tau = −.074). It appears possible that the relationship between lack of self-acceptance and employment status might collapse if controls on maternal age and age of children were introduced.

The finding most relevant to those interested in the effects of maternal employment on children is that the working mothers report more frequent feelings of inadequacy as mothers than housewives do. This relationship remains even when maternal age and education are controlled: The Tau coefficient for employment status and inadequacy as parent with the effects of education partialled out is not much smaller than the zero-order correlation, and as can be seen in Table 23.3, the relationship is evident within each educational level. The relationship persists within each of three age groupings even though the N's for younger and older working mothers are small; for the young, middle-aged, and older mothers, the percentage of women who often feel inadequate are 40 per cent versus 17 per cent, 26 per cent versus 18 per cent, and 25 per cent versus 15 per cent for working and non-working mothers, respectively.

Age of children is also significantly related to feelings of inadequacy as parent (Tau = .107); mothers with children of preschool age feel inadequate more frequently. Since working mothers feel more inadequate

TABLE 23.3 *Employment Status of Mothers and Feeling Inadequate as Parent, by Education Level*

FEELS INADEQUATE	EMPLOYMENT STATUS AND EDUCATION							
	GRADE		HIGH		COLLEGE		TOTAL	
	Working	Non-Working	Working	Non-Working	Working	Non-Working	Working	Non-Working
	Per Cent							
A lot	20	20	27	16	46	14	30	17
Once in a while	30	19	30	39	27	56	30	37
Never	50	58	35	42	18	30	33	43
Not ascertained	0	3	8	3	9	0	7	3
Total	100	100	100	100	100	100	100	100
Number	10	98	40	223	11	56	61	377

Tau: Employment status, Inadequacy as parent. Education = .082.

despite their lack of preschool age children, when the effect of age of children is partialled out, the correlation between employment status and inadequacy as a parent increases from .090 to .116 (Table 23.4).

Thus, to the extent that it is possible to make the relevant controls, the obtained relationship between employment status and inadequacy as parents is not appreciably changed: *working mothers feel more inadequate as parents than mothers who do not work outside the home.*

TABLE 23.4 *Employment Status of Mothers and Feeling Inadequate as Parent, by Age of Children*

FEELS INADEQUATE	EMPLOYMENT STATUS AND AGE OF CHILDREN					
	SOME PRESCHOOL		NO PRESCHOOL		TOTAL	
	Working	Non-Working	Working	Non-Working	Working	Non-Working
	Per Cent					
A lot	42	20	28	15	30	17
Once in a while	29	42	30	32	30	37
Never	29	35	35	50	33	43
Not ascertained	0	3	7	3	7	3
Total	100	100	100	100	100	100
Number	7	154	54	223	61	377

Tau: Employment status, Inadequacy as parent. Age of children = .116.

The working mothers clearly report fewer physical symptoms than mothers who do not work: only 7 per cent of the workers report any physical ill health symptoms, while 25 per cent of the housewives report some of these symptoms—pains and ailments in different parts of their bodies and not feeling healthy enough to carry out things they would like to do. The differences on the physical anxiety index are smaller: 36 per cent of the workers and 44 per cent of the housewives report these symptoms. The original factor analysis upon which these scores are based indicated that these indices are related; that is, the two items that define the physical anxiety index—shortness of breath and heart beating hard—are loaded on the physical ill health index as well. Therefore it was concluded that:

> when it is important to differentiate relationships between Factor 4 [physical anxiety] and other variables from the relationships obtained between Factor 2 [ill health] and these variables, we will control Factor 2 (2, p. 183).

When this is done in the present instance, the relationship between the physical anxiety index and employment status is drastically reduced (Tau = −.040). This eliminates the need to consider this relationship further. In contrast, when physical anxiety is partialled out of the correlation between physical ill health and employment status, the correlation remains high (Tau = −.139).

Three demographic variables are significantly related to the physical ill health factor—maternal education, age, and family income: more educated women, younger women, and women with higher family incomes report fewer physical ill health symptoms. Comparisons of the working and non-working mothers within the several demographic groups indicate that age of mother, her education, and family income do not account for the relationship between maternal employment status and the physical ill health factor. The zero-order correlation of −.153 between employment status and the physical health index is not appreciably reduced when the effect of education (−.143) or family income (−.146) is partialled out. And for all but the younger age group, working mothers more frequently have the lowest ill health scores (95 per cent and 100 per cent for the middle-aged and older groups) than do non-working mothers (71 per cent and 60 per cent). The relationship remains the strongest one obtained: *working mothers are less likely than housewives to complain of pains and ailments in different parts of their body and of not feeling healthy enough to carry out things they would like to do.*

It is also important to consider whether any of the non-significant correlations reported in Table 23.2 are spuriously low because of demographic differences between mothers who do and do not work. This possibility exists for the nervous breakdown, marital unhappiness, negative orientation to children, and problems in raising children indices. But a revision of the findings seems necessary only for the marital unhappiness index.

Feelings of an impending nervous breakdown are significantly less frequent among more educated women (Tau = .081). But the relatively more educated working mothers tend to be higher on the nervous breakdown index (Tau = .048). This latter correlation is increased only slightly when the effect of education is partialled out.

Marital unhappiness is significantly higher among women with low family incomes. (Tau = .203). But working women, despite higher family incomes than housewives, tend to be more unhappy with their marriages. Similarly, marital unhappiness is significantly higher among less educated women. (Tau = .196). But working women, despite more education than housewives, tend to report more marital unhappiness. Controlling on education does increase the correlation between marital unhappiness and maternal employment status, but not to a very high level (Table 23.5). How-

TABLE 23.5 *Employment Status of Mothers and Marital Unhappiness, by Education Level*

MARITAL UNHAPPI- NESS	EMPLOYMENT STATUS AND EDUCATION							
	GRADE		HIGH		COLLEGE		TOTAL	
	Working	Non- Working	Working	Non- Working	Working	Non- Working	Working	Non- Working
	Per Cent							
Not too happy	10	7	2	3	0	0	3	4
Just average	60	47	28	26	36	25	35	31
Little happier than average	20	17	30	23	18	23	26	21
Very happy	10	29	40	48	46	52	36	44
Total	100	100	100	100	100	100	100	100
Number	10	98	40	223	11	56	61	377

Tau: Employment status, Marital unhappiness. Education = .054.

ever, the control of family income does raise this correlation considerably. (Table 23.6). The simultaneous control of both these variables would raise the correlation even further, allowing the conclusion that *if educational level and family income were controlled, working mothers would report more marital unhappiness than their housewife counterparts.*

Negative orientation to children is significantly higher among more educated women (Tau = −.082). But working women, who are more educated than housewives, tend to be lower on this index (Tau = −.047). How-

TABLE 23.6 *Employment Status of Mothers and Marital Unhappiness,
by Family Income*

	EMPLOYMENT STATUS AND INCOME							
MARITAL UNHAPPI- NESS	UNDER $4,000		$4,000– $6,999		$7,000 OR MORE		TOTAL[1]	
	Working	Non- Working	Working	Non- Working	Working	Non- Working	Working	Non- Working
				Per Cent				
Not too happy	0	7	4	3	4	0	3	4
Just average	60	45	35	23	22	26	35	31
Little happier than average	10	20	15	25	48	14	26	21
Very happy	30	28	46	49	26	60	36	44
Total	100	100	100	100	100	100	100	100
Number	*10*	*127*	*26*	*168*	*23*	*70*	*61*	*377*

[1] Includes 2 working and 12 non-working mothers whose family incomes are not ascertained.
Tau: **Employment status, Marital** unhappiness. Family income = .075.

ever, even when the effect of education is partialled out from the correlation between employment status and negative orientation to children, the resulting partial correlation of –.053 is not appreciably higher; negative orientation to children does not appear to be significantly related to employment status.

Problems in raising children are reported significantly more frequently by younger than by older mothers (Tau = .126). Since working mothers are more middle-aged than housewives, the percentage of mothers reporting problems in raising their children was computed for each of the three age groups. These figures for working and non-working women do not differ appreciably in any age group; maternal employment status is not significantly related to problems in raising children.

DISCUSSION

The major conclusion that seems warranted by the findings is that whether a mother works is not an important variable in accounting for feelings of adjustment per se. Its relevance is seen in certain circumscribed, though important, areas of life functioning. The findings seem reasonable in light of the diversity of life experience, both past and present, observed among employed mothers. As Hoffman (Chapter Two) has pointed out, a number of facilitating and hindering social factors and a multiplicity of individual motivations are involved in the mother's decision to hold a job. All contribute to a diversity of characteristics among working mothers at the onset of their employment and further differentiate the women in terms of the kinds of jobs they get, their feelings toward their jobs, the child-care arrangements they make, and so forth. The succeeding events, the impact of the employment experience itself and the mother's absence from the home, can also differ. The type of job that is obtained can and does vary: from professional positions requiring a high degree of training, skill, and involvement to unskilled jobs requiring few of these qualities; from jobs requiring continuous contact with other people to those necessitating complete isolation. Thus, it would be surprising indeed to find that employment is *generally* associated with a disruption or facilitation of life functioning.

The exclusive reliance on self-report data raises the question of whether maternal employment status is related to willingness to report feelings of distress. While no final answer can be given here, the assumptions necessary in order for this factor to account completely for the present results do not seem compelling.

For instance, if we assumed that "honest" reports would reveal that maternal employment is associated with distress feelings, how could we account for the present results? The results indicate that working is associated with reports of marital unhappiness, but not with general life unhappiness, and that reports of feelings of inadequacy as a parent are associated with employment, but feelings of marital inadequacy are not. To account for these findings in terms of willingness to report distress, it would have to be assumed (a) that working mothers find it more acceptable to tell an unknown interviewer that they are unhappily married than that they are unhappy generally and (b) that it is more unacceptable for working than non-working mothers to report feelings of inadequacy as a wife but not more unacceptable to report similar feelings about their role as a parent. There seems to be no clear and consistent rationale for making such assumptions. In the total sample of women, for example, approximately the same proportion report feeling inadequate at some time in the wife role (54 per cent) and in the parent role (51 per cent).

Consideration of those indices of felt distress that appear to be significantly related to employment status when appropriate controls are used— lack of self-acceptance, marital unhappiness, inadequacy as parent, and physical ill health symptoms—leads to some interesting speculations regarding the potentially circular interplay between feelings of distress and employment.

The fact that working mothers have lower scores on the physical ill health index than non-working mothers, that they are not bothered by all sorts of pains and ailments in different parts of their body or by not feeling healthy enough to do the things they would like to do, lends itself to a variety of plausible interpretations. It may reflect the fact that physical disabilities sometimes act as barriers to employment. Or it may reflect psychological factors, such as differences in attitudes toward one's own strength and competence, differences in activity-passivity orientations to life that act as facilitating factors in the decision to work. Or it may indicate that the demands placed on a mother by adding outside employment to her housewife and mother duties effect a change in these attitudes toward the self. Or considering the housewives' relatively high level of physical ill health symptoms, these might be seen as reflections of a somatization of the anxieties and frustrations that have been theorized to exist in increasing degree in the modern mother's role.

The only evidence from the present study that is relevant to this issue stems from another series of questions asked about health problems. Similar findings were obtained: a greater proportion (34 per cent versus 20 per cent) of non-working than working mothers answered that they did not have "any particular physical or health troubles." And while nearly identical proportions of both groups (19 per cent versus 20 per cent) replied that they had had "any long illnesses in the past"—when asked "what was that?"— the working mothers were more likely to mention just one illness (18 per cent versus 11 per cent), and the housewives more likely to mention more than one illness (2 per cent versus 8 per cent).

Choices among these interpretations must rest upon additional research that directs itself to this issue in greater depth. It is not unlikely that a number of these factors enter into the correlation between ill health and employment status. These findings only reinforce the original results; they do not elucidate its meaning, since replies to these questions may reflect the same factors as the physical ill health symptoms. Public health surveys have shown that reports of illnesses and even hospitalization are subject to considerable error. It will perhaps be necessary to turn to data from public health community studies which provide periodic medical examinations for aid in interpreting these results. Clearly mothers' physical health or illnesses and their attitudes toward their physical well-being are fruitful areas for further study that require sophisticated medical and psychological treatment.

The association between maternal employment and self-acceptance may seem to support the view that many women choose outside work because of the lack of a sense of usefulness and of identity that confront mothers whose household chores are reduced and whose children are all in school. But despite the support for that view from tentative evidence that the relationship between employment status and lack of self-acceptance is clearest among middle-aged mothers and mothers with no children of preschool age, the issue of which comes first, the psychological characteristics or the outside employment, still confronts us. The possibility still remains that a more positive self-image facilitates a mother's decision to work outside the home; it may provide her with the confidence she needs to leave the most traditional arena of women's competence to test her worth in the dollars and cents terms of the labor market. A before-after study design and samples of sufficient size to explore the diverse content of these self-images are required to deal with this issue more definitively. Because the significance level of the partial correlation cannot be tested, and because the numerical value of the partial correlation between self-acceptance and employment status with the effect of age of children partialled out is below that required for significance for the zero order correlation, this finding is the most tentative of those discussed. Therefore it is most in need of replication before further speculations on its import are warranted.

Is marital unhappiness one of the factors motivating mothers toward outside employment, or is it the result of disruption caused by such employment? Once again, a firm conclusion is impossible; it is not necessary to go into detailed rationales for these two causal possibilities in view of their similarity to previous arguments presented. But the fact that working is significantly correlated with high marital unhappiness only when the total family income is controlled, does lend some support to the view (e.g., Nye, Chapter Nineteen) that working should increase marital happiness because employment improves the economic position of the family. But it may be more appropriate to think that this effect of maternal employment acts to decrease the level of unhappiness rather than increase the level of happiness. Since family income is only one among many correlates of marital unhappiness, the over-all impact of maternal employment must be viewed in terms of its influence upon the entire configuration of determinants of marital unhappiness. One important correlate of marital happiness or unhappiness is the relationship between the husband and wife; Gurin *et al.* (2, chap. 4) report that mentioning the relationship with the spouse as one of the "nicest things" about your marriage is associated with marital happiness, while mentioning this relationship as one of the things about your marriage that is "not quite as nice as you would like it to be" is associated with marital unhappiness. The type of marital relationship that may motivate mothers to work and the complex effects of maternal employment on this marital relationship, such as investigated by Hoffman (Chapter Fifteen), should be more thoroughly studied.

To conclude, let us consider the relationship between feeling inadequate as a parent and working. Feeling inadequate as a parent has been interpreted as reflecting an introspective attitude toward one's role functioning resulting from the meshing of aspirations and achievements (2, chap. 5). Thus, working mothers might feel more self-conscious about whether they have lived up to the goals they have set for themselves as mothers than non-working mothers. Perhaps the nature of the goals the mothers describe as unmet will provide some clues to the interpretation of this result.

When the women who said they have doubted their maternal role performance were asked "What kinds of things made you feel this way?" the majority of responses from all mothers dealt with their interpersonal relationships with their children rather than with economic or material considerations or with inadequacies in the children. About the same percentage of working and non-working mothers gave such responses: 65 per cent and 61 per cent, respectively. But when these responses are broken down, some interesting differences emerge: 35 per cent of the working mothers and 14 per cent of the housewives mention concern with parent-child affiliation ("We aren't close enough," "There isn't enough love," "I don't spend enough time with them "); 15 per cent of the working and 35 per cent of the non-working mothers mention parental intolerance for children's behavior ("I'm impatient with them," "I'm not understanding enough with them"); and, about the same proportion, 15 per cent and 12 per cent, mention concern with obedience or discipline. The differences between working and non-working mothers directly parallel differences between fathers and mothers; the parents who spend relatively little time with their children (fathers and working mothers) worry about lack of contact or closeness with the children; whereas the parents who are with their children relatively more of the time worry about their reactions to such constant interaction, and they feel guilty about their anger or impatience with the child.[7]

Thus, the reasons working mothers report for feeling inadequate as parents seem to be *reactions* to their absence from the home. It would seem more reasonable to interpret a mother's anxiety about lack of tolerance for her child's behavior as a possible precursor to a decision to work outside the home in order to reduce contact with the child. But, it is important to note that working mothers may have experienced such anxieties prior to working, and relieved them by reducing their contact with their children only to have this produce other problems. Certainly, the working mother must deal with society's concern about her "neglect" of her children when she is at work.

Yet the results from other questions on parenthood do not give any support to the view that working mothers have more difficulty with their children or are more negative in their feelings toward them. Working and non-working mothers do not differ in their reports of problems in rearing

---

[7] Since completion of this study, Yarrow *et al.* (11) have reported very similar findings: working mothers worry more about their maternal role, especially about whether working interferes with their relationships with and rearing of their children.

their children, and the working mothers tend to have more positive orientations to the changes that accompany parenthood. A separate coding of the replies to the question on what changes occur from having children shows that working mothers tend to be less likely to see parenthood as restricting, burdensome, or demanding. There is some overlap between the negative orientations to parenthood code and the restrictiveness of children code since, on the latter, all negative replies except non-specific ones like "it leads to unhappiness" were coded as restricting. But positive and neutral replies could also be coded as restricting, e.g., "You become a better person because you think of someone other than yourself," "You have more responsibility." The code is a summary of all responses to the question on life changes accompanying parenthood in terms of none, some, or all replies being restricting, burdensome, or demanding. The figures for working and non-working mothers, respectively, were as follows: none—39 per cent, 29 per cent; some—38 per cent, 38 per cent; all—23 per cent, 31 per cent. Differences are maintained when maternal age and education are controlled. These results are similar to those obtained by Hoffman (Chapter Two). Such attitudes may be reflected in the working mother's ability to take on the work role, or they may be a result of having done this. Once again the final question remains one of differentiating between the decision to work and the effects of this decision.

SUMMARY

Self-reports of feelings of adjustment in a variety of life areas were compared for a national representative sample of working and non-working mothers.

Of the nineteen indices of felt distress analyzed, only four were found to be correlated with employment status when appropriate controls were utilized. Working outside the home is associated with a positive view of the unique qualities of the self, lack of physical ill health symptoms, marital unhappiness, and feelings of inadequacy as a mother.

The results may indicate that maternal employment per se is not in itself a major variable accounting for feelings of adjustment. Those areas of life functioning where feelings of adjustment are related to employment status were considered in light of two major alternative interpretations: that feelings of adjustment are selective or motivating factors in the decision to work, or that the decision to work and its effects on the life situation influence feelings of adjustment. The distinction between these two types of interpretations were considered to be crucial to progress in research in this area.

REFERENCES

1. Allport, Gordon W. "Personality: Normal and Abnormal." In Gordon Allport. *Personality and the Social Encounter.* Boston: Beacon Press, 1960, pp. 155–68.
2. Gurin, Gerald, Veroff, Joseph, and Feld, Sheila. *Americans View Their Mental Health.* New York: Basic Books, 1960.
3. Jackson, Elton F. "Status Consistency and Symptoms of Stress," *American Sociological Review,* XXVII (August, 1962), 469–80.
4. Jahoda, Marie. *Current Concepts of Positive Mental Health.* New York: Basic Books, 1958.
5. Kendall, Maurice G. *Rank Correlation Methods.* London: Griffin, 1948.
6. MacMillan, Allister M. "The Health Opinion Survey: Technique for Estimating Prevalence of Psychoneurotic and Related Types of Disorder in Communities," *Psychological Reports,* III (September, 1957), 325–39.
7. National Manpower Council. *Womanpower..* New York: Columbia University Press, 1957.
8. Smith, M. Brewster. "Research Strategies toward a Conception of Positive Mental Health," *American Psychologist,* XIV (November, 1959), 673–81.
9. Stolz, Lois Meek. "Effects of Maternal Employment on Children: Evidence from Research," *Child Development,* XXXI (December, 1960), 749–82.
10. Veroff, Joseph, Feld, Sheila, and Gurin, Gerald. "Dimensions of Subjective Adjustment," *Journal of Abnormal and Social Psychology,* LXIV (March, 1962), 192–205.
11. Yarrow, Marian R., Scott, Phyllis, de Leeuw, Louise, and Heinig, Christine. "Child-rearing in Families of Working and Nonworking Mothers," *Sociometry,* XXV (June, 1962), 122–40.

Chapter Twenty-Four

*Adjustment to Children**

F. IVAN NYE

SOCIAL science research has been preoccupied with the personality development and socialization of children. The emphasis has usually been on the attitudes of the child or the effects of parental attitudes on his development. This is consistent with theories of personality and socialization which exclusively emphasize the importance of the earliest period of life.

Here and there a voice is heard that adults are people, too, and that they have socio-psychological needs which merit consideration in family research and in action programs which involve both parents and children. An example of this minority point of view is a report by Blood of his research on the effect of permissive child-rearing practices on *parents* (1). Landis also has consistently expressed concern for the adjustment of women to the role of mother as well as the welfare of their children:

> The girl who looked down upon the study of homemaking as a student is likely to look down upon the job of homemaking as a wife. Her years of study and training in an academic or professional field and the values she absorbed in the process make it difficult for her to subordinate her career values to those of homemaking. Meal planning, household management, child care, which would have been challenging and absorbing jobs had she learned to value them, become instead the dull routine of married life. Bitterness, marital frustration, boredom and discord are the common symptoms of disappointment (4, p. 75).

* Revision of a paper read before the American Sociological Society, Chicago, 1959.

Some of the dissatisfactions with the roles of wife and mother are, Landis thinks, the direct result of this socialization process. However, the values which underlie this process may be the result of the changes in the duties and responsibilities of mothers during the past two generations. That is, there must be a complex of behavior and attitudes which has *resulted* in the low value placed on proficiency in the tasks of the homemaker. Regardless of the exact nature of the value and socialization process which have produced the attitudes of contemporary educated women, Landis feels that the contemporary mother should not be limited to household tasks. Feelings of frustration, boredom, and isolation produced by separation from the occupational and intellectual world may produce a hostile, anxious, and nervous mother:

> . . . for many of the more intelligent women, the most frustrating aspect of marriage experience, is the mother's constant subservience to the demands of the young child. The average working mother, if she is interested in employment, and particularly if she is career-minded, cannot be content with dropping her career to become a housekeeper and child's nurse (4, p. 82) . . . [Finally] The demands of modern society are such that many intelligent and highly competent women cannot be happy devoting all their time to housekeeping and child care (4, p. 520–21).

Komarovsky, in discussing "The Homemaker and her Problems," describes two types of maternal discontent. Some wives are unhappy only with some particular aspect of their housewife role; others reluctantly give up jobs and yearn to return to them. She emphasized, however, that even women who have no desire for employment indicate considerable dissatisfaction with the homemaker role:

> Overwork, tired muscles, constant and almost exclusive association with young children, and monotony are among the frequently mentioned grievances. But even these women who had no yearning for careers complain not only about drudgery and fatigue, but also about the frustration of their days (3, p. 107).

It is interesting that some young women with one or two small children and all modern conveniences feel overworked. Dullness and monotony are also stressed by some, however, as in the following case:

> "Besides, I find life dull. I described my day to you. It isn't just one day—it is every day. Believe me, there is not enough stimulation in the incessant dishwashing, picking up, ironing, folding diapers, dressing and undressing the kids, making beds, day

in and day out. My social life with the other mothers on the park bench is depressing. I cannot get them away from the same old talk. They have nothing fresh to give me because they, too, are up to their neck in the same routine" (3, p. 110).

Both Komarovsky and Landis feel that for the talented, trained, and ambitious woman, the life of the non-employed mother is too limited and monotonous. Even if she is untrained and lacks talents and ambition, she may still find life dull. Both, however, are also aware of lack of adequate cultural adaptation to the innovation of the employed mother.

Interestingly enough, psychiatrists, who have done much to focus attention on young children, have in some instances expressed concern about the personal adjustment of adults as an important variable in the attitudes and behavior of parents toward children (5).

Lundberg and Farnham are, however, basically pessimistic concerning the effects of employment of the wife. Although they see it gratifying some of the needs of some women, they think that it encourages behavior incompatible with the wife's role as mother:

> Work that entices women out of their homes and provides them with prestige only at the price of feminine relinquishment, involves a response to masculine strivings. The more importance outside work assumes, the more are the masculine components of the woman's nature enhanced and encouraged. In her home and in her relationship to her children, it is imperative that these strivings be at a minimum and that her femininity be available both for her own satisfaction and for the satisfaction of her children and husband. She is, therefore, in the dangerous position of having to live one part of her life on the masculine level, another the feminine. It is hardly astonishing that few can do it with success (6, p. 235).

The general public seems to assume that the adjustment of mothers to children will be harmed by employment. It assumes that employed mothers will have more difficulty in controlling children, that mothers will resent the demands of children on their time, and that children are more likely to make them nervous or irritable (2).

It is the thesis of this investigation that the employment of women outside the home is a specific adjustment of the family to general changes in economic and family organization. Since employment is adjustive to changes in these institutions, it should provide increased satisfaction with the maternal role; however, some anxieties and guilt feelings are also thought to be characteristic of this transitional period.

Since research and theoretical ideas are fragmentary and not in agreement, it seems most appropriate to test the null hypothesis that the adjustment of mothers to children does not vary by employment status.

FINDINGS

Ten items intended to measure the adjustment of mothers to children were included in a longer questionnaire given to 1,993 mothers of children in grades one and ten in all the schools, public and parochial, in three Washington communities. This sample is described in detail in Chapter Nineteen.

To test the hypothesis that the adjustment of mothers to children does not differ by employment status, three sets of data are presented. These include five items considered indicative of unsatisfactory (to the mother) adjustment to children, five indicative of satisfactory adjustment, and a quasi-scale of seven items taken from the entire list of items.

TABLE 24.1 *Affirmative Responses of Mothers to Items Considered Indicative of Adjustment to Maternal Role*

ADJUSTMENT TO MATERNAL ROLE	MATERNAL EMPLOYMENT STATUS		
	NOT EMPLOYED	PART-TIME EMPLOYED	FULL-TIME EMPLOYED
	Per Cent		
Never have to punish children severely	52.6	55.9	52.3
Would have a larger family if had it to do over*	19.3	25.7	30.5
Children are willing to work around the house	27.2	25.7	26.9
Children don't hesitate to discuss their problems with their mother	80.8	78.2	70.7
Children behave when they're out of sight	36.7	40.2	39.1
Children don't appreciate what is done for them	17.3	18.4	22.3
Have difficulty understanding children	12.0	14.5	8.6
Children require time I would like to put into other activities	4.8	7.3	0.0
Children don't mind very well	29.7	30.2	22.8
Children make me nervous*	40.0	33.0	27.9

* Statistically significant.

The results of individual item analyses are shown in Table 24.1. Comparison of employed and non-employed mothers on the "satisfactory" items (items 1–5) reveals one significant difference; employed mothers more often desire more children. No other item approaches significance. The rationale of that item is that a wish for more children indicates favorable attitudes toward children. Since the groups are matched roughly for family size, the difference in attitudes probably cannot be explained by differences in present family size. Punishment, worrying about children, counseling children, and children's attitudes toward helping with household chores appear unrelated to the employment status of the mother.

The second group of five items (items 6–10) was intended to be indicative of unfavorable attitudes toward children. Of these, the item "children make me nervous" shows a significant difference; 40 per cent of the non-employed, compared to 28 per cent of the fully-employed, agree. None of the other negative items reveals significant differences, but three of the other four negative items are reported less frequently by full-time employed mothers than by those not employed.

These data lend support to the case studies reported by Komarovsky and Landis and agree with those of Feld (Chapter Twenty-Three) which report nervousness in mothers who spend long hours continuously with children.

As another test of the relationship, the responses to seven of the items were compiled into a score. These items were:

1. Never have to punish children severely.
2. Would have a larger family if had it to do over.
3. Children are willing to work around the house.
4. Children don't hesitate to discuss their problems with mother.
5. Don't worry about way children behave when they're out of sight.

TABLE 24.2 *Employment Status of Mothers and Attitude toward Children with a Quasi-Scale as the Criterion**

SCALE SCORES	MATERNAL EMPLOYMENT STATUS			
	NOT EMPLOYED	PART-TIME EMPLOYED	FULL-TIME EMPLOYED	TOTAL
	Per Cent			Number
0, 1, 2 (poorest)	22.5	17.3	16.2	153
3–4 (intermediate)	36.0	37.4	37.6	285
5–7 (best)	41.5	45.3	46.2	338
Total	100.0	100.0	100.0	776

* Not statistically significant.

6. Children don't mind very well.

7. Children make me nervous.

An application of Guttman's scaling technique (Cornell) to these items revealed a reproducibility coefficient of .86. The items also met the criteria of distribution of errors and marginal frequency indicating that the items conform to the criteria of a quasi-scale. It appears probable that a principal single dimension is present in the items, although something else is measured also. (Note: the items for the quasi-scale were selected prior to the item analysis described above.)

The analysis employing the single score as the criterion reveals non-significant differences between the attitudes toward children of employed and non-employed mothers. An examination of Table 24.2 reveals, however, that differences in the sample are in the direction of more favorable attitudes on the part of employed mothers.

CONTINGENT CONDITIONS

The general relationship of employment status of mothers to their adjustment to the maternal role analyzed within a heterogeneous sample may obscure or cancel important relationships within more homogeneous subcategories of the sample. Therefore, several test variables were introduced and the relationship re-examined.

FAMILY SIZE

Family size does alter the relationship of employment status to adjustment to children. In "small" families (1–3 children), employed mothers are more likely than non-employed to be well adjusted to children, but in large families, the reverse relationship is found (Table 24.3). In the latter families (4 or more children) employment tends to be related to poor adjustment to children. Employment may improve adjustment to the maternal role in small families. The statistical relationships appear reasonable in the light of the heavier maternal responsibilities of mothers of large families.

LENGTH OF TIME EMPLOYED

Length of employment also might affect the relationship of employment to adjustment to children. Non-employed women might be expected closely to approximate women employed only a short time, and it might be expected that longer employment would magnify these differences. The data fail to show significant differences, but the pattern of sample differences is interesting. Among mothers employed less than 15 months, adjustment to children is poorer than among mothers not employed. Among those who have worked 15 months to 27 months, adjustment is slightly better for the

TABLE 24.3 *Employment Status and Adjustment of Mothers to Children by Family Size*

SCALE SCORES: ADJUSTMENT TO CHILDREN	SMALL FAMILIES (1–3 CHILDREN) MATERNAL EMPLOYMENT STATUS		TOTAL
	NOT EMPLOYED	EMPLOYED	
	Per Cent		*Number*
0–2 (poorest)	21.3	13.6	*80*
3–4 (intermediate)	38.0	34.3	*157*
5–7 (best)	40.8	52.1	*190*
Total	100.1	100.0	*427*
	LARGE FAMILIES (4 + CHILDREN)		
0–2 (poorest)	25.2	23.2	*41*
3–4 (intermediate)	31.5	46.4	*61*
5–7 (best)	43.2	30.4	*65*
Total	99.9	100.0	*167*

Note: Relationship is statistically significant in the small family analysis but non-significant in the larger family analysis. Note also the *different direction* of the relationship in the two analyses.

employed group, and those who have worked 28 months or more show the best adjustment to children. If the sample indicates a pattern in the population, it suggests that employment initially produces poorer adjustment to children, probably related to role conflicts. As behavior becomes more congruent and as family expectations are modified, these conflicts are presumably decreased. In the sample, adjustment to children continues to improve up to the maximum of four years recorded in the study. An alternative explanation is that mothers finding it difficult to be both mothers and employees drop employment.

AGE OF CHILDREN

It might be anticipated that employed mothers would be best adjusted to older children who are more independent and better able to take care of themselves. The data show the reverse—that employed mothers with children between six and twelve compare most favorably with non-employed mothers. The reason for this is not clear. Can it be that the preadolescent child is more secure and more inclined to conform than the adolescent and therefore requires less attention from the mother? This finding is of interest because many women have thought that the best time to begin work is when their youngest child enters high school. This merits further investigation.

OTHER CONTINGENCIES

Analysis of the test variables of the education of the wife and the occupation of the husband disclosed no significant differences between the employed and non-employed mothers. Differences tend to favor employed over non-employed mothers in the highest socio-economic and educational categories, but they are neither significant nor entirely consistent.

ADJUSTMENT TO PRESCHOOL CHILDREN

A subsequent study of the adjustment of preschool children was made in another Washington city in which samples of 104 employed and 104 non-employed mothers of preschool children were questioned as part of a

TABLE 24.4 *The Association Between Marital Employment Status and Acceptance of the Child*

ITEM: ACCEPTANCE OF CHILD	SAMPLE DIFFERENCES FAVOR
Would have preferred to postpone having your child	Employed
§ Would have preferred child of other sex	Employed
§ Would like to have more children	Employed
§ Would like to have large family (at least 4)	Employed
Unplanned pregnancy	Employed
§ Number of reasons listed for wanting large family	Employed*
§ Number of reasons listed for not wanting more children	Employed
§ Number of things listed as enjoyable in child	Employed*
Number of annoying things listed	Employed
Does things that get on mother's nerves	Employed
Times child not allowed to bother parent	Employed
Had to postpone activity because of child	Non-employed
§ Since having child less satisfied with recreation	Non-employed
Total of Seven (§) *Items*	Employed

* Difference statistically significant.

larger study.[1] Another list of items was employed in an attempt to tap the dimension of the basic acceptance of the child by the mother. The rationale of these items was that women who were planning pregnancies, who would like to have several children, and who want more children, accept their children and are happy in this aspect of the maternal role. Also, mothers who indicate that children have interfered with or delayed desired activities, or that they reject the sex of the child, reveal dissatisfaction with their relationship to their children. The items and the differences between employed and non-employed mothers are shown in Table 24.4.

Two of the 12 items show significant differences favoring the employed mothers. More employed mothers indicated reasons for wanting larger families or for enjoying their present children. Most of the non-significant differences (8 of 10) support this data in that they suggest better adjustment of the employed mother. The two items significant for mothers of school-age children (discussed above), desire for more children and children make mother nervous, did not show significant differences for preschool mothers; however, the differences are in the same direction. Since the preschool sample is smaller, this might account for the lack of statistical significance of differences on these items.

Although the mothers of preschool children are from a different age group and a larger city and the data were collected by a different method, the findings are generally consistent with those from mothers of school-age children in that the employed mothers are more accepting of children and better satisfied with their relationships to them.

SUMMARY AND DISCUSSION

Although the differences are not great, some significant differences from each sample showed better adjustment to children among employed mothers. The non-significant differences in both studies generally favor the employed mother. The mothers of preschoolers knew that the study dealt with the employment of mothers; however, the mothers of school-age children did not. The findings for both groups favor the employed mother.

The introduction of test variables was unproductive—with two exceptions. Mothers seem to encounter initial parent-child problems as they take employment, some of which they resolve over time. The data are only suggestive on this point. More important, the positive relationship between employment and adjustment to children is increased to a significant level when the analysis is limited to small families and reversed when applied to large families. Statistically, the chances that a mother will be better satisfied if she

---

[1] For a description of this sample, see Chapter Five.

is employed are increased if she has a small family but decreased if she has a large family.

Generally, the data support the Komarovsky and Landis positions that the domestic roles of a mother of a small family are not sufficiently significant and interesting for many American women and that many are happier mothers if they can find employment under satisfactory conditions. They do not support the position of some that women who enter employment are hostile, frustrated women who can obtain no satisfaction from family or community relationships.

However, this evidence is insufficient for the assertion that all women would be better adjusted to children if they were employed. Presumably the women who are presently employed are those who are reaping the most significant rewards economically, socially, or psychologically or for whom employment holds the fewest penalties (Chapter Two). Those presently not employed would, in most instances, feel less rewarded by taking paid employment and have more difficulty handling other responsibilities, opposition from their husbands, or their own negative feelings.

REFERENCES

1. Blood, Robert O., Jr. "Consequences of Permissiveness of Parents of Young Children," *Marriage and Family Living,* XV (August, 1953), 209–12.
2. Hatch, Mary G., and Hatch, David L. "Problems of Married Working Women as Presented by Three Popular Working Women's Magazines," *Social Forces,* XXXVII (December, 1958), 148–53.
3. Komarovsky, Mirra. *Women in the Modern World.* Boston: Little, Brown, 1953.
4. Landis, Paul H. *Making the Most of Marriage.* New York: Appleton-Century-Crofts, 1955.
5. Levy, John, and Monroe, Ruth. *The Happy Family.* New York: Knopf, 1938.
6. Lundberg, Ferdinand, and Farnham, Marynia· F. *Modern Woman, The Lost Sex.* New York: Harper, 1947.

Chapter Twenty-Five

Recreation and Community

F. IVAN NYE

THIS chapter deals with the effects of the "provider role" on several familial and community roles, no one of which would in itself merit a separate chapter. The effects involve the recreational content of the roles of friend and confidante to husband, playmate and confidante of children, community member, and mother-in-law.

Since so much time is allocated to the provider role, presumably the time available to any of the above roles is reduced. The fact that the provider role is relatively dominant (or rigid) gives further sustenance to the idea that mothers would tend to reduce their recreational and community responsibilities in an attempt to reduce the tensions produced by role conflict. Such curtailment could be expected if (a) recreational and community roles are less rigid than the provider role and (b) recreational and community roles are not more rigid than other roles, such as supervisor and disciplinarian of children, housekeeper, and others in the wife-mother position. Those normative patterns within a role that compete directly in time with the provider role (usually from 8:00 A.M. to 5:00 P.M.) would be affected more than those not directly competing in time.

RECREATIONAL BEHAVIOR[1]

The popular stereotype of the mother employed full-time is that of a woman so overburdened with the combined duties of housekeeper and em-

---

[1] The portion of this paper dealing with recreational behavior is a revision of a previous paper by the writer (5).

ployee that she can hardly perform the minimum duties connected with these two roles and has no time for visiting or other types of recreation. By contrast, the mother who is not employed full-time is seen as possessing ample leisure for all types of recreation. It seems doubtful, however, that employed mothers (and by implication, their husbands) would deprive themselves entirely of visiting and other recreational activities.

Visiting requires the expenditure of considerable time. Daytime visiting, of course, requires that the mother have time available during the day, which employed mothers usually do not have. It should follow, therefore, that this type of social life will be sharply curtailed for employed mothers. This curtailment, however, may be followed by an expansion of recreational activity of a type which requires no advance planning, little expenditure of time and energy, but perhaps some expenditure of funds. Commercial spectator recreation would be such a type.

It is expected that employed mothers will participate least in recreational activity requiring the most time and most in types requiring the least time. Visiting is typical of the first type and attending movies is typical of the second. Bowling, tennis, and water sports might fall somewhere between the two types.

Present knowledge of the functions of recreation is limited. Available evidence supports the proposition that recreation is related to the absence of nervous symptoms and to the presence of happiness and life satisfactions (3, 4). The question therefore arises of whether or not recreation is sufficiently crucial to require an increase in recreational activities of one type as those of another type are curtailed. Several alternative hypotheses may be offered. Hypothesis One: Employed mothers will take part in less visiting and more spectator recreation than mothers not employed. Hypothesis Two: Employed mothers participate less in all types of recreation, with greatest differences in visiting and least differences in spectator sports. Hypothesis One requires the assumption that reduction in one type of recreation requires an increase in some other type; Hypothesis Two does not.

METHODOLOGY

Data were collected from 1,993 mothers in three Washington towns of from 10,000 to 30,000 population. The respondents were mothers of children in grades one and ten of the public and parochial schools. Names and addresses of mothers were obtained from school records, and the data were collected from them by mailed questionnaires. A 78 per cent return was obtained. Bias related to non-response was checked by comparing the returned questionnaires of mothers of tenth grade students with those collected from a 99 per cent sample of tenth grade students. Since previous research had shown that employed mothers were more likely to be highly educated, have smaller families and fewer preschool children, be remarried, and to be from low socio-economic levels, the samples were approximately matched on these variables by subsampling. The sample and other methodology of this study is described in more detail in Chapter Nineteen.

FINDINGS

The data show recreational patterns approximating those anticipated in Hypothesis Two (Table 25.1). Visiting relationships (with the exception of relatives) show considerable differences between those not employed and those employed full-time. As expected, the mothers employed full-time visit less, telephone less, attend fewer parties, and play cards less often. These are activities which require time, including time during the day. Some include advance planning and continuing commitments. Differences between the employed and non-employed are at a minimum or absent in spectator and commercial recreation.

It was expected that an intermediate recreational category would be found between visiting and spectator sports. This anticipated intermediate category included commercial recreation which requires some advance planning and participation from individuals outside of the family such as bowling, tennis, golf, and possibly dancing. All of these require the expenditure, also, of considerable physical energy. The data do not, however, support the idea that this is an intermediate category in relation to the employment of mothers. Employed mothers are not so physically fatigued that they participate less in "active" sports. In all of these types of recreation employed and non-employed mothers participate about equally.

It appears, therefore, that employed mothers do participate less in recreational activities involving time commitment but participate in commercial recreation about equally with non-employed mothers. Mothers employed part-time follow closely the recreational patterns of non-employed mothers.

Folk knowledge assumes that intrafamilial recreation is also curtailed when mothers take employment. This assumption does not, however, appear to be warranted. When family recreation items are dichotomized (Table 25.1) only one item shows significant differences. Non-employed mothers typically spend more time watching TV. Fifty-three per cent of non-employed mothers watched it more than 14 hours weekly compared with 39 per cent of mothers who were employed full-time. Card and game playing at home and family picnics and vacations do not differ significantly. One minor qualification might be made: No mother employed full-time engaged in family recreation as often as seven times weekly, but about 3 per cent

Table 25.1 *Frequent Participation in Selected Recreational Activities by Employment Status of Mothers*

FREQUENT PARTICIPATION IN RECREATION	MATERNAL EMPLOYMENT STATUS		
	NOT EMPLOYED (N = 400)	PART-TIME (N = 180)	FULL-TIME (N = 199)
	Per Cent		
Visiting			
Chatting with people on block*	83.8	82.8	64.4
Attending parties*	68.4	79.2	64.8
Telephoning friends*	52.5	53.5	41.2
Visiting outside block*	19.4	17.2	8.0
Playing cards*	48.0	51.2	38.8
Commercial Recreation			
Water sports	36.2	38.8	35.3
Bowling	10.9	16.8	10.8
Golf*	4.5	10.6	2.8
Tennis	4.7	6.2	3.9
Dancing	33.6	33.5	32.3
Movies	52.2	47.7	49.8
Family Recreation			
Visiting relatives	44.5	49.4	45.8
Organized games at home	61.1	60.6	52.1
Family picnics (summer)	45.1	45.2	44.7
TV*	53.4	52.9	39.1
Vacations	80.6	83.3	85.5

* Relationship is statistically significant.

Note: Frequent participation is measured as:
Chatting with people on block—weekly or oftener
Attending parties—more often than yearly
Telephoning friends—more often than weekly
Visiting outside block—more often than weekly
Playing cards—monthly or oftener
Playing water sports—three times monthly or oftener (summer)
Going bowling—monthly or oftener
Playing golf—monthly or oftener (summer)
Playing tennis—monthly or oftener (summer)
Dancing—twice monthly or oftener
Attending movies—all replies except "never"
Visiting relatives—more often than monthly
Playing organized games at home—all responses except "never"
Having family picnics (summer)—three times monthly or oftener
Watching TV—15 or more hours weekly
Vacationing—a vacation last year

of the non-employed mothers did. However, this might be a chance difference.

IMPLICATIONS

The role of companion to husband is different in one respect for employed mothers; that is, they attend fewer parties. Presumably couples including an employed wife also entertain others less often. Besides the obvious explanation that formal entertainment requires considerable time and advance commitment, the wife may substitute interpersonal relations in her occupation for those of formal entertainment to some extent. It is possible, too, that the two-income family has less need to entertain in order to advance the occupational status of the husband. Other spousal recreational activities are not affected by whether or not the mother is employed.

The analysis shows no reduction in mother-child recreational activity. However, the data probably do not reflect unorganized play activity between mothers and preschool children. Further research would be necessary to specify that relationship. Present data show no effect on the frequency of interaction with relatives. However, it might be anticipated that employed mothers would be less likely to take child relatives into their homes and more likely to invite widowed or divorced female adults who could share the responsibilities of the home-centered roles.

The role of community member appears to be essentially modified as mothers employed full-time reduce informal visiting, card playing, and telephoning friends. Of course some selectivity might be involved; less extroverted women might be more likely to seek employment. However, the findings can be explained in terms of the time required which directly conflicts with normal hours of employment.

Sociologists have long been aware of the decline of the neighborhood as a social unit. Those interested in personality and social control have generally taken a serious view of the loss of primary group relationships which have accompanied this change. Present findings suggest that the employment of mothers accelerates the decline of the neighborhood and tends also to limit the mothers' social relationships in the community beyond the neighborhood. Conversely, the mothers establish new sets of social relationships with business associates and clients. For example, mothers who become teachers establish relationships with their colleagues, students, and some parents. Perhaps the occupational world is increasing in importance in the areas of social control, status, and security for both the wife and the husband. Whether these new relationships are equivalent in emotional content to those of the neighborhood and community appears doubtful.

COMMUNITY ROLE

It has generally been assumed that employed mothers would participate less in formal organizations. By definition, such participation is time-consuming, and a major portion of the employed mother's time is occupied by her provider role. In addition, some organizations meet during working hours. Does such a decline occur, and, if so, does it affect all organizational activities equally?

FINDINGS

Data are available from two samples, the Washington sample of 1,993 mothers described earlier in this chapter and a smaller sample of 265 older mothers who had had a child married during the previous year. The latter sample has been described previously (Chapter Twenty-Three).

Contrary to common sense expectations, younger employed mothers (those with children of school age) belong to as many organizations as mothers who are not employed. One-fifth of each indicated no organizational membership; whereas 9 per cent of the non-employed and 7 per cent of the employed listed four or more memberships. The difference does not approach significance, and the small sample differences are associated with the part-time employed, more of whom belonged to several organizations than either the full-time employed or the non-employed.

The same pattern was found for attending organizational meetings. About one-third of both the non-employed and employed full-time said they attended no organizational meetings regularly. Almost the same proportion, 13 and 11 per cent, of the non-employed and full-time employed respectively, indicated regular attendance at meetings of three or more organizations. Again, a slightly greater proportion of those employed part-time regularly attended meetings of several organizations. No evidence supports the assumption that employment results in the curtailment of attendance at meetings of organizations to which the mothers belong. Although a third of the employed mothers attend no meetings, the same is true of those not employed.

Leadership in community organizations, however, *does* appear to be related to employment status. Less than two-fifths of the employed mothers hold an office or a committee chairmanship in any organization; whereas a majority of both non-employed and part-time employed indicated at least one of these leadership positions. The contrast is even greater for those holding two or more such positions—13 per cent of the non-employed compared to 4 per cent of the full-time employed. The part-time employed mothers appear to play a more prominent part in organizational leadership than either of the other two groups.

Some causal inference appears warranted from the above data. Leadership positions require considerably more time than membership or attendance. Since the three employment categories were matched by sociological variables, and since, on the whole, employed mothers should be at least as energetic as the others, it seems safe to conclude that employment does affect leadership roles in community organizations. A mediating sociological mechanism may be a redefinition of the community role of the mother who is a provider. Mothers employed full-time define their own community responsibilities as involving fewer leadership responsibilities—a redefinition with which the community concurs. The corollary of such redefinition is the placement of added community responsibility on the non-employed mother.

COMMUNITY ROLE IN THE "EMPTY NEST" PERIOD

The preceding data were from mothers of school-age children. Data are also available from 265 mothers who have had at least one child married. These women were typically in the forty-five to fifty-five age interval. Since the children of these mothers are adults or nearly so, it is possible that the role in the community of these older mothers is less affected by employment, since their roles as supervisor, disciplinarian of children, and (probably) housekeeper would demand considerably less time. The role of provider would seem to conflict less with their community role.

One preliminary finding is that these older women participate less than mothers of school-age children in formal community organizations. About one-fifth of both listed no membership in an organization. Of the younger mothers, two-fifths of the employed and over one-half of the non-employed held leadership positions. Only one-fourth of the older women indicated that they held committee chairmanships or offices. Older women do not appear to replace the responsibilities of their maternal roles with increased activity in the community.

The employment status of older women was unrelated to membership in organizations or to leadership positions. Having concluded that employment reduces the occupancy of leadership positions by mothers with school-age children, it can now be added that during the "empty nest" period, employment does not reduce the leadership by mothers.

Data on the question of whether employed women would tend to drop some types of community organizations and maintain others were not available from the younger mothers. However, such information was obtained from the older mothers.

Data from these older mothers do suggest some selectivity. The non-employed are more likely to be active in scouting organizations (16 per cent compared to 4 per cent of employed mothers). Scouting organizations meet in the daytime when employed mothers are working. Employed mothers, however, much more frequently belong to professional and occupational associations, as might be expected. No significant differences were found in membership in P.T.A., church auxiliary, community welfare, self-betterment groups, or groups in a residual "other" category. The number of these who belonged to the country club, WCTU, League of Women Voters, Federated Clubs, or Grange was too small to warrant a test of significance.

In reviewing the community role of older mothers, we note no quantitative difference either in membership or leadership of community organizations as a whole between the employed and non-employed. In looking at specific organizations, differences in organizational participation are found only in organizations peculiarly related to the working hours and occupational activity of the mothers. Earlier, it was noted that mothers of school-age children are less likely to lead community organizations than mothers who are not employed. This general difference disappears after children leave home. Apparently mothers whose children are grown can manage the duties of community leadership along with the housekeeper role. Therefore, it is concluded that the stage in the family life cycle is an important contingent condition mediating the relationship between employment and role in the community.

It should be remembered, however, that the data do not show that older women accept more community responsibilities after their children are grown. Since present data are cross-sectional rather than longitudinal, it is not certain that the opposite is true. Community organizations have proliferated in recent years, and the more widespread participation of the younger women may be a result of modification of the norms of the community role rather than the result of less physical energy or less interest on the part of older women. With respect to this apparent lessened community activity, Gass (2) found that although middle-aged wives liked to be amused and interested, they felt no sense of loss in having few duties and responsibilities.

EMPLOYED MOTHERS AND THE MOTHER-IN-LAW ROLE

Young couples often complain of interference in their family affairs on the part of the mother-in-law. Sometimes such interference takes the form of competition by the latter with the new spouse for the affection of her former child; sometimes it is unwanted advice and pressure to conduct family affairs as she thinks they should be conducted. It seems logical that if the role of provider occupies a major part of the time and energy of the mother-in-law and provides her with another set of interests, she should participate less in the family relationships of her former child, and the relationship between her and her son or daughter-in-law should be improved.

Present data from the 265 mothers of children recently married provide only a partial test of these ideas in that the in-law relationship is reported by the mothers only and not by their children and spouses. Questions were asked concerning: frequency of seeing married children; whether the young couple had lived with the parents after marriage; frequency of giving advice on buying furniture and clothing, on cooking and housekeeping, and on child rearing; and frequency of loaning money to the young couple.

In general, the data failed to support the idea that employed mothers-in-law would interact and interfere less in the affairs of married children. All differences were non-significant, and not all were in the anticipated direction. Employed mothers more frequently loaned money to their children and more frequently gave advice on personal problems. Non-employed mothers were more likely to advise on household and child-rearing matters.

The second idea, that the emotional relationship between the employed mother and her married child and his spouse would be improved by the employment of the mother-in-law, was based on the assumption that the responsibilities of the provider role would lessen her preoccupation with her married children. Since the pattern of interaction between mother and married children does not appear to be substantially affected by her employment, there is no reason to expect that the emotional relationship will be different. The data show no differences in emotional tone related to employment of the mother-in-law.

SUMMARY AND DISCUSSION

Data presently available lead us to believe that the addition of the provider role reduces the mother's TV viewing time, her informal visiting both in neighborhood and community, and her participation in formal entertaining. Only the latter involves her roles with other family members.

The community leadership activity of mothers of school-age children appears to be limited by her occupation of the provider role, although employment does not reduce the number of organizations to which she belongs or the number she attends. Even the difference in leadership activity disappears for the older women; that is, the older employed woman is as likely to be a member or an officer of an organization as one not employed. No evidence indicates less interaction between employed mothers and their married children or other members of the extended family group. Present data fail to show that the recreational content of roles involving family members is affected to any degree by the addition of the provider role and that only the leadership aspect of the community (organizational) role is affected.

REFERENCES

1. Axelson, Leland J. "Personal Adjustment in the Postparental Period," *Marriage and Family Living*, XXII (February, 1960), 66–69.
2. Gass, Gertrude Zemon. "Counseling Implications of Woman's Changing Role," *Personnel and Guidance*, XXVII (March, 1959), 482–87.
3. Havinghurst, R. J. "Leisure Activities of the Middle-Aged," *American Journal of Sociology*, LXIII (September, 1957), 161.
4. Jameson, Samuel Haig. "Recreation and Morale," *Sociology and Social Research*, XXVIII (January, 1944), 200–205.
5. Nye, F. Ivan. "Employment Status and Recreational Behavior of Mothers," *Pacific Sociological Review*, I (Fall, 1958), 69–72.

Chapter Twenty-Six

Employers' Attitudes toward Working Mothers*

JAMES E. CONYERS

CULTURAL change and the heterogeneity of American life have modified the mother's economic and social roles. Many social scientists, aware of this change, have noted and reflected upon its implications. Myrdal and Klein (9), Landis (6, chap. 4), Nye (12), Mead (7), and Nilsen and Weiss (11) have called attention to the lack of consensus about the mother's role under these new conditions. One of the principal changes has been the removal of the traditional economic functions of the mother to establishments outside the home. The traditional position holds that she should continue her former wife and mother roles, though many of the responsibilities of this role have been removed from her (12, pp. 12–13).

These changes and the increased employment of women (10, p. 10; 12, p. 4),[1] have moved some writers to concern themselves with the social and psychological consequences of the employment of mothers. Mueller suggests that the general problems of working women are like those of minority groups, and that integration of self and work should be regarded as legitimate aims of employment (8, pp. 64–90). On the question of whether or not mothers should work, Joselyn and Goldman contend that

* Expanded and revised from "Employers' Attitudes toward Working Mothers," *Sociology and Social Research*, XLV (January, 1961), 145–56. This exploratory study is a supplementary project in a research program on the employed mother supported in part by grants from the College Committee on Research of Washington State University. The writer wishes to acknowledge the assistance of Professor Ivan Nye in planning the study and preparing the report.

[1] As of April, 1958, 36 per cent of women fourteen and over were in the labor force. The National Manpower Council states that only one-fourth of the labor force today consists of single women compared with seven-tenths in 1890. They further state that about two-fifths of the mothers with children of school age are in the labor force.

some mothers are possibly better mothers and citizens *because* they work (5, p. 82). Hansl and Hatch call attention to part-time work as a solution to the problem of working while raising young children (3, pp. 27–32; 4). Others do not regard maternal employment as of grave consequence because the jobs women seek do not compete with fathers' roles as wage-earners (13, pp. 13–16). It should be noted here' that many of the ideas about the social products of the employment of mothers are speculative and await further refinement and additional documentation.

THE PROBLEM

No studies have yet been made of the effects of the mother role on the employee role. Whether employers see special problems for business in the hiring of mothers, their resulting attitudes toward employed mothers, and whether or not employers modify their expectations of women workers are not known.

The employers' reaction to mothers is both intrinsically interesting and possesses considerable significance for future trends in maternal employment. If employer attitudes are unfavorable because of a traditional family ideology or because mothers are less productive or dependable as employees, one might forecast a decreasing rate of the flow of mothers into employment. Conversely, either neutral or positive attitudes would be favorable to the continued and rapid movement of mothers into factory, office, classroom, and other paid employment. Attitudes of employers whether positive, negative, or neutral undoubtedly have a bearing on the work adjustment of mothers and an indirect bearing on their family relationships.

A number of studies have shown that the statuses of wife and of mother have been altered by simultaneous assumption of the status of employee. The reverse question should also be asked: Do the family statuses affect employers' expectations concerning the employee role? Are mothers accorded special privileges because of their other responsibilities, or are the expectations for all women workers affected by the increasing proportion of them who are mothers? If the answer to these latter questions is "Yes," one might forecast an increased congruence of the maternal and employee roles and a sharing of the necessary adjustments between family and economic organization.

Finally, this study will pose the question of whether recent structural changes affecting the employment of mothers[2] have challenged ideological

---

[2] Some of the common changes have been increased longevity, decreased family size, greater educational training for women, lowered average age of marriage, increased leisure time, and concentration of childbearing activities in the early and middle twenties. Of equal importance is the cultural orientation (possibly emanating from the Protestant Ethic) that work pays off in income, status, and power.

commitment to the ideas of the "weaker sex" and "mother's place is in the home."[3]

METHOD

THE RESPONDENTS

This study was conducted in a western city of about 200,000 population during the summer of 1959. A random sample of 20 was selected from a list of 100 businesses or service concerns employing the largest number of females. From the 20 businesses, 18 managers were interviewed.[4]

These managers act as employment agents and personnel managers, though most have additional responsibilities. Thirteen of the respondents are males; five are females.

Eleven of the wives of the male respondents are mothers, three of whom had worked since motherhood, and one of whom is presently employed. Whether or to what extent this may have influenced their answer is unknown.

The respondents' businesses employ approximately 5,900 employees, of which approximately 3,000 are females. Of the 3,000 females, the respondents estimated that approximately 1,850 are mothers. The sex ratio for employees is approximately 97. It was further estimated that 50 per cent of the mothers employed by the businesses studied have children under eighteen years of age.

THE INSTRUMENT

The information in this study was obtained through a structured interview. (A pretest was conducted at an earlier date in another city.) Prior

---

[3] The National Manpower Council, in examining the employers' appraisal of working women, stated that employers often exaggerate the failings of women workers and are more tolerant of those of men. Considering the wide range of characteristics of women employees, NMC stated, "generalizations about feminine traits and employment policies based on stereotypes of women's behavior could be costly to employers and wasteful of the abilities of potentially valuable individuals."

[4] An attempt was made to group the 100 businesses into occupational categories and, according to the number of concerns in each group, to select a representative number of businesses from each category. The 100 businesses were classified according to the principal occupations of women: (a) professional, (b) clerical and kindred, (c) sales workers, (d) service workers, and (e) operatives. From the first category, a college, a school district, and a sanitarium were selected. From the clerical category, two banks, a post office, the main district office of a petroleum company, and a welfare department were chosen. From the sales workers' category, three well-established merchandise retail department stores and a grocery store were interviewed. From the service-work category, a motel-inn and a private club of the city were selected. From the operative category, a laundry, a wholesale meat company, a linen supply company, and a wholesale lumber company were chosen. Two concerns refused—a dental operation from the clerical category and a merchandise retail department from the sales workers category.

to the interview, a letter was written telling the managers of the project and asking for their cooperation. Respondents were assured of anonymity as to person, business, and exact location of business.

EMPLOYMENT PRACTICES

In all instances a formal application is a prerequisite for employment. Six of the businesses—the two banks, the petroleum company office, the post office, the welfare department, and the grocery store—require examinations as a condition of employment. These examinations are designed to test the prospective employee's qualification for a particular job, and serve as a basis for deciding who is to be considered for employment. Six of the businesses require a physical examination or a health certificate. The twelve businesses with written policies governing employment have *no* policies regarding the employment of mothers. Formalized procedures would probably lessen the effects of the personal philosophies of the personnel managers.

The respondents were asked, "From what age categories do you prefer to hire women, and why?" The modal response was twenty to forty-five. This indicates a preference for an age during which most women are married and rearing children, an age when women are generally psychologically and physically mature and adept, and an age when women may have completed training or preparation for jobs. Employers seeking these work virtues in women are unavoidably confronted with the fact that most mature young women are also mothers. Thus, the two dimensions are largely inseparable and are two aspects of the same thing, i.e., a preferential age category.

GENERAL ATTITUDES

It has been suggested that attitudes such as those of employers toward working mothers are reflections of social situations. Myrdal and Klein in their book, *Women's Two Roles,* state the position in these words: "Peoples' personal attitudes are a reflection of the social situation and, at the same time, an important factor in it" (9). This point is particularly germane to this study.

Personnel managers were asked, "When you think of mothers as employees, what comes to your mind?" This question was basically unstructured and designed to tap general attitudes. The responses were grouped into four broad categories.

First were positive responses associating mothers and valued personal attributes (e.g., "Mothers are stable, dependable, steady, and mature").

Second were responses picturing the working mother as a person who had responsibilities other than those for which she had been employed (i.e., children). In this connection, the employers were concerned with "baby sickness," "child care," etc. The majority of responses were in this category.

Third were negative responses (e.g., "I think of someone who should stay home with children"). According to this position, the best, most profitable, and only place for a mother is at home, especially if her children are young.

Fourth were responses based upon the "necessity to work." Typical were that many mothers work because "they have to": some mothers have no husbands, or husbands who are incapacitated, bring home a marginal income, or are negligent.

Two particular responses could not be classified in any of these four categories. The first pragmatically suggested that mothers fulfill a need for industry as well as herself: this respondent said the first thing that came to his mind was, "Where would I hire female help if I did not hire mothers?" Considering his business—elementary and high school education —an important question has been posed. Highly qualified women are needed; he employs about 1,300 women, approximately half of which have children under eighteen. Apparently, when a business needs scarce skills, considerations of sex and motherhood are subordinated to the task of "getting the job done."

A female personnel manager also gave an atypical reply. She said, "I think of God . . . And God watches over the working mother." She seemed to be saying that a mother has many problems, and if someone does not watch over her, she cannot "make it." She indicated that business looks out for itself, . . . so God must be helping the working mother. Many of the mothers she employs have handicapped, alcoholic, or negligent husbands; some are husbandless; yet she has never lost a mother from work for an extended period of time. To her, God is responsible for this miracle.

To the question of what comes to the employers' minds when they think of mothers as employees, we may interpret and summarize the responses as follows:

(a) Mothers are stable, mature, steady, and dependable.
(b) Mothers have responsibilities other than those associated with gainful employment which may interfere with their work.
(c) Mothers should stay home with their children, especially if they are very young.
(d) There are some mothers who understandably must work because of extenuating circumstances.

ADVANTAGES OF EMPLOYING MOTHERS

The respondents were asked, "What to you would be the advantage to your business to employ mothers?" The majority of responses stated that the advantages of employing mothers come from their stability and reliability. Some of the common responses favorable to employing mothers were: "A well-adjusted business needs a cross-section of the community for both the individual and collective good"; "Mothers have an understanding of people"; "Mothers are mentally adapted to meeting and serving the needs of people"; "They are good public relations people"; and "Mothers are excellent for holiday and part-time work." Other responses stated that motherhood is of little relevance in employment.

It does appear that there are some advantages to the business in employing mothers. We should suggest, nevertheless, that employers feel some ambivalence, and that one of the principal reasons both for employing and not employing mothers is one and the same—stability. Mothers have responsibilities other than those incurred on the job which may interfere with job regularity; yet the responsibilities themselves encourage dependability.

PROBLEMS AND CONFLICTS IN EMPLOYING MOTHERS: QUALIFYING VARIABLES

MAXIMUM NUMBER OF CHILDREN

Concerning the maximum number of children a working mother should have, half of the respondents stated that they do not have any opinion on this point or that they do not want to concern themselves with this issue. These respondents feel that such a question depends upon the moral, economic, and religious values of the husband and wife. Three managers stated that if the mother had two or three children of preschool age, she should not be working.

A female respondent was willing to specify definitely the maximum (and minimum) number of children a working mother should have—two. Her reasoning was that one child would be lonely, and more than two would overwork the mother. Some evidence suggests that a working mother with two or three children decidedly increases her work-week hours over those of childless wives—from an average of 28 to 39 hours per week (9, p. 36).

AGE OF YOUNGEST CHILD

To the question, "If a woman has children, do you have any feeling concerning the age of her youngest child?", the majority of respondents indicated that the mother should be at home with children of preschool age. Though the notion that mothers with children under preschool age should stay home is apparently widespread, there are almost 2.5 million mothers in the labor force with children under six years. This group constitutes one-eighth of the entire female labor force (10, p. 69) and one-fifth of all mothers with preschool children.

Three respondents had no particular feeling concerning this point. One said she would rather see a mother work before the baby is two years old than during the years following this age. According to this respondent, a baby about two years old can be cared for by almost anyone. She suggested, however, that some teen-agers may need more guidance and care than the very young.

NEED AS A FACTOR IN DECIDING TO EMPLOY MOTHERS

To the question, "With respect to working mothers is their *need* for a job often a factor in deciding to employ them?", eleven respondents said "no" and seven said "yes"; however, very few of these responses were categorical. Instead, they were conditional (1, p. 11–17).[5] For example, a respondent who said "yes," also said that the mother's ability to do the job comes first; but, "if two mothers are equally qualified, the 'needy' mother would get the job." The same was true for some of the "no" responses.

Of the atypical responses to the question of need, one respondent said: "It is difficult for me to determine need. One person may buy clothes to get a job, while another who may not be in as great a need may be poorly clad." Then, too, this respondent said, "There are different kinds of needs and purposes."

Another atypical response stated that the need perspective is not a sound basis for employment: "Hiring on the basis of need is not a good policy. If you hire on the basis of need, then firing becomes difficult." He added that when a "needy" person looks for a job, some business managers may think: "Here comes a sucker, someone I can 'use' like I want to because he or she is in need."

The post office and welfare department said they cannot employ from a need perspective. Referrals to them are regulated by federal and state laws, and selection for consideration is then made on the basis of scores from examinations, qualification, or seniority. These include no consideration of need.

It is difficult to generalize whether need is or is not a definite factor in deciding to employ a mother. It seems, nevertheless, that the employers of this study are not insensitive to need, but need is not a primary consideration.

REQUESTS FOR SPECIAL PRIVILEGES AND OTHER
QUALIFYING VARIABLES

The respondents were asked to compare single and childless married women with mothers in reference to: (a) requests for special privileges, (b)

[5] For a study of the factors a manager might take into consideration in employing women, see Brown and Arensen (1).

complaints and grievances, (c) health, (d) accidents, (e) temperament and disposition, and (f) job morale.

Through these comparisons, the employers suggest that there is no appreciable difference between the three classes of women, or at least that the employers have not evaluated them in this light. With the exception of requests for special privileges, the respondents have stated that mothers compare favorably with the other two classes of women. The respondents seem to regard even their requests for special privileges as legitimate and expected. It does not appear, therefore, that mothers' complaints, health, accidents, temperament and disposition, and job morale, exist as problems any more than do those of their single or childless married counterparts.

CONFLICTS BETWEEN HOME AND WORK

The respondents were asked three questions about conflicts between home and work: (a) "What appears to you to be the most important single reason why one might not employ mothers?" (b) "With respect to the mothers you have employed, what conflicts, if any, between home and work have you found to occur most frequently as a job conflict?" (c) "In your business how frequent and serious are these conflicts?"

The principal objections were young children and problems of providing for their care. Also, responses to the second question indicate that the principal area of conflict between home and work for the businesses studied relates to children—their illnesses, accidents, general care, and preparation for school. Such conflicts occur in a majority of the businesses studied. They often require time-off from the mother's job.

Another area of conflict between home and work mentioned by the respondents is related to the husband's adjustment to his wife, home, and children. Though conflicts of this type are less direct, they are real to the respondents of this study. One stated that indirect conflict exists when the husband is ambivalent toward his wife's working.

Two respondents said fights between husband and wife, court cases, etc., have caused conflicts. One said, "I had a woman here who was working to help support children and family, and for a while she couldn't come to work because of a broken jaw inflicted by her husband." This employer also stated that this same woman had to be away from work because of divorce proceedings. "This type of conflict can even be of more trouble than a babysitting problem, for it might involve some of my time talking to police or court officials," the respondent stated. The other respondent who gave a similar answer replied promptly, saying that a source of conflict between home and work would be a "son-of-a-bitch who fights wife and will not cooperate with wife and children." These respondents manage establishments in which women are employed as operatives.

The conflicts mentioned above are not very frequent or serious. The respondents would not or could not state exactly how many occur in their businesses, but one suggested that there might be four a month. The conflicts mentioned were generally more characteristic of mothers than non-mothers.

PREGNANCY AND EMPLOYMENT

The majority of the respondents stated that five months was the usual terminating point for employment of a pregnant woman. They say a state law requires that a pregnant woman must have a doctor's permission to continue work after the fifth month of pregnancy. Some of the respondents said they have allowed women to work until the last month of pregnancy. Typically, however, pregnant women are discouraged from working when their pregnancy begins "to show."

There are several reasons for this, varying from the point that "our work is not conducive to pregnant women, i.e., lifting, bending, heat," to the most typical response, "a pregnant woman does not 'look good' before the public." A manager of one of the service concerns (motel) asked the question, "Just how would you feel having a pregnant woman 'wait' on you?" In addition to the belief that pregnant women do not create a "good" public image, two respondents said that fear of injury and liability are reasons for their not wanting women in their later months of pregnancy to work for them.

The respondents were also asked about their policy toward pregnant woman after childbirth. They replied that when a pregnant woman leaves employment to have a baby, she usually takes complete severance. She is hired again if there is an opening and she was a "good worker"; even this is done "in order to be fair." In some cases, however, leaves of absence or maternal leaves are granted, and an attempt is made to keep the job open.

CHILD-CARE FACILITIES FOR CHILDREN OF
WORKING MOTHERS

The most frequent area of conflict between home and work is centered on children—sometimes their illnesses, but often provision for their care, i.e., babysitting. The respondents, therefore, were asked their opinion as to the adequacy of child-care facilities for children of working mothers. Thirteen said that they are adequate or that they do not know if they are adequate or not. By "adequate" or "don't know," the majority of the respondents meant: "Mothers seem to be doing okay here"; or "I don't know what mothers here are doing; my wife is home taking care of mine";

or again, "They are adequate as far as I'm concerned—I have not had any calls or complaints."

Such responses seem to indicate management's non-involvement in the problems of mothers as they seek work outside the home. To them, child-care facilities are adequate as long as the mother comes to work. If they think that a mother will have child-care problems, they will hesitate to hire her; nevertheless, mothers are hired, and one of the principal areas of conflict remaining between home and work is child care.

Several respondents stated that the present child-care facilities are not adequate. Respondents reporting inadequate facilities were asked in what way they should be changed and by whom. A school district official suggested that social welfare classes and day nurseries might help and that business and private donors could help to finance its operations. Another respondent suggested help by individuals and the community, then hastened to add, "This is not an obligation of the employer or state. It is the mother's duty to take care of home and children, and father's, to make enough money."

Two of the respondents suggested that child-care facilities could be established on a private basis. These respondents would not like to see the federal government involved in this area (10, p. 10).[6] One of them said that things are too "socialistic" now, and neither wants to see what is happening to children in Russia take place in the United States. They believe that children of working mothers are treated like calves in the U.S.S.R.

The personnel managers were asked, "Does your company help mothers with their special problems as mothers in reference to their adjustment to working conditions?" Responses were negative, though in some cases sympathetic. Practically all suggested that nothing is done or that they help by granting small favors to mothers when possible. One summarized, "I help them no more than what I can do individually or what can be handled through policy."

SUMMARY AND DISCUSSION

This study indicates that managers are not identical in their policies concerning working mothers. In many instances they are ambivalent. This study has also suggested that:

1. Managers are skeptical of hiring women over forty-five.
2. Employers perceive working mothers as employees who have responsibilities other than those for which they are employed; yet mothers are stable and dependable workers because of these responsibilities. Stability is a reason both for and against the employment of mothers.

---

[6] For a discussion of the role played by the federal government with respect to child-care facilities for children of working mothers, see National Manpower Council (10).

3. Employers do not agree about the maximum number of children a working mother should have. Many state that this is an issue with which they do not want to get involved.
4. Employers think that mothers with preschool children should not be working, but they will employ them. This may indicate a difference between employers' attitudes as citizens and as employers, as well as an understanding that some mothers particularly need to work for economic reasons. Equally important is that mothers with young children may have specific qualifications for jobs which management must fill, consideration for the mother's young children notwithstanding.
5. A majority of the employers prefer not to employ mothers because of the mother's need—unless other considerations are first taken into account; however, both those who would and those who would not employ from a need perspective qualified their responses.
6. Usually, pregnant women must stop work after five months of pregnancy. Usually they take complete severance, returning to their former employment only if management needs them.
7. In reference to complaints, health, accidents, temperament, and job morale, employers do not think mothers are more trouble than non-mothers. They do, however, report that mothers request more special privileges.
8. Concerning conflicts between home and work, the managers indicated that the principal area of conflict is centered on children, i.e., illness, accidents, school exercises, babysitting, etc., and is more characteristic of mothers than non-mothers; nevertheless, other conflicts were mentioned not related to the motherhood variable as such. The managers did not consider any of the conflicts to be very serious or frequent.
9. Child-care facilities for children of working mothers are adequate as far as most of the managers are concerned. If they are inadequate, the managers stated that they do little to help the mothers they employ with their adjustment to working conditions.
10. The managers interviewed in this study have few data on working mothers.

One objective of the exploratory study was to determine whether employers are modifying their expectations of employees who are also mothers. In the conflict between employee and family roles, are *all* adjustments made by family? This limited study has failed to show substantial or consistent action in this direction by management. Some stated that mothers need and are granted time off from the job when children require the mothers' special attention. This appears to be a matter for a personal decision by the supervisor rather than generally agreed-upon policy. Managers mention that mothers "make up" for these "favors" by more efficient and responsible work.

It is possible that consistent and continued action by supervisors will lead to official recognition by employers that mothers' responsibilities require a modification of the employee role. The United States government implicitly recognizes such responsibilities by granting sick leave to an employee whose presence is required to care for a member of the family who is seriously ill. Other modifications of the employee role may follow, but the present study does not suggest that extensive modification may be expected in the near future. The attitudinal questions indicate that employers expect the modifications to occur in family roles—not in the employee role.

REFERENCES

1. Brown, Clara M., and Arensen, Ruth V. *Employment Opportunities for Women with Limited Home Economics Training.* Minneapolis: Burgess, 1944.
2. *Handbook on Women Workers, 1958.* United States Department of Labor, Women's Bureau. Washington, D. C.: Government Printing Office, 1958.
3. Hansl, Eva B. *Trends in Part-Time Employment of College Trained Women.* New York: .Women's Press, 1949.
4. Hatch, Mary G. and Hatch, David L. "Problems of Married Working Women as Presented by Three Popular Working Women's Magazines," *Social Forces,* XXXVI (December, 1959), 48–53.
5. Joselyn, Irene M., and Goldman, Ruth Schley. "Should Mothers Work?" *Social Service Review,* XXIII (March, 1940), 82.
6. Landis, Paul H. *Making the Most of Marriage.* New York: Appleton-Century-Crofts, 1955.
7. Mead, Margaret. *Male and Female.* Part IV; New York: New American Library, 1955.
8. Mueller, Kate Hevner. *Educating Women for a Changing World.* Minneapolis: University of Minnesota Press, 1954.
9. Myrdal, Alva, and Klein, Viola. *Women's Two Roles: Home and Work.* London: Routledge & Kegan Paul, 1956.
10. National Manpower Council. *Womanpower.* New York: Columbia University Press, 1957.
11. Nilsen, Norman O., and Weiss, Eric J. *The Self-Supporting Woman in Oregon.* Salem, Ore.: State Bureau of Labor, no date (probably 1960).
12. Nye, F. Ivan. "What Patterns of Family Life?" *Coordinator,* IV (November, 1955), 12–17.
13. Parsons, Talcott, and Bales, Robert F. *Family, Socialization and Interaction Process.* Glencoe, Ill.: Free Press, 1955.

Chapter Twenty-Seven

Adjustment of the Mother: Summary and A Frame of Reference

F. IVAN NYE

PART IV has dealt with (a) employed mothers' feelings of satisfaction or dissatisfaction with relationships to people about external objects; (b) their self-feelings of anxiety, guilt, satisfaction, and achievement, either expressed verbally or through psychosomatic symptoms; (c) their more serious mental-emotional disturbances resulting in commitment to an institution; (d) physical health; (e) participation in recreational and community life; and (f) the community images of the employed mother.

FEELINGS OF SATISFACTION AND DISSATISFACTION WITH RELATIONSHIPS AND OBJECTS

One chapter by Feld (Twenty-Four) and two by Nye (Twenty-Three and Twenty-Five) considered maternal satisfaction. Both writers reported direct verbal responses and recognized the possibility of bias through socially acceptable answers; however, since both report that some comparisons favored employed and other non-employed, they discounted the possibility that serious systematic bias favored one group or the other.

Concerning *relationships to children,* both Feld and Nye found that the employed and non-employed did not differ significantly concerning number of problems. However, both reported differences favoring the employed mothers' attitudes toward relationships with children. Feld found this true, particularly in that the employed mothers did not feel restricted by the duties of motherhood; she also found employed mothers ahead when the items "restricting," "burdensome," and "demanding" were pooled. Nye found that employed mothers had more favorable attitudes toward children and motherhood in two different samples: those with school-age children and those with preschool children. This was true, however, only for mothers with three or fewer children.

Concerning *relationships to husbands,* both Feld and Nye found more dissatisfaction and Nye found a poorer marital relationship among the employed-mother couples—whether satisfaction was measured by a conflict scale or by a broader measure of the marital relationship (Chapter Nineteen). Blood also reported more husband-wife conflicts in employed-wife families. Blood found that role conflict was more likely in the higher income levels; while conflict concerning money was more characteristic in the lower income groups. Although Nye found fewer differences between the employed and non-employed among highly educated couples and *no* relationship between employment and marital adjustment among remarried couples, the findings of all three studies agree that marital relationships tend to contain more negative elements for employed-mother couples.

On the subject of *other relationships and feelings toward objects,* Nye obtained feelings about community, daily work, recreation, income, and house and furniture (Chapter Twenty-Three). The employed mothers showed significantly more satisfaction with their daily work and the community as a place in which to live; other differences (including income) were non-significant. A satisfaction quasi-scale favored the employed—but only for mothers of school-age and preschool children. Among the older women in the post-parental period, the opposite was discovered; the non-employed mothers more frequently indicated satisfaction with their recreation and income; and most non-significant sample differences also favored them.

DISCUSSION

It appears that the association between maternal employment and broader feelings of satisfaction and dissatisfaction differs with the relationship studied—whether it is parent-child, husband-wife, or person-community. For younger women, the employed mothers appear to be more satisfied with these relationships—except for the husband-wife relationship. We cautiously propose, therefore, that relationship problems associated with maternal employment are more likely to be found in the husband-wife relationship than elsewhere. The redefinition of the mother's roles and the changes in power relationships (Hoffman, Chapter Fifteen; and Heer, Chapter Eighteen) presumably produce conflict and dissatisfaction. We cannot rule out the possibility that wives enter employment because they are dissatisfied with the marital relationship. However, no study has shown this to be a cause for entering employment.

The role of contingent conditions in satisfactions in the above relationships should be stressed. Employed mothers are better satisfied with their relationship to children only when they have three or fewer. Poorer marital adjustment is not found among remarried employed mothers. Higher education and socio-economic level appear to decrease differences between the employed and non-employed in marital relationships. Differences favoring employed younger mothers are *not* found among mothers in the post-parental period. While the general relationships needed to be established, the determination of the contingent conditions for the existence (and direction) of the relationships is equally or even more crucial.

SELF-FEELINGS OF GUILT, ANXIETY, SATISFACTION, AND ACHIEVEMENT

The data on *self-feelings* consisted of statements from mothers regarding their feelings and psychosomatic symptoms considered indicative of anxiety. Feld reported that employed mothers supplied more positive and fewer negative statements about themselves as persons (Chapter Twenty-Four). This seems to indicate that high self-esteem is somewhat more prevalent among the employed women. However, Feld also found that more employed mothers felt inadequate in particular (role) situations: that is, as mothers. Though these two findings appear contradictory, they are actually compatible; that is, employed mothers tend toward higher self-esteem as *individuals,* but in situations involving conflict between the roles of employee and domestic roles, they often feel inadequate.

The Feld and the Sharp and Nye studies used different lists of psychosomatic complaints. Neither study found significant differences between employed and non-employed women. Sharp and Nye also asked whether the mother had consulted a psychiatrist in the past five years or had felt the need to consult one. Almost identical proportions of the employed and non-employed responded affirmatively to the two questions. Sharp and Nye's use of several contingent conditions was unproductive.

DISCUSSION

High self-esteem might encourage a woman to seek employment, and success as an employee might encourage a favorable self-image; but at the same time, a woman might feel inadequate concerning those responsibilities that conflict with the employee role. This hypothesis should be tested in further research.

Role conflict by itself might be expected to produce more psychosomatic symptoms among the employed mothers. However, anxieties about working may be counter-balanced in several ways: (a) Since the housekeeping and economic production roles of the non-employed mother have been so reduced, homemakers may feel guilty about *not* working. As one of the contributors to this volume said when she gave up a paid position, "I want to become a part of that great American leisure class—the non-employed mother." (b) Certain familial rivalries and hostilities may be dissipated through creative work in employment. Feld found that employed mothers had fewer anxieties concerning the *nature* of parent-child interaction. (c) Two incomes provide additional financial independence and security which may alleviate anxieties. (d) Since most psychosomatic complaints involve some degree of physical incapacity, women with severe symptoms may never enter employment or may more frequently leave the labor force. (e) Finally, a possible clue may lie in a personal and, to some extent, social redefinition of the domestic roles by the employed mother. There is considerable evidence that American husbands are acknowledging that the provider role revises the housekeeper role (Hoffman, Chapter Fifteen; Blood, Chapter Twenty) and that, to a lesser extent, employers acknowledge that the supervisor and nursemaid for children role modifies the employee role (Conyers, Chapter Twenty-Six). Therefore, the conflict between the provider and domestic roles may be less sharp than one might expect.

MENTAL DISTURBANCES RESULTING IN INSTITUTIONALIZATION

Data bearing on the relationship between the employment experience and commitment to a mental institution are limited to the results of one study based on secondary data (Sharp and Nye, Chapter Twenty-One). The data did show differences among the mentally ill who had or had not had prior employment experiences. Those with employment histories were more likely to have been classed psychoneurotic than psychotic and to have had chronic rather than acute onsets. These data suggest that employed women who become mentally ill are more likely to have extended histories of personality instability.

This information is not sufficient to permit even tentative conclusions concerning cause and effect relationships, but it raises some interesting questions. Did employment serve as a release for neurotic feelings and dissipate conflict related to these feelings, thus delaying the onset of illness, or did it provide added burdens which finally precipitated an emotional crisis? Probably neither is true for all cases, and a search for crucial social and psychological contingent conditions would be an important part of continuing research in this area.

PHYSICAL HEALTH

Feld found that ". . . working mothers have lower scores on the physical ill health index than non-working mothers . . . they aren't bothered by all sorts of pains and ailments in different parts of their body or by not feeling healthy enough to do the things they would like to . . ." (Chapter Twenty-Three). As Feld pointed out, healthy mothers may be more likely to take employment, or employment may have a beneficial effect on their health. Also, those whose health becomes poor may drop employment.

Perhaps the most important conclusions that can be drawn are that the health of employed mothers does not appear to *suffer* from their dual set of tasks and that the stereotype of the employed mother as an exhausted, "bedraggled," physically debilitated "wreck" can be safely stowed in the intellectual garbage can along with an increasing number of common sense myths. Whether feminine health is typically improved by adding employment to domestic roles is an intriguing question, but one requiring additional research. Women currently demand and receive much more medical care than men, even though they typically outlive them by several years. It is possible that the regular full-time employment of married women might change these patterns.

PARTICIPATION IN RECREATIONAL AND ORGANIZATIONAL LIFE

The recreational life of employed mothers was discovered to contain less non-familial interaction: that is, less visiting with neighbors, formal entertaining, card playing, and TV watching (Nye, Chapter Twenty-Five). Participation in family recreation, visiting relatives, and commercial recreation was *not* significantly different for the two groups. Yarrow (21) found that employed mothers were more likely consciously to plan to spend recreation time with family members. Such conscious planning may compensate for less total time in the home. The effects of employment are concentrated on the daytime recreational activity of mothers, and evening and week-end recreation is not very much affected—except in the reduction of formal entertaining and perhaps the decrease of TV time. This apparently reduces recreational contacts outside the family in the mother's peer group. In place of this outside activity employed mothers develop relationships with their work associates and tend to limit their recreation to that shared with their families.

Concerning *organizational participation,* fewer differences than anticipated were found (Nye, Chapter Twenty-Five). No significant differences appeared either in the number of organizations to which the two groups belong or in the frequency with which they attend meetings. Their leadership roles are different, however; fewer employed mothers hold offices or committee chairmanships. As expected, differences were greatest for organizations which function primarily in the daytime.

Employed mothers were found to be likely to play passive or supporting roles rather than active leadership roles in organized community life. Probably community expectations have modified with respect to leadership functions, and this redefinition has come to be shared by the employed mothers themselves. Employed mothers perform more leadership functions in the provider role and assume more responsibility for decision-making within the family; consequently, they may have less desire to lead voluntary organizations.

It is interesting to review here an earlier finding that employed mothers tend to be *better* satisfied with their communities than those not employed (Chapter Twenty-Five). This suggests that reduced participation in voluntary organizations does not lead to feelings of deprivation and that there may be more frustration than satisfaction in working for voluntary community organizations. Voluntary work, in general, may be giving way to professional work; if so, the employed mother is in harmony with this trend.

COMMUNITY IMAGE OF THE EMPLOYED MOTHER

Conyers investigated the employers' attitudes toward working mothers, their problems in employing mothers, and the modifications they permit in the employee role in recognition of the demands of the domestic roles on the mothers (Chapter Twenty-Six). He found that employers shared the traditional view that a mother's place is in the home but did not hesitate to employ a mother if they thought that she would be an effective employee. Although they defined the same job responsibilities for mothers as for anyone else, in practice, most employers allowed mothers to take time off for emergencies related to their children. They usually rationalized the practice by stating that mothers were better employees in other respects. One formal change was occurring in that the illness of a child was being considered legitimate sick leave.

Although the employee role is rigid, it shows evidence of being somewhat redefined in deference to the other roles of the employed mothers. Employers are clearly ambivalent toward employed mothers: as community members they view them with concern because of presumed negative effects of employment on family life; as employers they find them satisfactory, even necessary.

Glenn (3) and Nolan (15) studied attitudes toward working women. Both found a very great difference between the attitudes of the family members of employed and non-employed mothers. Almost all adults in families with non-working mothers disapproved of maternal employment; most of those with working mothers approved. Of course, this factor might influence a mother's decision to accept or not accept a job opportunity. However, the families of employed mothers were reaping the economic benefits of the mother's employment, while the other families were gaining no benefits and could only lose if there were negative effects. Some non-employed mothers may also have rationalized their own lack of economic contribution by attributing probable ill-effects of working to other family members. Nye found a sizeable minority of non-employed mothers who said they would like to have a job. A smaller proportion of working mothers said they would like to quit (Chapter Nineteen). Hoffman has discussed the attitudes of children toward employed mothers in Chapter Fourteen.

American society is widely split and often ambivalent about the employment of mothers. As mothers continue to seek employment on a large scale and current research fails to reveal catastrophic consequences of such employment, the future image will become less negative—and perhaps positive.

SUGGESTIONS FOR RESEARCH

All present research is cross-sectional in design (except the data dealing with institutionalized mothers, which are ex post facto), and all could benefit by testing by longitudinal design. This appears crucial for the relationship of physical health to employment, since reasonably good health is a prerequisite to regular employment. Longitudinal design is also desirable in other cases—such as the study of marital relationships—where selective factors that influence the seeking of employment may not be operative but cannot be ruled out on the basis of present knowledge. In still other cases—such as the apparent curtailment of leadership in community organizations and reduction in time spent watching TV by employed mothers—the findings seem so consistent with other facts that research time might be better invested in some other way.

The concept and technique of the contingent condition (or test variable) has proven useful and probably will be employed in future research with increasing frequency and finesse.[1] Some contingent conditions which have been valuable in specifying types of relationship are: number of children, presence of preschool children, income of husband, previous marital status of husband and wife, and education and age of mother. Broad occupational categories have not yet proven useful, but more specific categories—such as those of public school teacher or waitress—might be illuminating. However, the potential usefulness of a contingent condition is closely tied to the particular relationship being studied. Moreover, extensive use of contingent conditions requires large samples.

The "neglected populations" discussed by Hoffman with respect to

---

[1] We are using the concept *contingent condition* as developed by Selltiz, Jahoda, Deutsch, and Cook (17, pp. 82–84). This includes antecedent as well as intervening variables. This conceptualization closely parallels Lazarsfeld's concept *specification*.

effects on children (Chapter Fourteen) are appropriate to the research on the employed mother herself. In addition to the non-white families and families with a solo parent mentioned by Hoffman is the population of older women. Approximately one-third of the average woman's life remains after her last child marries. What are the effects of employment or its absence during this period? Only one study reported here presented data separately on women in the post-parental or "empty-nest" period of the life cycle (Nye, Chapter Twenty-Two). It failed to confirm the widely held belief that this is an ideal time for mothers to enter the labor force. Data available were not sufficient to indicate whether biological changes, occupational differences, or other social factors were involved.

The study of employment as a variable in the post-hospital adjustment of mothers who had been confined in mental institutions could benefit by the use of the longitudinal technique, and a careful study of work experiences prior to commitment might shed light on the function of employment in decreasing or increasing severe emotional problems.

TOWARD A SOCIOLOGICAL CONCEPTUALIZATION OF MATERNAL EMPLOYMENT

Although there is no necessary conflict between conceptualization, measurement, analysis, and other parts of the scientific process, more specific attention is usually given to measurement and analysis than to conceptualization and theory building. Theoretically oriented sociologists complain that much research makes little or no use of existent theory. Of course, such use is difficult because present theory is diffuse and fragmentary. However, as the present research is presented and as interested family researchers look past it to additional research, it seems appropriate briefly to differentiate some disciplinary frames of reference and to propose a socio-psychological scheme which may be useful as further research develops.

FRAMES OF REFERENCE

In viewing the employed mother, early writings by psychologically oriented scholars emphasized personality attributes as selective factors in the decision to enter employment. Hostile or rejecting feelings toward husband or children or strong anxiety, insecurity, or drives toward self-realization were seen as motivating women who entered employment. The conceptual equipment of these scholars lacked concepts relating to cultural change, particularly to the effects of change in one area of social organization on the content of roles in another. In viewing social organization as a constant and personality attributes and needs as the variables, early psychologically oriented writers viewed the employed mother with alarm (11).

The economists viewed mothers as new and valued (perhaps even necessary) additions to the labor force. Their tasks were classified in detail and their earnings analyzed. The number of hours employed, rates of unemployment, and similar data have ben studied and published in numerous releases from the Children's Bureau (19) and the Bureau of the Census (18). These have been further supplemented recently by a monograph from the National Manpower Council (14). In the economic frame of reference, the mother is a production resource—and a rather important one.

A third frame of reference was contributed from social work. This viewpoint has stressed the employment of mothers as contributing to the neglect of children and, in some instances, to poor health in the mother (18). Social work has often seen the employment of mothers as a social problem and sought to discourage it or, if this is not possible, to alleviate its presumed consequences. Though the children of some mothers no doubt are neglected and some employed mothers have poor health, social work did not raise the question of whether neglect or ill health is actually more prevalent in families in which the mother is employed or in those in which she is not employed.

The sociological frame of reference has encompassed a complexity of concepts and assumptions which have led to diverse and sometimes ambivalent reactions, and often to a "let's wait and see what the research shows" attitude. Aware of the interrelationships between the economic and familial organization, sociologists see the economic responsibilities of the mother reduced by the transfer of economic and service functions to commercial agencies. Inevitably many women compensate for the loss of these tasks by entering the factory, office, and classroom. At the same time, sociologists have been acutely aware of the conflict between the new role as a provider and the roles of housekeeper and supervisor of children. Evaluations have varied from Bossard (2), who thought this conflict led inevitably to the neglect of children, to Parsons and Bales (16), who thought it would have little effect of any kind on family relationships, to Komarovsky (7) and Landis (8), who saw it as an opportunity for married women to follow their interests more closely and to utilize their talents and training. Perhaps the most serious shortcoming in sociological perspective has been a failure to see clearly that someone other than the biological mother can play the role of supervisor of children in many instances as effectively, and in some, more effectively, than the mother.

A SOCIOLOGICAL POINT OF DEPARTURE [2]

The work on position, status, and role of Frederick Bates (1) and Neal

[2] From the paper, "The Employed Mother: Basic Change in Family Structure," read before the Family Section of the American Sociological Association, St. Louis, Missouri, in August, 1961.

Gross (4) provides a useful point of departure for sociological conceptual analysis of the employed mother.[3]

According to the Bates model, "a position is a location in a social structure which is associated with a set of social norms." In the present formulation, the central position is that of wife-mother. Positions are composed of a number of related social roles, which are defined "a more or less integrated or related sub-set of social norms." A norm is "a patterned or commonly held behavior expectation; a learned response held in common by members of a group" (1, p. 314).

Considering the wife-mother as a position, some of her principal roles are housekeeper, supervisor of children, playmate, teacher of children, and sex partner to husband. In this model, role becomes *a subunit in the structure* of her position as wife-mother. Her various roles are delimited by the norms which define them.

The concept of role conflict, which is crucial to the study of employed mothers, can readily be delineated from the above structure. Such conflict may be said to occur when two or more roles within a single position: (a) require the actor to *be* in two different places at the same time (b) require the actor to do two or more different actions at the same time, (c) require the actor to behave in ways that are by social definition incompatible even though they occur at different times and could otherwise be performed by the same person, and (d) require the actor to perform psychologically contradictory (although socially compatible) behaviors such as Motz describes in her paper, "The Roles of the Married Woman Scientist" (13).

Bates assumes that the presence of incompatible roles within a position results in tension which leads to modifications in behavior in attempts to reduce it. If modification is impossible, personality of the actor must change (1). The assumption that role conflict is tension-producing is not documented; however, this writer is willing to accept this assumption and thinks that it could be readily supported. If the assumptions of role conflict and tension are made, several testable hypotheses are deducible: (a) mothers who have internalized the norms of the conflicting roles will experience guilt feelings; (b) mothers who think that their performance of the responsibilities of the roles are deficient will experience feelings of anxiety; and (c) mothers who are unable to modify their roles to reduce the tension related to role conflicts will develop neurotic symptoms.

From the assumption that incompatible roles produce tension, it is postulated that within a position roles display a "strain toward consistency." In the short run, individuals improvise means to reduce such conflicts; in

---

[3] The following discussion draws heavily on Bates (1); however, the Gross *et al.* (4) discussion of position and role is also recommended.

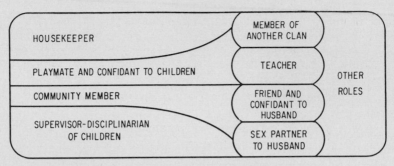

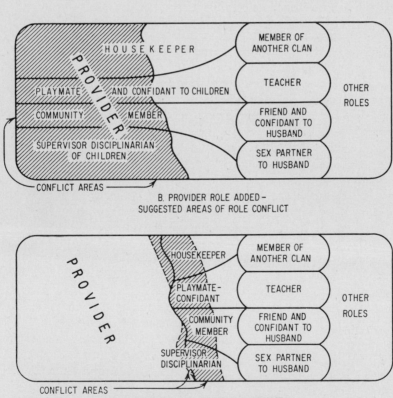

FIGURE 1. *Role Conflict and Improvision in the Wife-Mother Position*

the long run, consistency is achieved through changes in the normative content of the roles (1). Figure I-A shows a conception of the position of wife-mother including major traditional roles—but not that of provider. Figure I-B shows the initial conflict between the provider and the other major roles. Figure I-C reflects typical improvision to reduce tension resulting from role conflict.

Role definitions vary in rigidity, so changes in incompatible roles do not occur equally. The provider role is more rigidly defined than the other roles of wife-mother. From the above can be deduced the hypotheses that: (a) conflicts between the provider and the other roles of the wife-mother have lessened during the past decade and will continue to lessen during the next; (b) mothers will attempt to reduce role conflict by decreasing their responsibilities in both the provider and the other roles; (c) roles within the home will be changed more than the provider role.

It has been found that the general model of position, role, and norm provides theoretical materials for a more specific conceptualization dealing with the women who have added the role of provider to the other roles in the position of wife-mother. However, some important parts of the scheme are missing. How can one account sociologically for the addition of the provider role to the wife-mother position?

It has been suggested that tension (from role playing) in individual actors furnishes the "motive power" which creates change (1). The tension and motive power for the addition of the provider role has come largely from changes in two other roles: the housekeeper role of the wife-mother and the provider role of the husband-father. The housekeeper role has been gradually redefined until the norms no longer include gardening, care of domestic animals, making cloth or clothing, canning fruits and vegetables, churning butter, baking bread, and many other tasks. (In a sense, these were equivalent to the provider role of the present-day employed mother.) Equally important, the role has incorporated labor-saving equipment into the definition of the performance of most remaining tasks. These tasks have been added to the husband-father role of provider; not, of course, in the sense that he makes clothing or churns butter but in the sense that he must earn enough money to pay someone to perform these tasks and to buy the labor-saving equipment used by the mother.

To provide reasonable completeness to this discussion, attention must be shifted to two non-structural elements in the society: (a) a developing equalitarian ideology of marriage which asserts equality of privilege and implies equality of responsibility and (b) a dominant value of upward social mobility and a higher level of living. Sociologically, therefore, we see mothers as adding the provider role as a result of tensions arising from the reduced responsibilities in the housekeeper role and the added duties in the provider role of the father. The addition of the provider role to the mother-wife position restores the economic contribution of the mother and shares the heavier responsibilities of the provider role of the father. In so doing, it reduces tension in two roles while it may simultaneously increase tension by conflicting with other wife-mother roles. Of course the relative increase or decrease is different for various categories of individuals. To specify these results more closely, another conceptual and research tool is required.

Contingent Conditions and Test Variables. Although it is possible to describe the general nature of role change, role conflict, role improvision, and personality reaction to the addition of the provider role, the relationship can be specified much more accurately by the introduction of other variables.

It has been known for some time that test variables and contingent conditions are useful in more closely specifying the relationship between variables or attributes, but how they fit into a general model of position and role or the present more specific one for employed mothers has not been explored. First, they modify the normative description of the role. For example, the responsibilities of a mother of a preschool child are considerably different from those of a mother with children of school age only. Thus, age of the child is a condition that not only modifies the normative content of the role but also modifies the extent of the conflict between the provider and supervisor-of-child roles. Contingent conditions also affect the effectiveness of the improvisations aimed at reducing role conflict and reduction of tension in the actors. A high income of the mother which permits the hiring of a competent mother substitute would illustrate this. Thus, a number of contingent conditions modify the incorporation of the provider role into the wife-mother position by individual mothers and determine the extent of role conflict and tension in individual actors.

One further question must be considered. Is the provider role being incorporated into the wife-mother position, becoming a part of the definition of the wife-mother position as is housekeeper or supervisor of children? Will it become the dominant pattern and its absence in the wife-mother position considered deviant? The latter may, indeed, come to pass eventually if present technological and social trends continue. In the immediate future, however, the provider role in the wife-mother position appears as an "alternative" in the Lintonian sense (10). For now, it appears that an appreciable minority of women will continuously occupy the role of provider, commencing before marriage and continuing until retirement. A larger minority will occupy the role intermittently during marriage, depending on age of children and other conditions. This group may become the largest without necessarily constituting a majority. Finally, a large minority of women will never occupy the role of provider or will abandon it before the birth of the first child and never reoccupy it.

Cross-Cultural Considerations. The present proposal is devised for the study of the employed mother in American culture in the mid-twentieth century. Brief attention should be directed to some contrasting societies.

In non-industrial societies, the provider role of the wife-mother is integrated with her housekeeping and supervisor roles. In most societies, children participate with the parents in common economic tasks, and the problem of separation of mother and child is infrequently encountered. This was generally true of American society until the twentieth century.

In contemporary societies, the greatest contrasts to the American situation are the communist societies and the kibbutz communities in Israel. In the U.S.S.R., the government has encouraged mothers to take employment. Simultaneously, they have almost eliminated the conflict between her roles as provider and supervisor and disciplinarian of her children by providing nurseries and day care centers and by keeping her children at school until she returns home from work. She retains responsibility for them only before and after work. In contrast, it appears that the communists have made little progress in reducing her housekeeping responsibilities, and a considerable area of conflict may remain with that role (12).

The kibbutz have eliminated any such conflict by eliminating the roles of supervisor and disciplinarian of children and by virtually eliminating the role of housekeeper from the wife-mother position. The children are cared for by nurse-teachers, and everyone eats in communal dining halls. One recent observer has stated that the relationship between parent and child in the kibbutz is not parental but grandparental (5).

It is apparent from the experience of these societies that major conflicts between the roles of provider and of supervisor-disciplinarian and housekeeper can be avoided or greatly reduced. The price, however, is a major modification of day care, nursery and school systems, and the support of these facilities by the society.

SUMMARY

The social-cultural change involved in the occupancy of the provider role by mothers is far-reaching and complex. An attempt has been made to describe it very briefly. The major points may be summarized as follows:

(a) The general conceptual scheme for the analysis of position and role provides useful conceptual material for a more limited and specific scheme for studying the employed mother.

(b) The role of provider has become an "alternative" in the wife-mother position. Insofar as the immediate future can be anticipated, more women in this position will occupy the role non-continuously than will occupy it continuously or not at all.

(c) The addition of the provider role to the wife-mother position represents a *major* structural change in that it requires more of the woman's time than any other role. Furthermore, it is a rigid (or dominant) role which will modify her other roles more than it will be modified by them.

(d) The provider role will affect the other wife-mother roles differentially, having a major impact on the roles of supervisor of children and housekeeper. Other roles appear to be less affected.

(e) A number of contingent conditions modify the normative definitions of the roles in the wife-mother position. These include age and number of children, occupation and age of the mother, income of the husband, remarriage, length of time employed, family ideology of husband, and others. Modifications by these conditions affect the compatibility between the provider and other roles. As a consequence, these also affect the level of tension of individuals and the adequacy of their attempts to improvise means of reducing tension.

(f) The addition of the provider role acts to *reduce* tension by restoring the economic contribution of the wife and by reducing the burden of the provider role of the husband. Further, it is instrumental in implementing the dominant American values of upward mobility and a higher level of living.

The employed mother is a permanent and significant addition to the familial and economic structure of American society. The correlates and consequences of the situation are the subject of a growing body of research. Conceptual schemes for the study of the employed mother have lagged far behind empirical research. Future research might profitably devote additional time to theoretical considerations, improved measurement, and the more sophisticated use of test variables and contingent conditions.

REFERENCES

1. Bates, Frederick. "Position, Role and Status: A Reformulation of Concepts," *Social Forces,* XXXIV (May, 1956), 313–21.
2. Bossard, James H. S. *The Sociology of Child Development.* New York: Harper, 1954.
3. Glenn, Hortense M. "Attitudes of Women Regarding Gainful Employment of Married Women," *Journal of Home Economics,* LI (April, 1959), 247–52.
4. Gross, Neal, Mason, Ward S., and McEachern, Alexander W. *Explorations in Role Analysis: Studies of the School Superintendency Role.* New York: Wiley, 1958.
5. Halpern, Howard. "Alienation from Parenthood in the Kibbutz and America," *Marriage and Family Living,* XXIV (February, 1962), 42–46.

6. Kendall, Patricia L., and Lazarsfeld, Paul F. "Problems of Survey Analysis." In Robert K. Merton and Paul F. Lazarsfeld, eds. *Continuities in Social Research,* Glencoe, Ill.: Free Press, 1950, pp. 148–58.

7. Komarovsky, Mirra. *Women in the Modern World.* Boston: Little, Brown, 1953.

8. Landis, Paul H. *Making the Most of Marriage.* 2nd ed.; New York: Appleton-Century-Crofts, 1960.

9. Lazarsfeld, Paul F., and Rosenberg, M. *The Language of Social Research.* Glencoe, Ill.: Free Press, 1955.

10. Linton, Ralph. *The Study of Man.* New York: Appleton-Century-Crofts, 1936.

11. Lundberg, Ferdinand, and Farnham, Marynia F. *Modern Woman, the Lost Sex.* New York: Harper, 1947.

12. Mace, David. "The Employed Mother in the U.S.S.R.," *Marriage and Family Living,* XXIII (November, 1961), 330–34.

13. Motz, Annabelle Bender. "The Roles of the Married Woman Scientist," *Marriage and Family Living,* XXIII (November, 1961), 574–77.

14. National Manpower Council. *Womanpower.* New York: Columbia University Press, 1957.

15. Nolan, Francena. "Certain Practices, Satisfactions, and Difficulties in Families with Employed Homemakers," Bulletin 455, Pennsylvania State University, Agricultural Experiment Station, University Park, Pennsylvania, August, 1959.

16. Parsons, Talcott, and Bales, Robert F. *Family, Socialization and Interaction Process.* Glencoe: Free Press, 1955.

17. Selltiz, Claire, and others. *Research Methods in the Social Sciences.* New York: Henry Holt, 1959.

18. United States Department of Commerce, Bureau of the Census, Series P-50, especially Bulletins Nos. 22, 62, 73, 76, 81, 87. Washington, D.C.: Government Printing Office.

19. United States Department of Health, Education and Welfare, Bulletins Nos. 20, 218, 232, 275. Washington, D.C.: Government Printing Office.

20. Wright, H. R. *Children of Wage Earning Mothers.* United States Department of Labor, Children's Bureau Bulletin 102, Washington, D.C.: Government Printing Office, 1922.

21. Yarrow, Marion Radke. "Effects of Maternal Employment on Children." *Children.* New York: Holt, 1959.

Index